And I asked myself about the present:
how wide it was, how deep it was,
how much was mine to keep.

Published by
ARCHAIA™

SLAU

HOUS

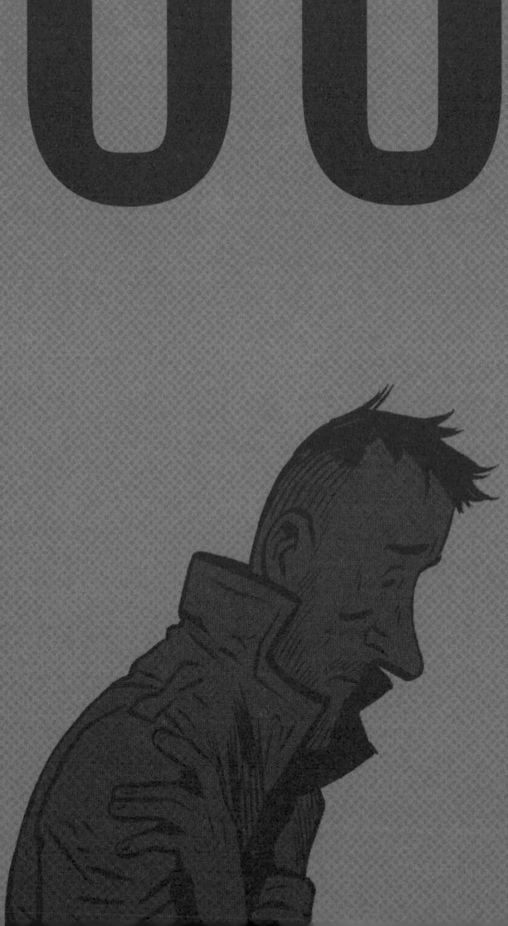

HTER

or the children's crusade: a duty-dance with death

-FIVE

™

Story by **Kurt Vonnegut**

Written by **Ryan North**

Illustrated by **Albert Monteys**

Cover by **Scott Newman** and **Albert Monteys**

ARCHAIA™
Los Angeles, California

Colored by **Albert Monteys**
with color assistance by **Ricard Zaplana**
Lettered by **Albert Monteys**

Assistant Editors **Gwen Waller** and **Allyson Gronowitz**
Editor **Sierra Hahn**
Designer **Scott Newman**

Special thanks to **Stephen Christy**,
Katie Cacouris of the **Wylie Agency**,
and the **Vonnegut Estate**.

ARCHAIA™

BOOM! Studios, 5670 Wilshire Boulevard, Suite 400, Los Angeles, CA 90036-5679. Printed in China. First Printing.

ISBN: 978-1-68415-625-2, eISBN: 978-1-64668-037-5

For Kurt.

For the lives lost.

For those who have
come unstuck.

The Dresden atrocity, tremendously expensive and meticulously planned, was so meaningless, finally, that only one person on the entire planet got any benefit from it. I am that person. I wrote this book, which earned a lot of money for me and made my reputation, such as it is.

One way or another, I got two or three dollars for every person killed.

Some business I'm in.

—Kurt Vonnegut

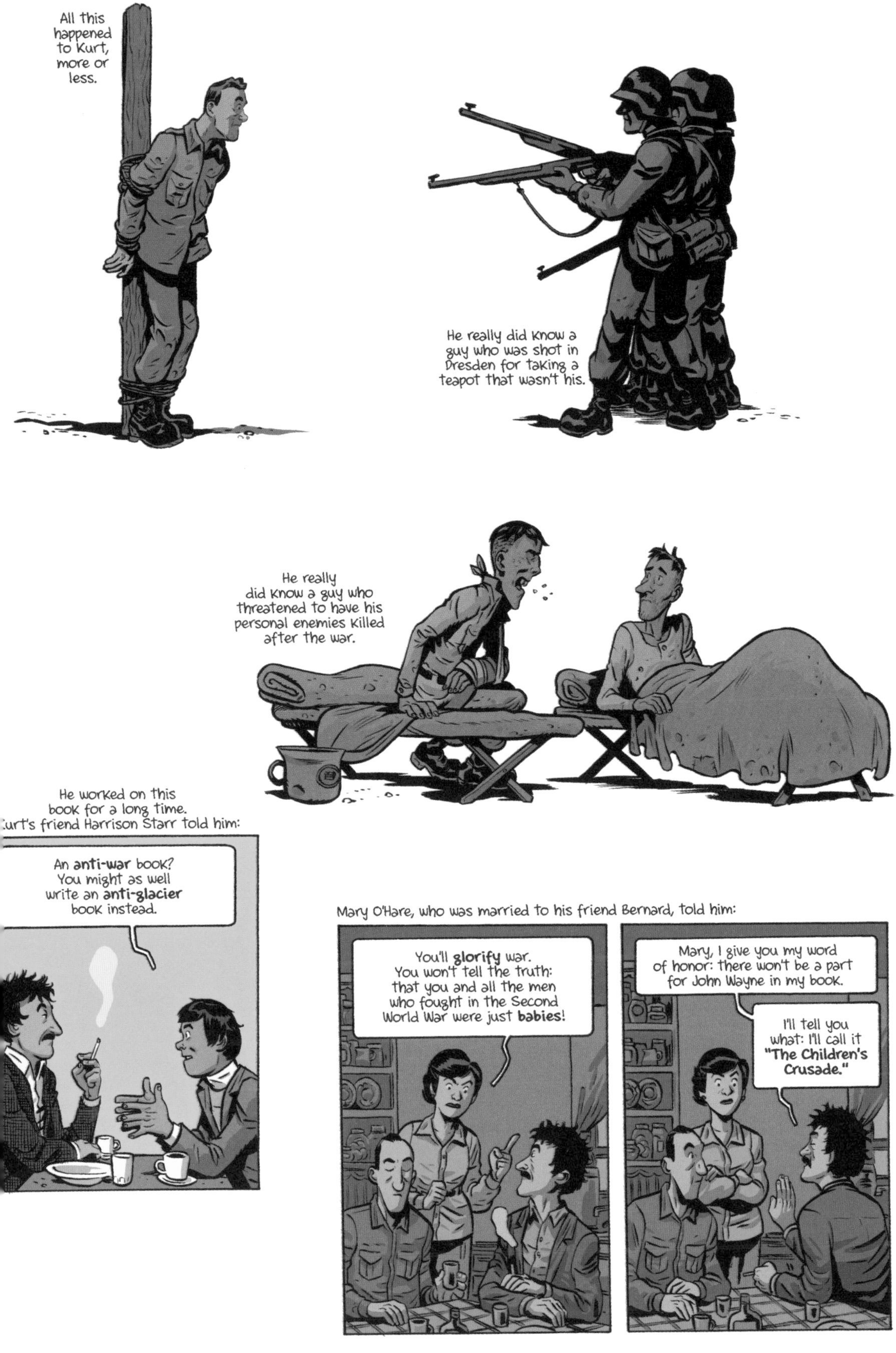
All this happened to Kurt, more or less.
He really did know a guy who was shot in Dresden for taking a teapot that wasn't his.
He really did know a guy who threatened to have his personal enemies killed after the war.
He worked on this book for a long time.
urt's friend Harrison Starr told him:
An **anti-war** book? You might as well write an **anti-glacier** book instead.
Mary O'Hare, who was married to his friend Bernard, told him:
You'll **glorify** war. You won't tell the truth: that you and all the men who fought in the Second World War were just **babies**!
Mary, I give you my word of honor: there won't be a part for John Wayne in my book.
I'll tell you what: I'll call it **"The Children's Crusade."**

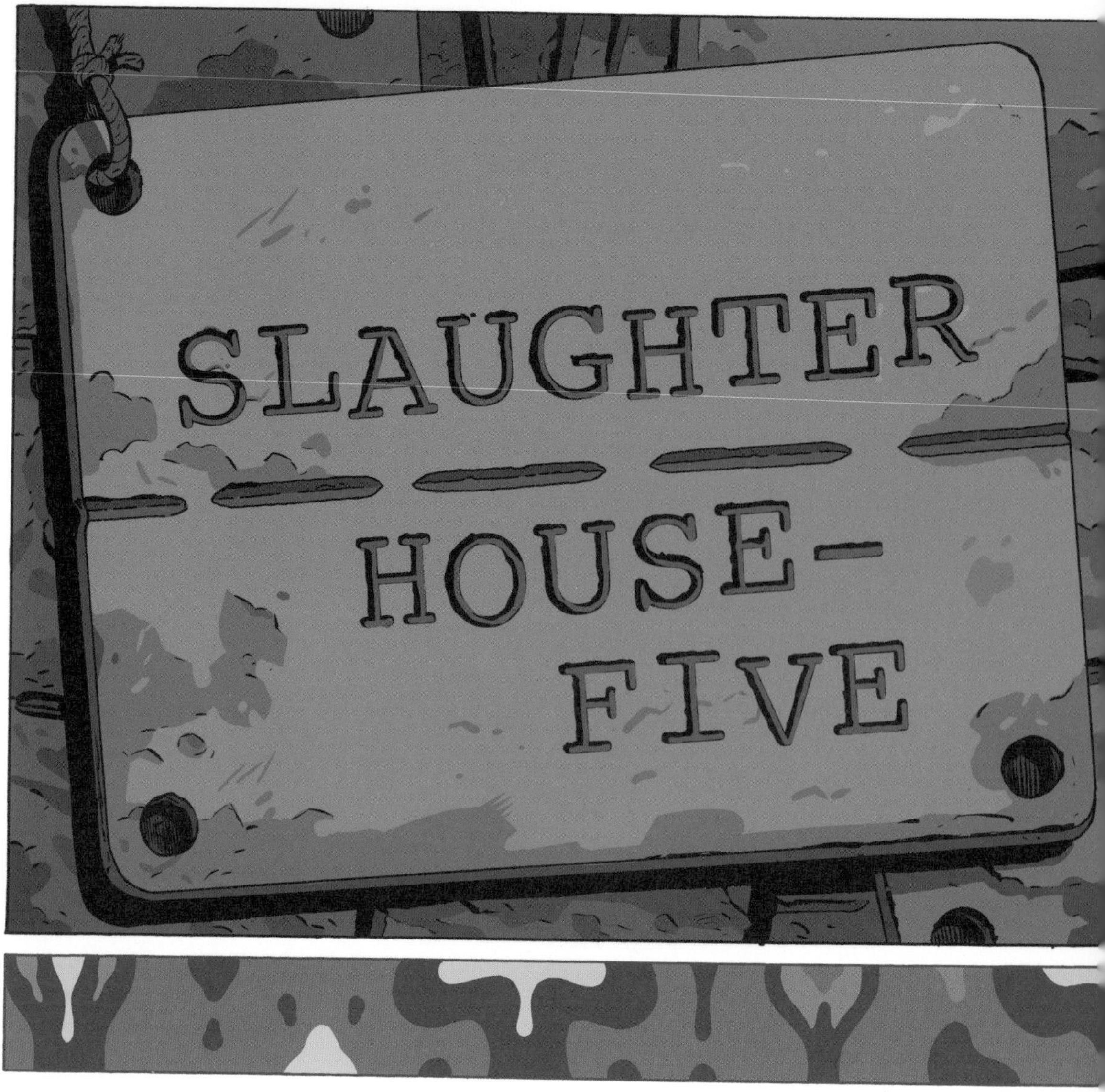
SLAUGHTER
HOUSE-
FIVE

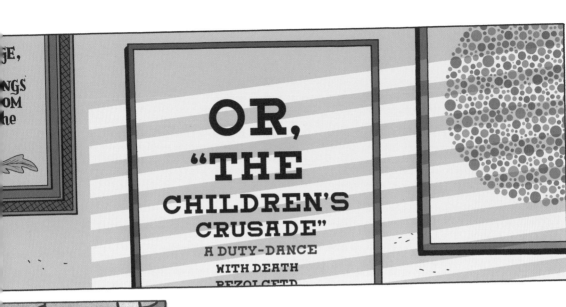

OR, "THE CHILDREN'S CRUSADE"

A DUTY-DANCE
WITH DEATH

by KURT VONNEGUT

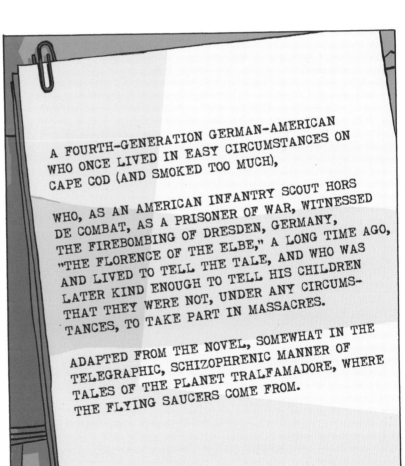

A FOURTH-GENERATION GERMAN-AMERICAN WHO ONCE LIVED IN EASY CIRCUMSTANCES ON CAPE COD (AND SMOKED TOO MUCH),

WHO, AS AN AMERICAN INFANTRY SCOUT HORS DE COMBAT, AS A PRISONER OF WAR, WITNESSED THE FIREBOMBING OF DRESDEN, GERMANY, "THE FLORENCE OF THE ELBE," A LONG TIME AGO, AND LIVED TO TELL THE TALE, AND WHO WAS LATER KIND ENOUGH TO TELL HIS CHILDREN THAT THEY WERE NOT, UNDER ANY CIRCUMSTANCES, TO TAKE PART IN MASSACRES.

ADAPTED FROM THE NOVEL, SOMEWHAT IN THE TELEGRAPHIC, SCHIZOPHRENIC MANNER OF TALES OF THE PLANET TRALFAMADORE, WHERE THE FLYING SAUCERS COME FROM.

PEACE.

EVERYTHING WAS BEAUTIFUL, AND NOTHING HURT

Mary and Kurt were friends after that. But Kurt, Mary, and Bernard are all long gone now.

So it goes.

Kurt's book is still in print, though. And now you're reading a new version of it, in a different medium.

This is the comic book adaptation of
"Slaughterhouse-Five, or The Children's Crusade."

The two versions of the story are very similar, only ours has more pictures.
For example, both begin like this:

Listen: Billy Pilgrim has come unstuck in time.

And both end like this:

Poo-tee-weet?

OUR SUPPORTING CAST

Roland Weary: stupid, mean, unpopular, unhappy eighteen-year-old obsessed with glory.

Paul Lazzaro: insane car thief from Cicero, Illinois, with a revenge list.

Kilgore Trout: failed author of science fiction.

Edgar Derby: decent man, a high school teacher and tennis coach whose death is the climax of this book.

Howard W. Campbell, Jr.: American Nazi.

Valencia Merble: Billy's wife, mother to their two children, Robert and Barbara.

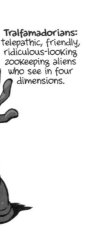

Tralfamadorians: telepathic, friendly, ridiculous-looking zookeeping aliens who see in four dimensions.

Montana Wildhack: sex worker, mother to Billy's third child.

Eliot Rosewater: millionaire fan of Kilgore Trout.

And if you're ever in Cody, Wyoming, just ask for Wild Bob.

Listen: Billy Pilgrim has come unstuck in time.

He has no control over where he's going.
He is in a constant state of stage fright,
because he has no idea what part of his
life he's going to have to act in next.

BILLY'S TIMELINE

1922	1928	1933	1943	1944	1945	194
AGE 0	AGE 6	AGE 11	AGE 21	AGE 22	AGE 23	AGE 2
a funny-looking baby.	a funny-looking kid being taught to swim.	a funny-looking owner of a gory crucifix.	a chaplain's assistant in the war, powerless to harm the enemy or help his friends. (In fact, he has no friends.)	a prisoner of war after the Battle of the Bulge, and when he first comes unstuck in time.	an honorably-discharged veteran with PTSD, and later, an optometry student.	a men patient a veter hospit in Lai Placi New Yc engag to Vale Merbl

1967 is when the Tralfamadorians first reveal to Billy how time works: that all moments exist in parallel. The Tralfamadorians see the different moments in time like a stretch of mountains.
This is what Billy Pilgrim looks like to them:

1955
AGE 33
a rich [o]ptometrist [fa]ther of [tw]o who [m]akes [m]ost of [his] income [selling [fr]ames, [wh]ich are [wh]ere the [m]oney is.

1961
AGE 39
a disgra-ceful drunk at a New Year's Eve party.

1964
AGE 42
a new friend of Kilgore Trout, who is a bitter man.

1967
AGE 45
a successful optometrist, rich as Croesus, kidnapped by a flying saucer from the planet Tralfamadore.

1968
AGE 46
the sole survivor of a plane crash full of optome-trists, and later thought to be senile by his daughter Barbara and son Robert.

1975
AGE 53
a lecturer and thought leader in the post-breakup United States.

1976
AGE 54
a corpse.

So it goes.

When a Tralfamadorian sees a corpse, all they think is that the dead person is in a bad condition at that particular moment, but that same person is just fine in plenty of other moments. When they see a dead person, the Tralfamadorians shrug, and say "So it goes."

(The Tralfamadorians didn't have anything to do with Billy coming unstuck in time. They were simply able to give him insight into what was really going on.)

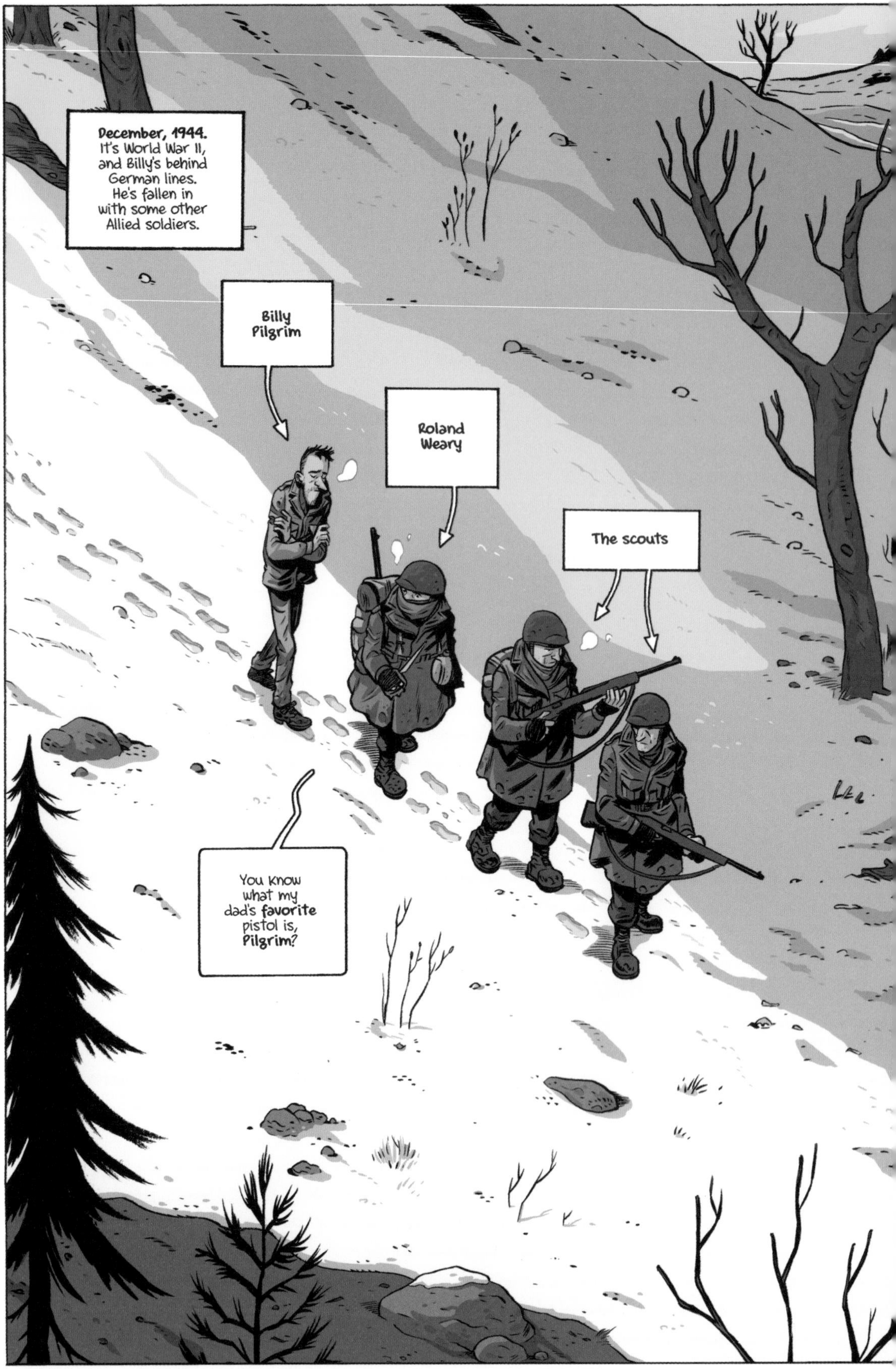
December, 1944. It's World War II, and Billy's behind German lines. He's fallen in with some other Allied soldiers.
Billy Pilgrim
Roland Weary
The scouts
You know what my dad's **favorite** pistol is, **Pilgrim?**

LAND WEARY IN THREE PANELS

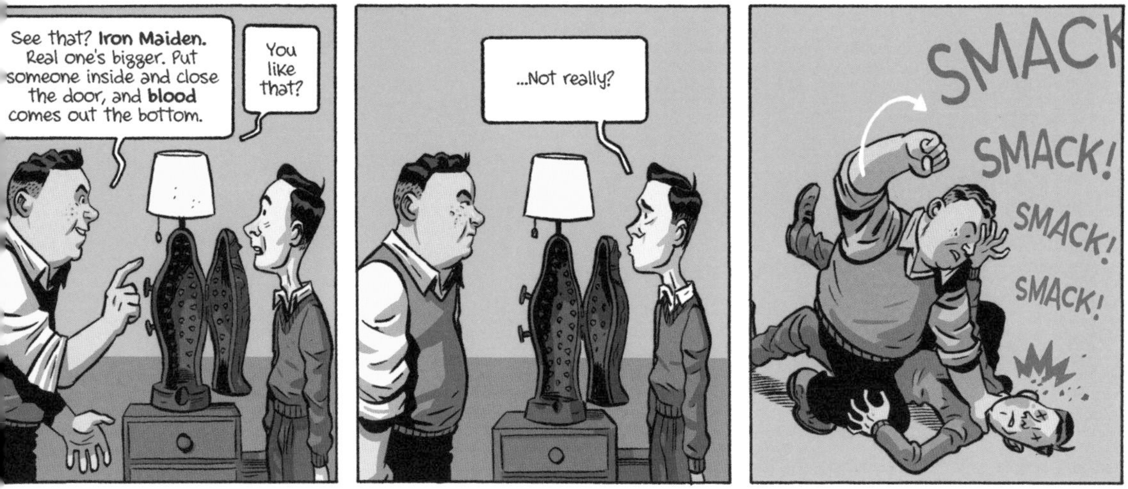

See that? **Iron Maiden.** Real one's bigger. Put someone inside and close the door, and **blood** comes out the bottom.
You like that?
...Not really?
SMACK
SMACK!
SMACK!
SMACK!

LLY PILGRIM IN THREE PANELS

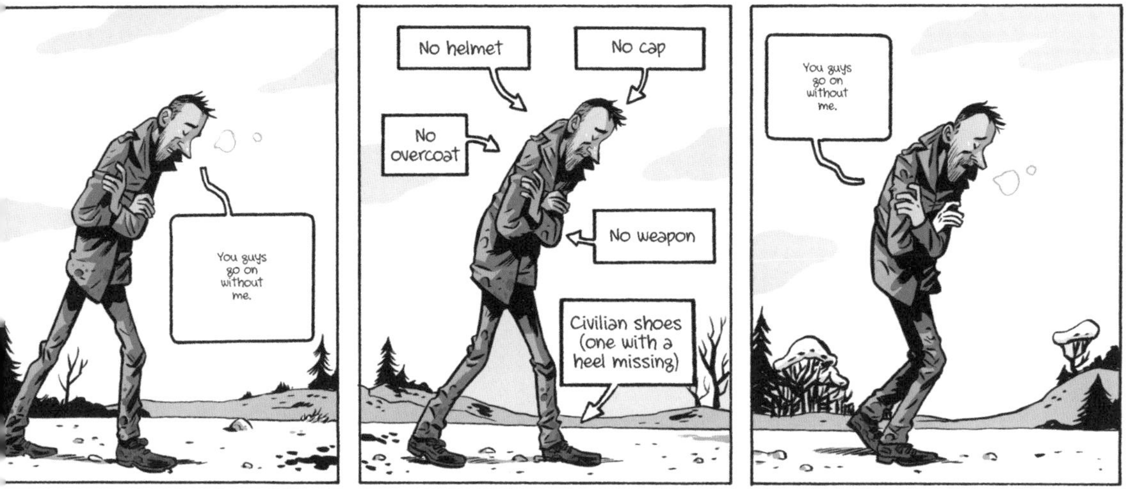

You guys go on without me.
No helmet
No cap
No overcoat
No weapon
Civilian shoes (one with a heel missing)
You guys go on without me.

E SCOUTS IN THREE PANELS

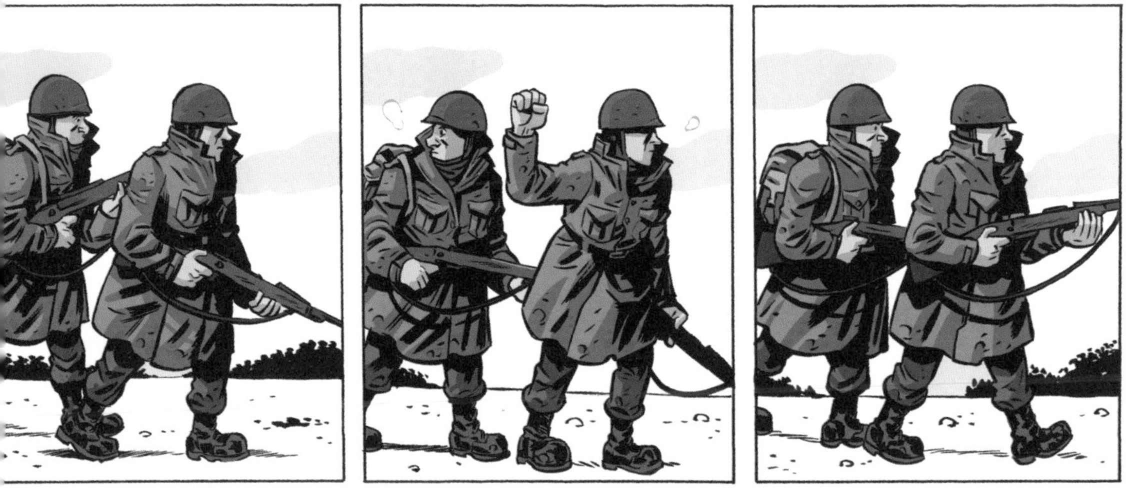

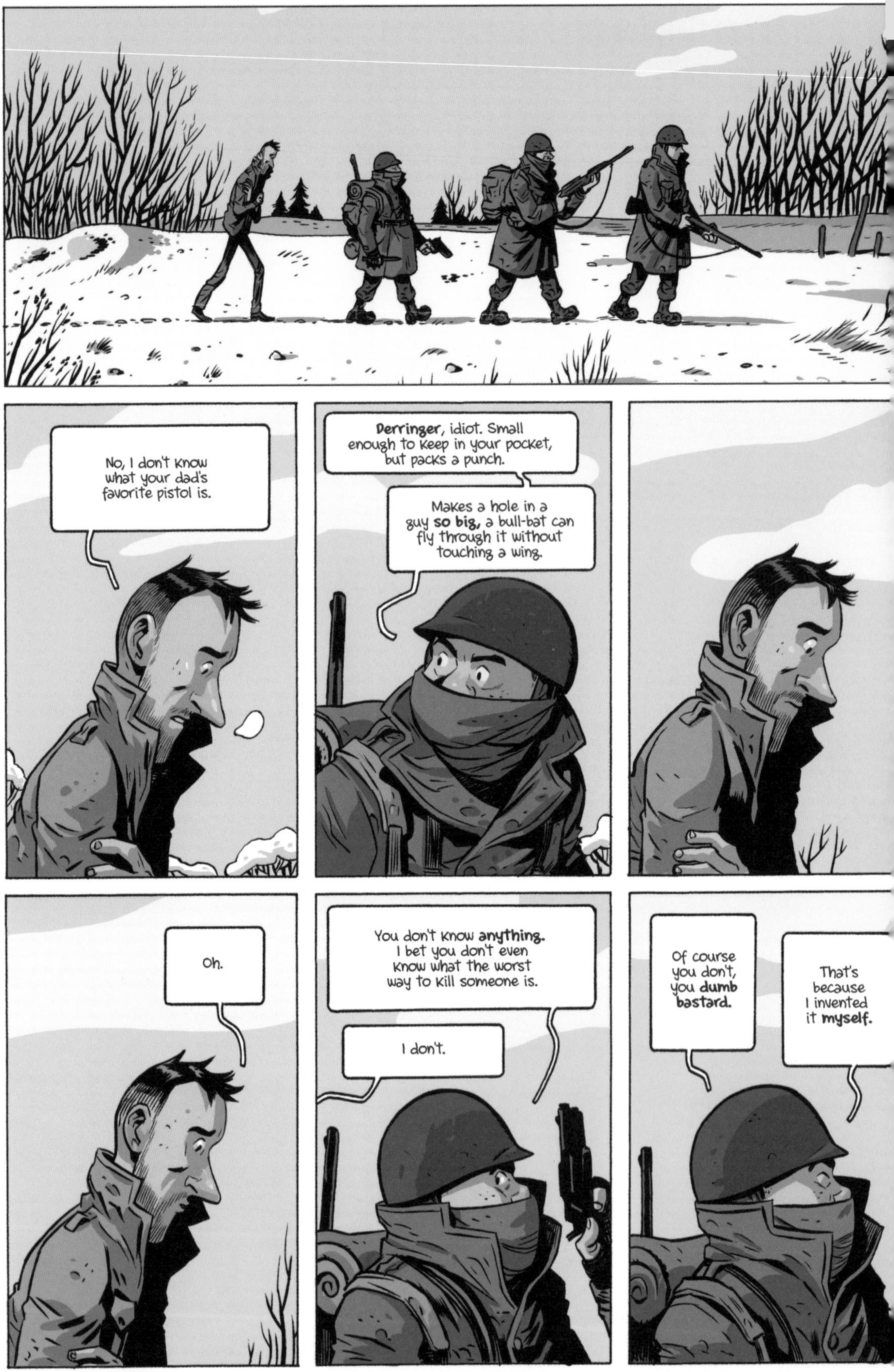
No, I don't know what your dad's favorite pistol is.
Derringer, idiot. Small enough to keep in your pocket, but packs a punch.
Makes a hole in a guy **so big,** a bull-bat can fly through it without touching a wing.
Oh.
You don't know **anything.** I bet you don't even know what the worst way to kill someone is.
I don't.
Of course you don't, you **dumb bastard.**
That's because I invented it **myself.**

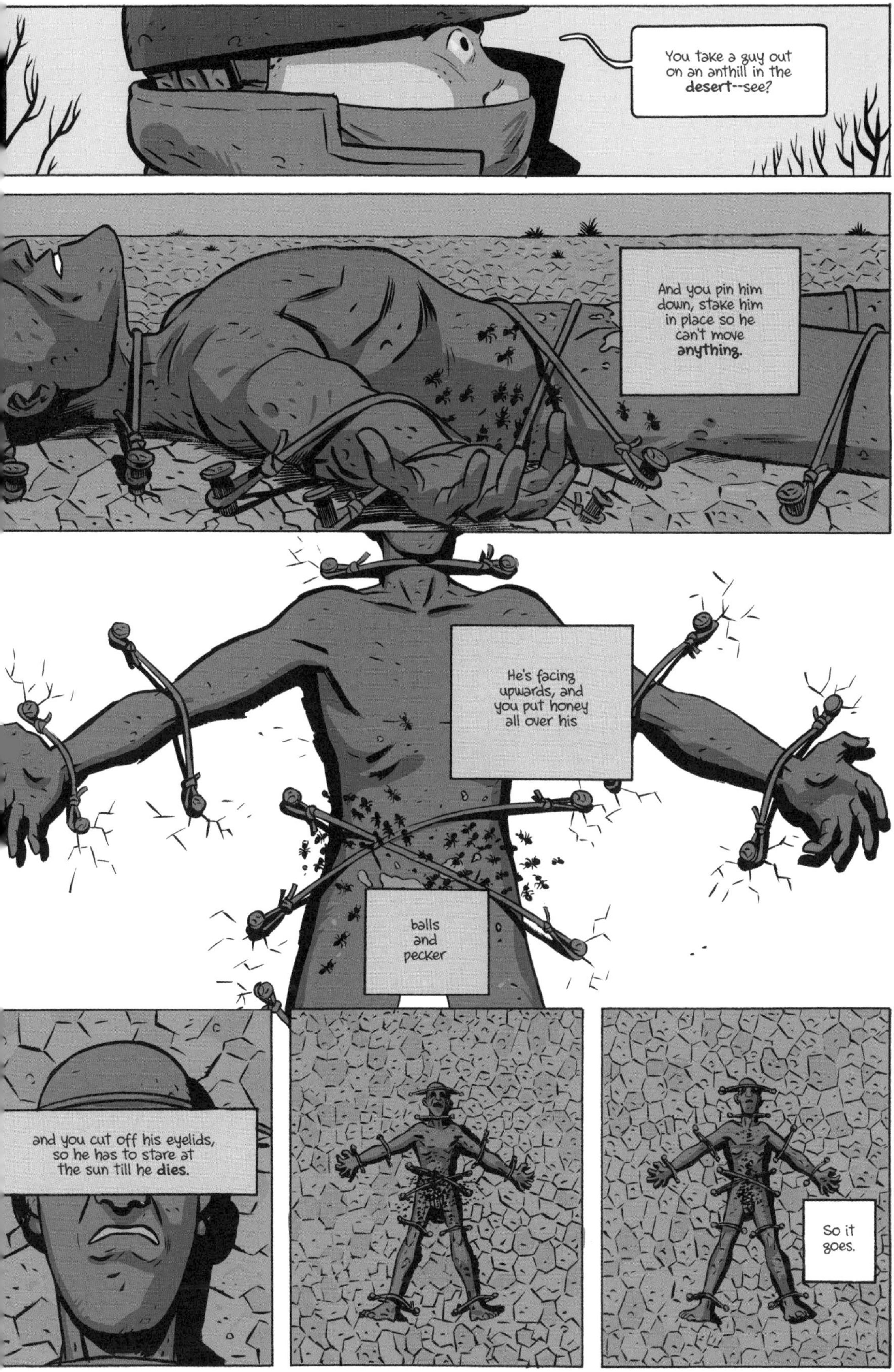
You take a guy out on an anthill in the **desert**--see?
And you pin him down, stake him in place so he can't move **anything.**
He's facing upwards, and you put honey all over his
balls and pecker
and you cut off his eyelids, so he has to stare at the sun till he **dies.**
So it goes.

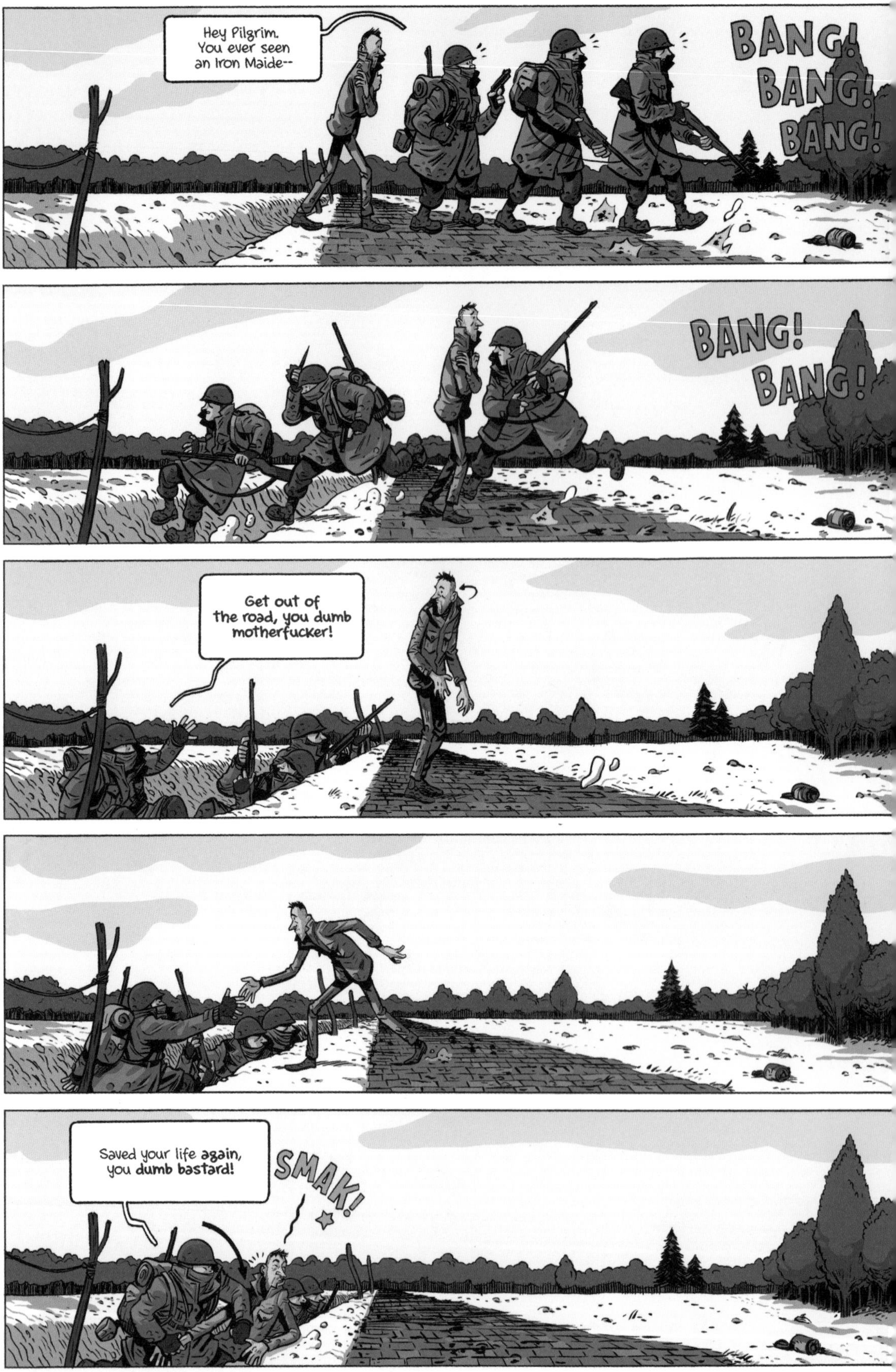
Hey Pilgrim. You ever seen an Iron Maide--
BANG! BANG! BANG!
BANG! BANG!
Get out of the road, you dumb motherfucker!
Saved your life **again**, you **dumb bastard!**
SMAK!

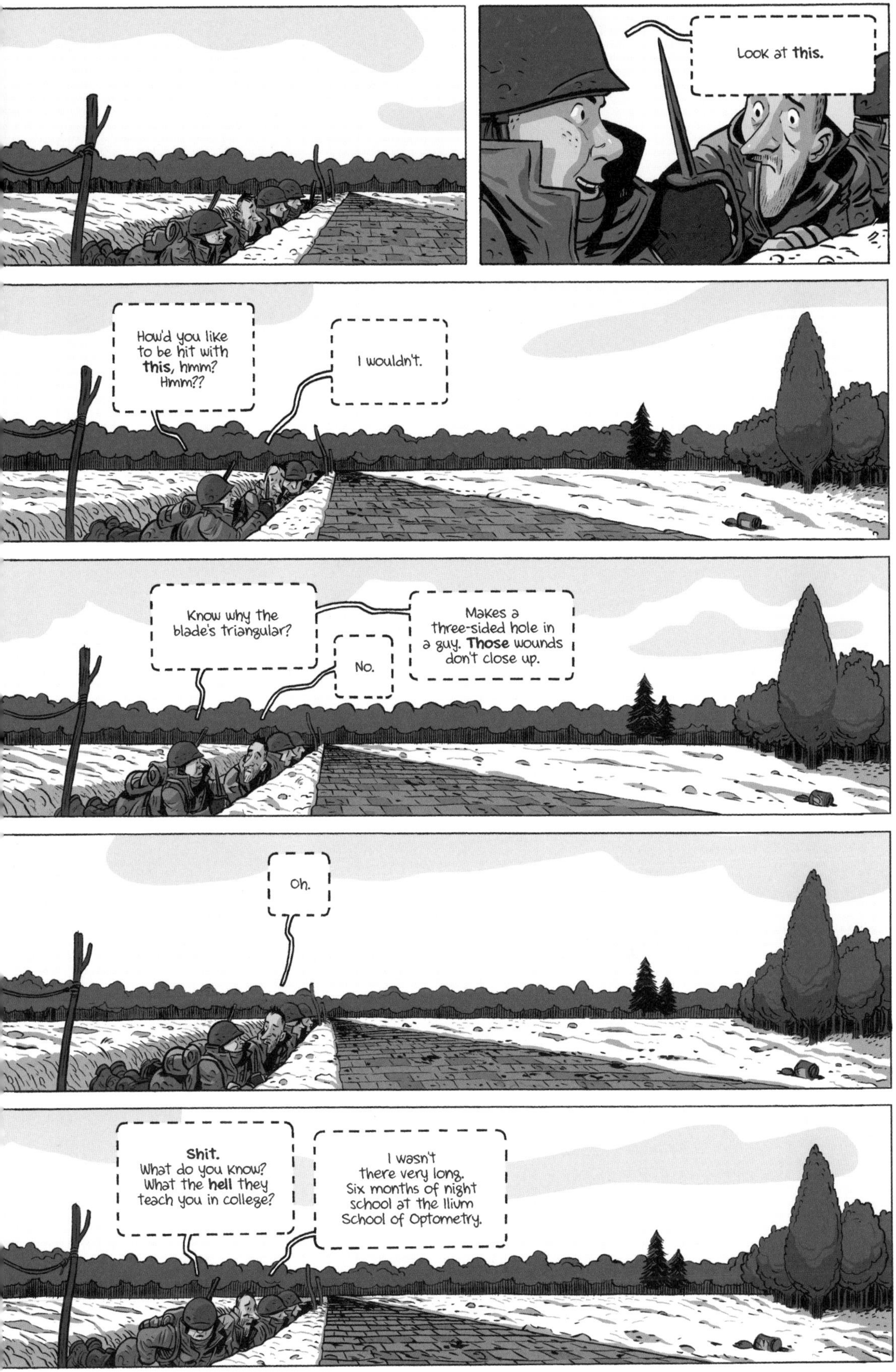
Look at this.
How'd you like to be hit with **this**, hmm? Hmm??
I wouldn't.
Know why the blade's triangular?
No.
Makes a three-sided hole in a guy. **Those** wounds don't close up.
Oh.
Shit. What do you know? What the **hell** they teach you in college?
I wasn't there very long. Six months of night school at the Ilium School of Optometry.

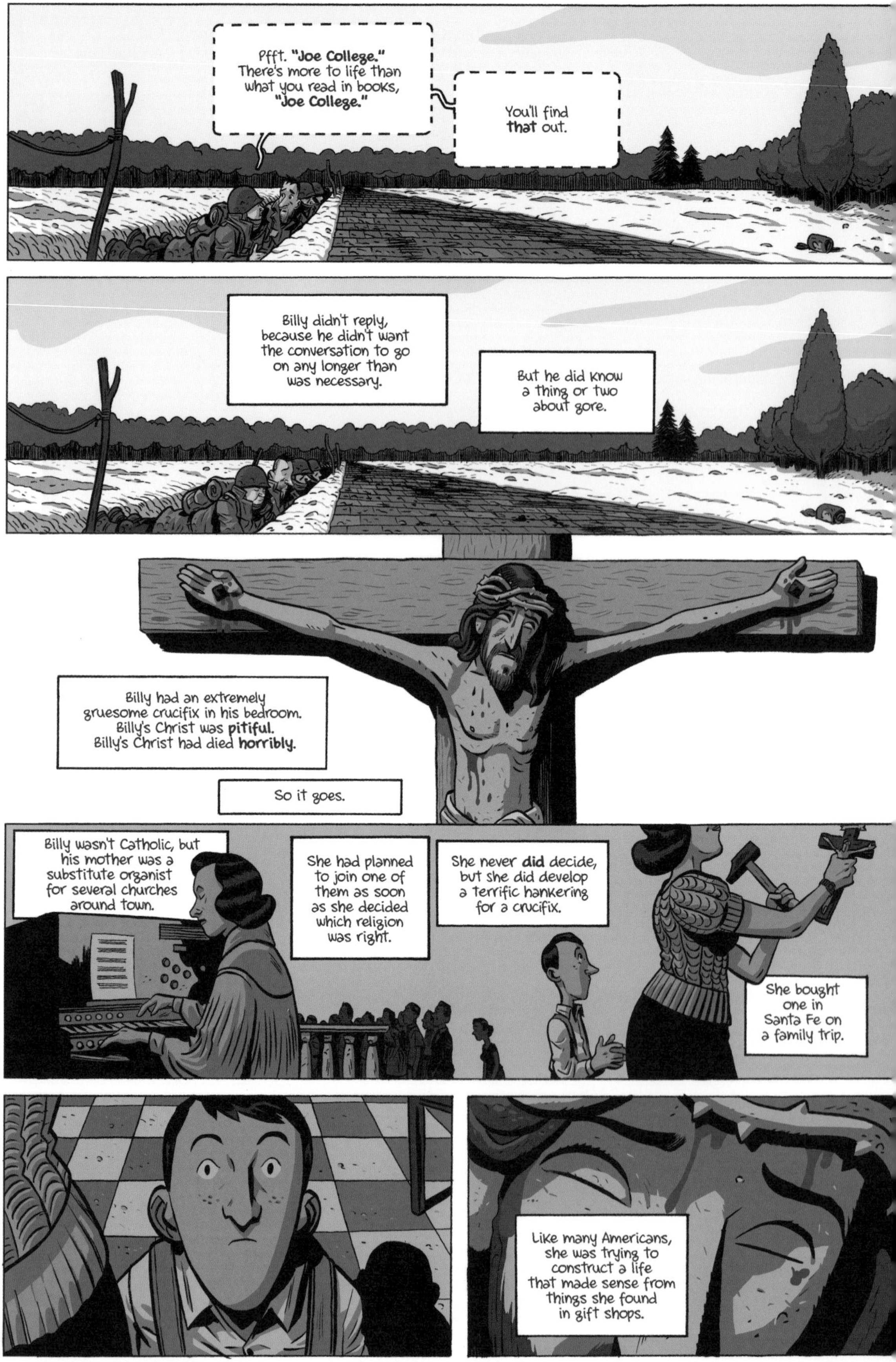
Pfft. "Joe College." There's more to life than what you read in books, "Joe College."
You'll find that out.
Billy didn't reply, because he didn't want the conversation to go on any longer than was necessary.
But he did know a thing or two about gore.
Billy had an extremely gruesome crucifix in his bedroom. Billy's Christ was pitiful. Billy's Christ had died horribly.
So it goes.
Billy wasn't Catholic, but his mother was a substitute organist for several churches around town.
She had planned to join one of them as soon as she decided which religion was right.
She never did decide, but she did develop a terrific hankering for a crucifix.
She bought one in Santa Fe on a family trip.
Like many Americans, she was trying to construct a life that made sense from things she found in gift shops.

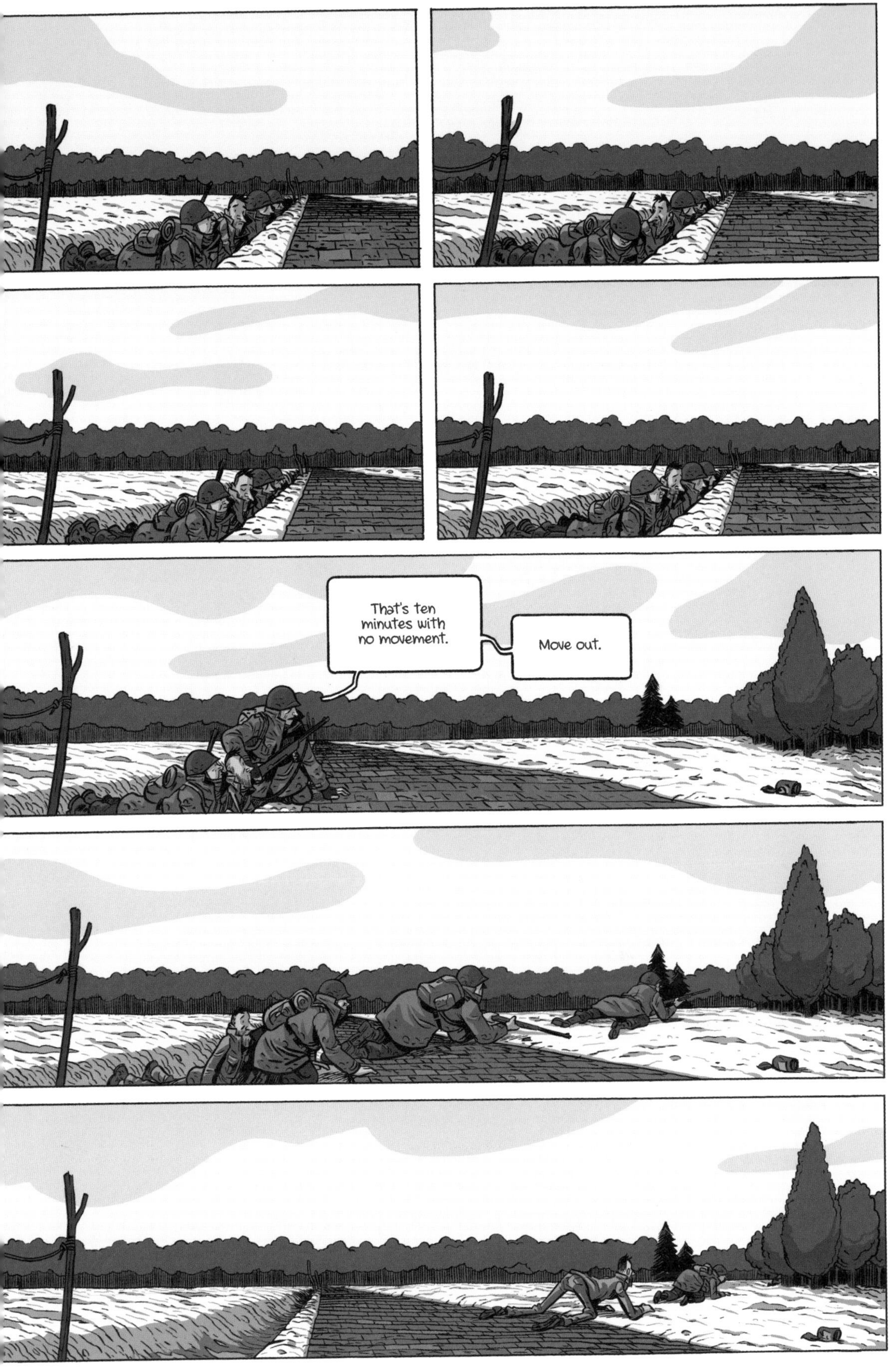
That's ten minutes with no movement.
Move out.

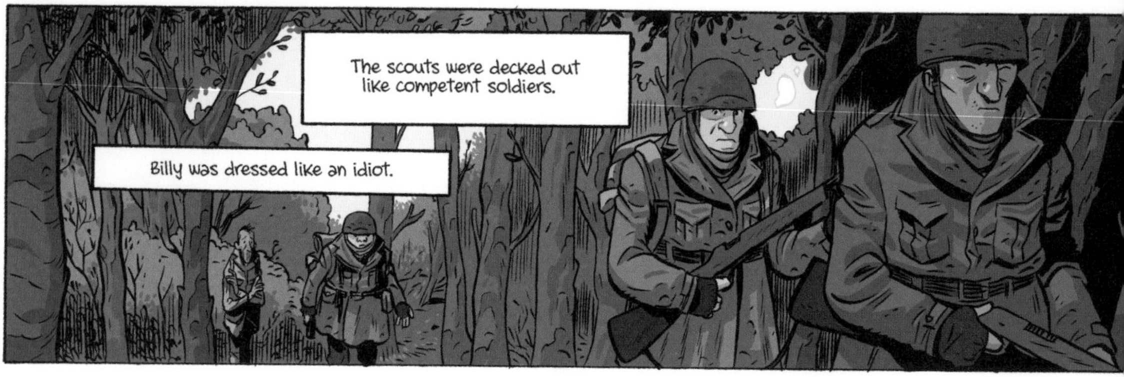
The scouts were decked out like competent soldiers.
Billy was dressed like an idiot.

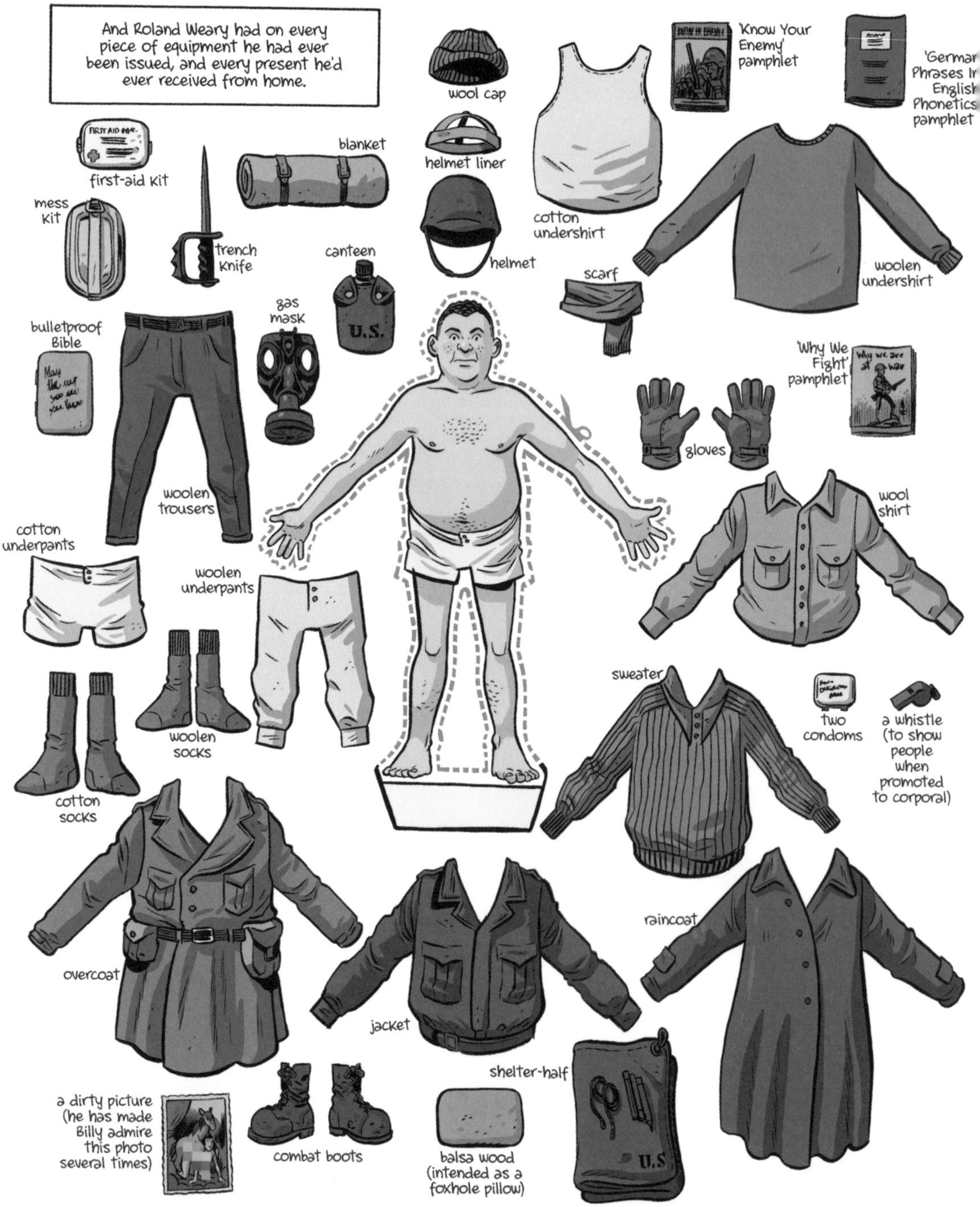
And Roland Weary had on every piece of equipment he had ever been issued, and every present he'd ever received from home.
wool cap
'Know Your Enemy' pamphlet
'Germa Phrases I English Phonetics pamphlet
first-aid kit
blanket
helmet liner
cotton undershirt
mess kit
trench knife
canteen
helmet
scarf
woolen undershirt
gas mask
bulletproof Bible
'Why We Fight' pamphlet
gloves
woolen trousers
wool shirt
cotton underpants
woolen underpants
sweater
two condoms
a whistle (to show people when promoted to corporal)
woolen socks
cotton socks
raincoat
overcoat
jacket
shelter-half
a dirty picture (he has made Billy admire this photo several times)
combat boots
balsa wood (intended as a foxhole pillow)

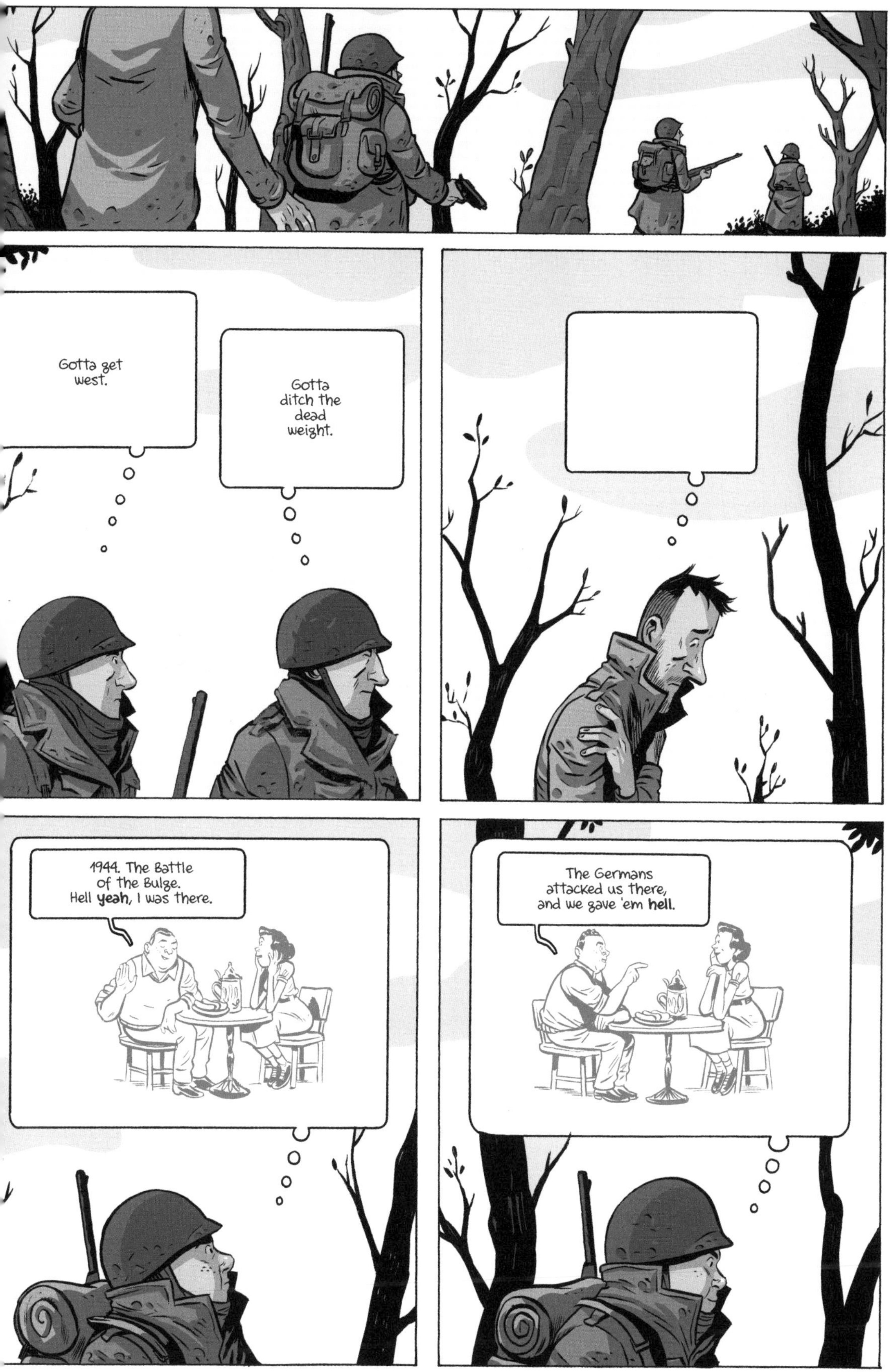

Gotta get west.
Gotta ditch the dead weight.
1944. The Battle of the Bulge. Hell **yeah**, I was there.
The Germans attacked us there, and we gave 'em **hell**.

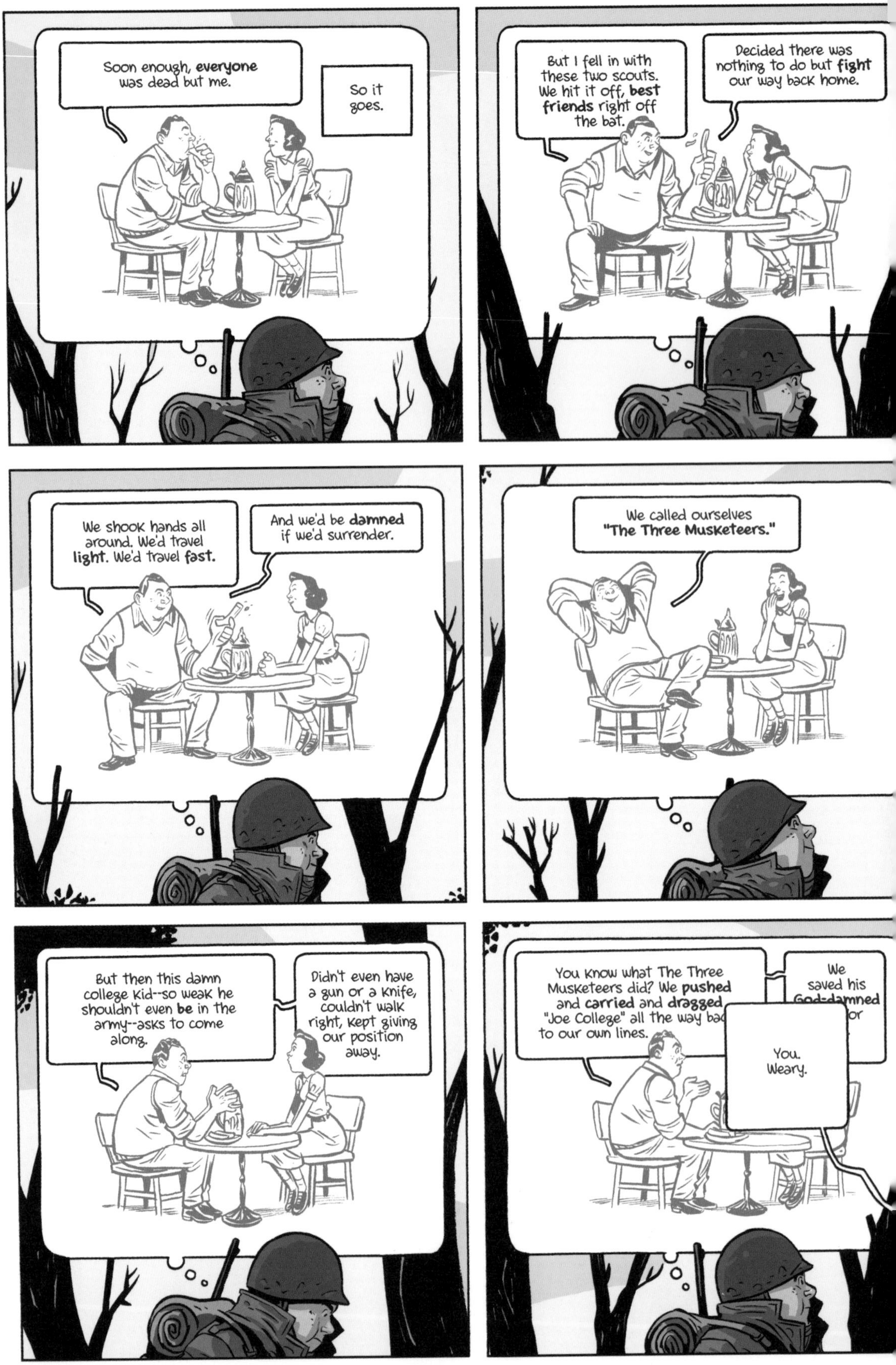

Soon enough, **everyone** was dead but me.
So it goes.
But I fell in with these two scouts. We hit it off, **best friends** right off the bat.
Decided there was nothing to do but **fight** our way back home.
We shook hands all around. We'd travel **light**. We'd travel **fast**.
And we'd be **damned** if we'd surrender.
We called ourselves **"The Three Musketeers."**
But then this damn college kid--so weak he shouldn't even **be** in the army--asks to come along.
Didn't even have a gun or a knife, couldn't walk right, kept giving our position away.
You know what The Three Musketeers did? We **pushed** and **carried** and **dragged** "Joe College" all the way ba
to our own lines.
We saved his
or
You. Weary.

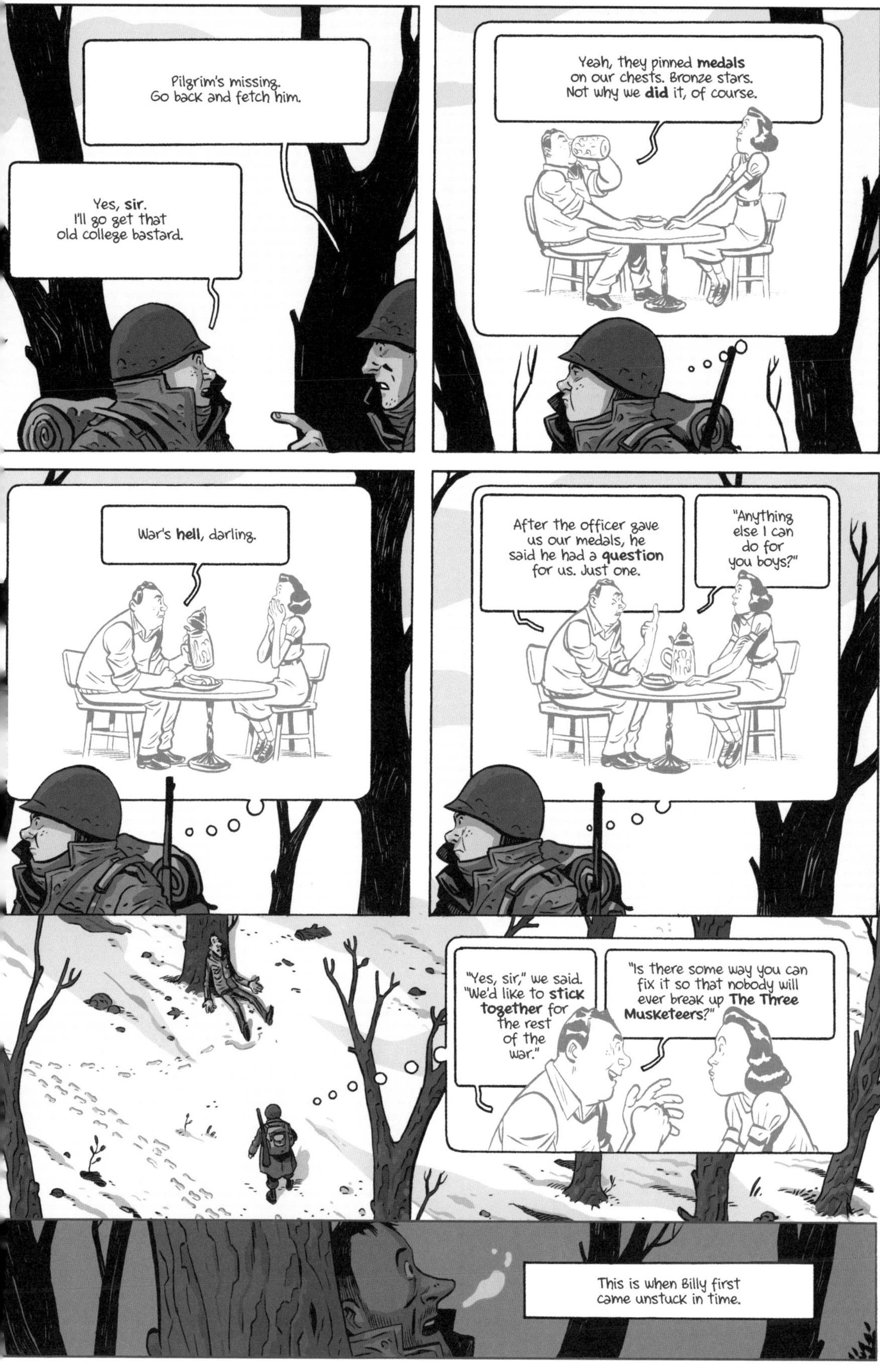

Pilgrim's missing. Go back and fetch him.
Yes, **sir**. I'll go get that old college bastard.
Yeah, they pinned **medals** on our chests. Bronze stars. Not why we **did** it, of course.
War's **hell**, darling.
After the officer gave us our medals, he said he had a **question** for us. Just one.
"Anything else I can do for you boys?"
"Yes, sir," we said. "We'd like to **stick together** for the rest of the war."
"Is there some way you can fix it so that nobody will ever break up **The Three Musketeers?**"
This is when Billy first came unstuck in time.

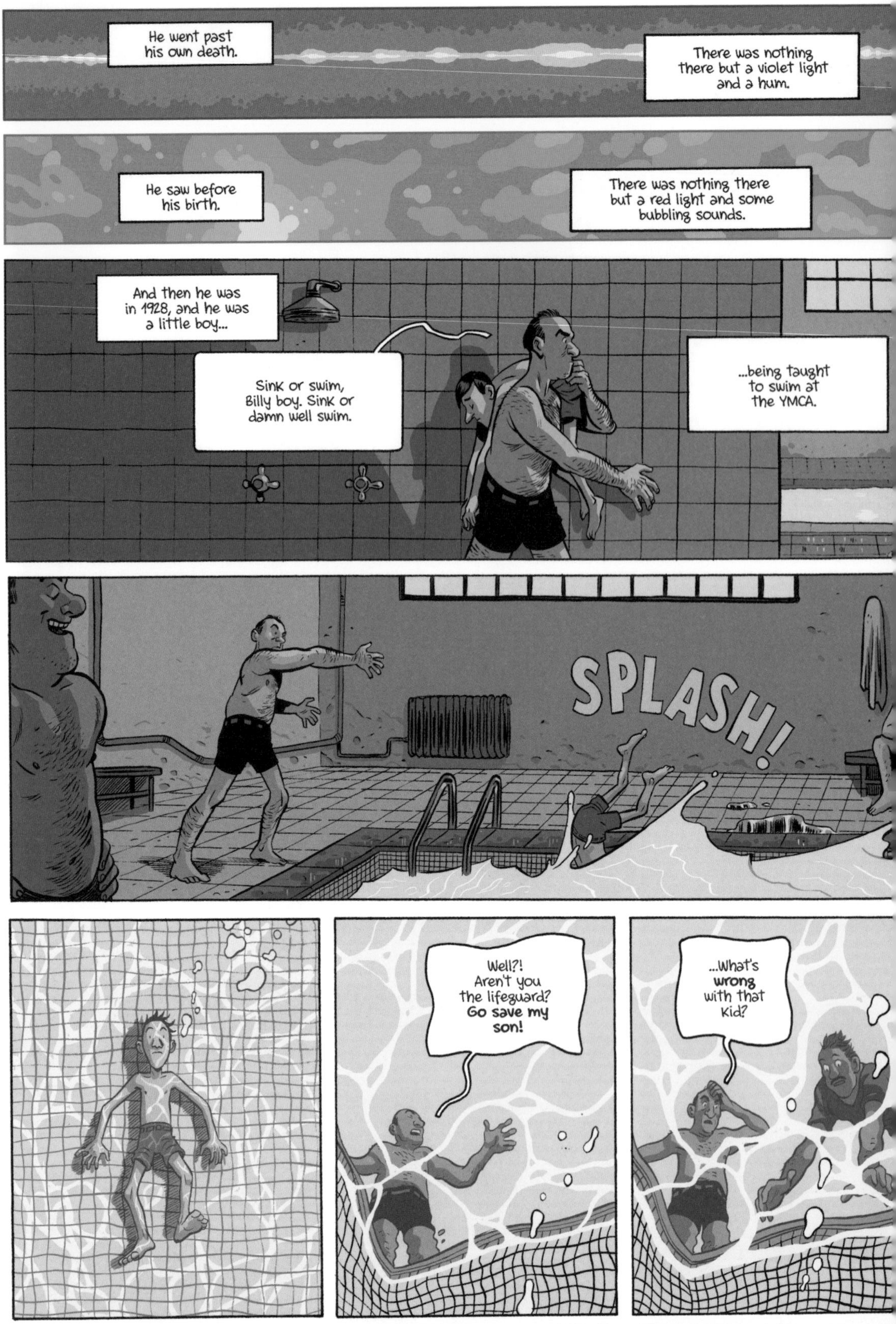
He went past his own death.
There was nothing there but a violet light and a hum.
He saw before his birth.
There was nothing there but a red light and some bubbling sounds.
And then he was in 1928, and he was a little boy...
Sink or swim, Billy boy. Sink or damn well swim.
...being taught to swim at the YMCA.
SPLASH!
Well?! Aren't you the lifeguard? **Go save my son!**
...What's **wrong** with that kid?

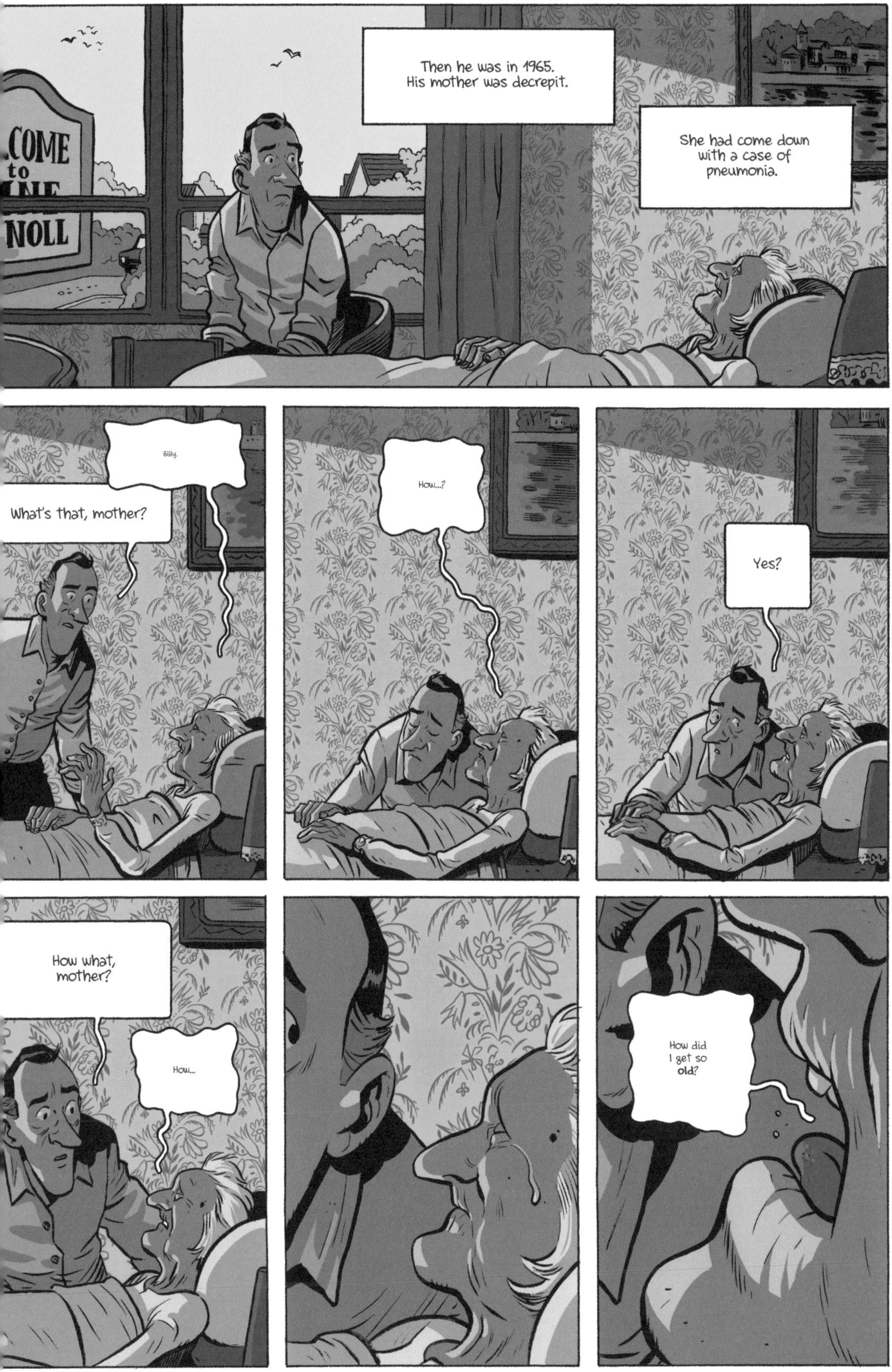

COME
to
NOLL
Then he was in 1965. His mother was decrepit.
She had come down with a case of pneumonia.
What's that, mother?
Billy.
How...?
Yes?
How what, mother?
How...
How did I get so **old**?

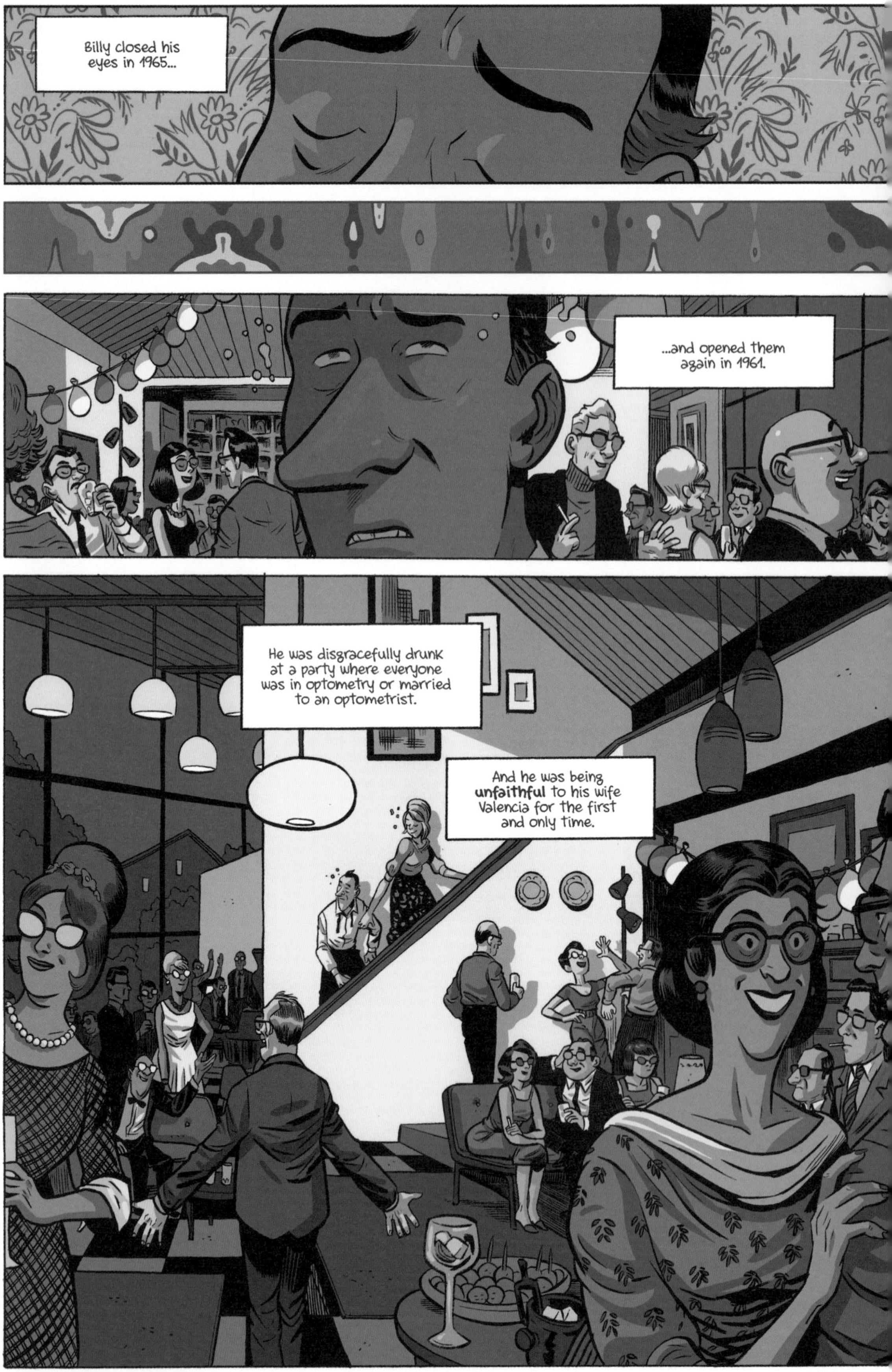
Billy closed his eyes in 1965...
...and opened them again in 1961.
He was disgracefully drunk at a party where everyone was in optometry or married to an optometrist.
And he was being **unfaithful** to his wife Valencia for the first and only time.

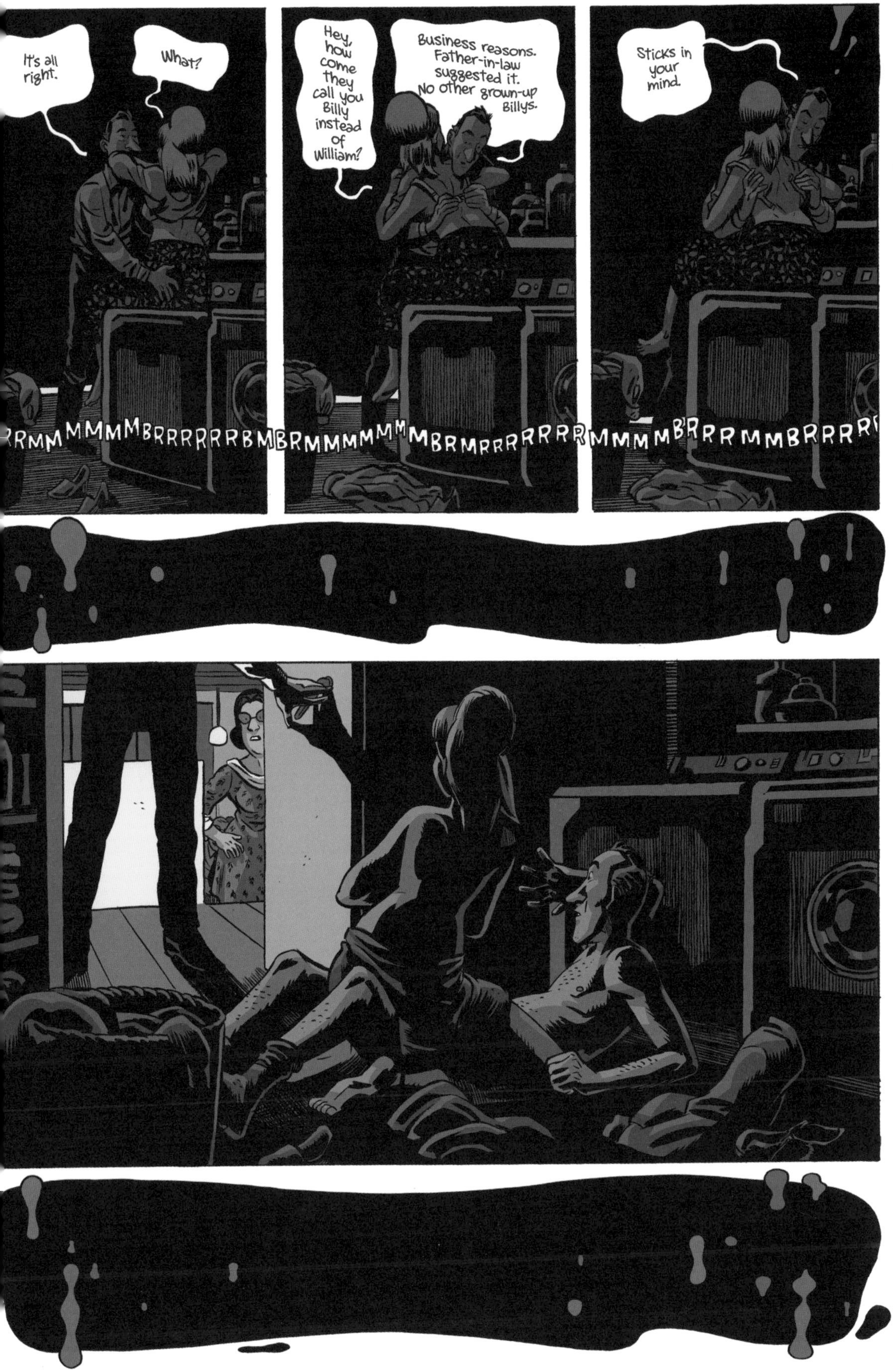
It's all right.
What?
RMMMMMMMBRRRRRRRBM
Hey, how come they call you Billy instead of William?
Business reasons. Father-in-law suggested it. No other grown-up Billys.
BRMMMMMMMBRMRRRRRR
Sticks in your mind.
MMMMBRRRMMBRRRR

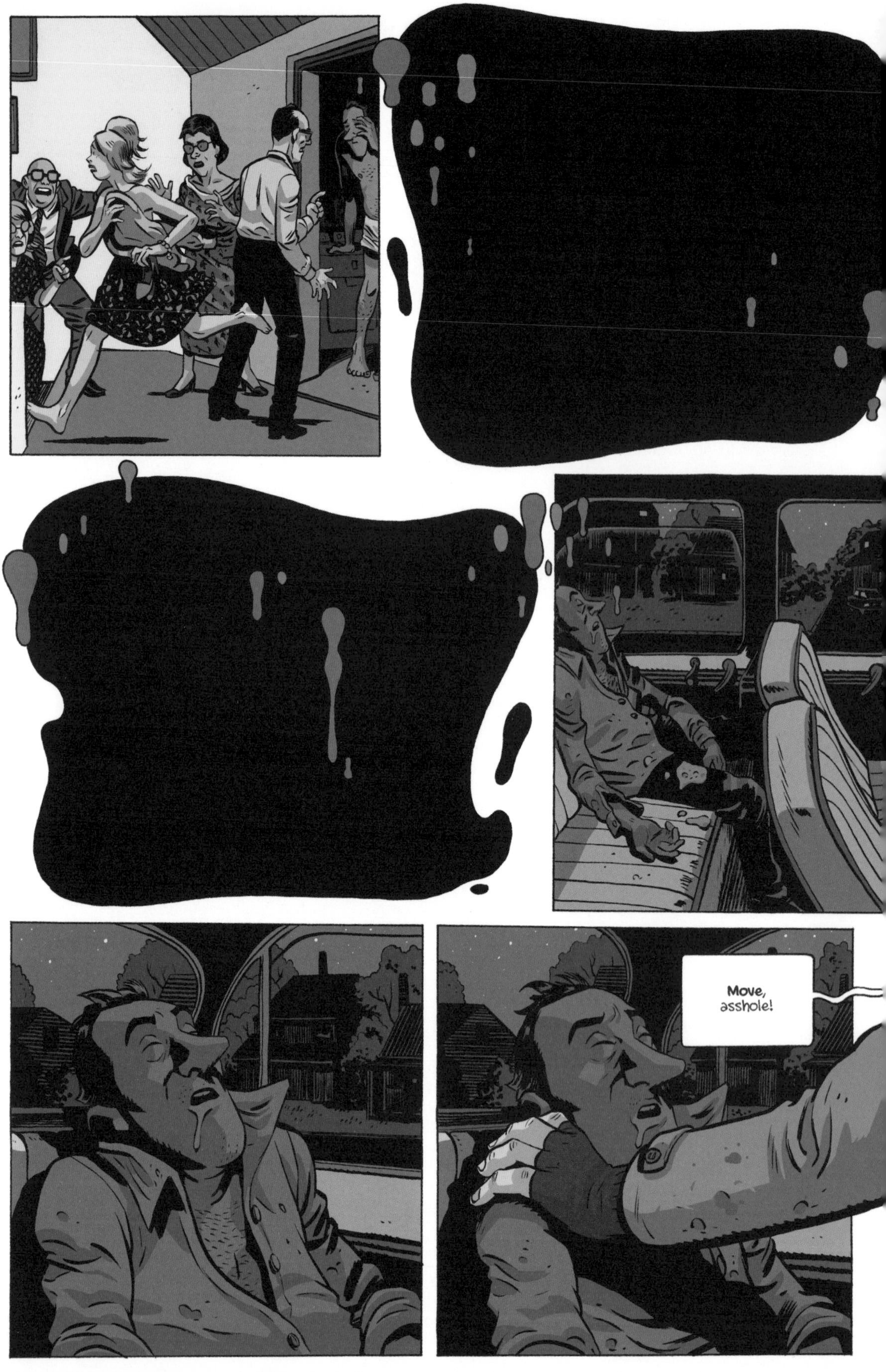
Move, asshole!

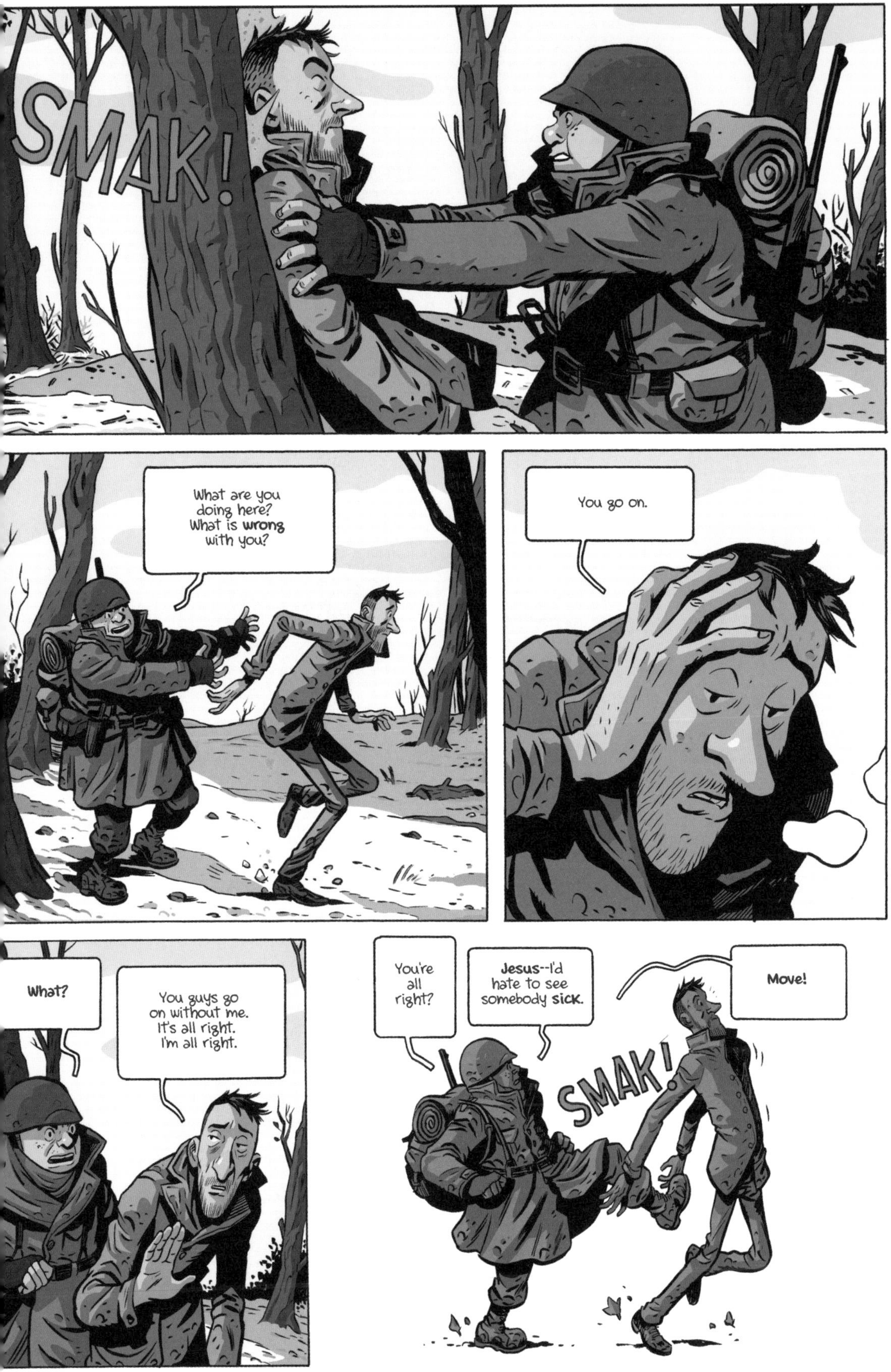
SMAK!
What are you doing here? What is **wrong** with you?
You go on.
What?
You guys go on without me. It's all right. I'm all right.
You're all right?
Jesus--I'd hate to see somebody **sick**.
SMAK!
Move!

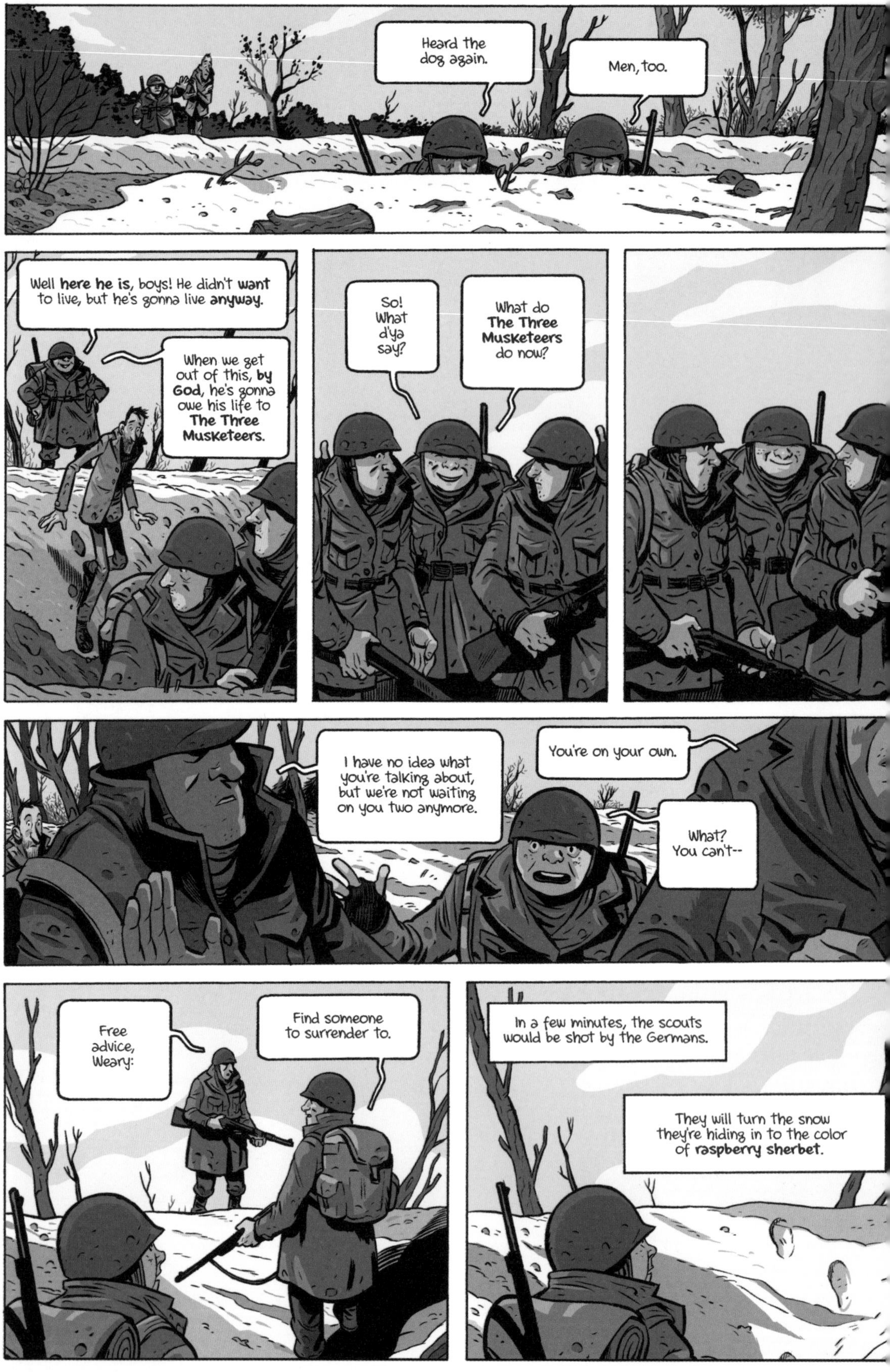

Heard the dog again.
Men, too.
Well **here he is**, boys! He didn't **want** to live, but he's gonna live **anyway**.
When we get out of this, **by God**, he's gonna owe his life to **The Three Musketeers**.
So! What d'ya say?
What do **The Three Musketeers** do now?
I have no idea what you're talking about, but we're not waiting on you two anymore.
You're on your own.
What? You can't--
Free advice, Weary:
Find someone to surrender to.
In a few minutes, the scouts would be shot by the Germans.
They will turn the snow they're hiding in to the color of **raspberry sherbet**.

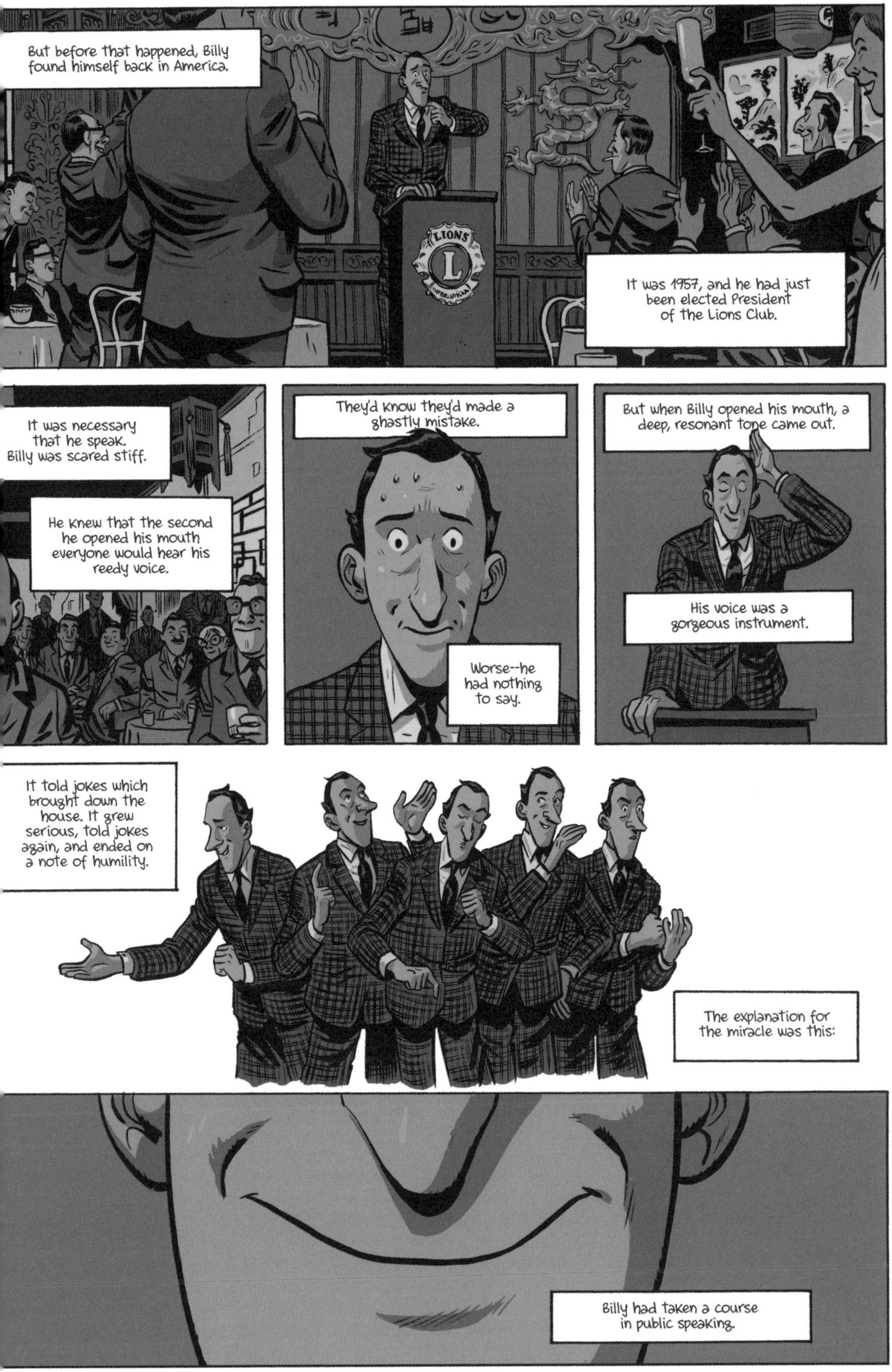
But before that happened, Billy found himself back in America.
LIONS
It was 1957, and he had just been elected President of the Lions Club.
It was necessary that he speak. Billy was scared stiff.
He knew that the second he opened his mouth everyone would hear his reedy voice.
They'd know they'd made a ghastly mistake.
Worse--he had nothing to say.
But when Billy opened his mouth, a deep, resonant tone came out.
His voice was a gorgeous instrument.
It told jokes which brought down the house. It grew serious, told jokes again, and ended on a note of humility.
The explanation for the miracle was this:
Billy had taken a course in public speaking.

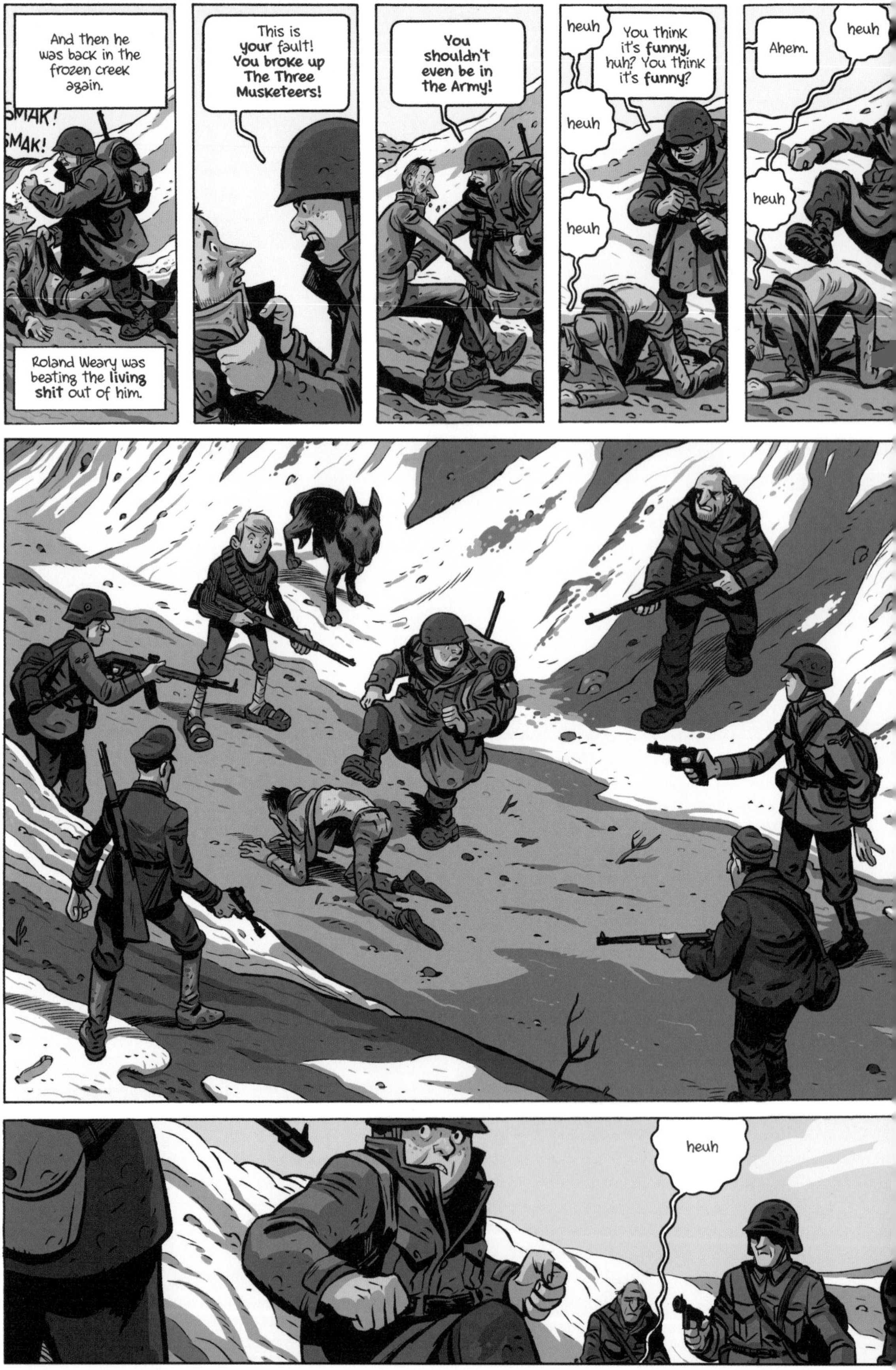

And then he was back in the frozen creek again.
SMAK!
SMAK!
Roland Weary was beating the **living shit** out of him.
This is **your** fault! **You broke up The Three Musketeers!**
You shouldn't even be in the Army!
heuh
You think it's **funny,** huh? You think it's **funny?**
heuh
heuh
Ahem.
heuh
heuh
heuh

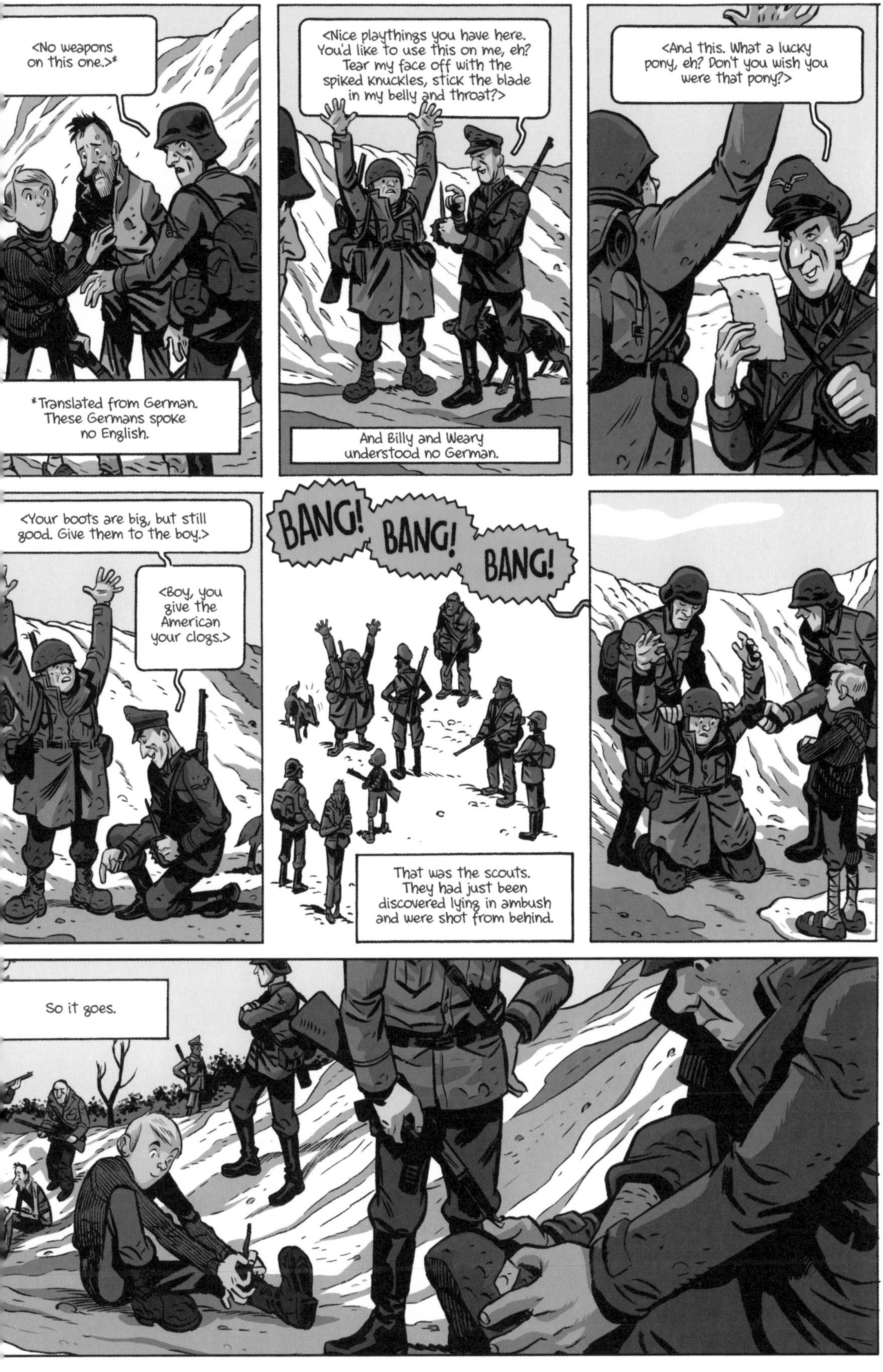

<No weapons on this one.>*
*Translated from German. These Germans spoke no English.
<Nice playthings you have here. You'd like to use this on me, eh? Tear my face off with the spiked knuckles, stick the blade in my belly and throat?>
And Billy and Weary understood no German.
<And this. What a lucky pony, eh? Don't you wish you were that pony?>
<Your boots are big, but still good. Give them to the boy.>
<Boy, you give the American your clogs.>
BANG!
BANG!
BANG!
That was the scouts. They had just been discovered lying in ambush and were shot from behind.
So it goes.

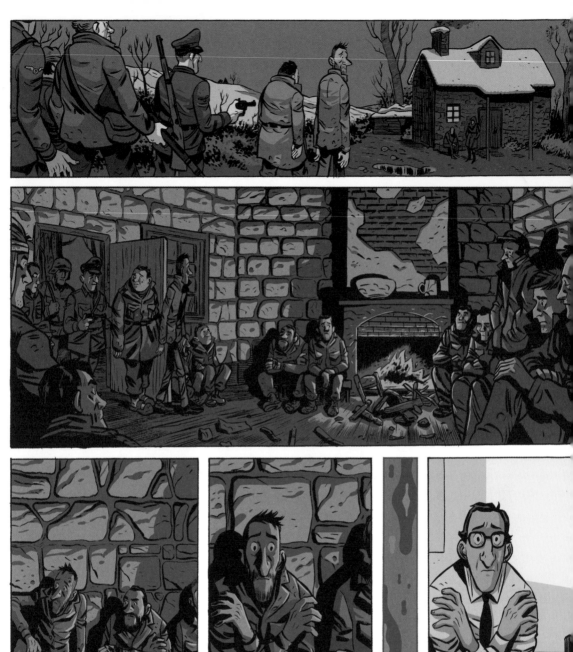

Doctor...?
Are you
still there?

Hm?

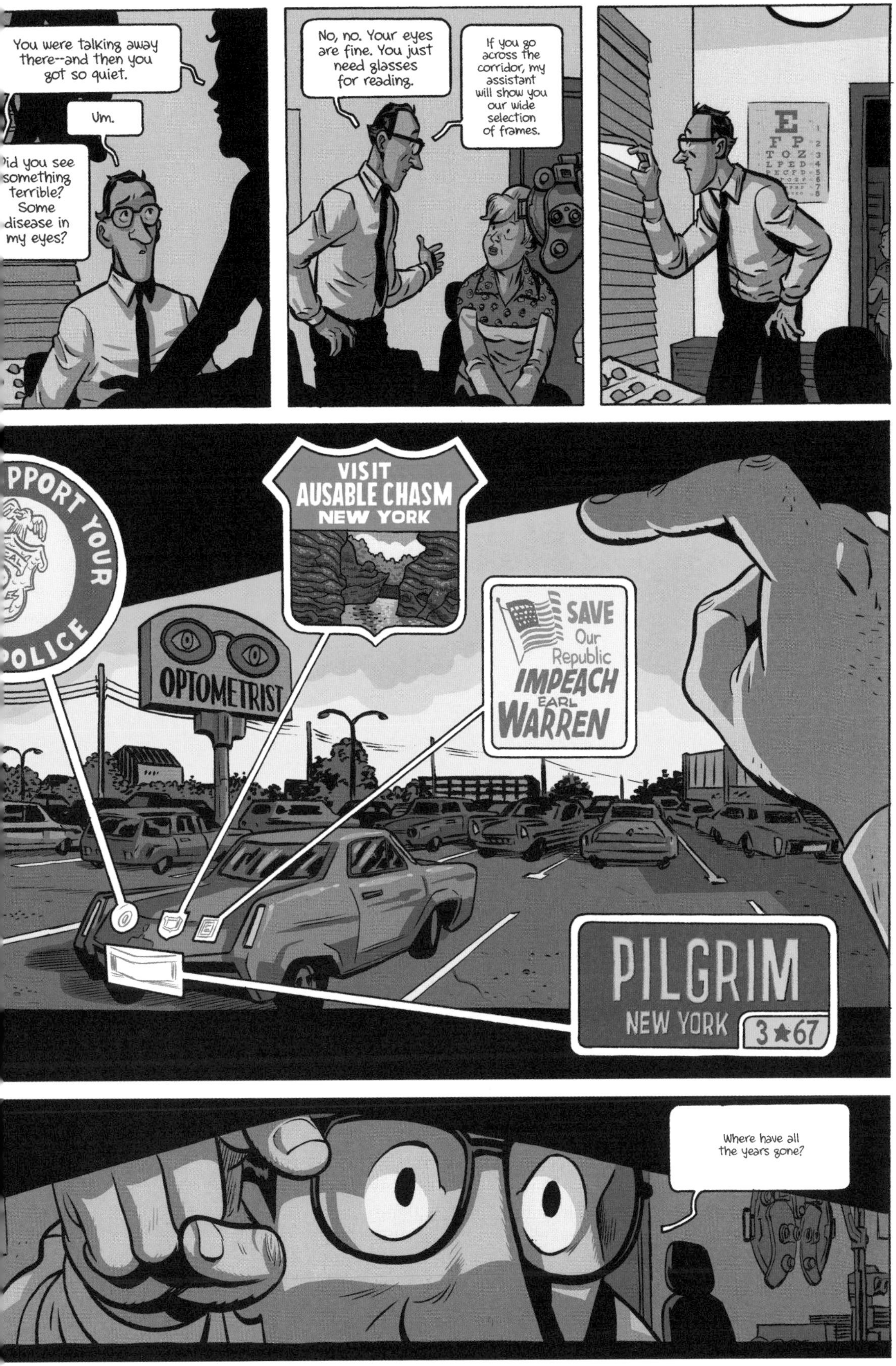

You were talking away there--and then you got so quiet.
Um.
Did you see something terrible? Some disease in my eyes?
No, no. Your eyes are fine. You just need glasses for reading.
If you go across the corridor, my assistant will show you our wide selection of frames.
E
F P
T O Z
L P E D
PPORT YOUR POLICE
VISIT AUSABLE CHASM NEW YORK
OPTOMETRIST
SAVE Our Republic IMPEACH EARL WARREN
PILGRIM
NEW YORK
3★67
Where have all the years gone?

Billy had a framed prayer on his wall.

It expressed his method for keeping going, even though he was unenthusiastic about living.

A lot of his patients who saw the prayer said it helped **them** keep going too.

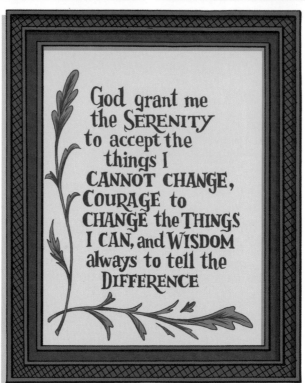

God grant me the SERENITY to accept the things I CANNOT CHANGE, COURAGE to CHANGE the THINGS I CAN, and WISDOM always to tell the DIFFERENCE

Among the things Billy Pilgrim could not change were the past, the present, and the future.

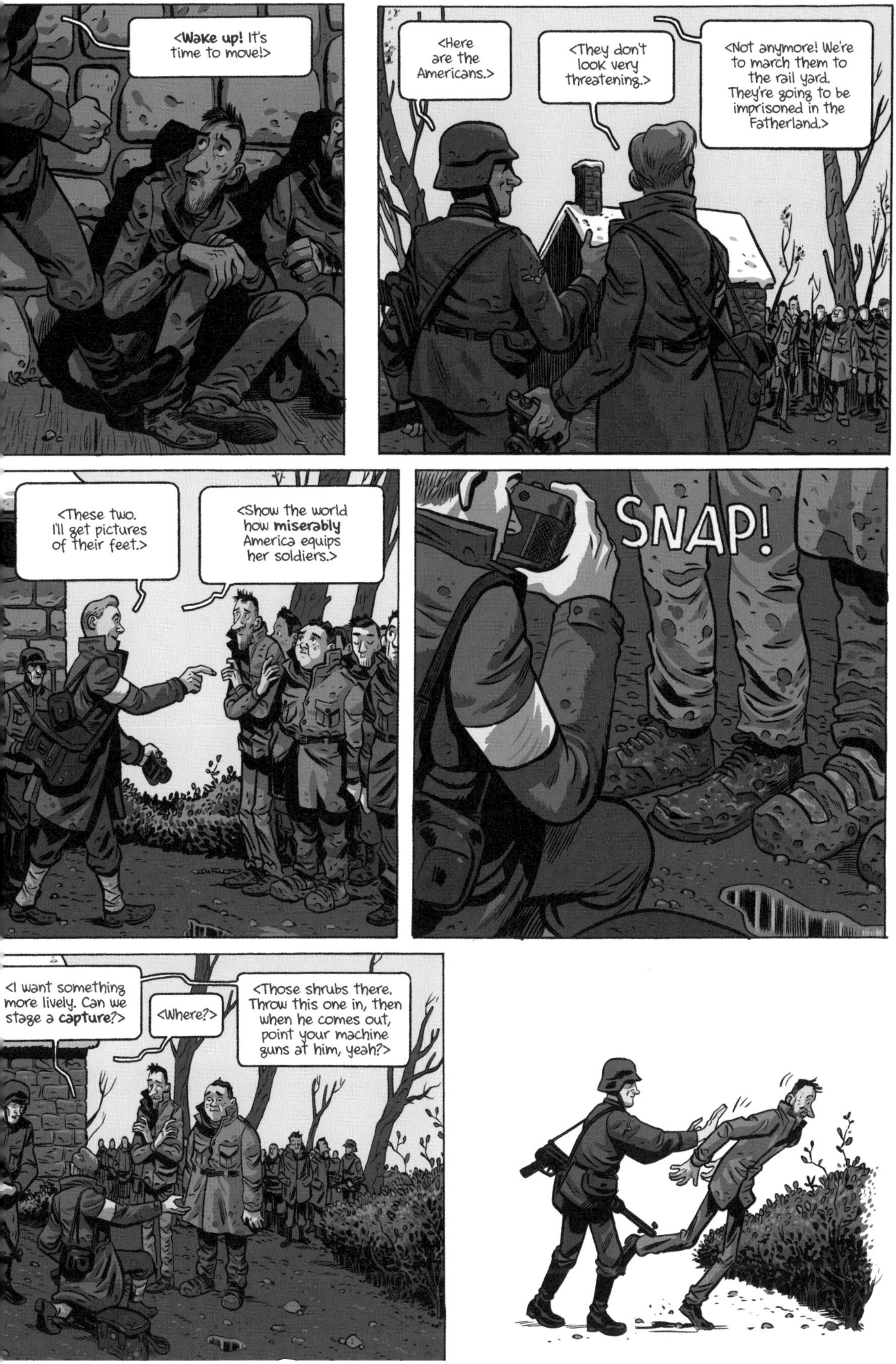
<**Wake up!** It's time to move!>
<Here are the Americans.>
<They don't look very threatening.>
<Not anymore! We're to march them to the rail yard. They're going to be imprisoned in the Fatherland.>
<These two. I'll get pictures of their feet.>
<Show the world how **miserably** America equips her soldiers.>
SNAP!
<I want something more lively. Can we stage a **capture**?>
<Where?>
<Those shrubs there. Throw this one in, then when he comes out, point your machine guns at him, yeah?>

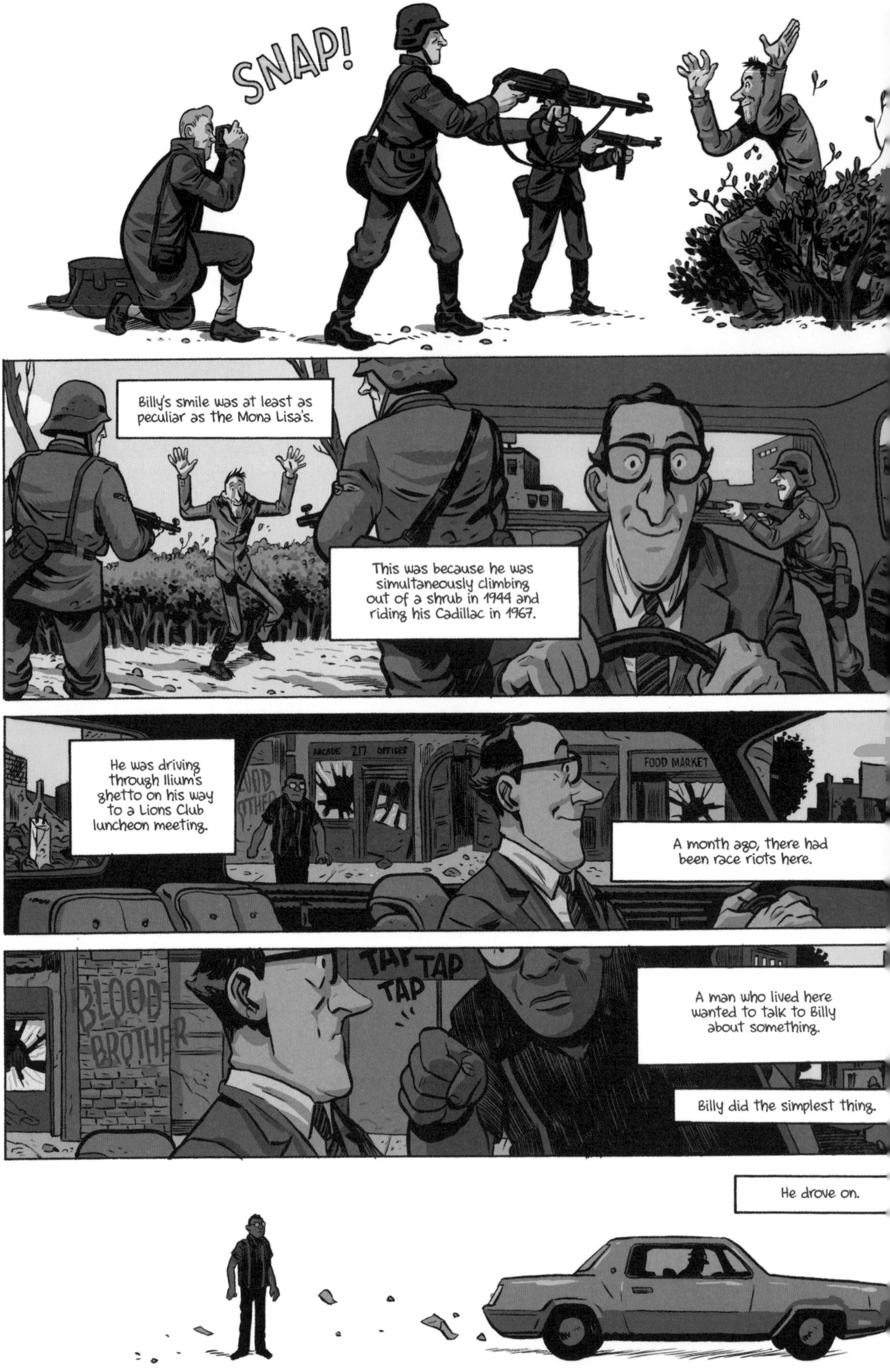
SNAP!
Billy's smile was at least as peculiar as the Mona Lisa's.
This was because he was simultaneously climbing out of a shrub in 1944 and riding his Cadillac in 1967.
He was driving through Ilium's ghetto on his way to a Lions Club luncheon meeting.
ARCADE 217 OFFICES
FOOD MARKET
A month ago, there had been race riots here.
BLOOD BROTHER
TAP TAP TAP
A man who lived here wanted to talk to Billy about something.
Billy did the simplest thing.
He drove on.

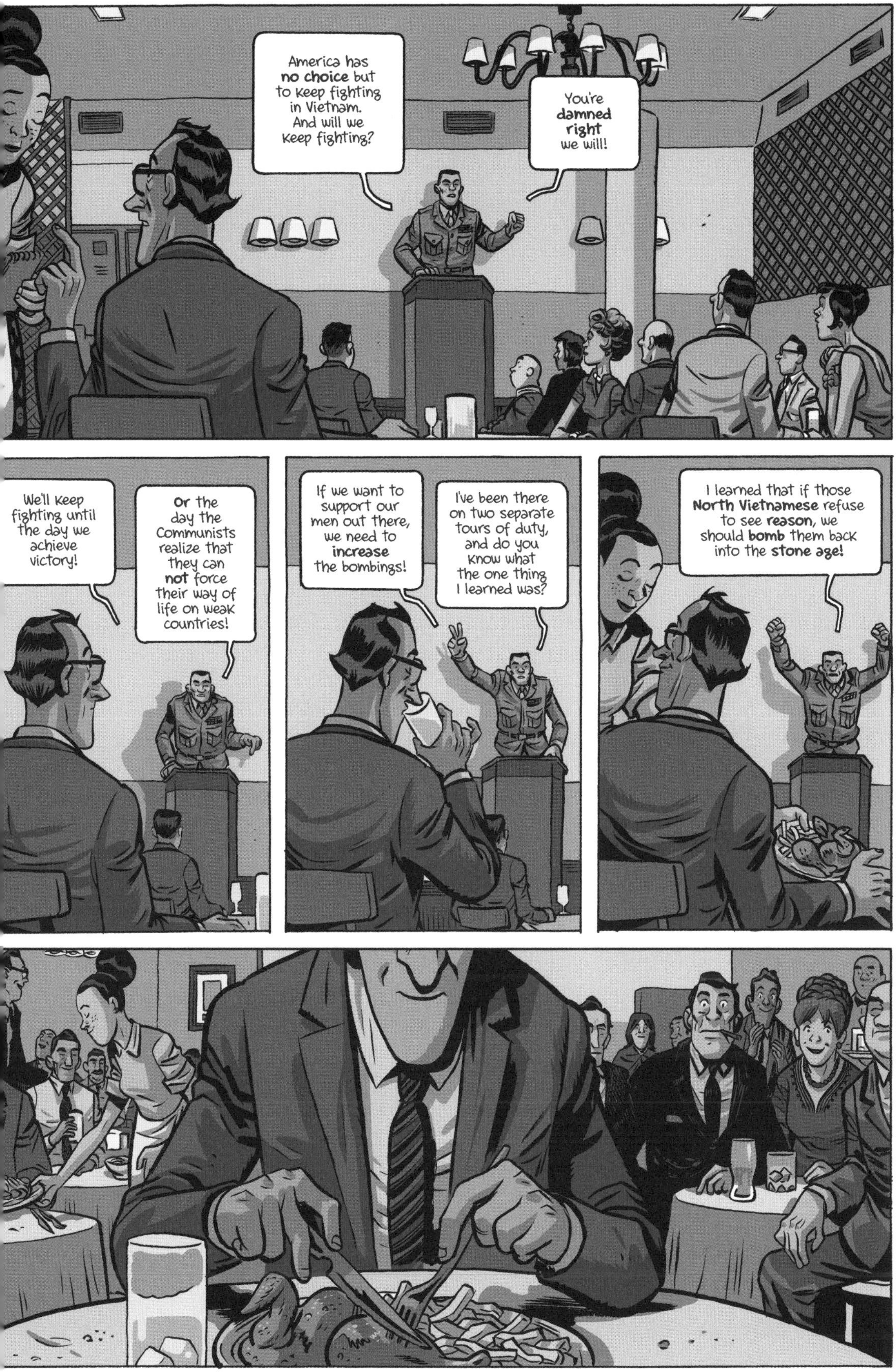
America has **no choice** but to keep fighting in Vietnam. And will we keep fighting?
You're **damned right** we will!
We'll keep fighting until the day we achieve victory!
Or the day the Communists realize that they can **not** force their way of life on weak countries!
If we want to support our men out there, we need to **increase** the bombings!
I've been there on two separate tours of duty, and do you know what the one thing I learned was?
I learned that if those **North Vietnamese** refuse to see **reason**, we should **bomb** them back into the **stone age!**

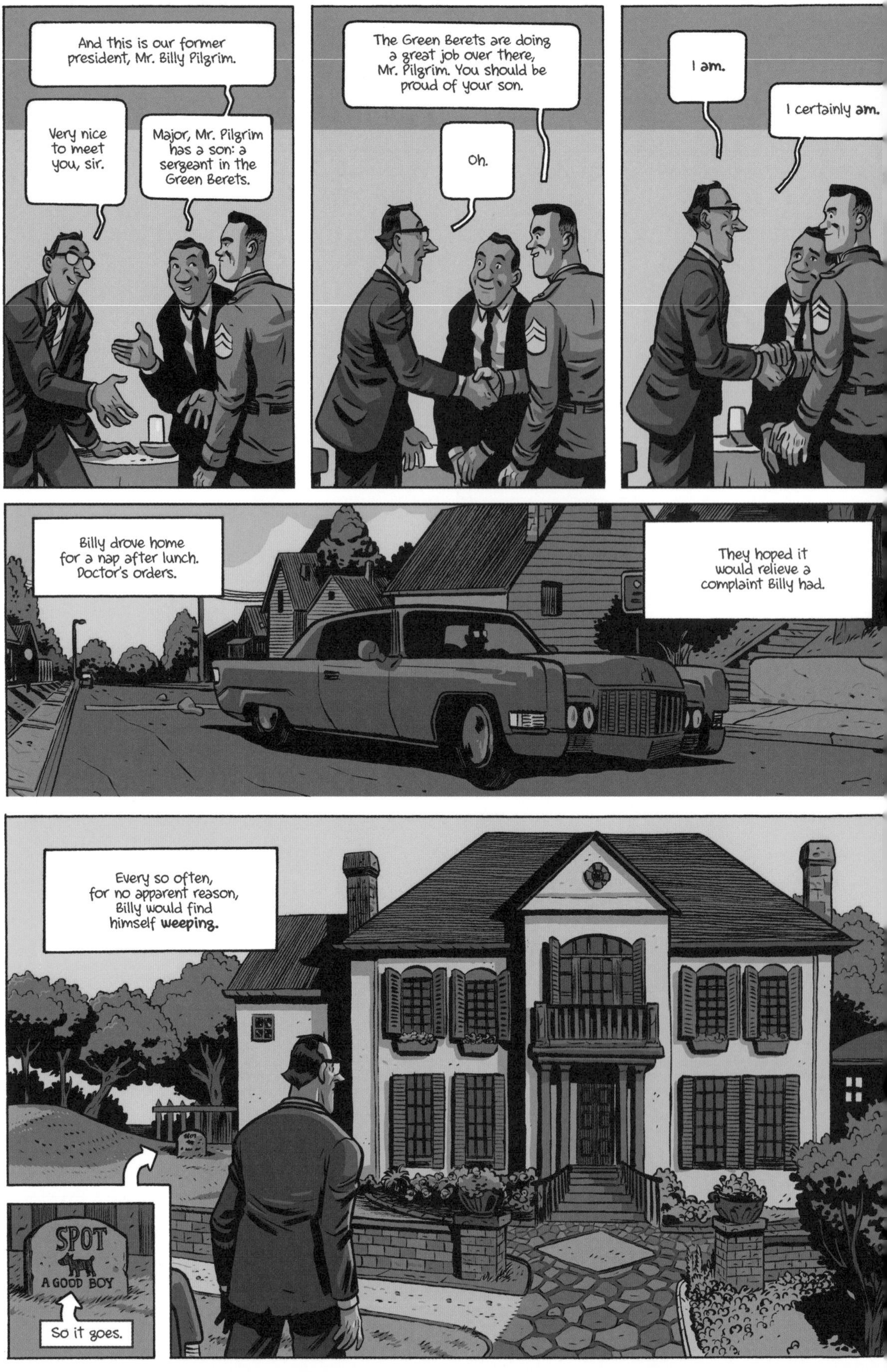

And this is our former president, Mr. Billy Pilgrim.
Very nice to meet you, sir.
Major, Mr. Pilgrim has a son: a sergeant in the Green Berets.
The Green Berets are doing a great job over there, Mr. Pilgrim. You should be proud of your son.
Oh.
I am.
I certainly am.
Billy drove home for a nap after lunch. Doctor's orders.
They hoped it would relieve a complaint Billy had.
Every so often, for no apparent reason, Billy would find himself weeping.
SPOT
A GOOD BOY
So it goes.

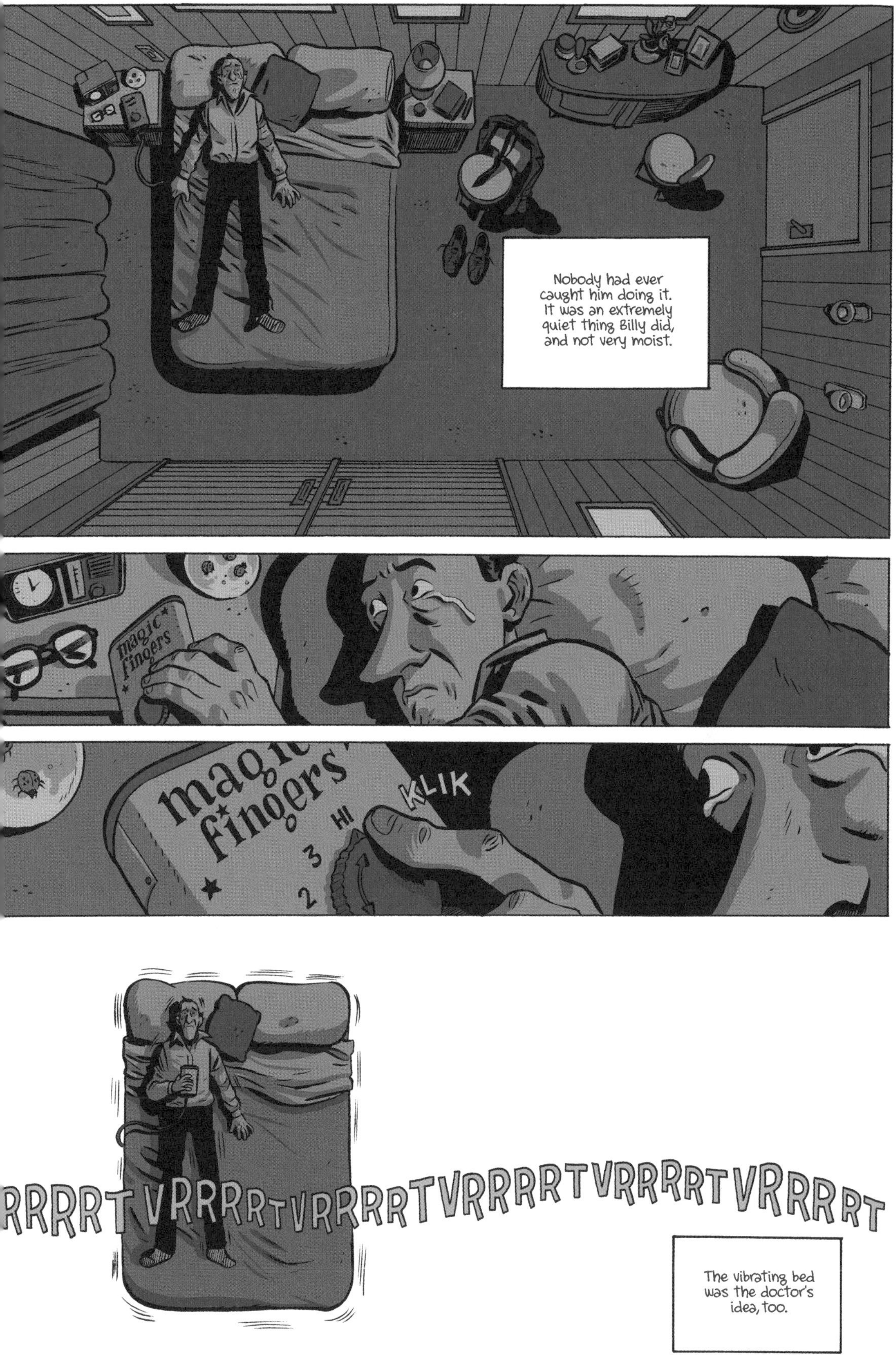
Nobody had ever caught him doing it. It was an extremely quiet thing Billy did, and not very moist.
magic fingers
magic fingers
HI
3
2
KLIK
RRRRTVRRRRTVRRRRTVRRRRTVRRRRTVRRRRT
The vibrating bed was the doctor's idea, too.

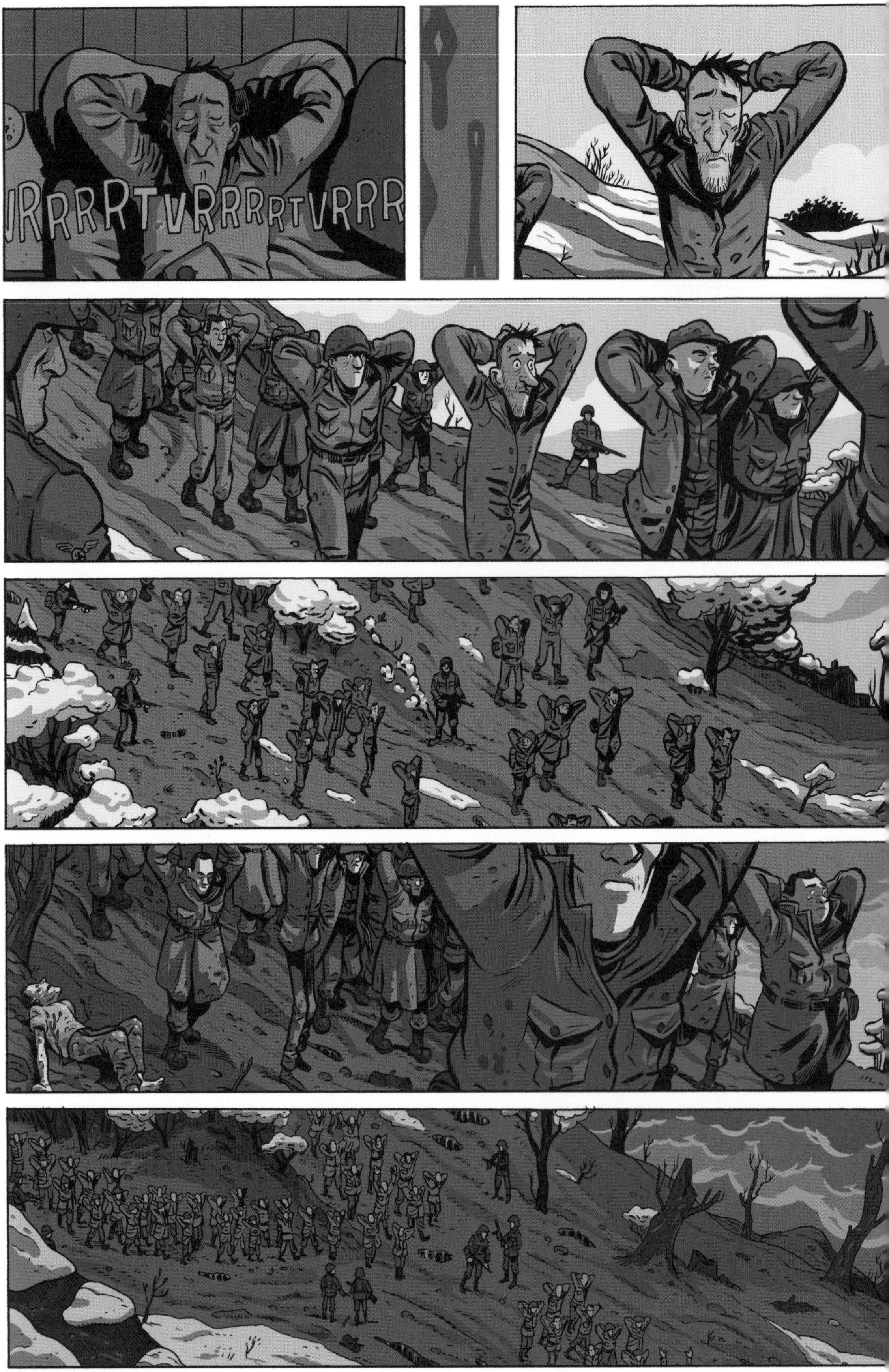
VRRRRTVRRRRRTVRRR

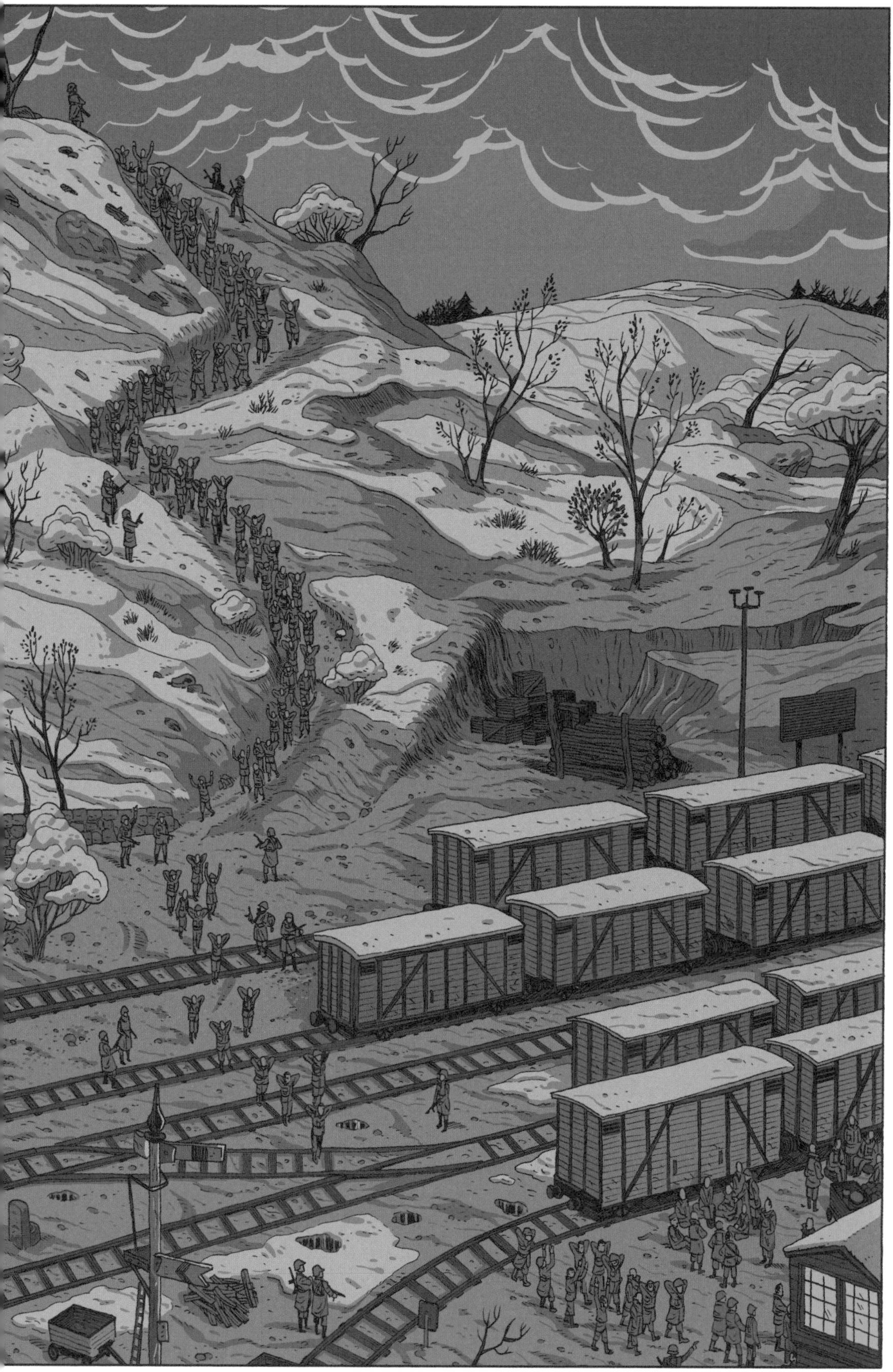

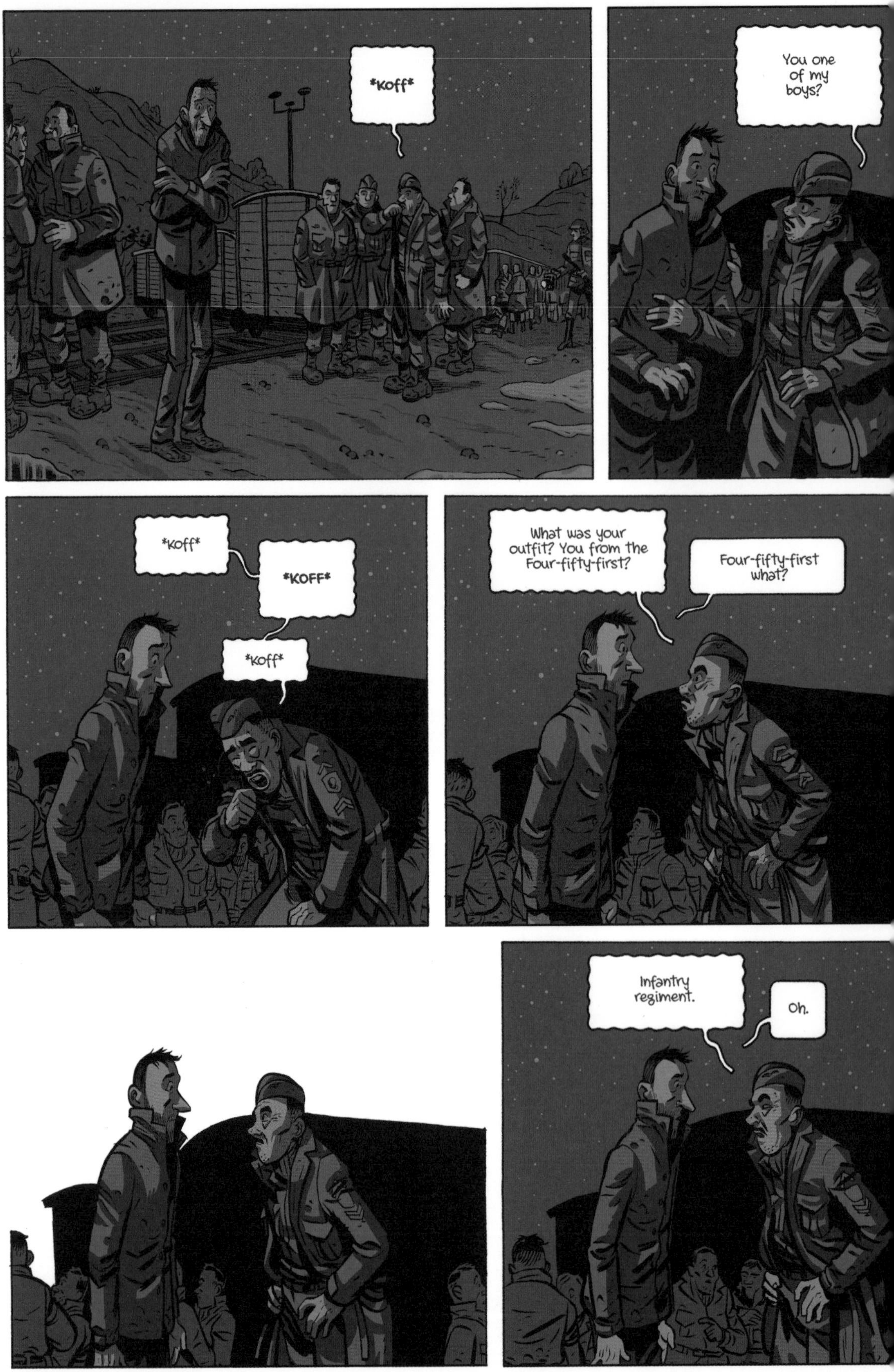
koff
You one of my boys?
koff
KOFF
koff
What was your outfit? You from the Four-fifty-first?
Four-fifty-first what?
Infantry regiment.
Oh.

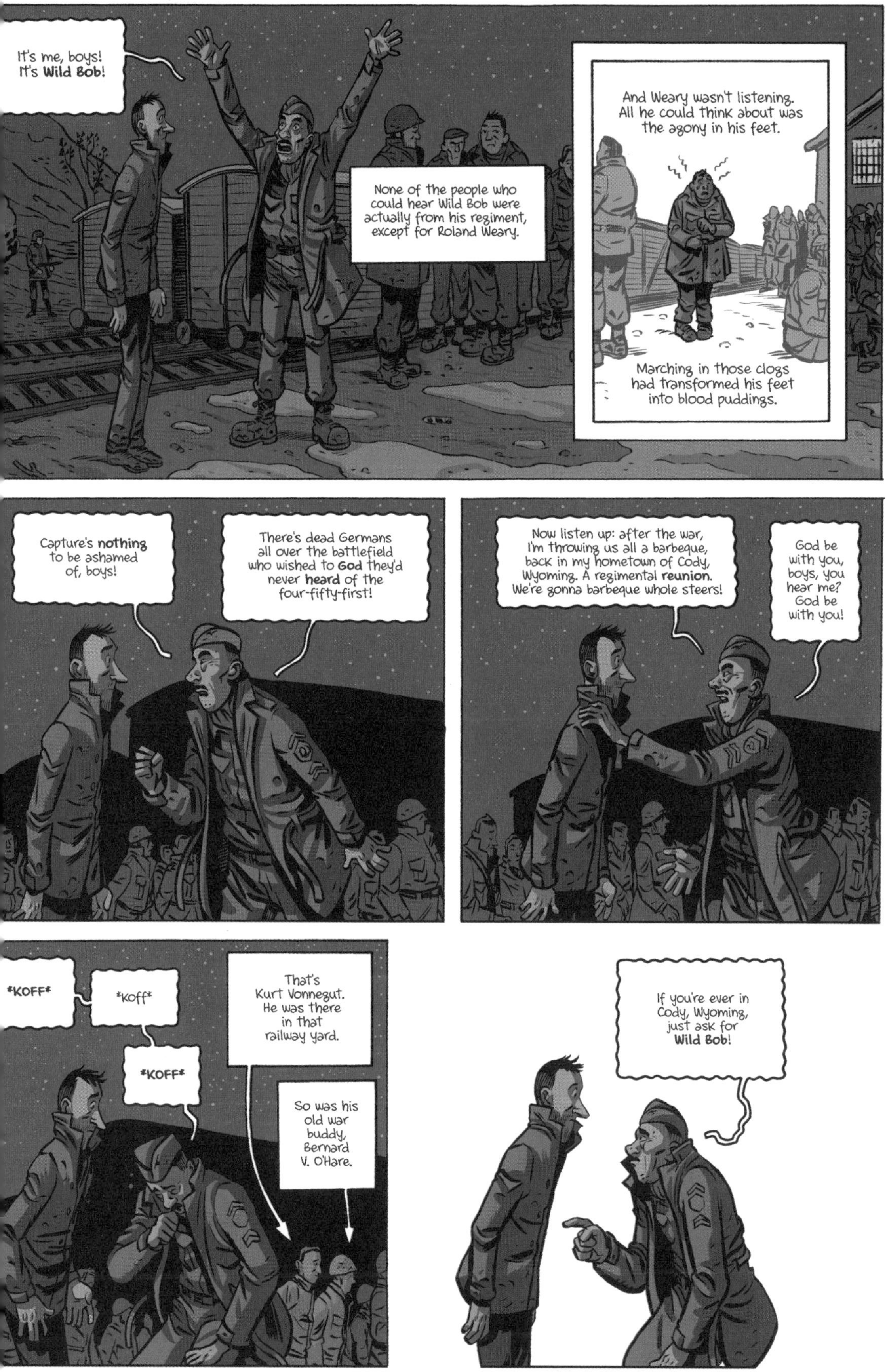

It's me, boys! It's **Wild Bob**!
None of the people who could hear Wild Bob were actually from his regiment, except for Roland Weary.
And Weary wasn't listening. All he could think about was the agony in his feet.
Marching in those clogs had transformed his feet into blood puddings.
Capture's **nothing** to be ashamed of, boys!
There's dead Germans all over the battlefield who wished to **God** they'd never **heard** of the four-fifty-first!
Now listen up: after the war, I'm throwing us all a barbeque, back in my hometown of Cody, Wyoming. A regimental **reunion**. We're gonna barbeque whole steers!
God be with you, boys, you hear me? God be with you!
KOFF
koff
KOFF
That's Kurt Vonnegut. He was there in that railway yard.
So was his old war buddy, Bernard V. O'Hare.
If you're ever in Cody, Wyoming, just ask for **Wild Bob**!

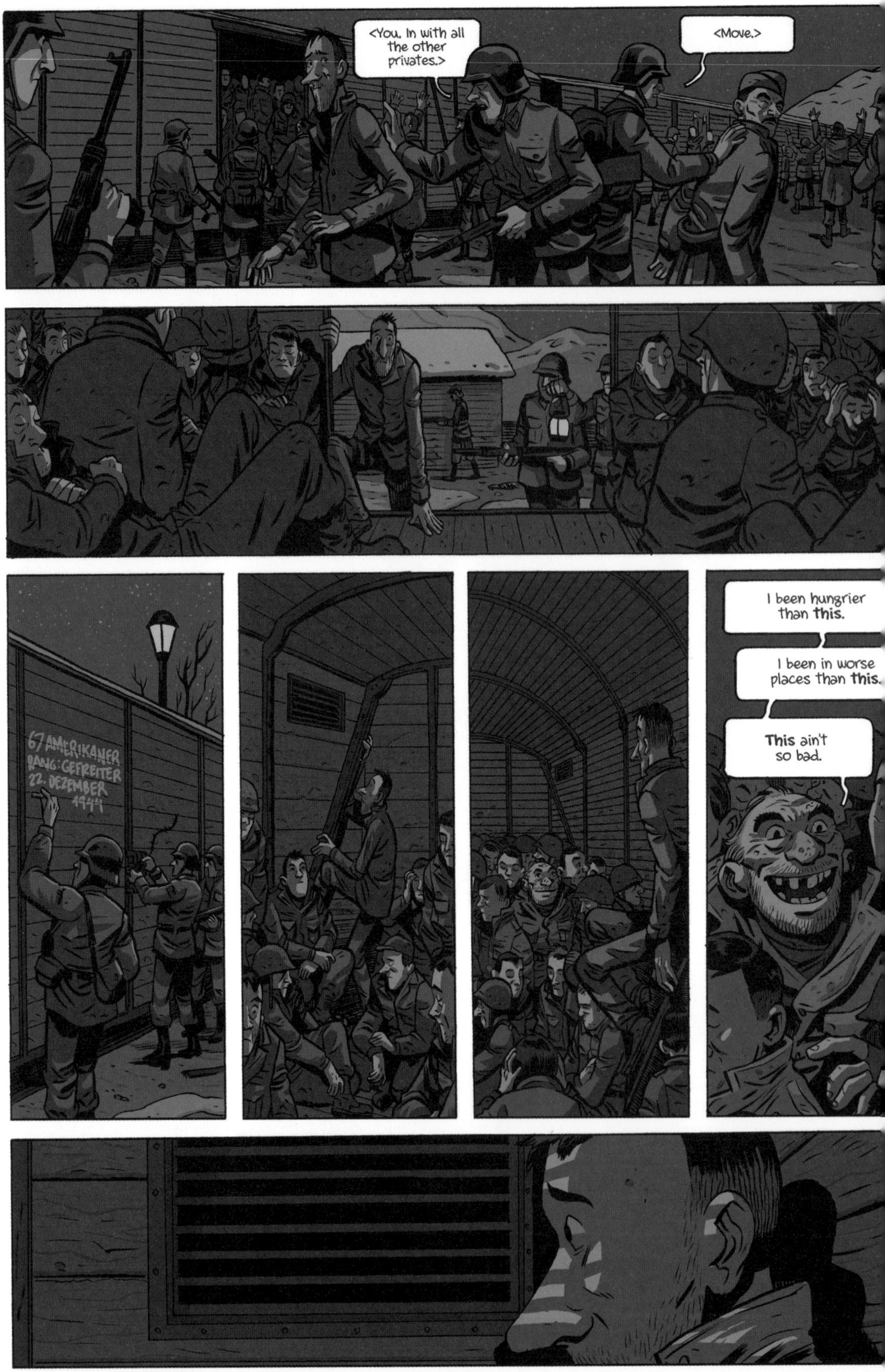

<You. In with all the other privates.>
<Move.>
67 AMERIKANER
RANG: GEFREITER
22. DEZEMBER
1944
I been hungrier than this.
I been in worse places than this.
This ain't so bad.

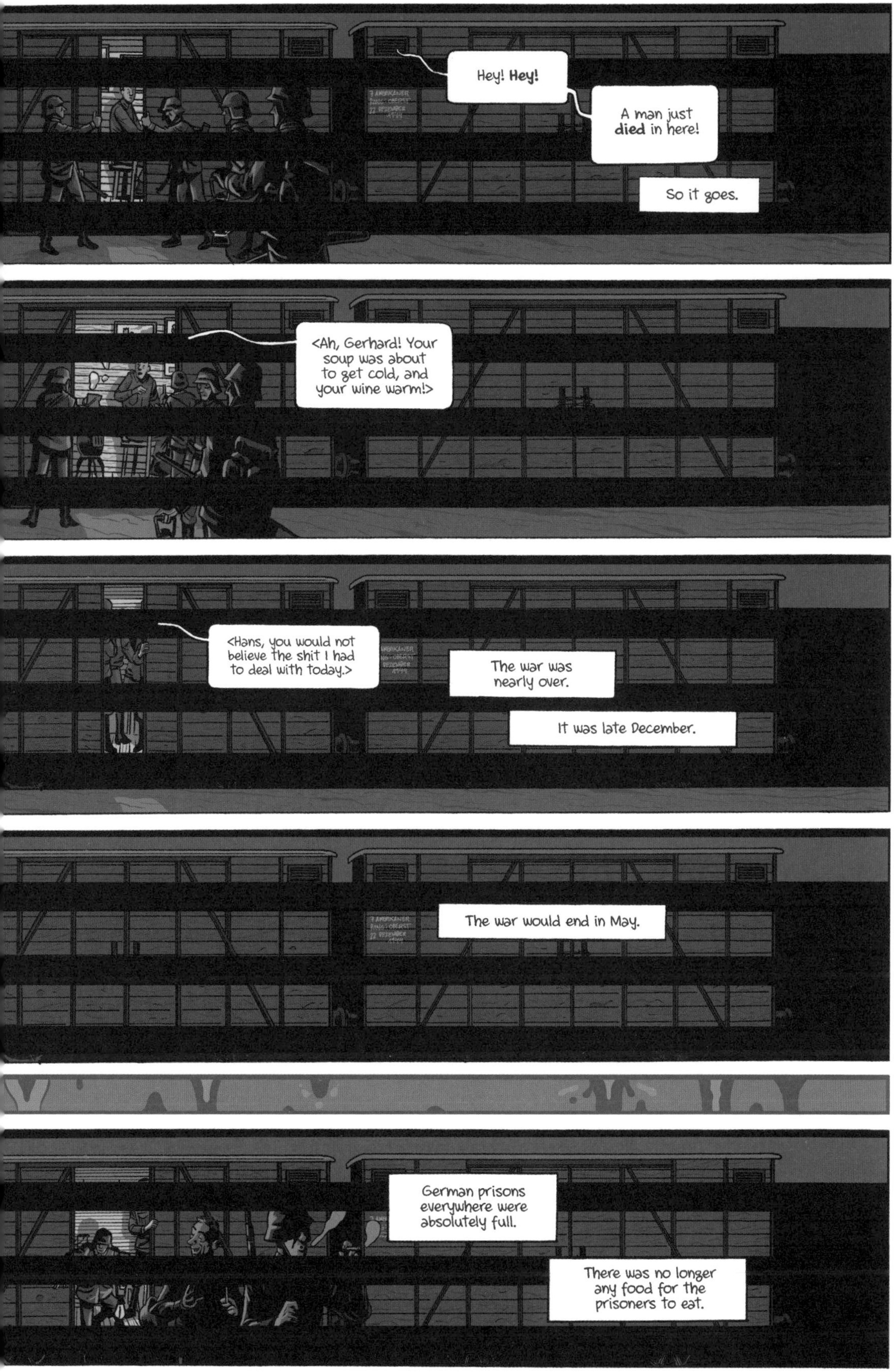
Hey! **Hey!**
A man just **died** in here!
So it goes.
<Ah, Gerhard! Your soup was about to get cold, and your wine warm!>
<Hans, you would not believe the shit I had to deal with today.>
The war was nearly over.
It was late December.
The war would end in May.
German prisons everywhere were absolutely full.
There was no longer any food for the prisoners to eat.

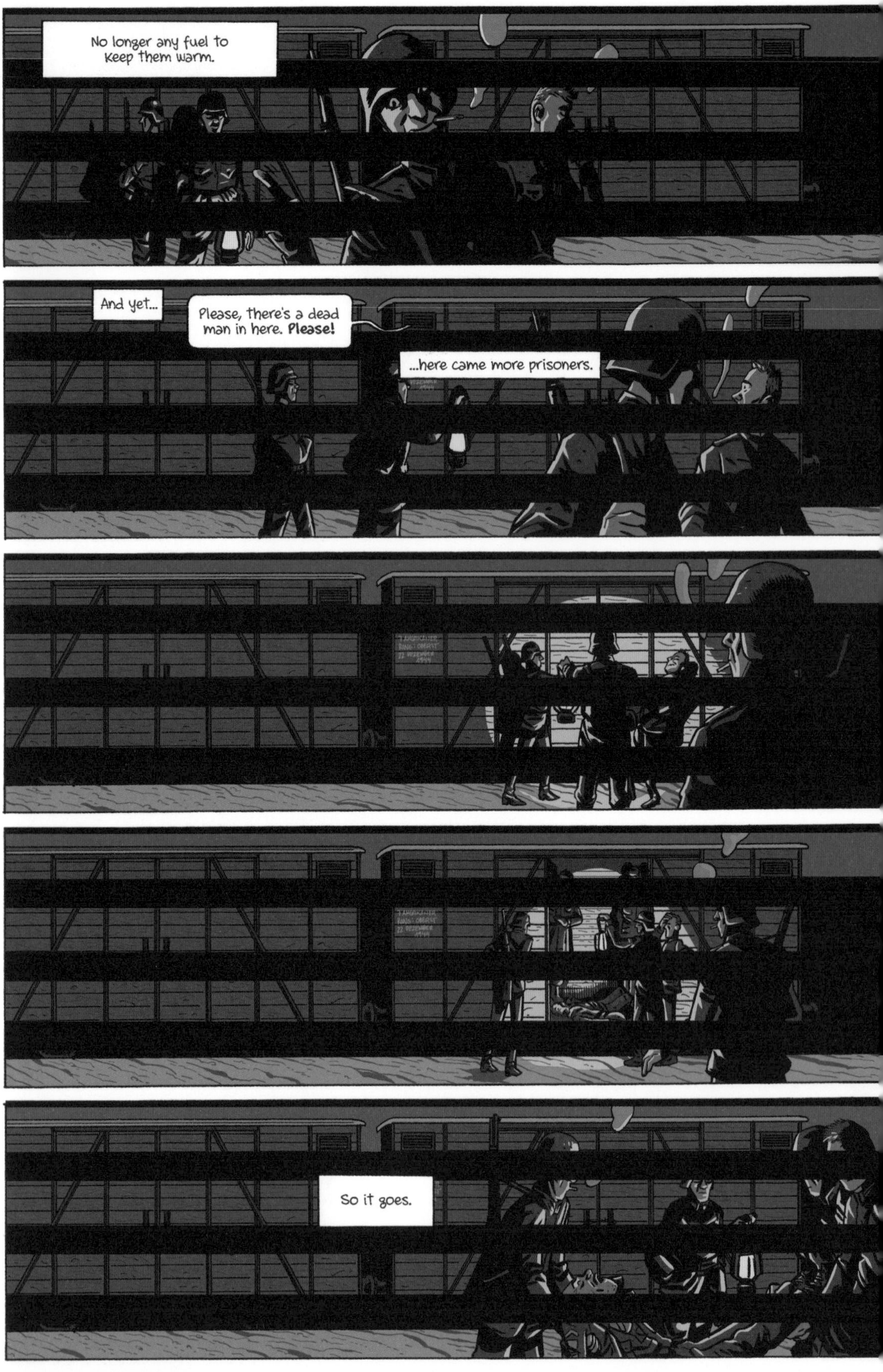
No longer any fuel to keep them warm.
And yet...
Please, there's a dead man in here. Please!
...here came more prisoners.
So it goes.

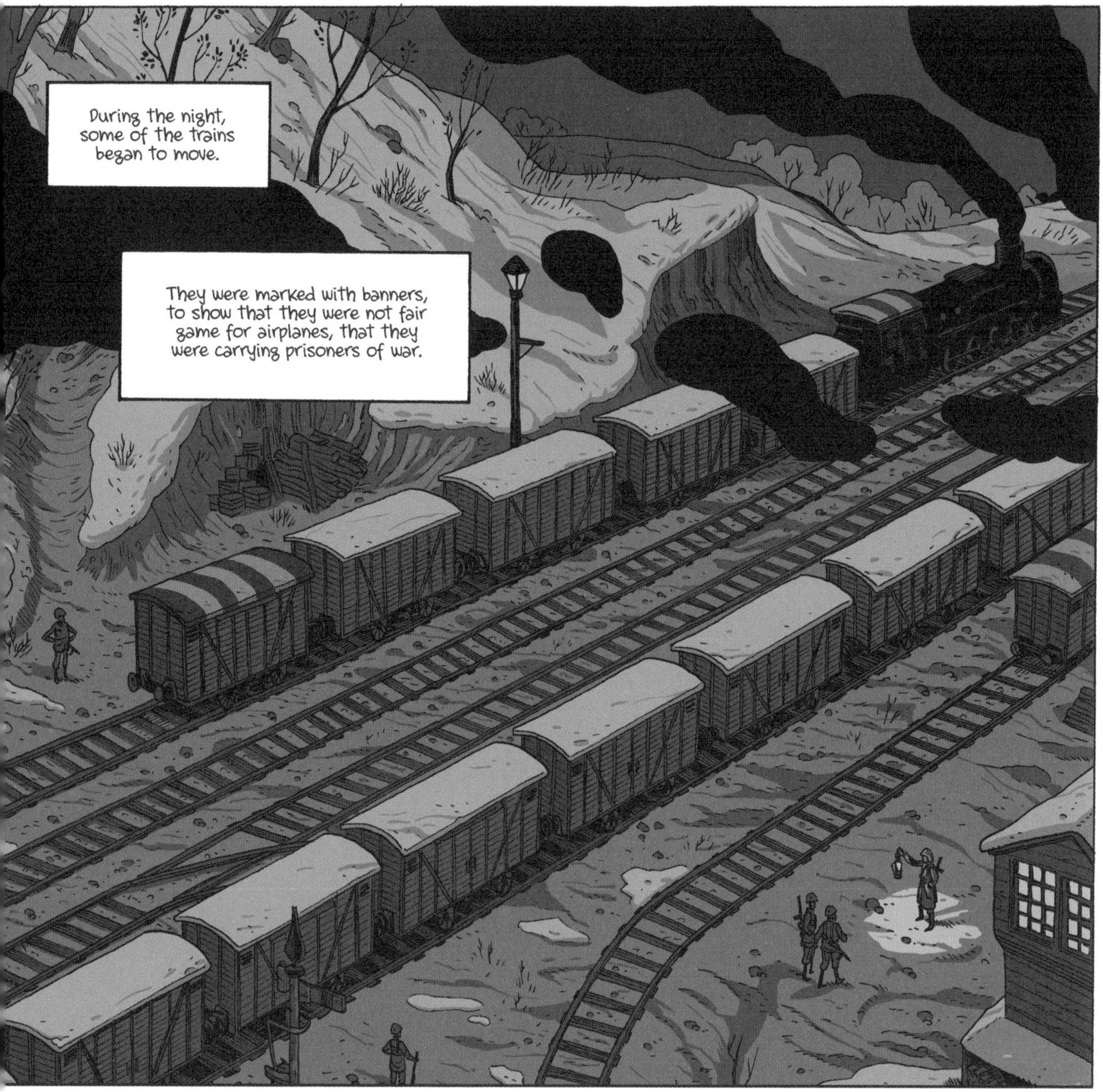
During the night, some of the trains began to move.
They were marked with banners, to show that they were not fair game for airplanes, that they were carrying prisoners of war.

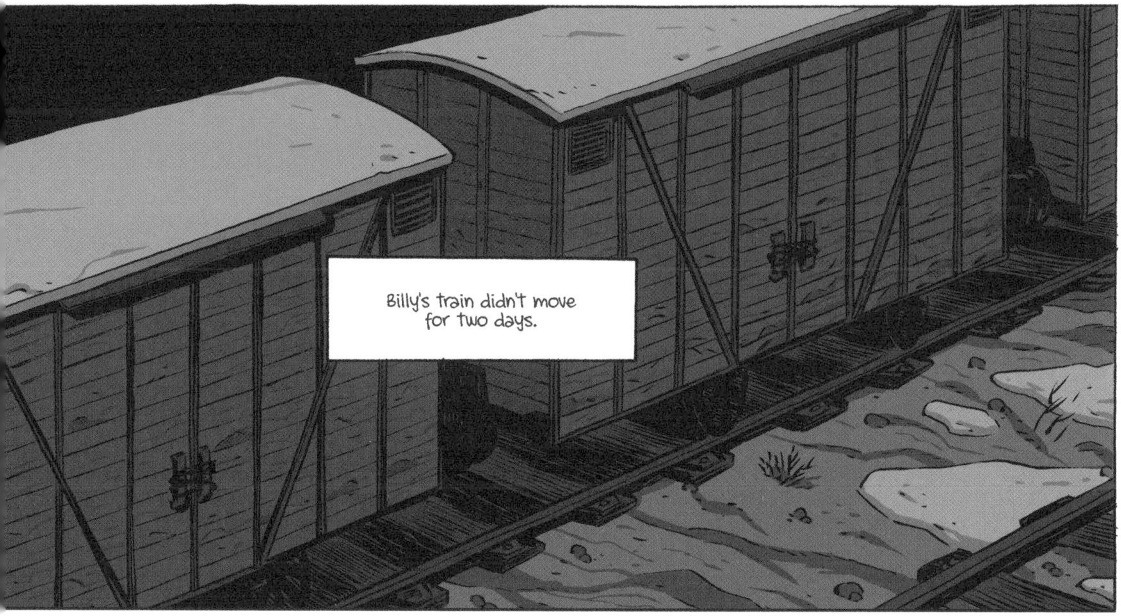
Billy's train didn't move for two days.

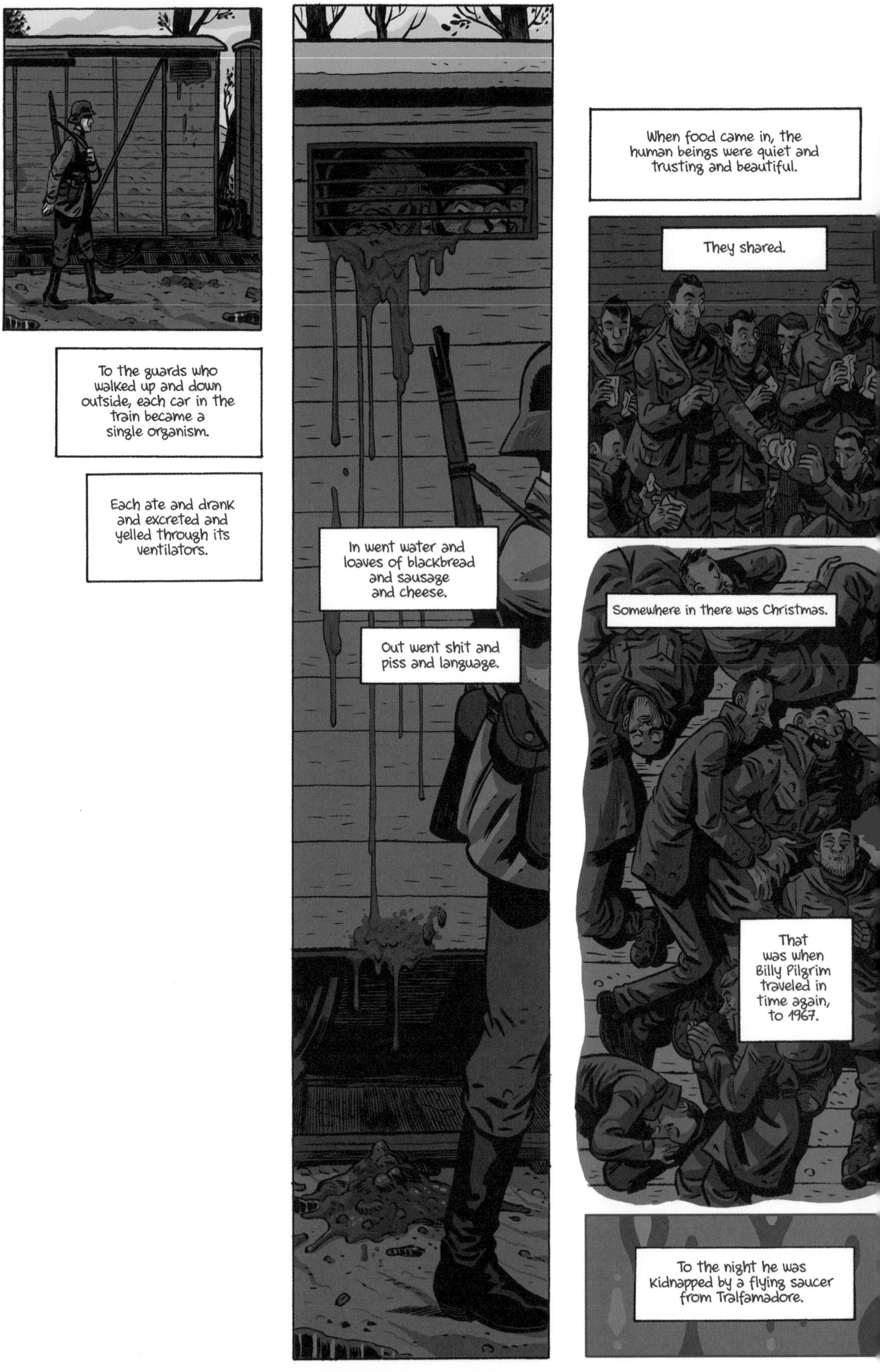
To the guards who walked up and down outside, each car in the train became a single organism.
Each ate and drank and excreted and yelled through its ventilators.
In went water and loaves of blackbread and sausage and cheese.
Out went shit and piss and language.
When food came in, the human beings were quiet and trusting and beautiful.
They shared.
Somewhere in there was Christmas.
That was when Billy Pilgrim traveled in time again, to 1967.
To the night he was kidnapped by a flying saucer from Tralfamadore.

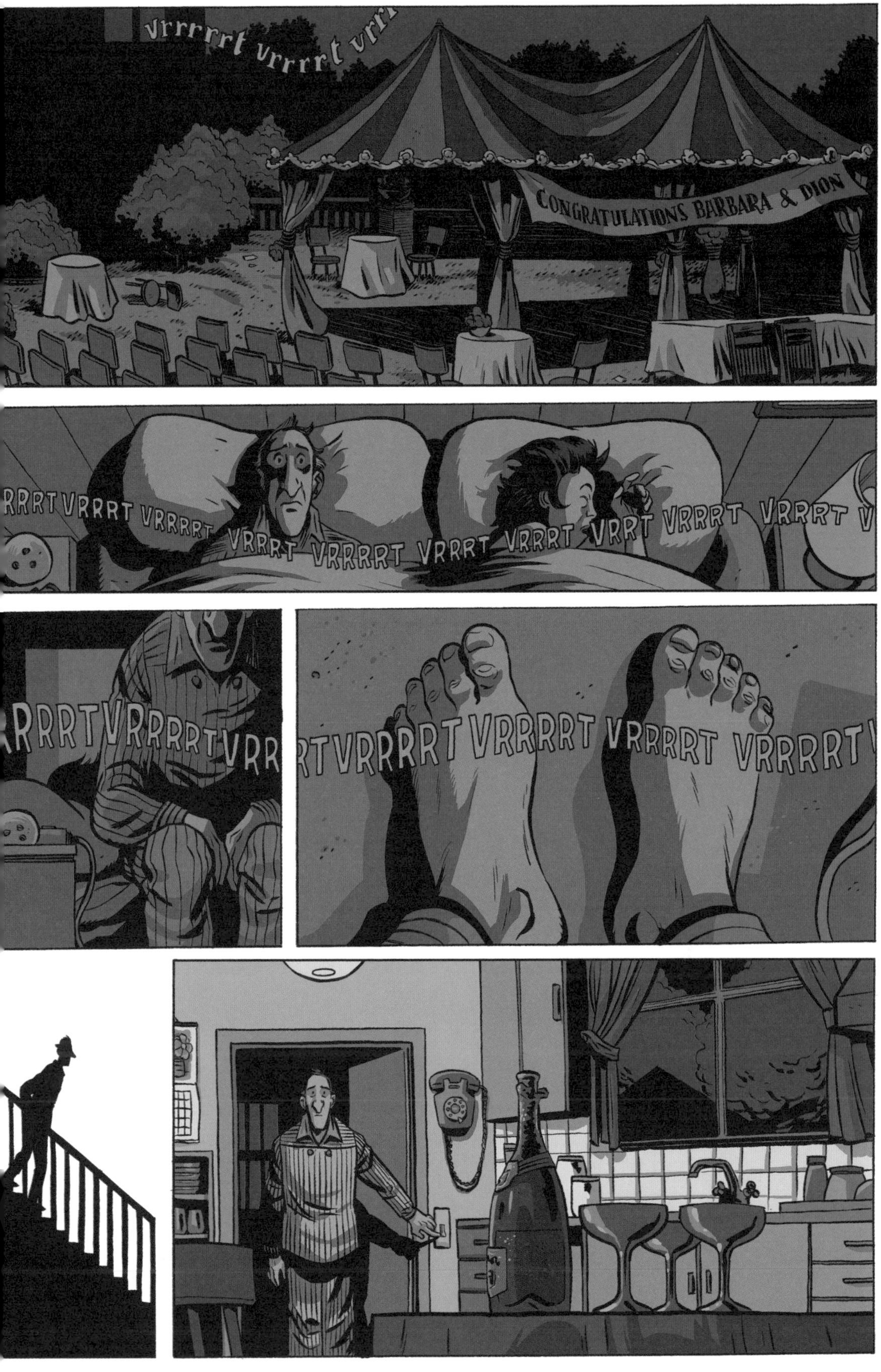
vrrrrrt vrrrrt vrr
CONGRATULATIONS BARBARA & DION
RRRT VRRRT VRRRRT VRRRT VRRRRT VRRRT VRRRT VRRT VRRRT VRRRT V
RRRTVRRRRRTVRR
RTVRRRRT VRRRRT VRRRRT VRRRRT V

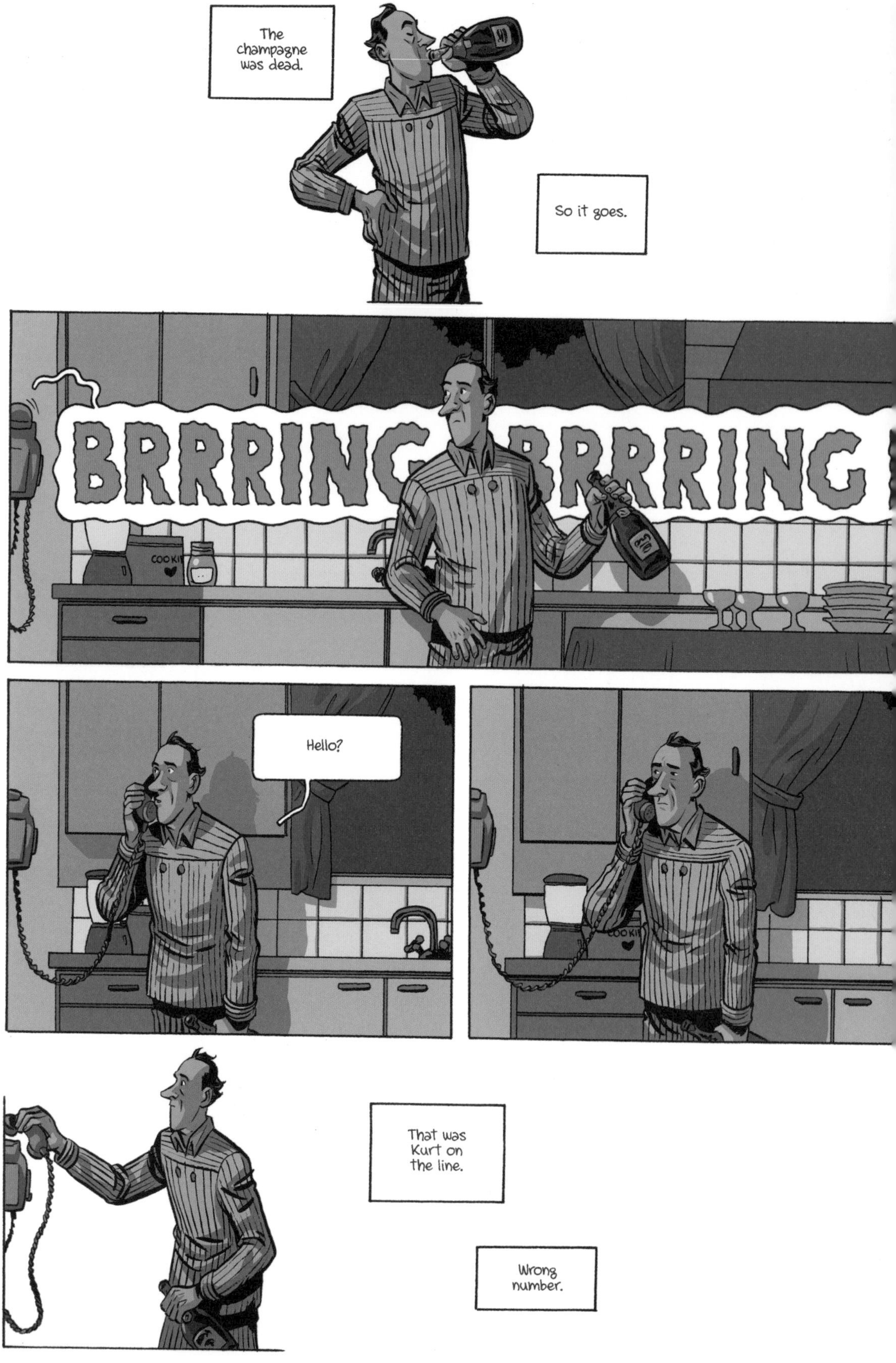
The champagne was dead.
So it goes.
BRRRING BRRRING
COOKI
Hello?
COOKI
That was Kurt on the line.
Wrong number.

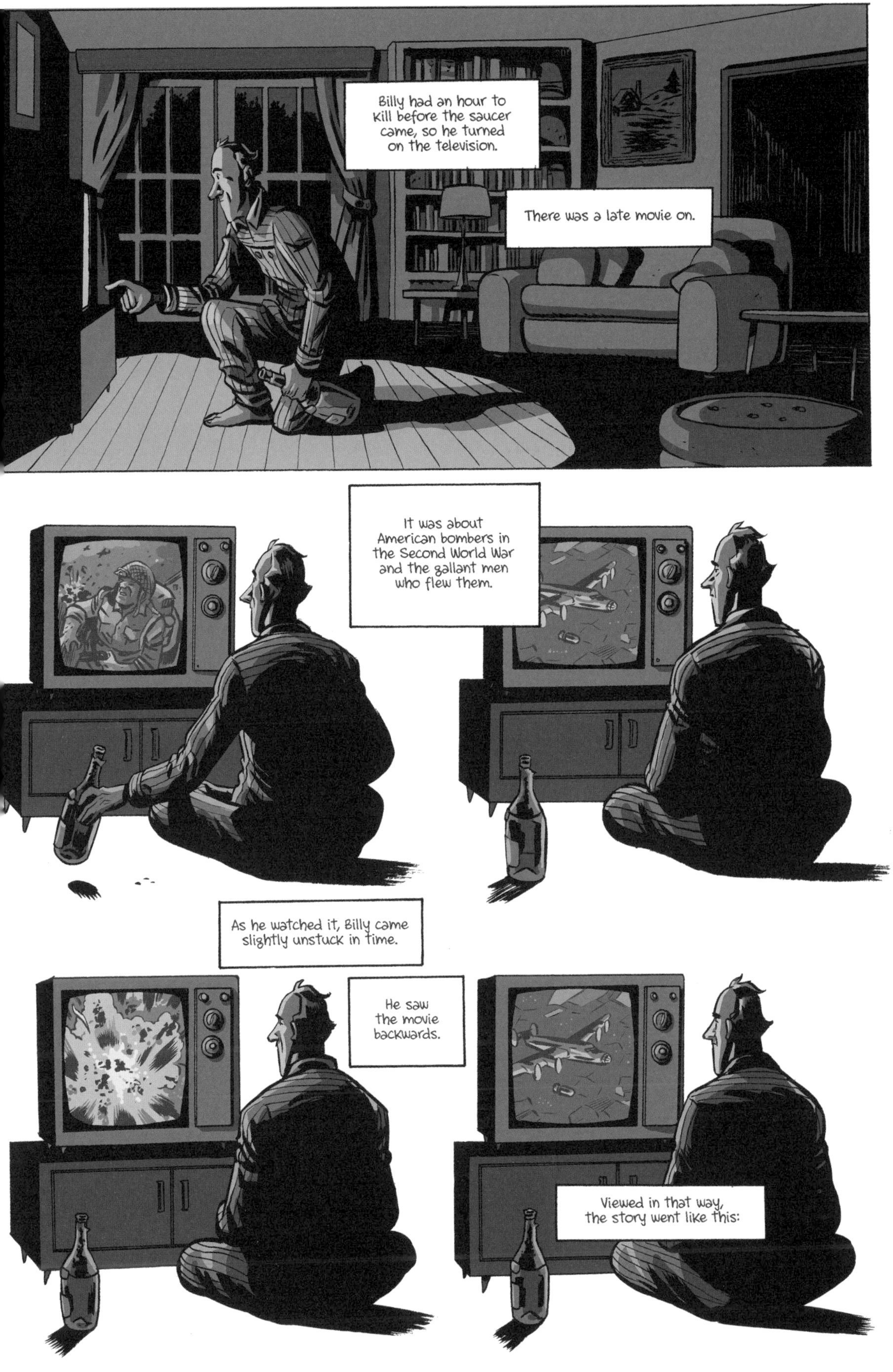
Billy had an hour to kill before the saucer came, so he turned on the television.
There was a late movie on.
It was about American bombers in the Second World War and the gallant men who flew them.
As he watched it, Billy came slightly unstuck in time.
He saw the movie backwards.
Viewed in that way, the story went like this:

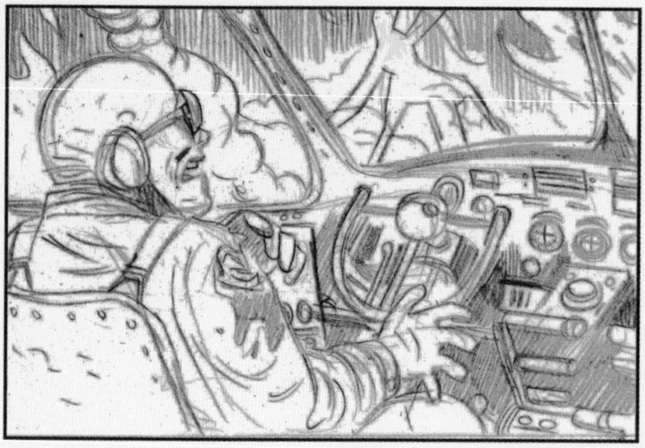

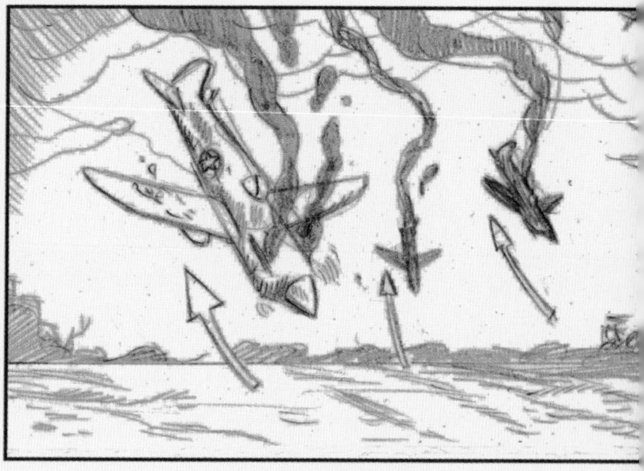

Action:

American planes, full of holes and wounded men and corpses

take off backwards from an airfield in England.

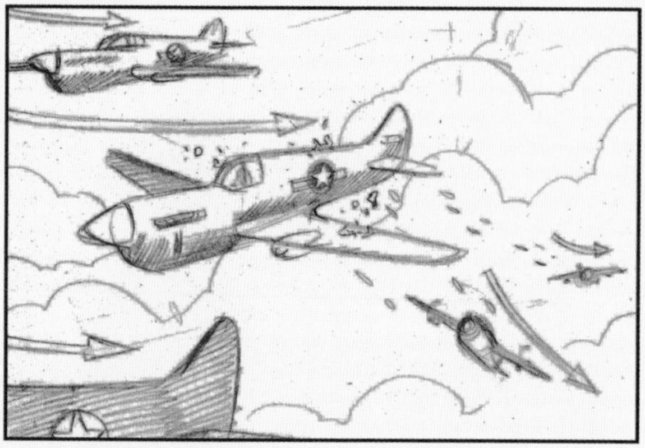

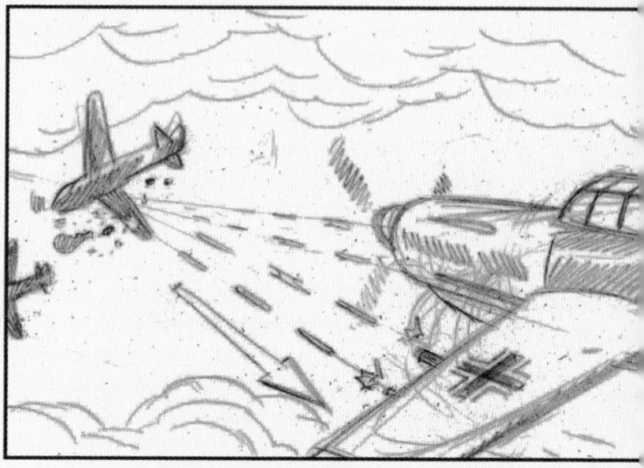

Action:

Over France, a few German fighter planes fly at them backwards,

sucking bullets and shell fragments from some of the planes and crewmen.

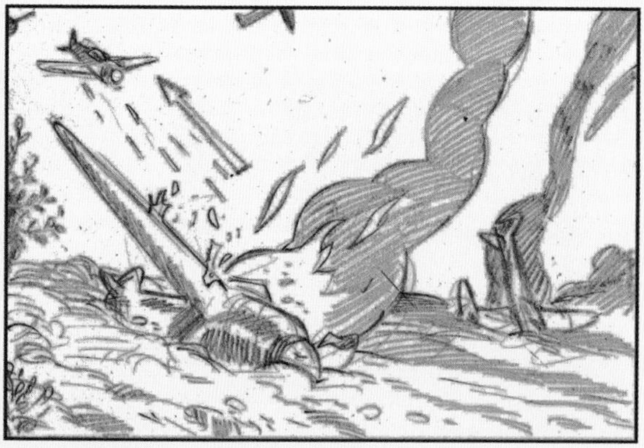

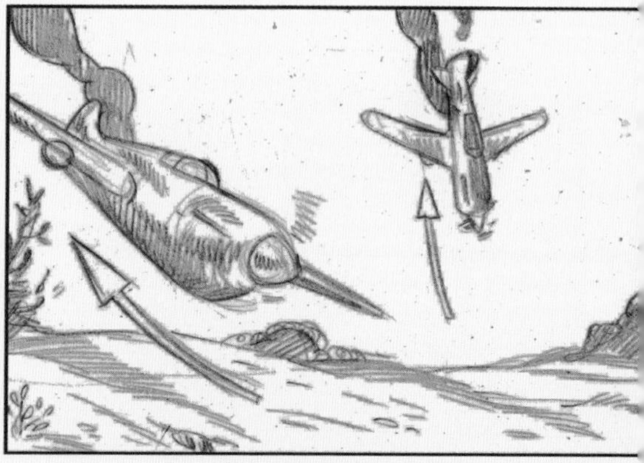

Action:

They do the same for wrecked American bombers on the ground,

which then fly up backwards to join the formation.

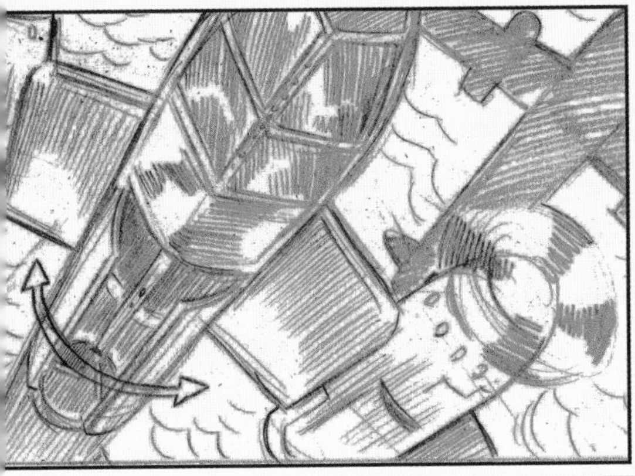

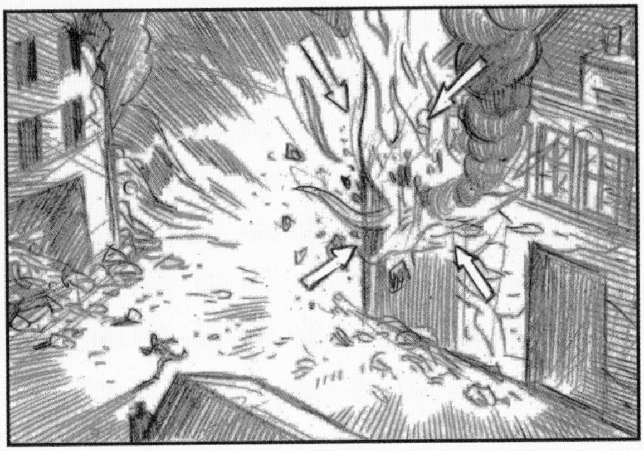

Action:

The bombers open their bomb bay doors above a burning German city,

and exert a miraculous magnetism which shrinks the fires.

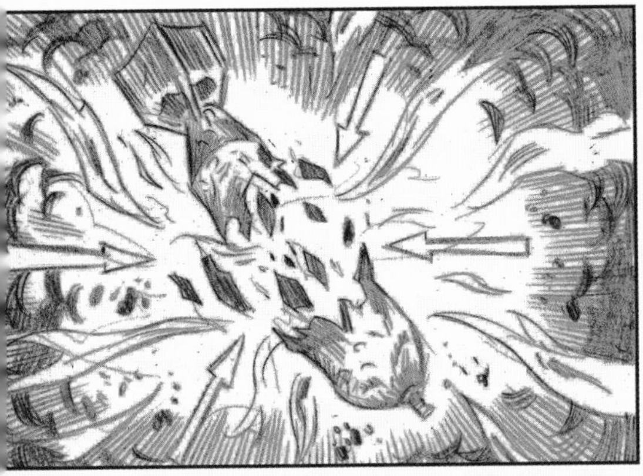

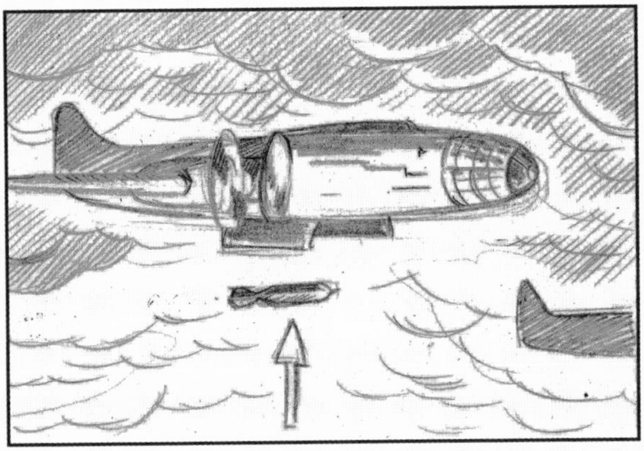

Action:

They gather them up into cylindrical steel containers,

and lift them into the bellies of the planes.

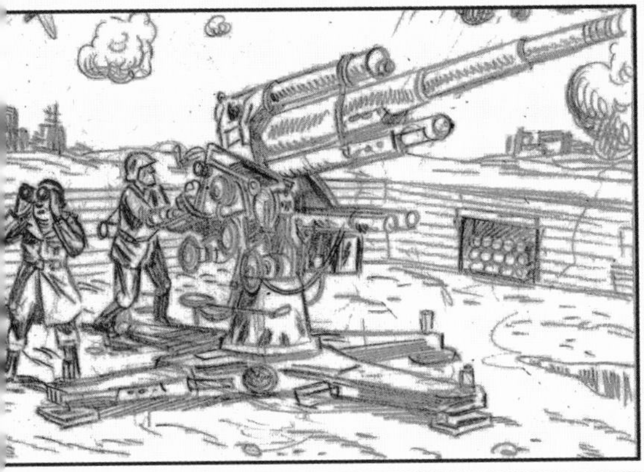

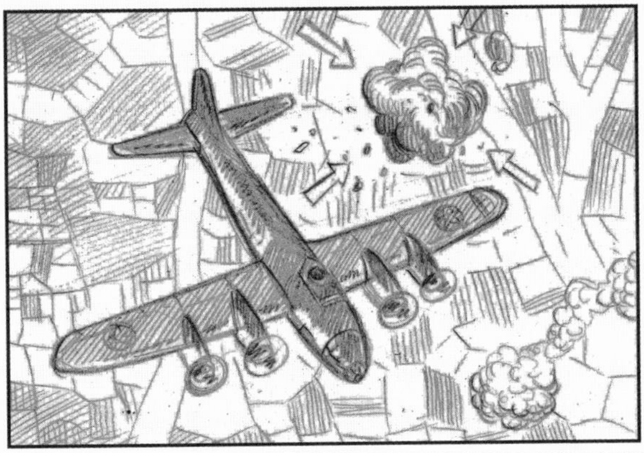

Action:

Below, the Germans have miraculous devices of their own,

which they use to suck more fragments from the American crewmen and their planes.

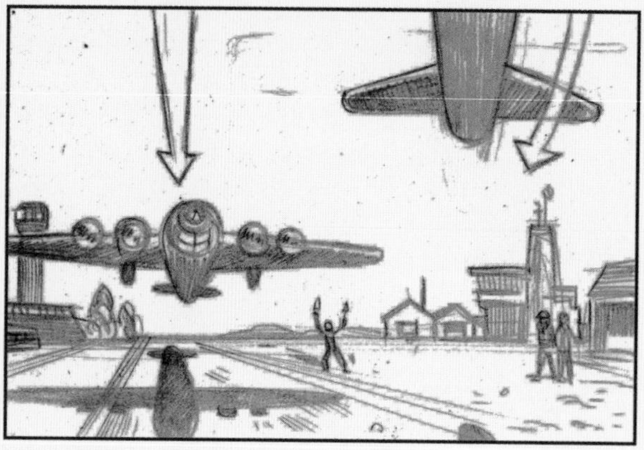

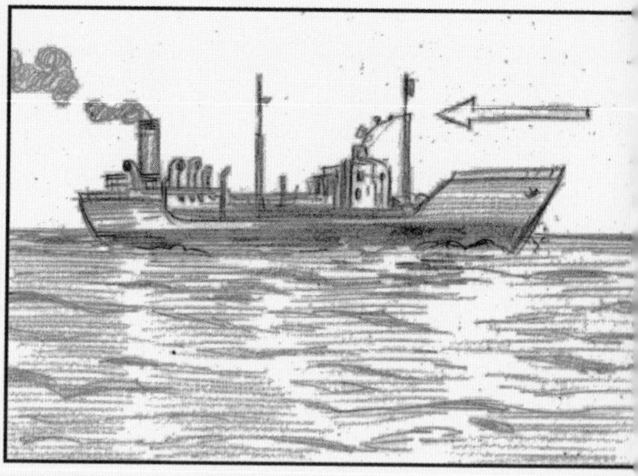

Action:

The American bombers
fly back to their base,

and ship their steel cylinders
back to the United States of America.

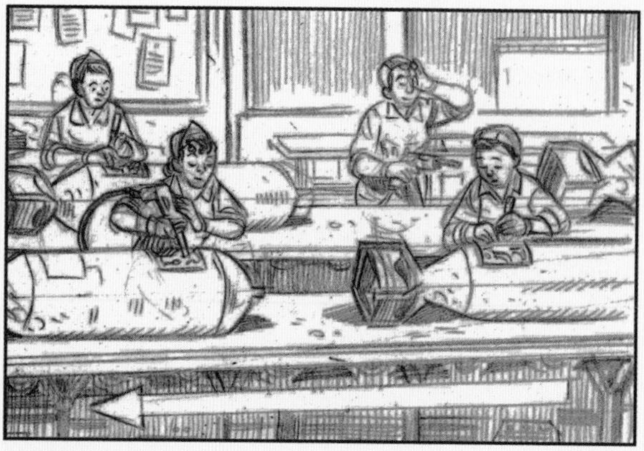

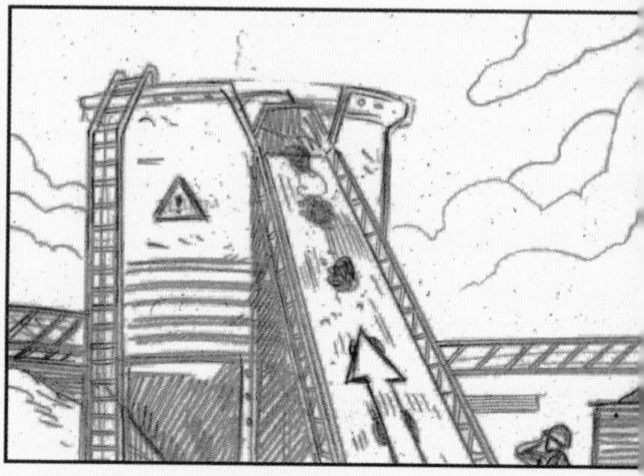

Action:

Factories staffed by women
operate there night and day,
dismantling the cylinders,

separating the dangerous
contents into minerals.

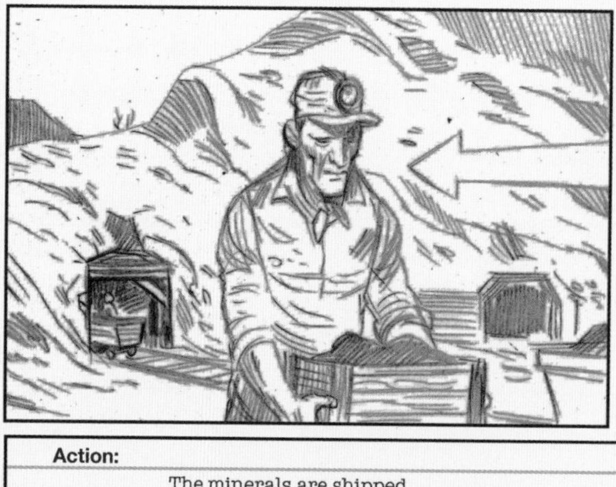

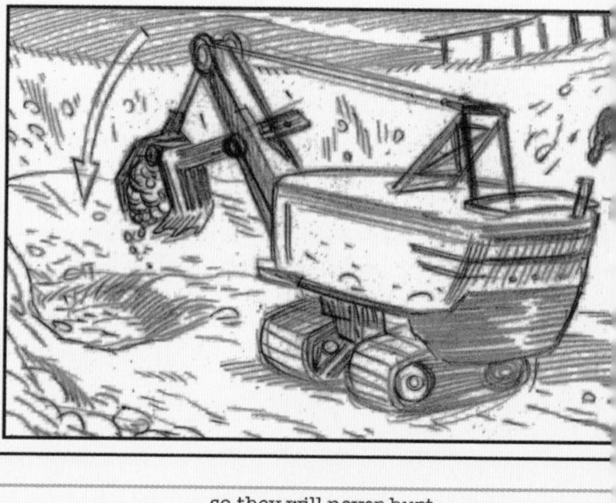

Action:

The minerals are shipped
to remote areas, where specialists
hide them cleverly in the ground,

so they will never hurt
anybody ever again.

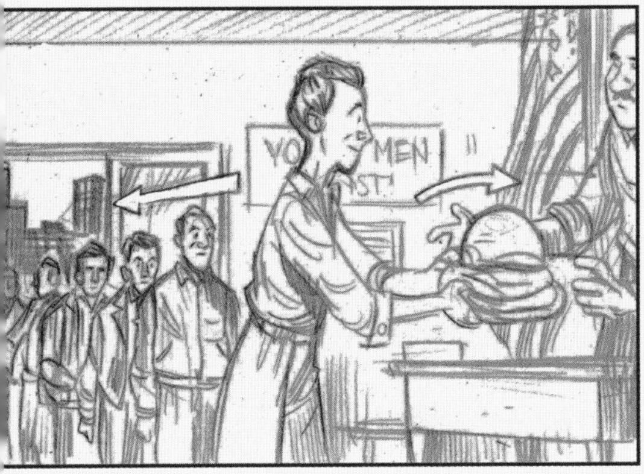

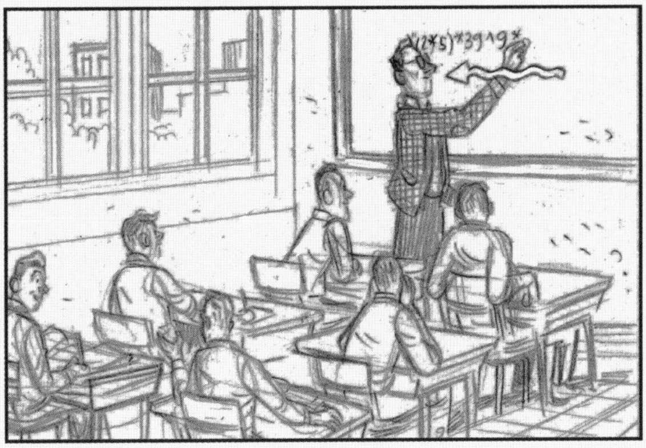

Action:

The American fliers
turn in their uniforms,

and they become
high school kids.

(That wasn't in the movie.
Billy was extrapolating.)

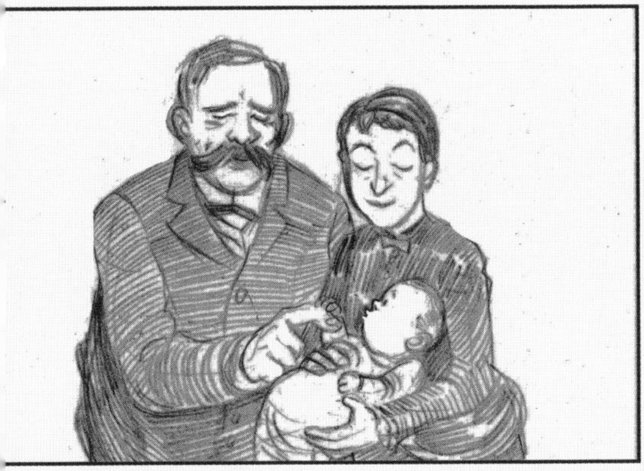

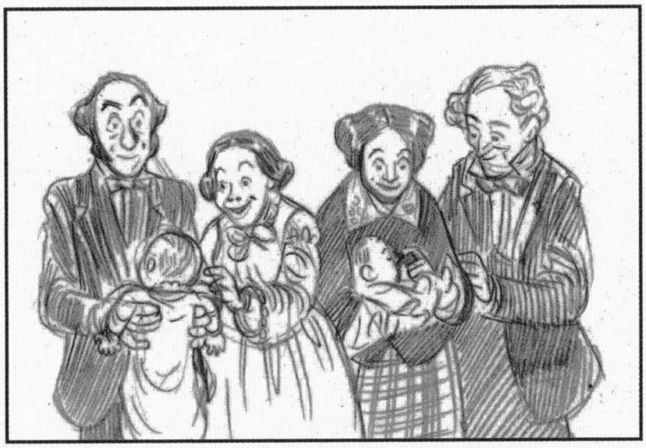

Action:

And Hitler turns
into a baby.

In fact, everyone
turns into a baby.

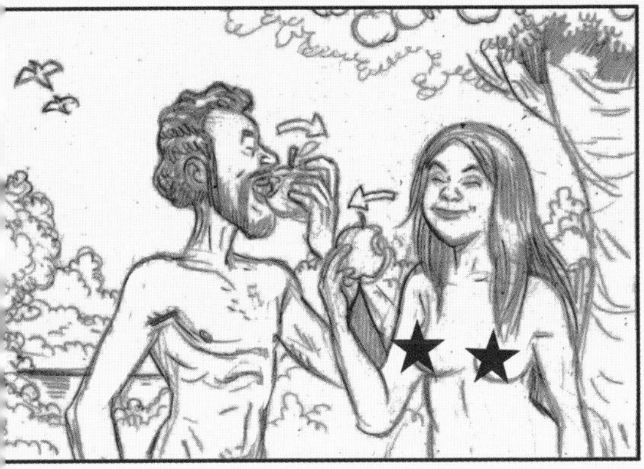

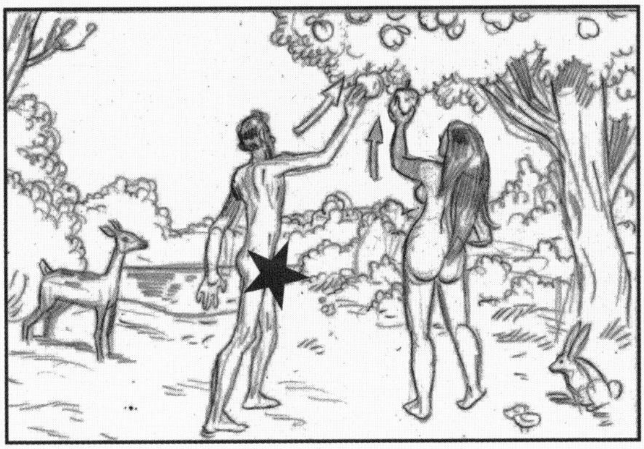

Action:

And all humanity, without exception,
conspires biologically to produce
two perfect people.

They are named
Adam and Eve.

THE END

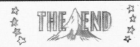

And then the movie was over and it was time for Billy to go out into his backyard and meet the flying saucer.

vrrrtvrrrtvrrrtvvvrr

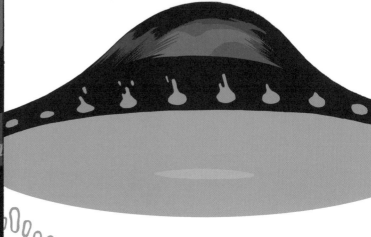

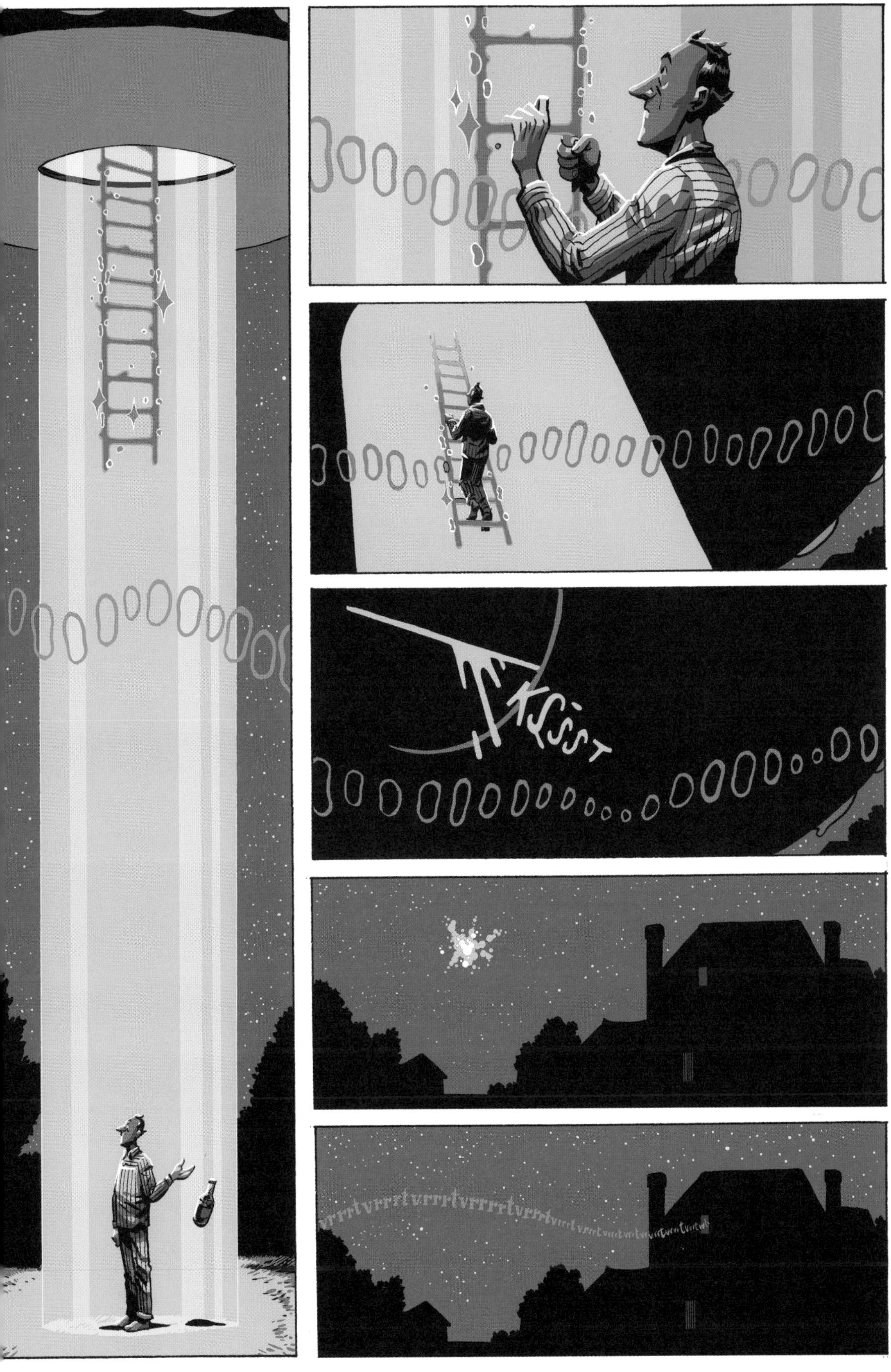
KSSST
vrrrtvrrrrtvrrrrtvrrrrrtvrrrrt

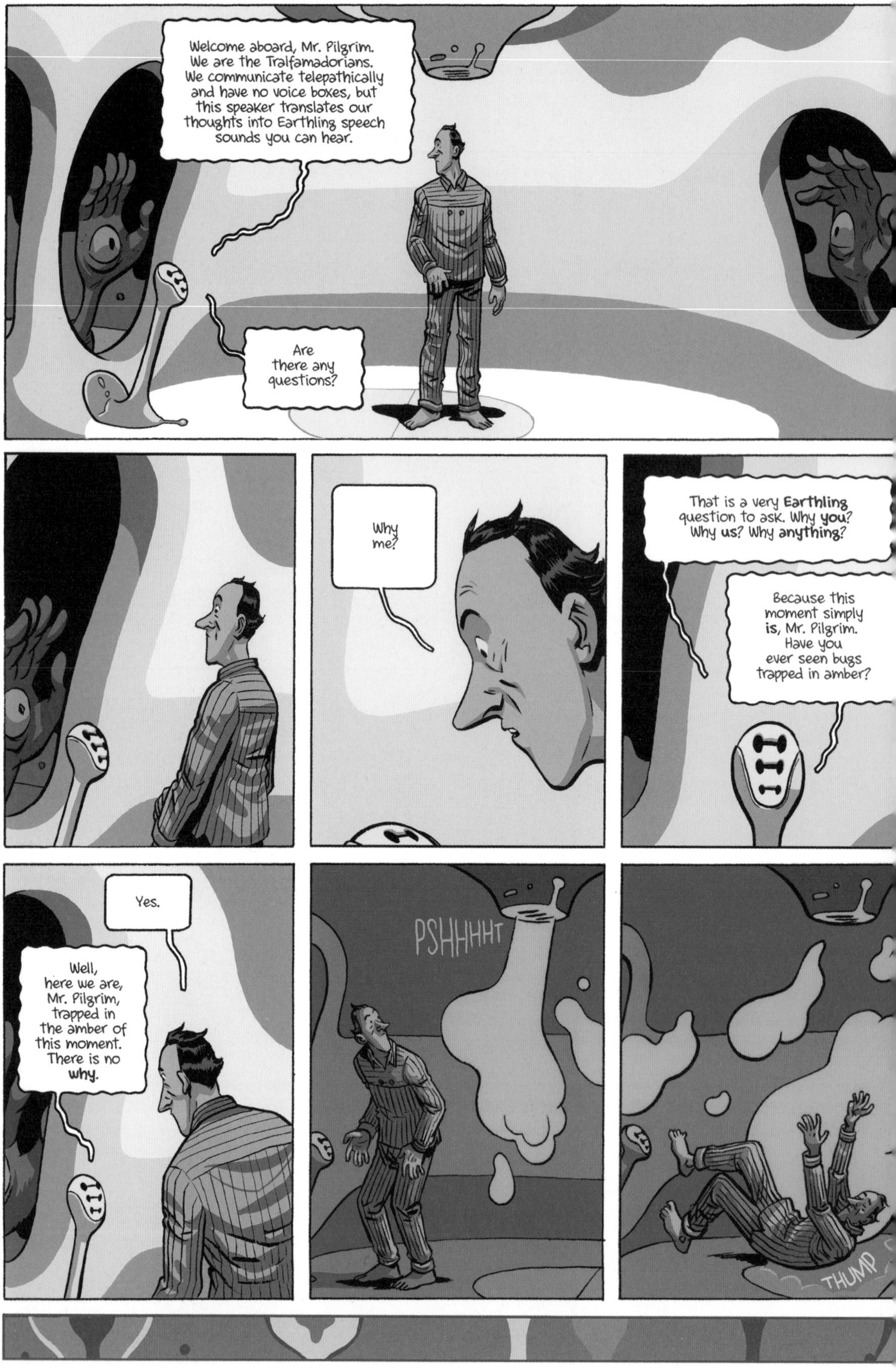
Welcome aboard, Mr. Pilgrim. We are the Tralfamadorians. We communicate telepathically and have no voice boxes, but this speaker translates our thoughts into Earthling speech sounds you can hear.
Are there any questions?
Why me?
That is a very **Earthling** question to ask. Why **you**? Why **us**? Why **anything**?
Because this moment simply **is**, Mr. Pilgrim. Have you ever seen bugs trapped in amber?
Yes.
Well, here we are, Mr. Pilgrim, trapped in the amber of this moment. There is no **why**.
PSHHHHT
THUMP

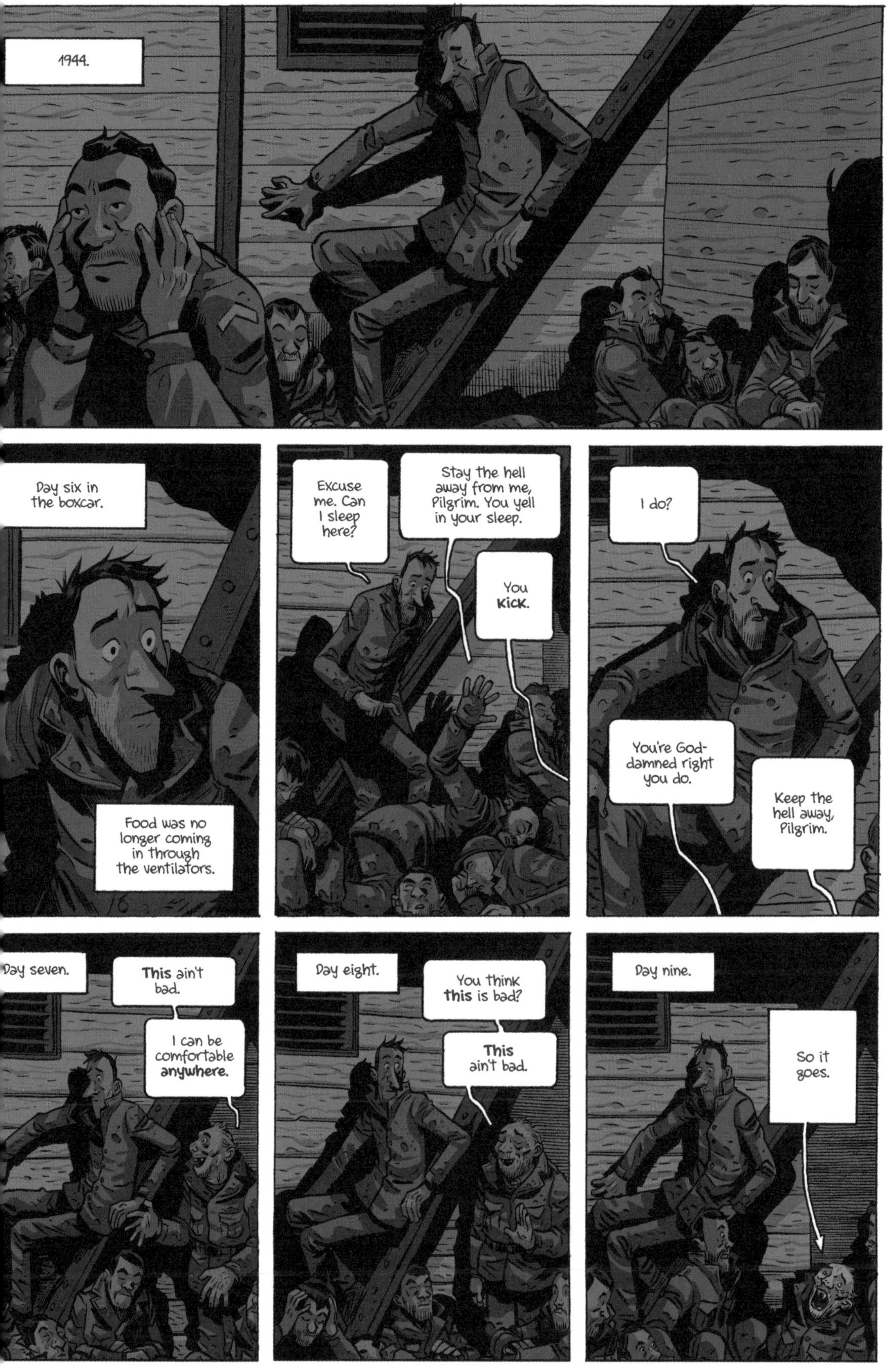

1944.
Day six in the boxcar.
Food was no longer coming in through the ventilators.
Excuse me. Can I sleep here?
Stay the hell away from me, Pilgrim. You yell in your sleep.
You **kick.**
I do?
You're God-damned right you do.
Keep the hell away, Pilgrim.
Day seven.
This ain't bad.
I can be comfortable **anywhere.**
Day eight.
You think **this** is bad?
This ain't bad.
Day nine.
So it goes.

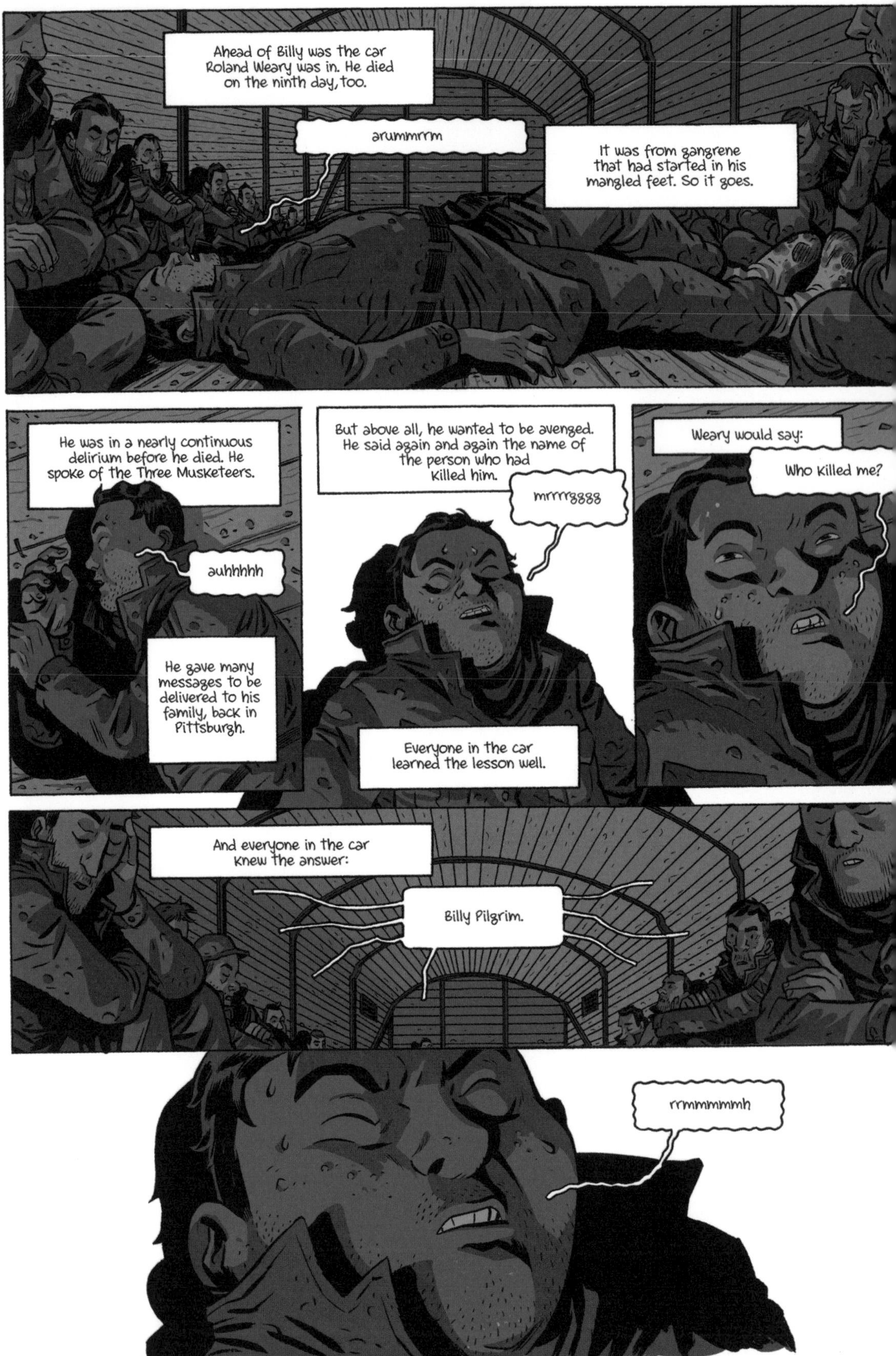

Ahead of Billy was the car Roland Weary was in. He died on the ninth day, too.
arummrrm
It was from gangrene that had started in his mangled feet. So it goes.
He was in a nearly continuous delirium before he died. He spoke of the Three Musketeers.
auhhhhh
He gave many messages to be delivered to his family, back in Pittsburgh.
But above all, he wanted to be avenged. He said again and again the name of the person who had killed him.
mrrrrgggg
Everyone in the car learned the lesson well.
Weary would say:
Who killed me?
And everyone in the car knew the answer:
Billy Pilgrim.
rrmmmmmh

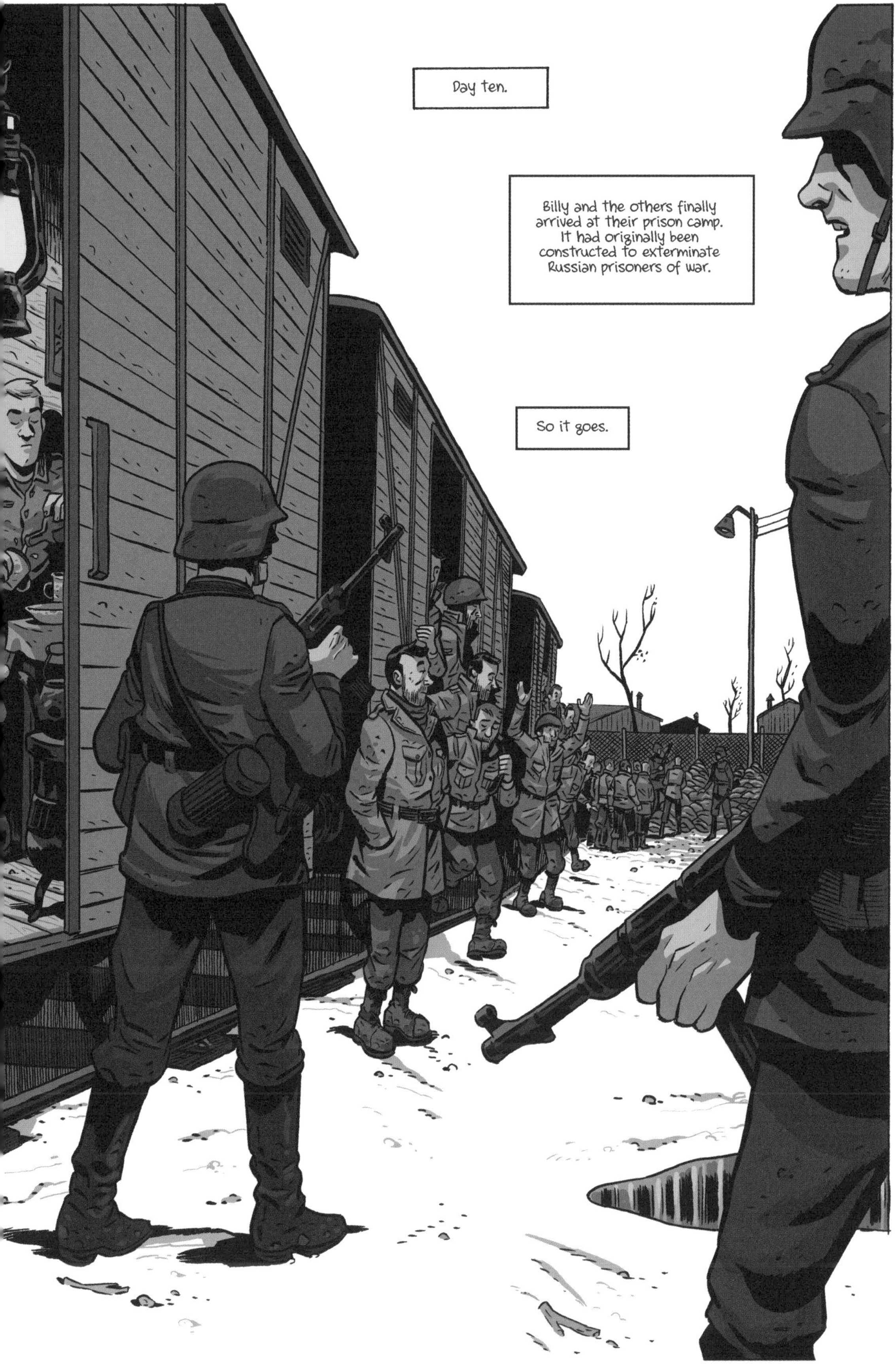
Day ten.
Billy and the others finally arrived at their prison camp. It had originally been constructed to exterminate Russian prisoners of war.
So it goes.

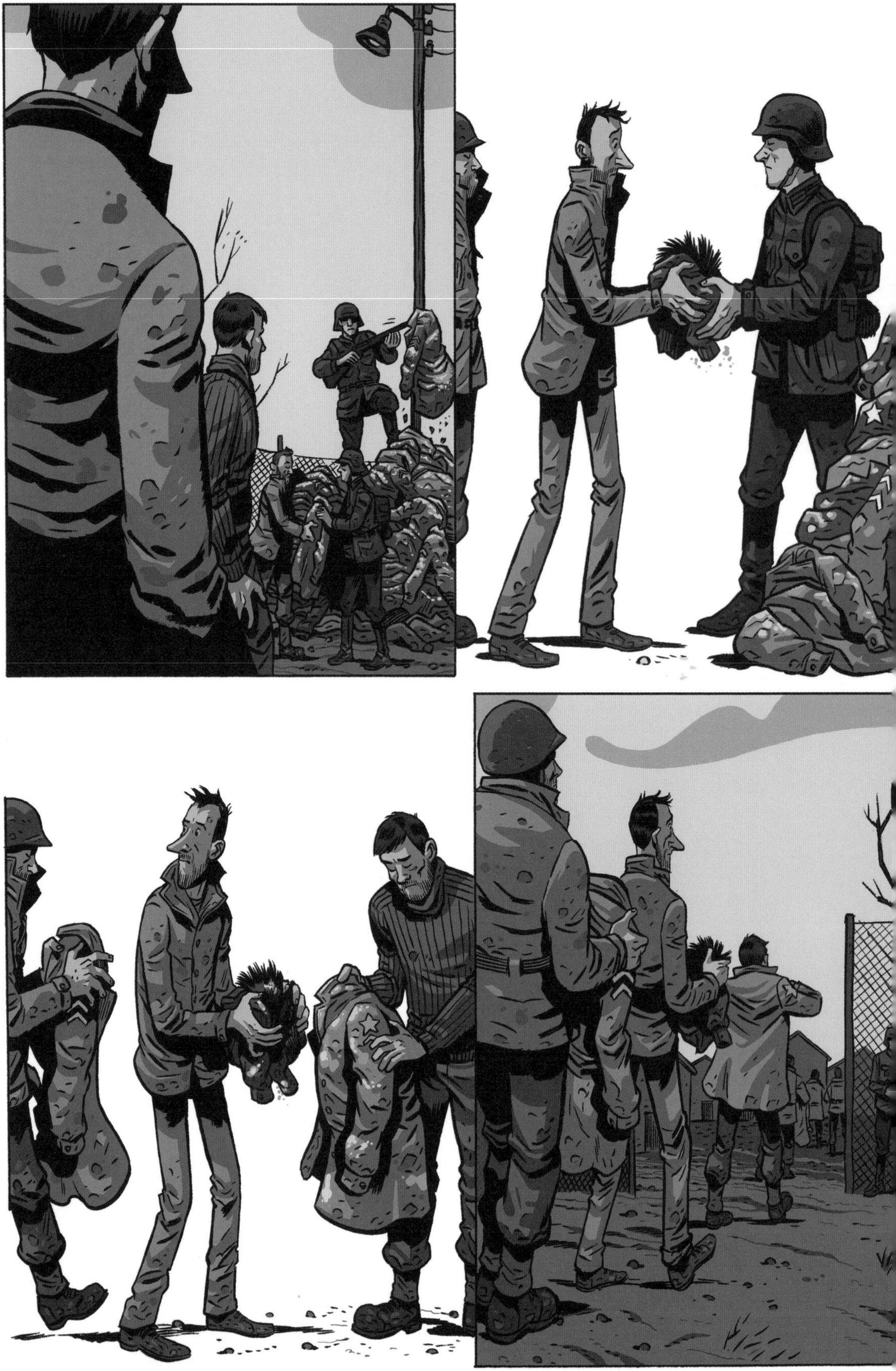

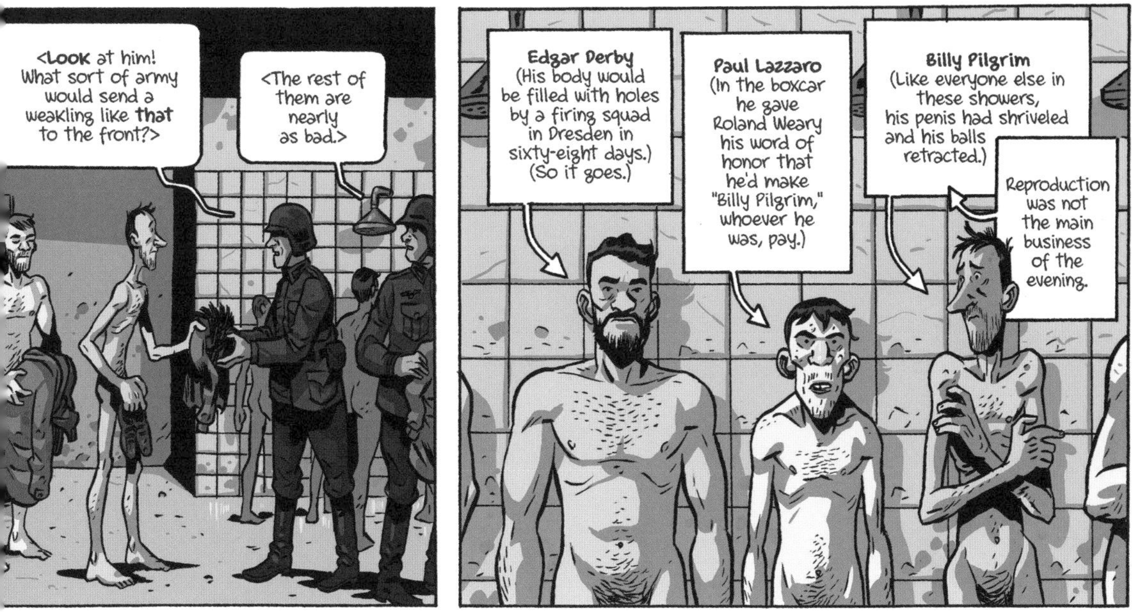
<**Look** at him! What sort of army would send a weakling like **that** to the front?>
<The rest of them are nearly as bad.>
Edgar Derby (His body would be filled with holes by a firing squad in Dresden in sixty-eight days.) (So it goes.)
Paul Lazzaro (In the boxcar he gave Roland Weary his word of honor that he'd make "Billy Pilgrim," whoever he was, pay.)
Billy Pilgrim (Like everyone else in these showers, his penis had shriveled and his balls retracted.)
Reproduction was not the main business of the evening.

GAR DERBY IN THREE PANELS

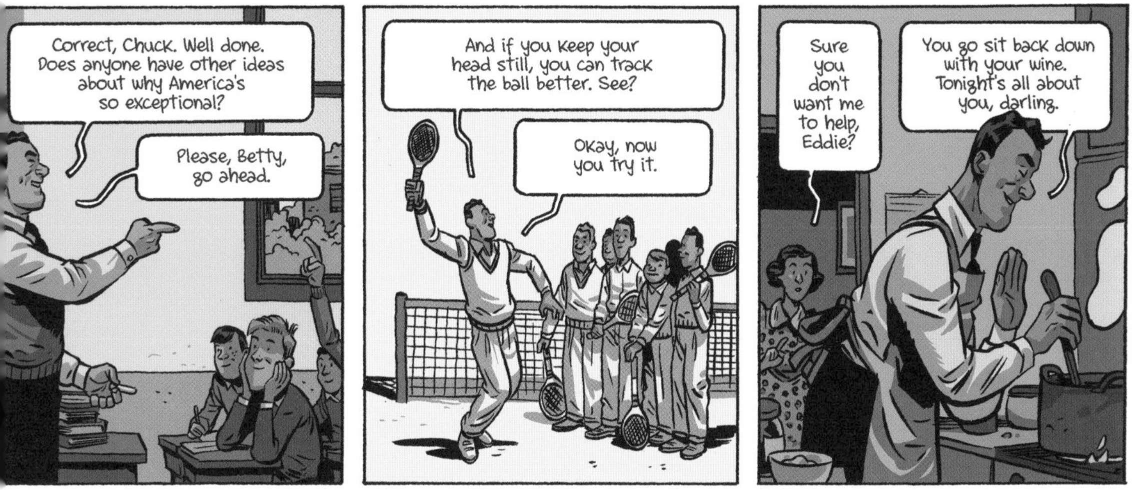
Correct, Chuck. Well done. Does anyone have other ideas about why America's so exceptional?
Please, Betty, go ahead.
And if you keep your head still, you can track the ball better. See?
Okay, now you try it.
Sure you don't want me to help, Eddie?
You go sit back down with your wine. Tonight's all about you, darling.

UL LAZZARO IN THREE PANELS

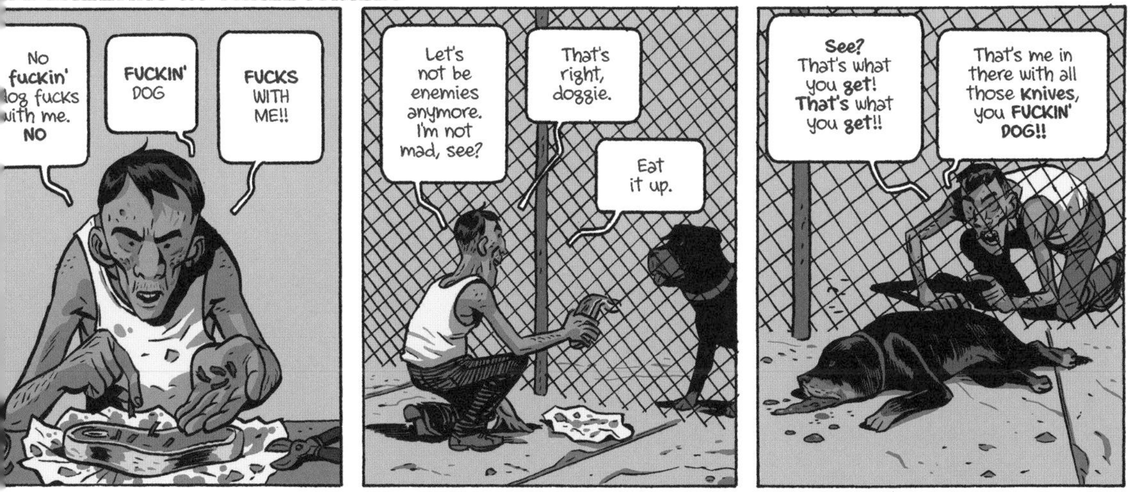
No **fuckin'** log fucks ith me. **NO**
FUCKIN' DOG
FUCKS WITH ME!!
Let's not be enemies anymore. I'm not mad, see?
That's right, doggie.
Eat it up.
See? That's what you **get**! **That's** what you **get**!!
That's me in there with all those **knives**, you **FUCKIN' DOG!!**

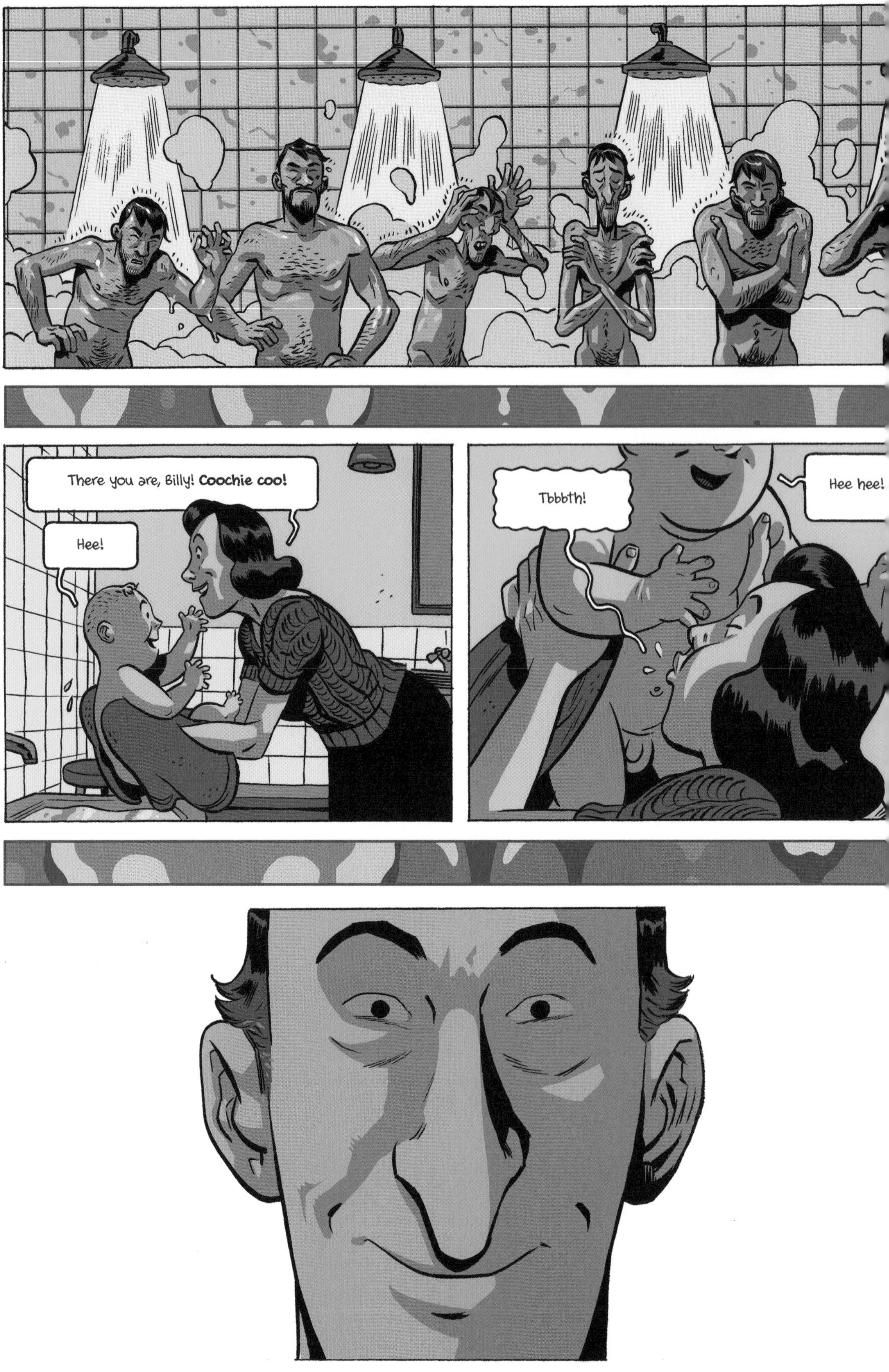

There you are, Billy! **Coochie coo!**
Hee!
Tbbbth!
Hee hee!

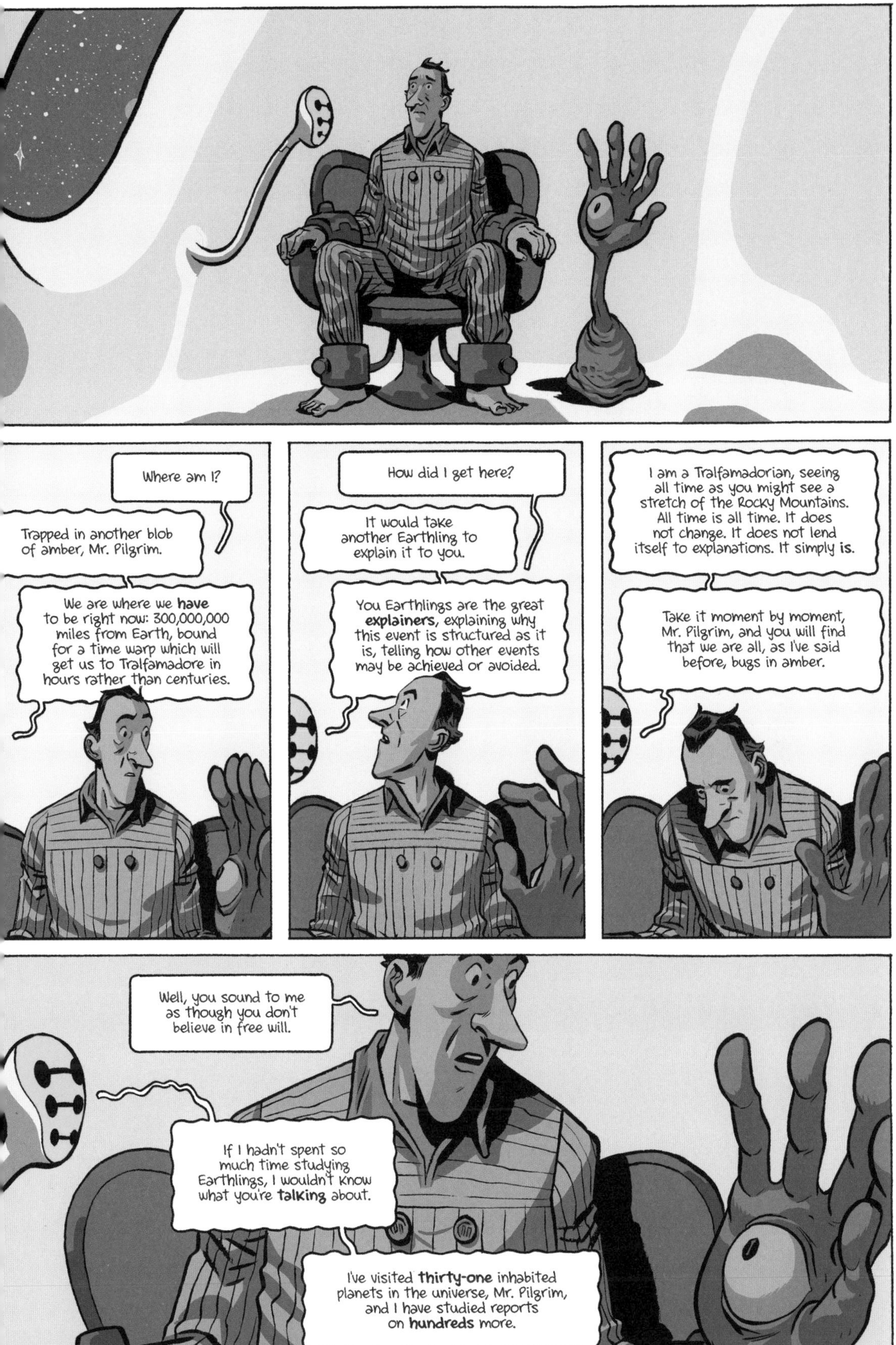
Where am I?
Trapped in another blob of amber, Mr. Pilgrim.
We are where we **have** to be right now: 300,000,000 miles from Earth, bound for a time warp which will get us to Tralfamadore in hours rather than centuries.
How did I get here?
It would take another Earthling to explain it to you.
You Earthlings are the great **explainers**, explaining why this event is structured as it is, telling how other events may be achieved or avoided.
I am a Tralfamadorian, seeing all time as you might see a stretch of the Rocky Mountains. All time is all time. It does not change. It does not lend itself to explanations. It simply **is**.
Take it moment by moment, Mr. Pilgrim, and you will find that we are all, as I've said before, bugs in amber.
Well, you sound to me as though you don't believe in free will.
If I hadn't spent so much time studying Earthlings, I wouldn't know what you're **talking** about.
I've visited **thirty-one** inhabited planets in the universe, Mr. Pilgrim, and I have studied reports on **hundreds** more.

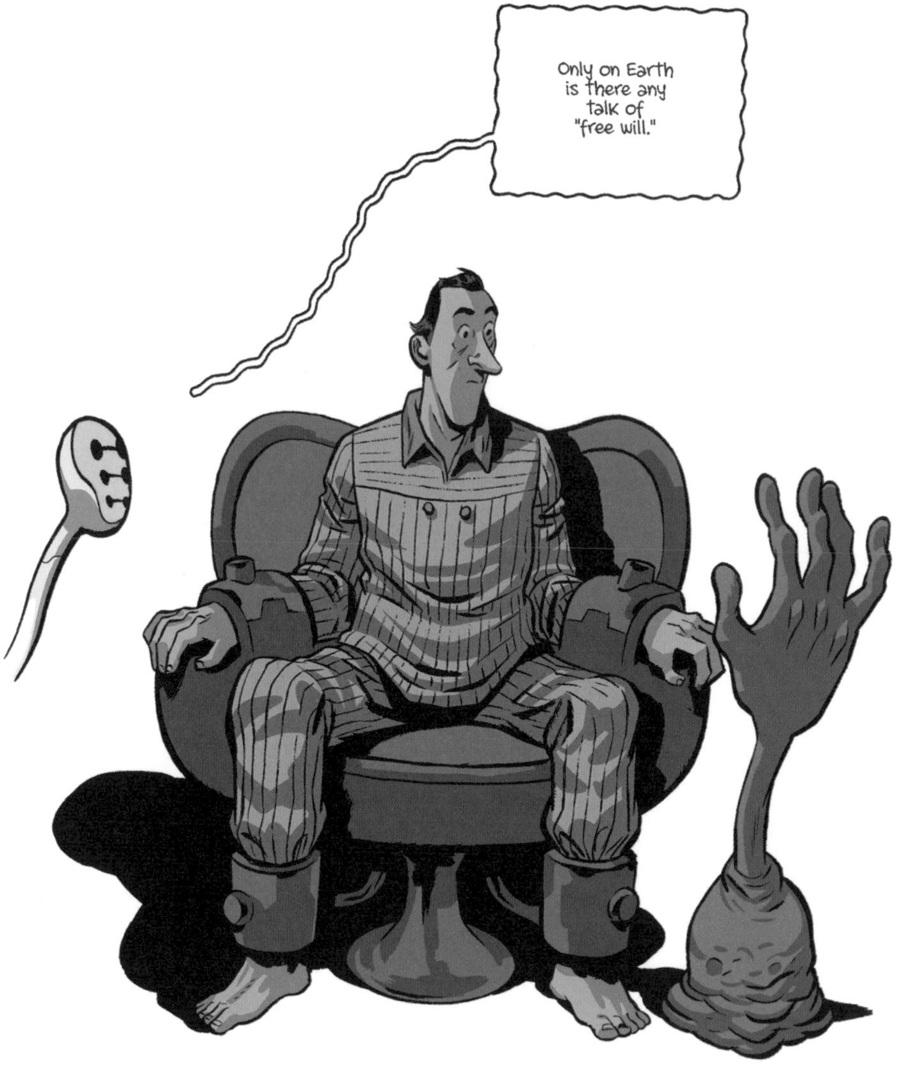
Only on Earth is there any talk of "free will."

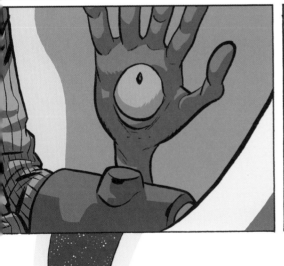

So...

...do you have something I can read?

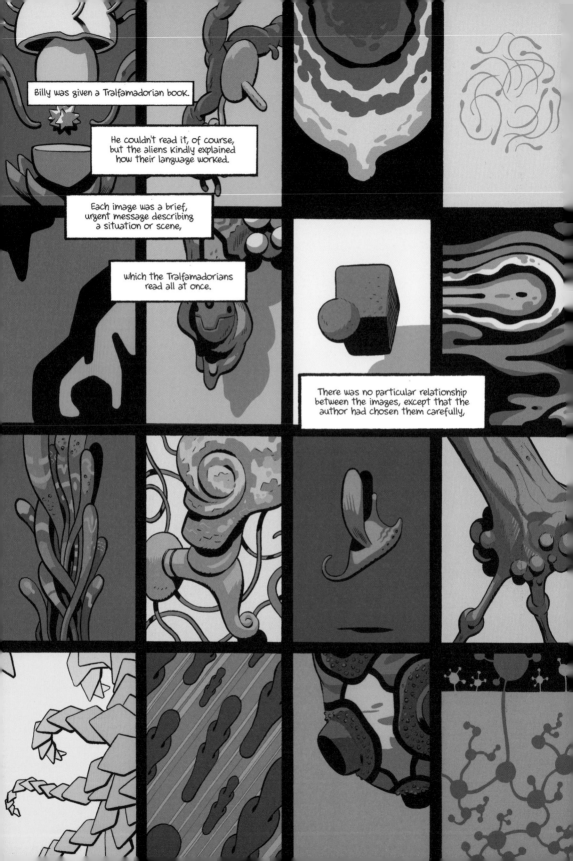

Billy was given a Tralfamadorian book.

He couldn't read it, of course, but the aliens kindly explained how their language worked.

Each image was a brief, urgent message describing a situation or scene,

which the Tralfamadorians read all at once.

There was no particular relationship between the images, except that the author had chosen them carefully,

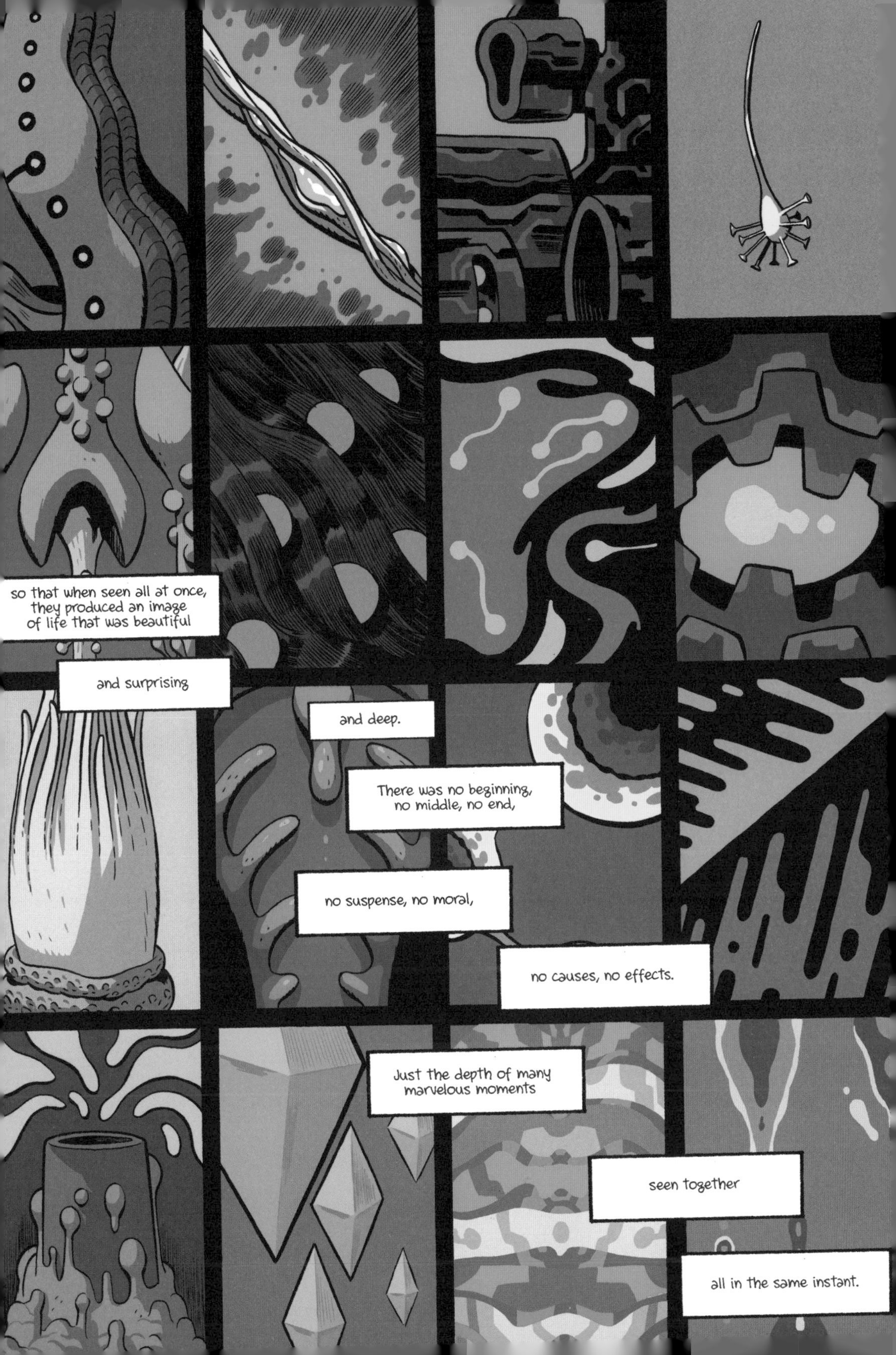
so that when seen all at once, they produced an image of life that was beautiful
and surprising
and deep.
There was no beginning, no middle, no end,
no suspense, no moral,
no causes, no effects.
Just the depth of many marvelous moments
seen together
all in the same instant.

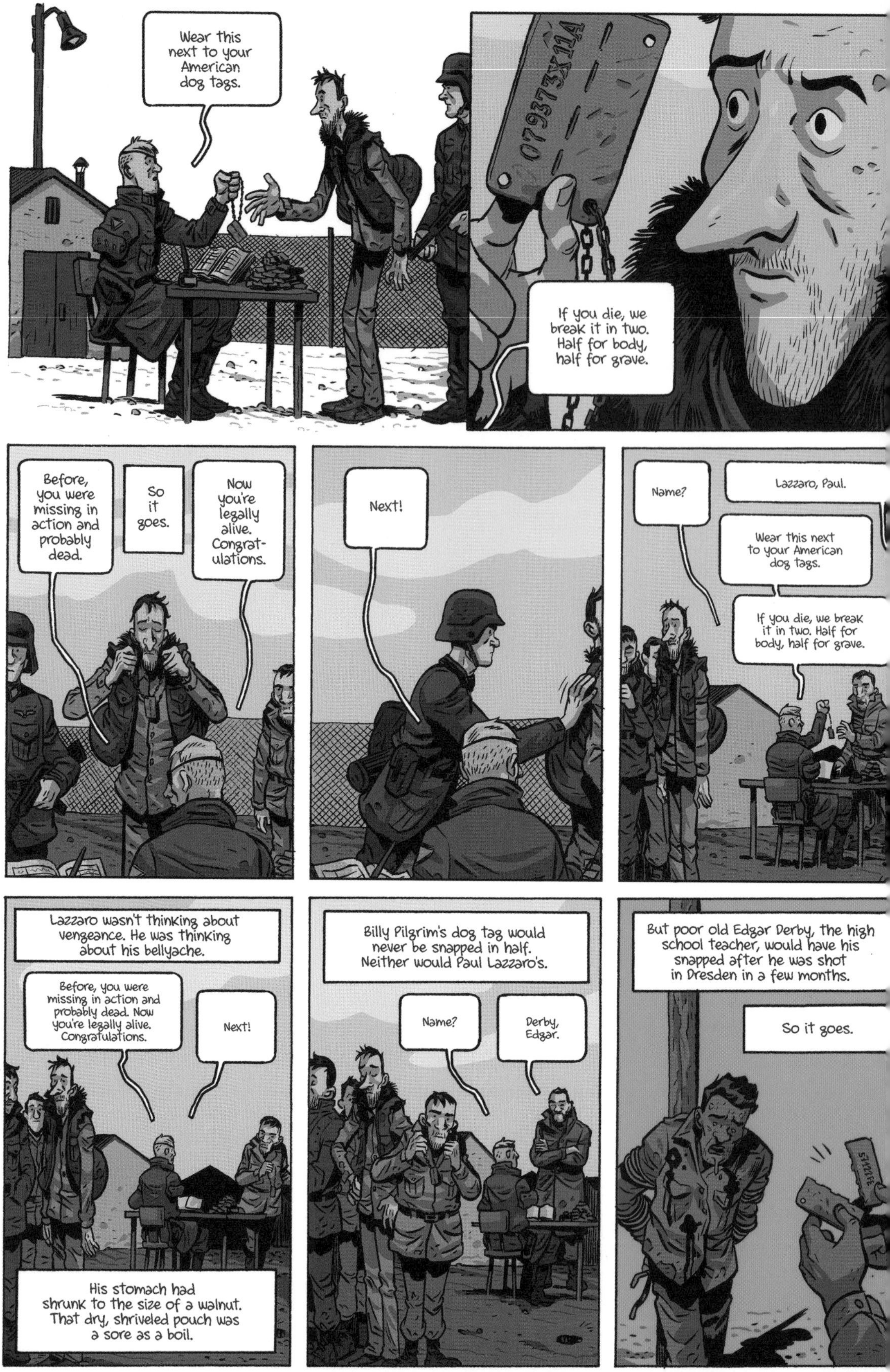
Wear this next to your American dog tags.
079375X11A
If you die, we break it in two. Half for body, half for grave.
Before, you were missing in action and probably dead.
So it goes.
Now you're legally alive. Congrat-ulations.
Next!
Name?
Lazzaro, Paul.
Wear this next to your American dog tags.
If you die, we break it in two. Half for body, half for grave.
Lazzaro wasn't thinking about vengeance. He was thinking about his bellyache.
Before, you were missing in action and probably dead. Now you're legally alive. Congratulations.
Next!
His stomach had shrunk to the size of a walnut. That dry, shriveled pouch was a sore as a boil.
Billy Pilgrim's dog tag would never be snapped in half. Neither would Paul Lazzaro's.
Name?
Derby, Edgar.
But poor old Edgar Derby, the high school teacher, would have his snapped after he was shot in Dresden in a few months.
So it goes.

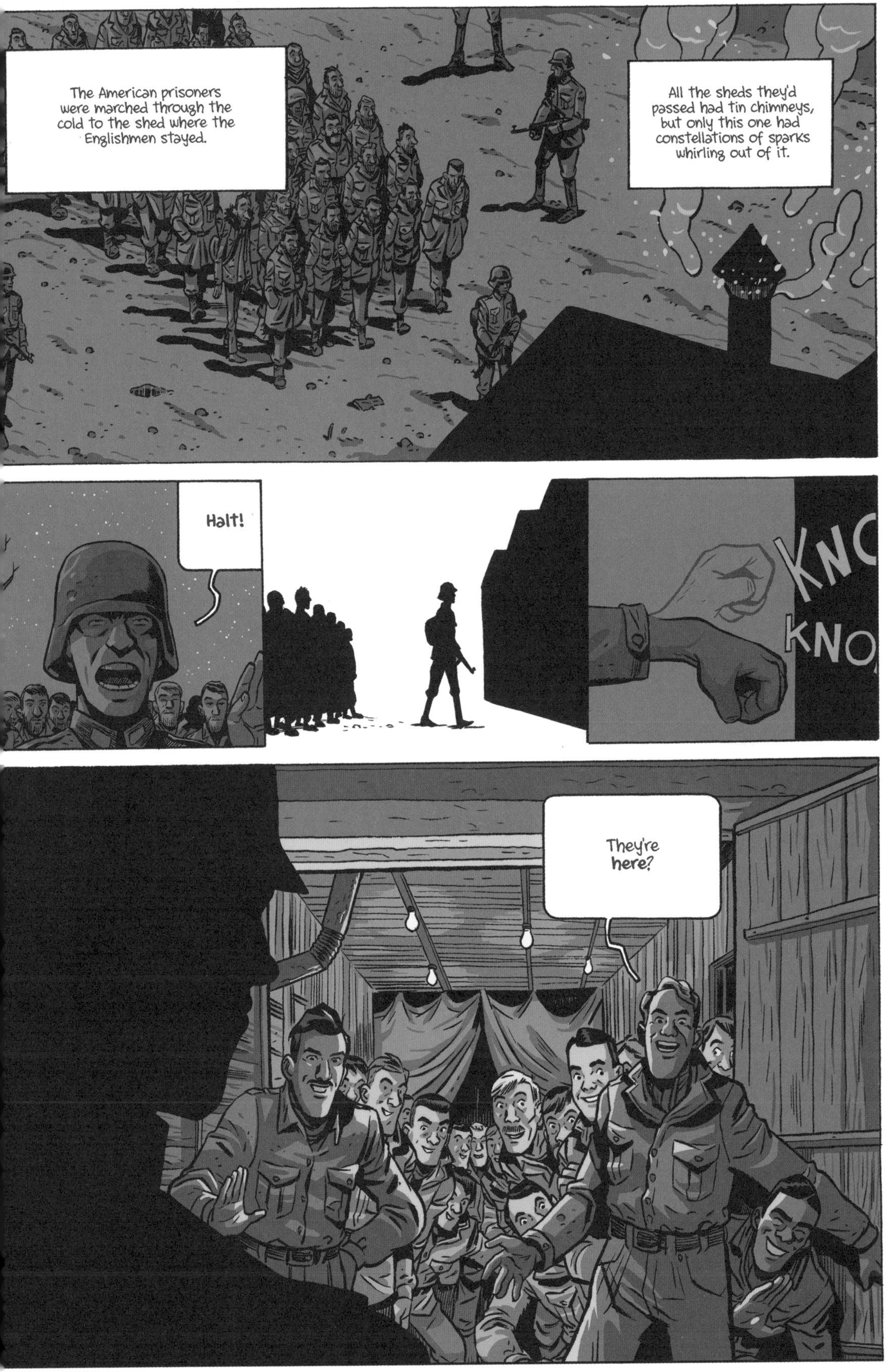
The American prisoners were marched through the cold to the shed where the Englishmen stayed.
All the sheds they'd passed had tin chimneys, but only this one had constellations of sparks whirling out of it.
Halt!
KNO
KNO
They're here?

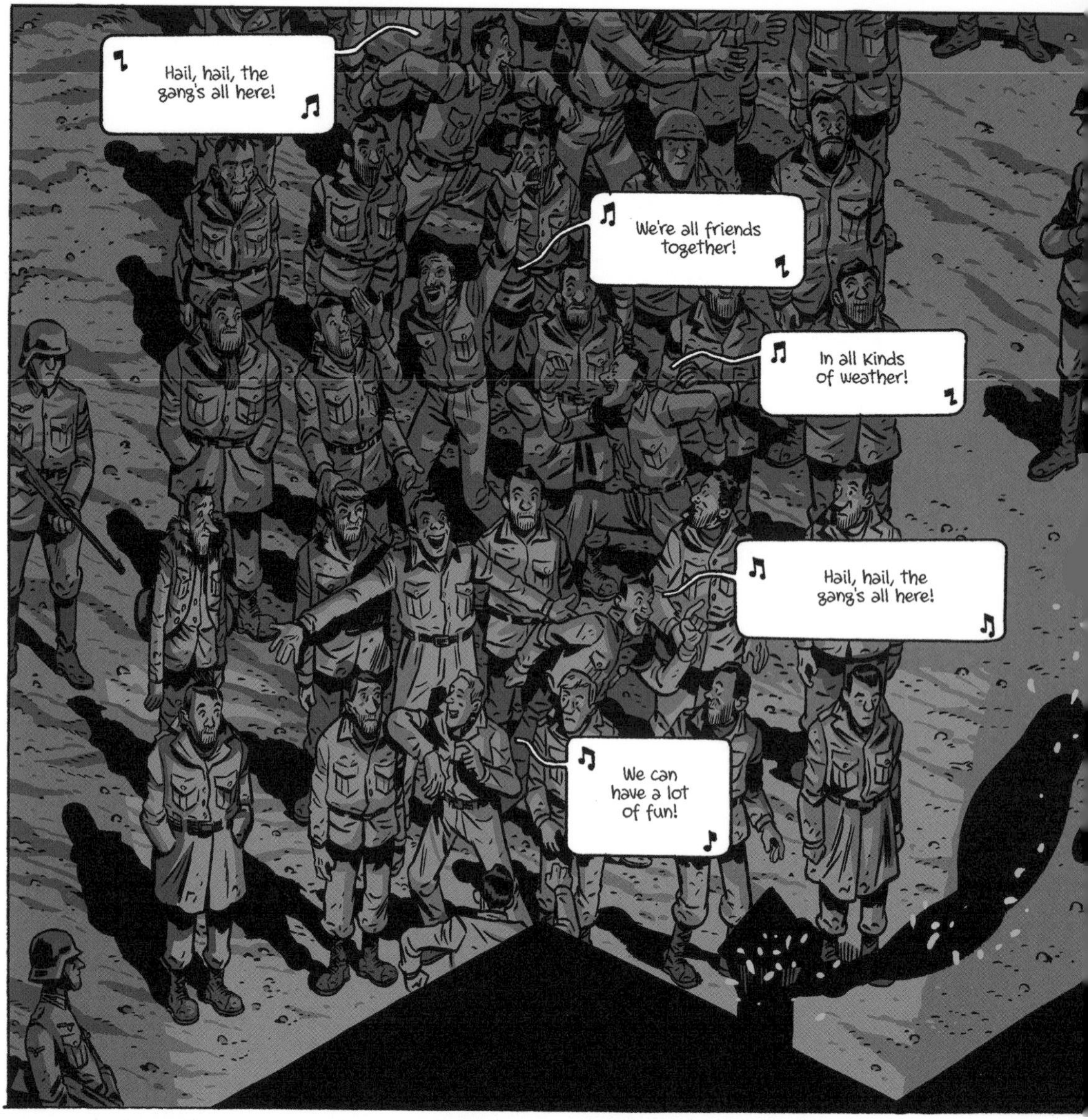
Hail, hail, the gang's all here!
We're all friends together!
In all kinds of weather!
Hail, hail, the gang's all here!
We can have a lot of fun!

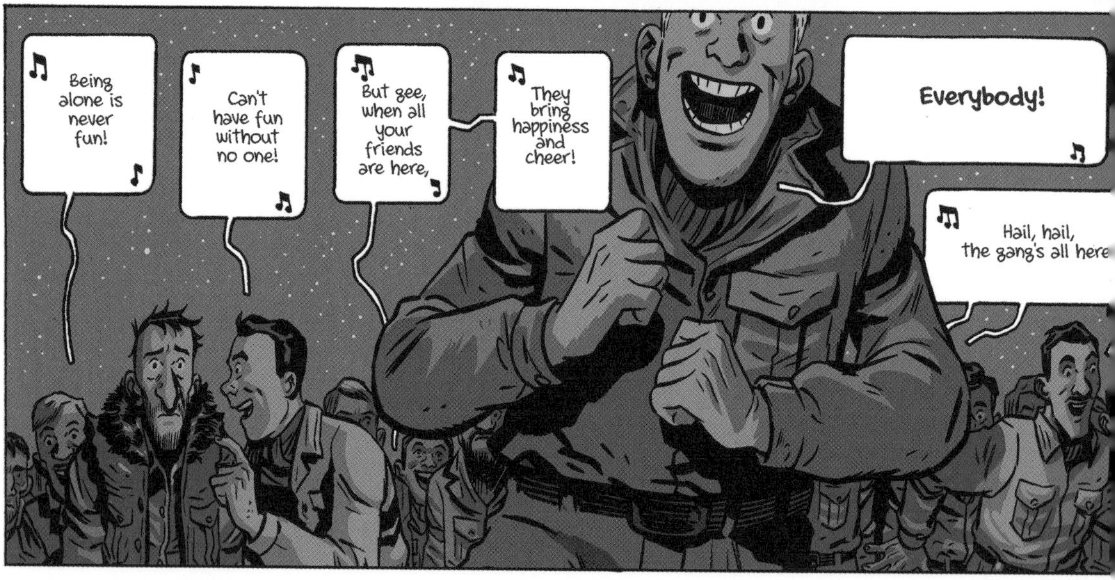
Being alone is never fun!
Can't have fun without no one!
But gee, when all your friends are here,
They bring happiness and cheer!
Everybody!
Hail, hail, the gang's all here

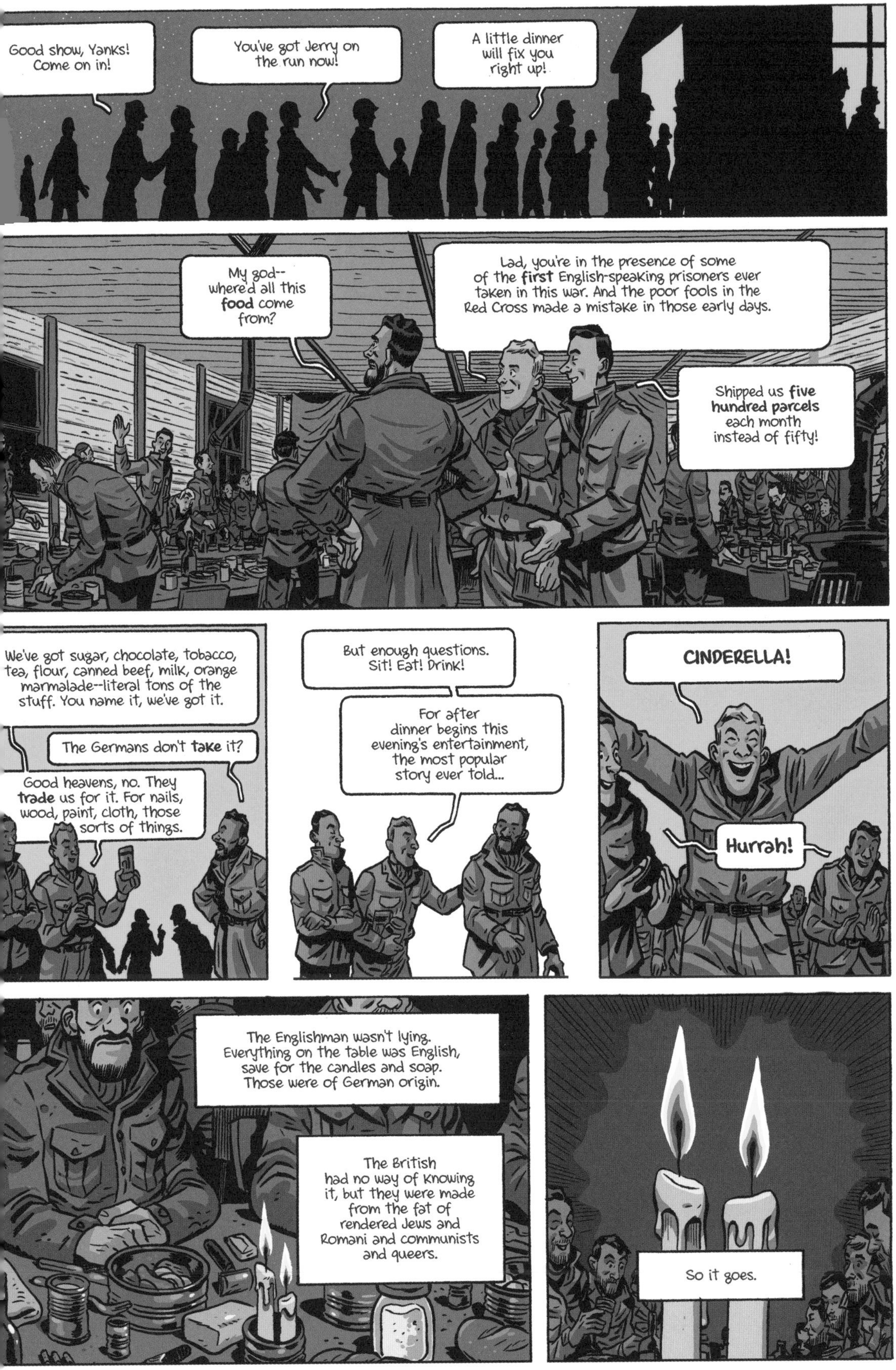
Good show, Yanks! Come on in!
You've got Jerry on the run now!
A little dinner will fix you right up!
My god--where'd all this **food** come from?
Lad, you're in the presence of some of the **first** English-speaking prisoners ever taken in this war. And the poor fools in the Red Cross made a mistake in those early days.
Shipped us **five hundred parcels** each month instead of fifty!
We've got sugar, chocolate, tobacco, tea, flour, canned beef, milk, orange marmalade--literal tons of the stuff. You name it, we've got it.
The Germans don't **take** it?
Good heavens, no. They **trade** us for it. For nails, wood, paint, cloth, those sorts of things.
But enough questions. Sit! Eat! Drink!
For after dinner begins this evening's entertainment, the most popular story ever told...
CINDERELLA!
Hurrah!
The Englishman wasn't lying. Everything on the table was English, save for the candles and soap. Those were of German origin.
The British had no way of knowing it, but they were made from the fat of rendered Jews and Romani and communists and queers.
So it goes.

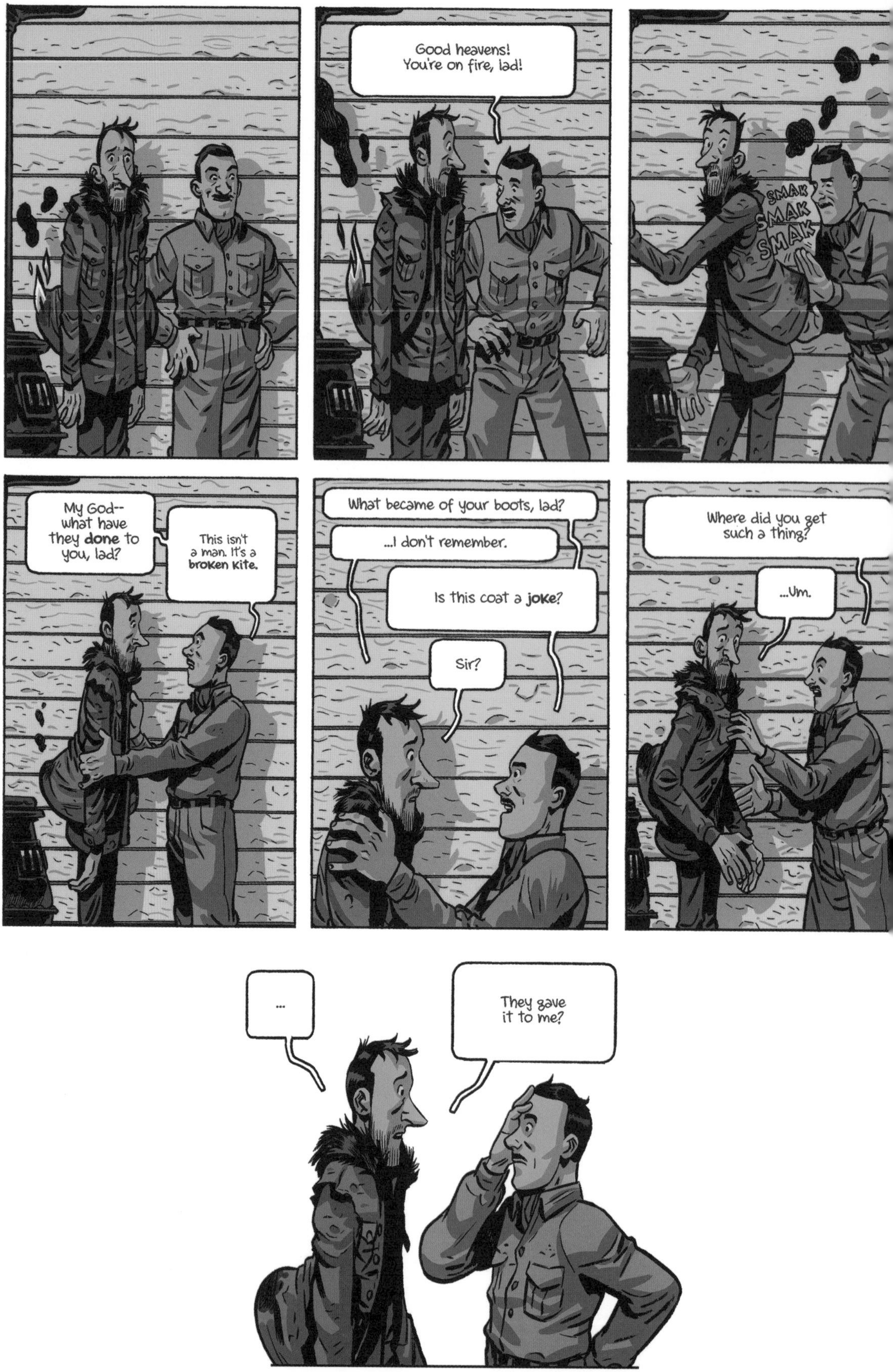
Good heavens! You're on fire, lad!
SMAK SMAK SMAK
My God-- what have they **done** to you, lad?
This isn't a man. It's a **broken kite.**
What became of your boots, lad?
...I don't remember.
Is this coat a **joke**?
Sir?
Where did you get such a thing?
...Um.
...
They gave it to me?

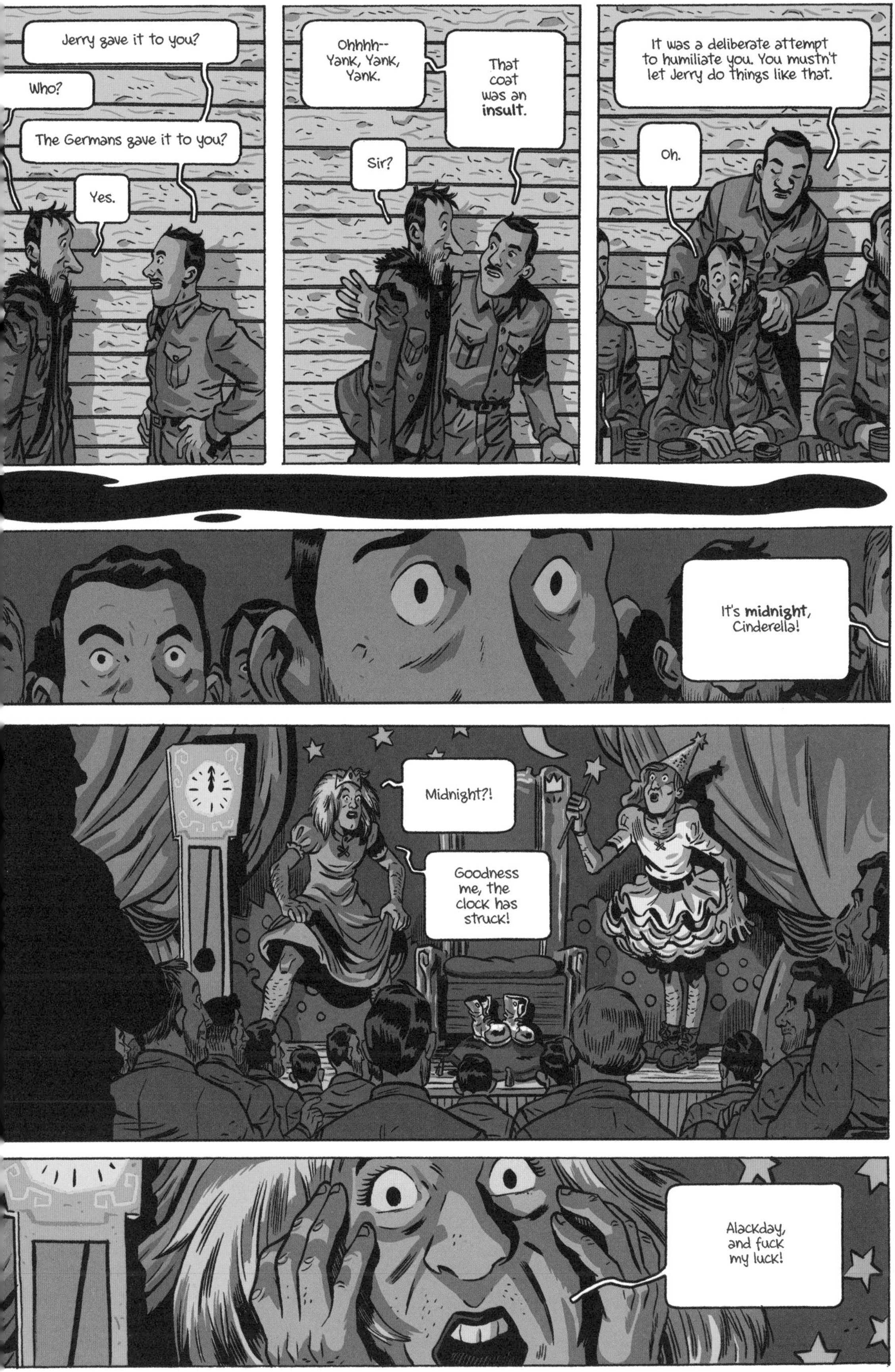

Jerry gave it to you?
Who?
The Germans gave it to you?
Yes.
Ohhhh--
Yank, Yank, Yank.
That coat was an **insult**.
Sir?
It was a deliberate attempt to humiliate you. You mustn't let Jerry do things like that.
Oh.
It's **midnight**, Cinderella!
Midnight?!
Goodness me, the clock has struck!
Alackday, and fuck my luck!

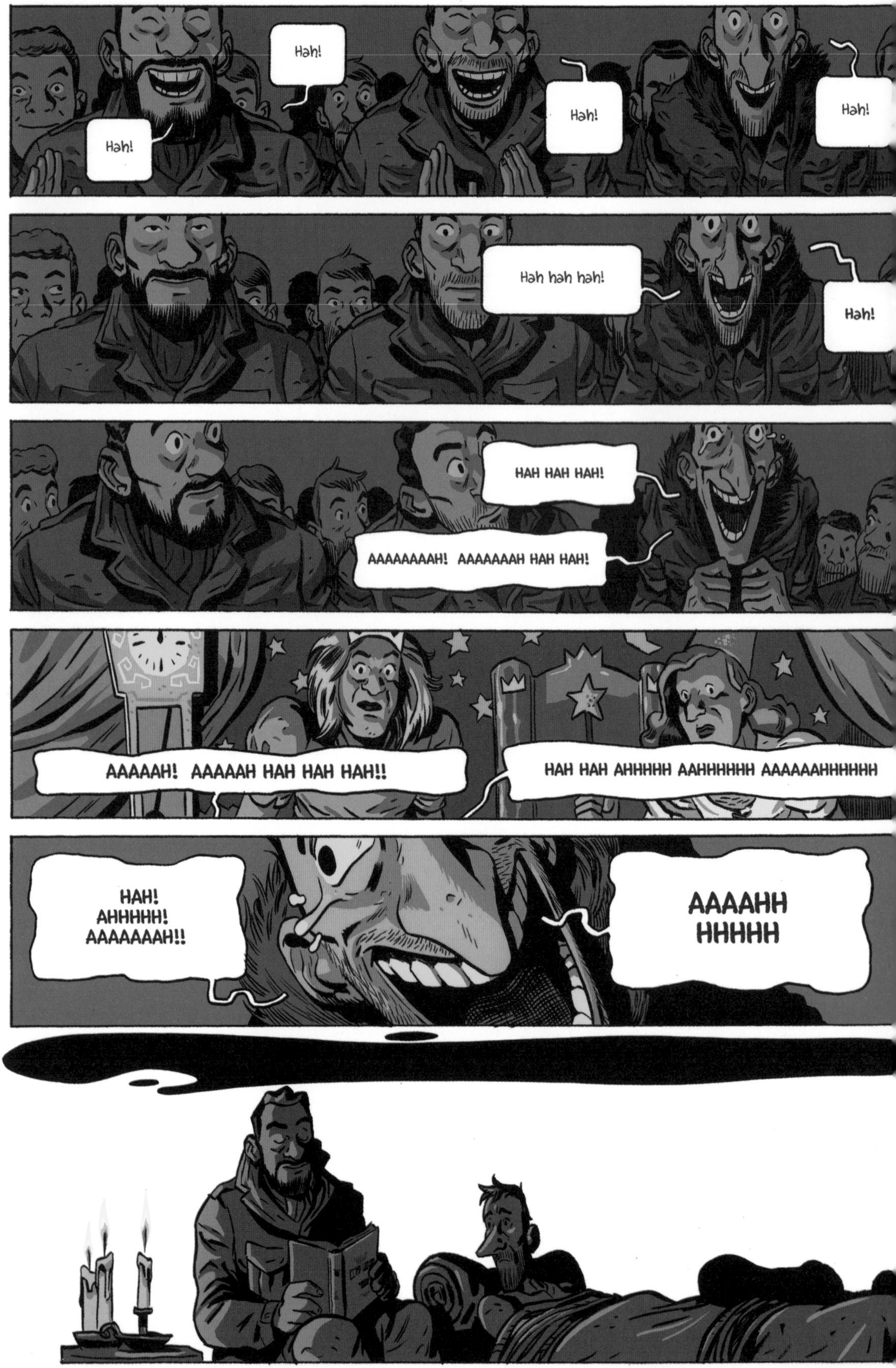
Hah!
Hah!
Hah!
Hah!
Hah hah hah!
Hah!
HAH HAH HAH!
AAAAAAAAH! AAAAAAAH HAH HAH!
AAAAAH! AAAAAH HAH HAH HAH!!
HAH HAH AHHHHH AAHHHHHH AAAAAAHHHHHH
HAH!
AHHHHH!
AAAAAAAH!!
AAAAHH
HHHHH

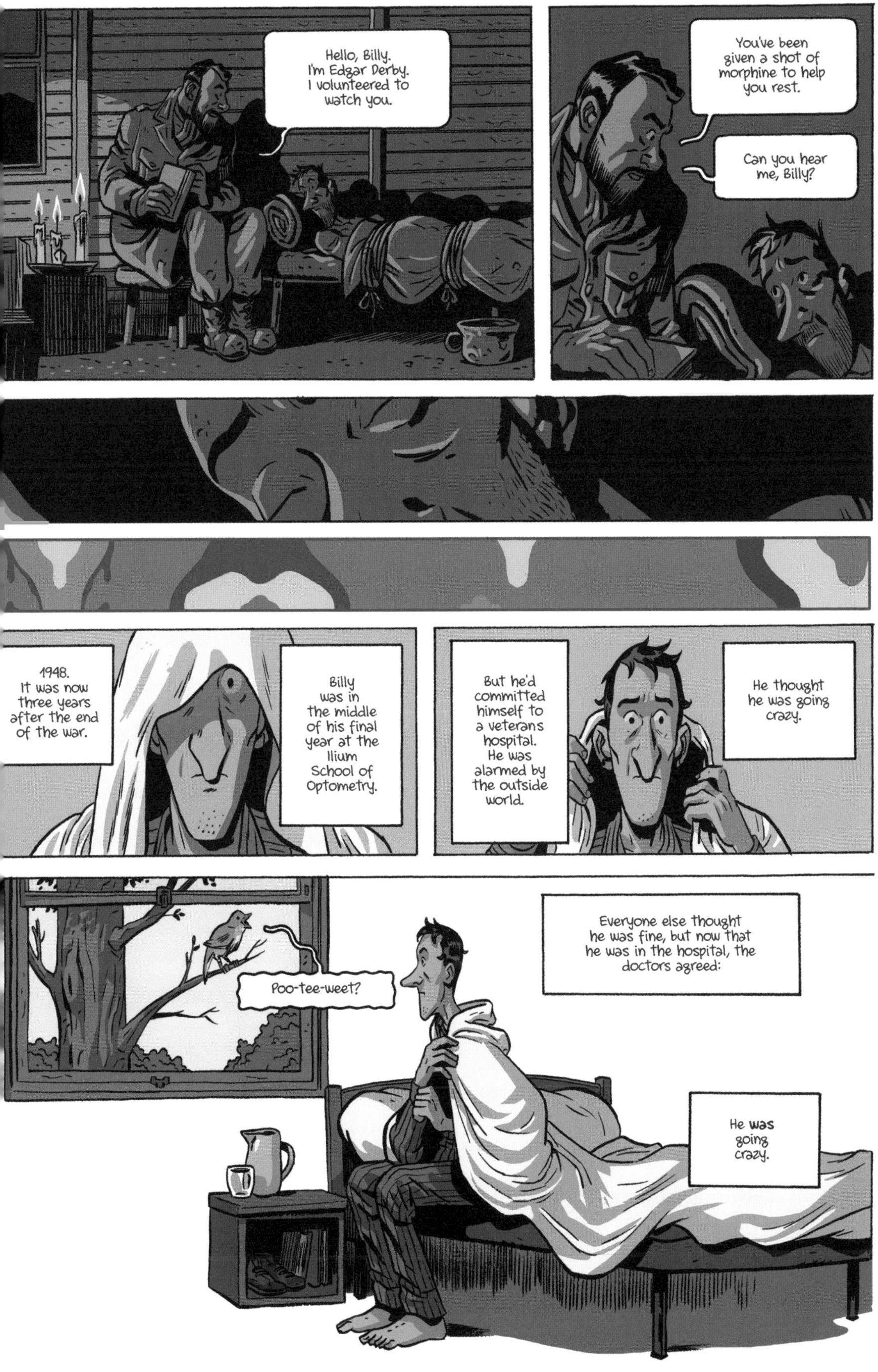
Hello, Billy. I'm Edgar Derby. I volunteered to watch you.
You've been given a shot of morphine to help you rest.
Can you hear me, Billy?
1948. It was now three years after the end of the war.
Billy was in the middle of his final year at the Ilium School of Optometry.
But he'd committed himself to a veterans hospital. He was alarmed by the outside world.
He thought he was going crazy.
Poo-tee-weet?
Everyone else thought he was fine, but now that he was in the hospital, the doctors agreed:
He **was** going crazy.

The doctors didn't think it had anything to do with the war.

They were sure it was because his father had thrown him into the deep end of the Y.M.C.A. swimming pool when he was a little boy.

There was a man assigned to the bed beside Billy. He was a former infantry captain named Eliot Rosewater.

Mr. Rosewater! How are you today?

I'm just fine, Mrs. Pilgrim. And how are **you** today?

Eliot was experimenting with being ardently sympathetic with everyone he met. He thought it might make the world a slightly more pleasant place to live in.

Why, I'm just fine, thank you for asking. God bless you, Mr. Rosewater.

God bless **you**, dear.

He was also experimenting with calling everybody "dear."

Some day I'm going to come in here, and Billy is going to uncover his head, and you know what he's going to say?

What's he going to say, dear?

He's going to say "Gee, it's good to see you, Mom. How have you been?"

Today could be the day.

Every night I pray.

That's a **good** thing to do.

People would be surprised if they knew how much in this world was due to prayers.

You never said a truer word, dear.

Billy was at the top of his class when this happened.

Maybe he was **working** too hard.

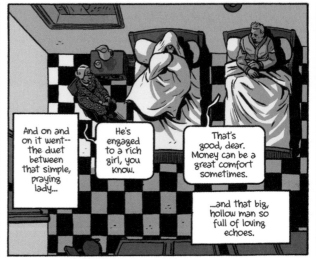

And on and on it went-- the duet between that simple, praying lady...

He's engaged to a rich girl, you know.

That's good, dear. Money can be a great comfort sometimes.

...and that big, hollow man so full of loving echoes.

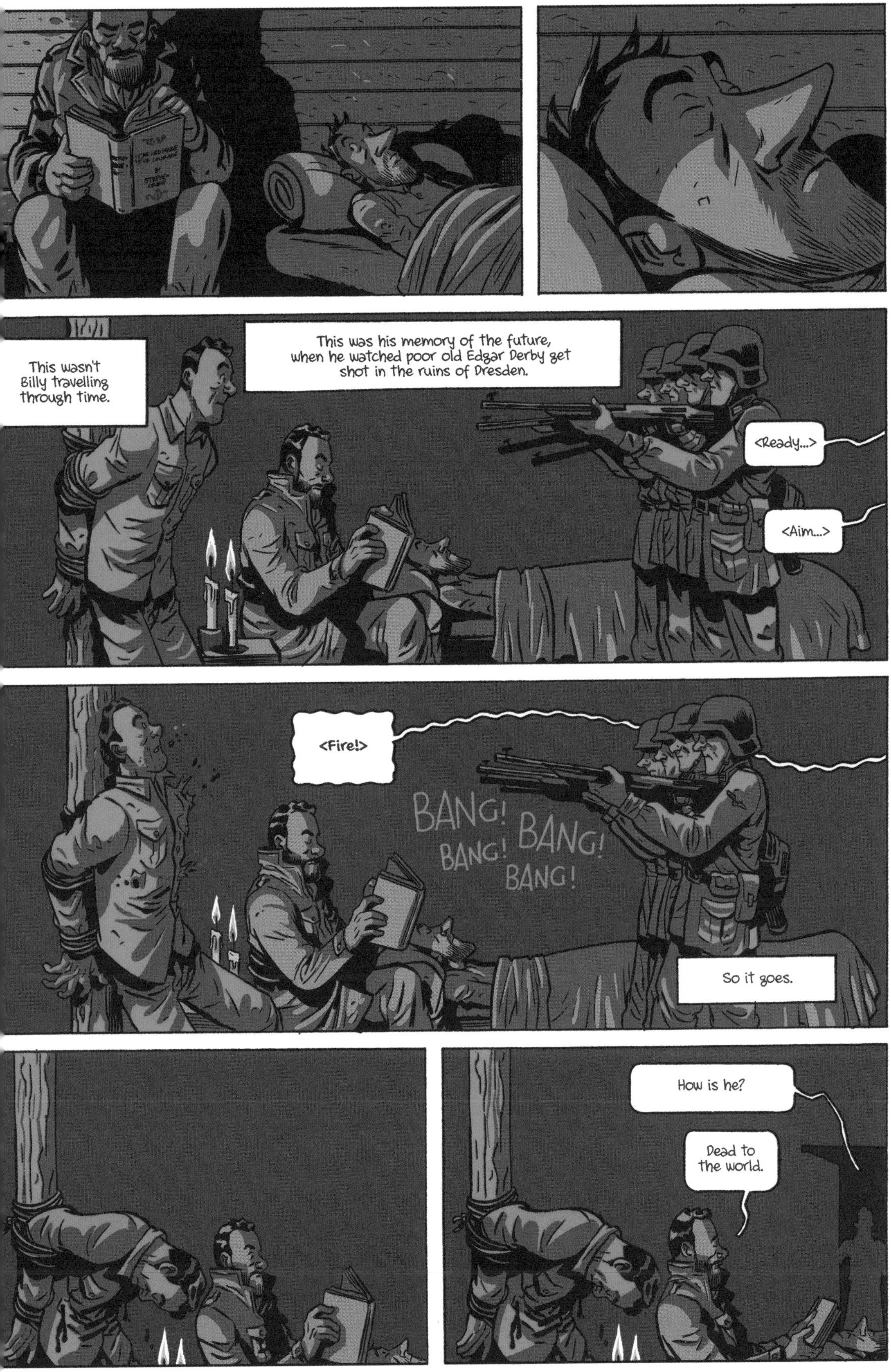
This wasn't Billy travelling through time.
This was his memory of the future, when he watched poor old Edgar Derby get shot in the ruins of Dresden.
<Ready...>
<Aim...>
<Fire!>
BANG! BANG! BANG! BANG!
So it goes.
How is he?
Dead to the world.

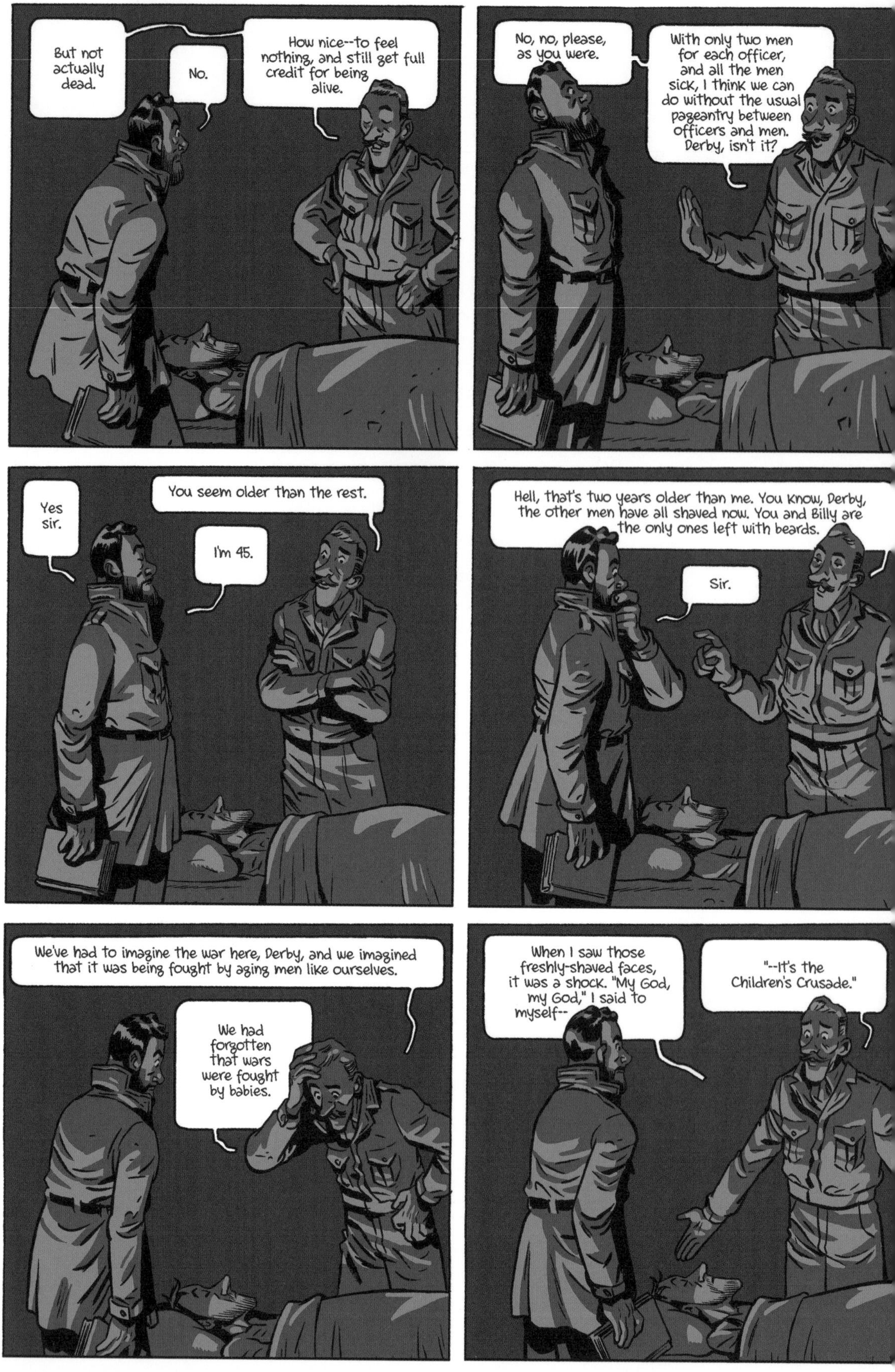
But not actually dead.
No.
How nice--to feel nothing, and still get full credit for being alive.
No, no, please, as you were.
With only two men for each officer, and all the men sick, I think we can do without the usual pageantry between officers and men. Derby, isn't it?
Yes sir.
You seem older than the rest.
I'm 45.
Hell, that's two years older than me. You know, Derby, the other men have all shaved now. You and Billy are the only ones left with beards.
Sir.
We've had to imagine the war here, Derby, and we imagined that it was being fought by aging men like ourselves.
We had forgotten that wars were fought by babies.
When I saw those freshly-shaved faces, it was a shock. "My God, my God," I said to myself--
"--It's the Children's Crusade."

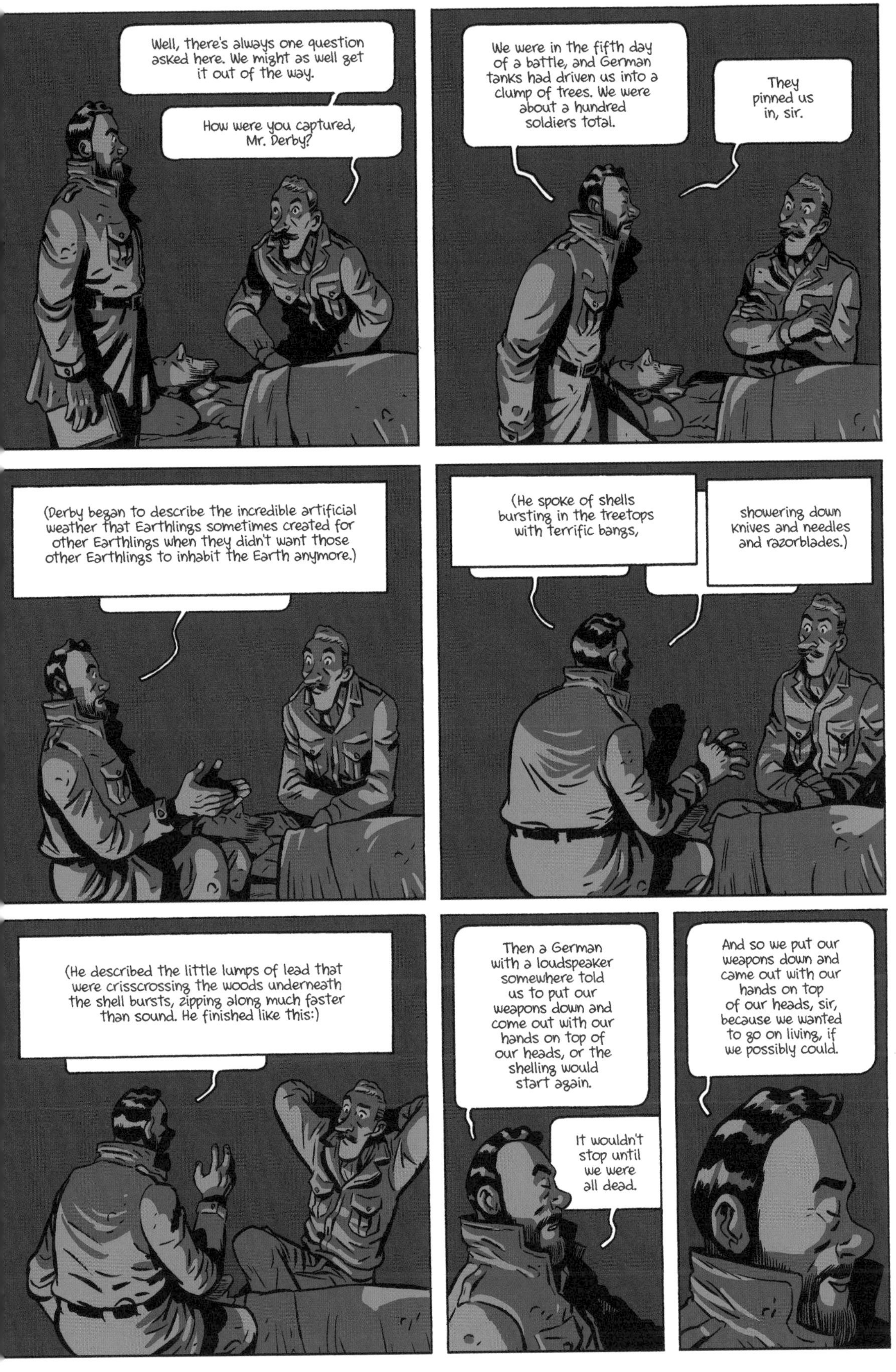

Well, there's always one question asked here. We might as well get it out of the way.
How were you captured, Mr. Derby?
We were in the fifth day of a battle, and German tanks had driven us into a clump of trees. We were about a hundred soldiers total.
They pinned us in, sir.
(Derby began to describe the incredible artificial weather that Earthlings sometimes created for other Earthlings when they didn't want those other Earthlings to inhabit the Earth anymore.)
(He spoke of shells bursting in the treetops with terrific bangs,
showering down knives and needles and razorblades.)
(He described the little lumps of lead that were crisscrossing the woods underneath the shell bursts, zipping along much faster than sound. He finished like this:)
Then a German with a loudspeaker somewhere told us to put our weapons down and come out with our hands on top of our heads, or the shelling would start again.
It wouldn't stop until we were all dead.
And so we put our weapons down and came out with our hands on top of our heads, sir, because we wanted to go on living, if we possibly could.

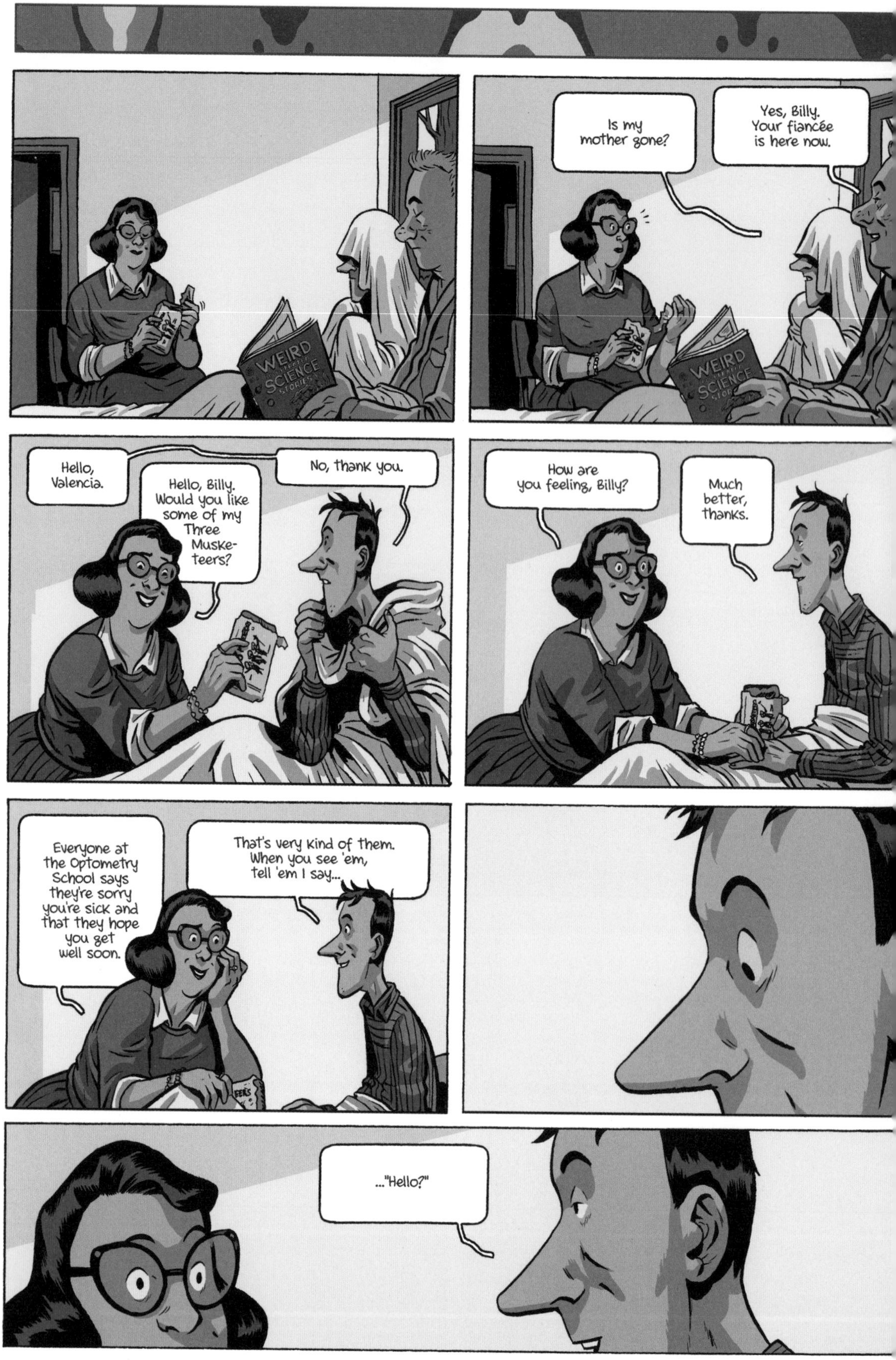
Is my mother gone?
Yes, Billy. Your fiancée is here now.
Hello, Valencia.
Hello, Billy. Would you like some of my Three Musketeers?
No, thank you.
How are you feeling, Billy?
Much better, thanks.
Everyone at the Optometry School says they're sorry you're sick and that they hope you get well soon.
That's very kind of them. When you see 'em, tell 'em I say...
..."Hello?"

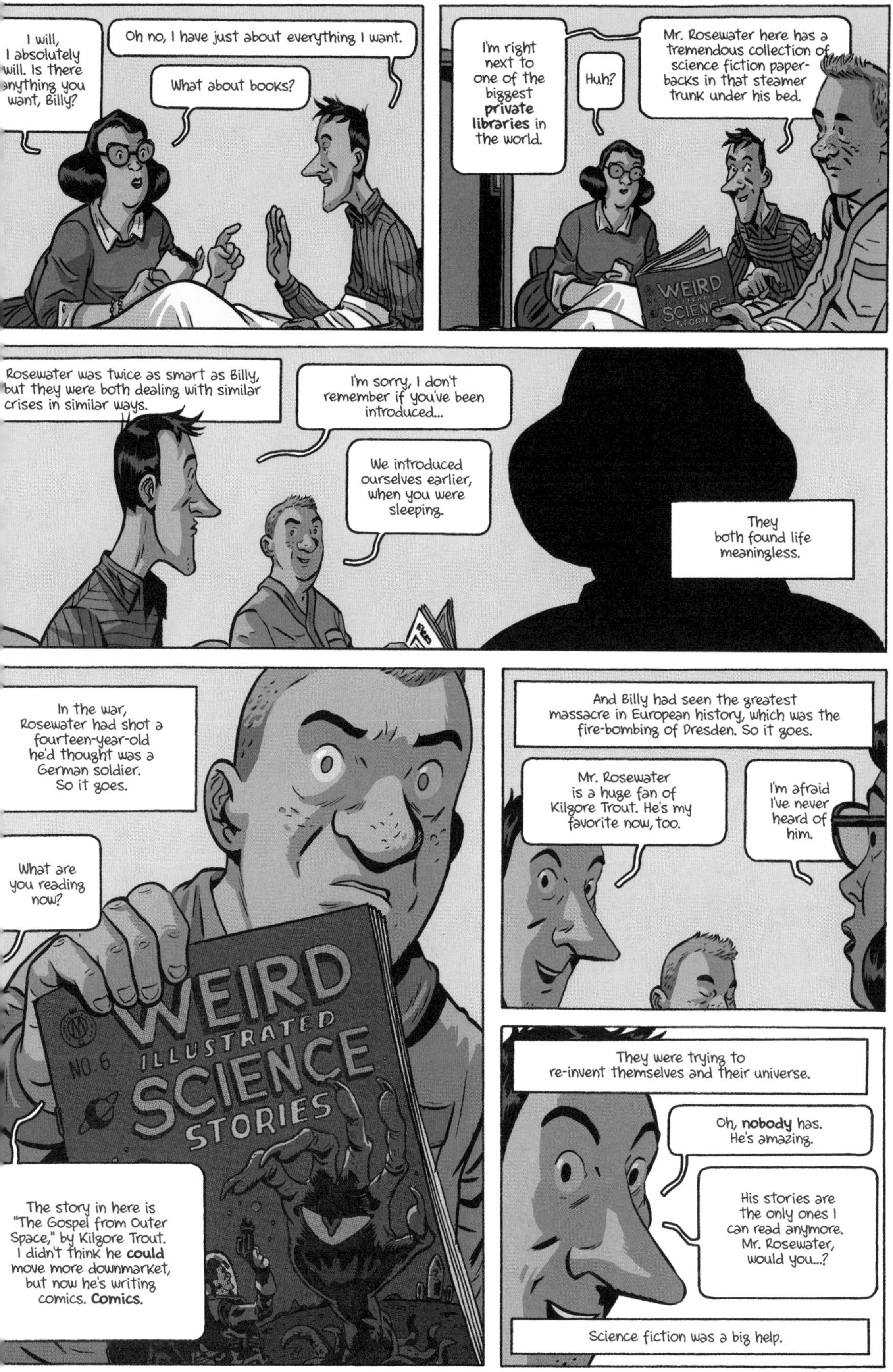
I will, I absolutely will. Is there anything you want, Billy?
Oh no, I have just about everything I want.
What about books?
I'm right next to one of the biggest **private libraries** in the world.
Huh?
Mr. Rosewater here has a tremendous collection of science fiction paperbacks in that steamer trunk under his bed.
WEIRD SCIENCE
Rosewater was twice as smart as Billy, but they were both dealing with similar crises in similar ways.
I'm sorry, I don't remember if you've been introduced...
We introduced ourselves earlier, when you were sleeping.
They both found life meaningless.
In the war, Rosewater had shot a fourteen-year-old he'd thought was a German soldier. So it goes.
What are you reading now?
NO. 6
WEIRD ILLUSTRATED SCIENCE STORIES
The story in here is "The Gospel from Outer Space," by Kilgore Trout. I didn't think he **could** move more downmarket, but now he's writing comics. **Comics.**
And Billy had seen the greatest massacre in European history, which was the fire-bombing of Dresden. So it goes.
Mr. Rosewater is a huge fan of Kilgore Trout. He's my favorite now, too.
I'm afraid I've never heard of him.
They were trying to re-invent themselves and their universe.
Oh, **nobody** has. He's amazing.
His stories are the only ones I can read anymore. Mr. Rosewater, would you...?
Science fiction was a big help.

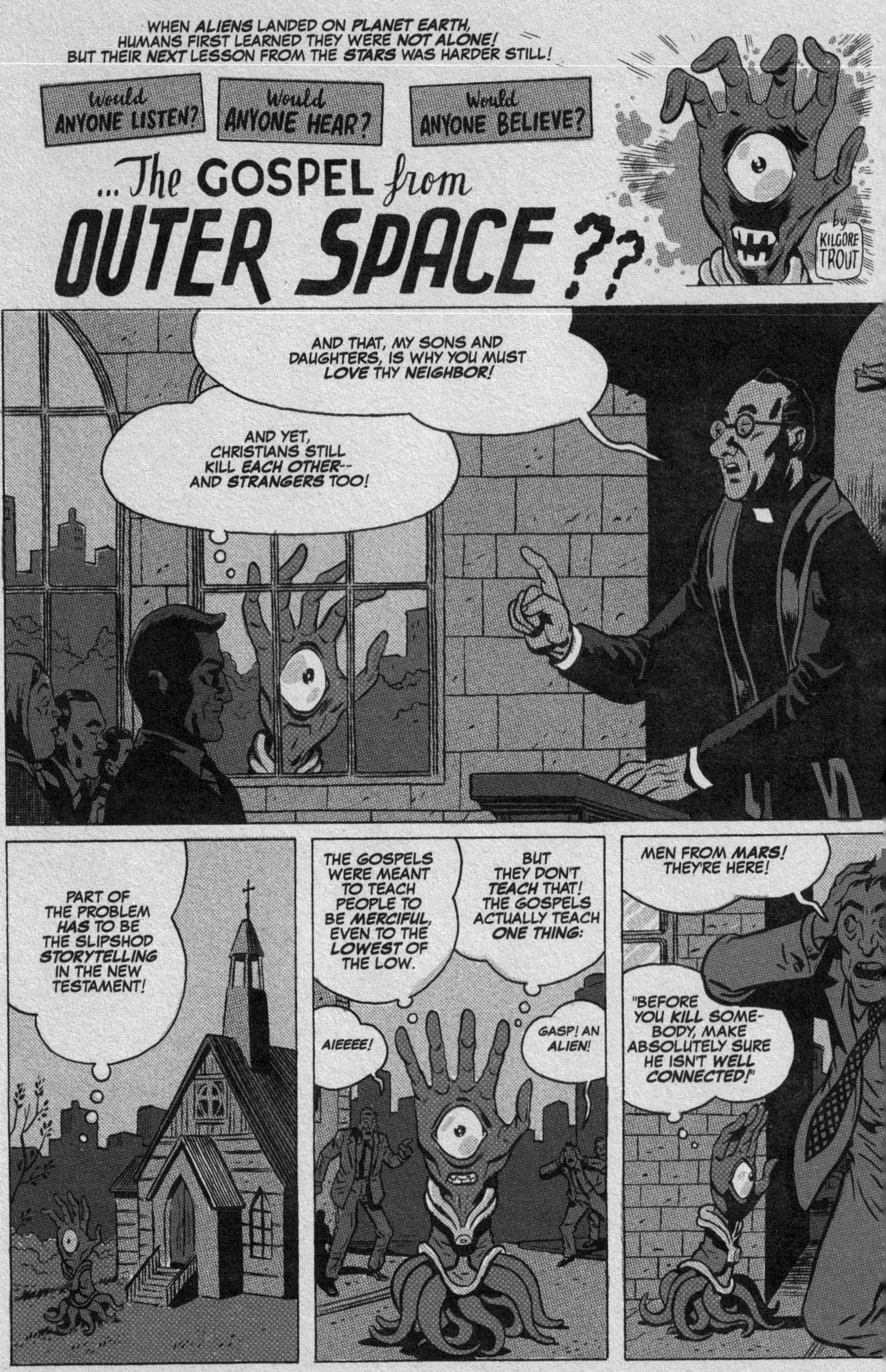
WHEN ALIENS LANDED ON PLANET EARTH, HUMANS FIRST LEARNED THEY WERE NOT ALONE! BUT THEIR NEXT LESSON FROM THE STARS WAS HARDER STILL!
Would ANYONE LISTEN?
Would ANYONE HEAR?
Would ANYONE BELIEVE?
...The GOSPEL from OUTER SPACE??
by KILGORE TROUT
AND THAT, MY SONS AND DAUGHTERS, IS WHY YOU MUST LOVE THY NEIGHBOR!
AND YET, CHRISTIANS STILL KILL EACH OTHER-- AND STRANGERS TOO!
PART OF THE PROBLEM HAS TO BE THE SLIPSHOD STORYTELLING IN THE NEW TESTAMENT!
THE GOSPELS WERE MEANT TO TEACH PEOPLE TO BE MERCIFUL, EVEN TO THE LOWEST OF THE LOW.
BUT THEY DON'T TEACH THAT! THE GOSPELS ACTUALLY TEACH ONE THING:
AIEEEE!
GASP! AN ALIEN!
MEN FROM MARS! THEY'RE HERE!
"BEFORE YOU KILL SOMEBODY, MAKE ABSOLUTELY SURE HE ISN'T WELL CONNECTED!"

THE *FLAW* IN THE STORIES IS THAT *CHRIST*, WHO DOESN'T LOOK LIKE MUCH, IS ACTUALLY THE *SON* OF THE *MOST POWERFUL* BEING IN THE UNIVERSE!

SO WHEN IT COMES TO THE *CRUCIFIXION*, EARTHLINGS READING THE *STORIES* NATURALLY THINK *ONE* THING:

THERE! THE *ALIEN!*

"OH BOY! THEY SURE PICKED THE *WRONG GUY* TO LYNCH *THIS* TIME!"

IT'S NO USE! HE'S GOT SOME SORT OF DEFENSE SHIELD!!

PING! PING! PING!

AND THAT THOUGHT HAS A SIBLING: "THERE ARE *RIGHT PEOPLE* TO LYNCH."

SAINTS PRESERVE US!!

PING! PING!

WHO ARE THEY? THE PEOPLE *NOT* WELL CONNECTED, OF COURSE.

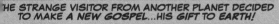

THE STRANGE VISITOR FROM ANOTHER PLANET DECIDED TO MAKE A *NEW GOSPEL*...HIS GIFT TO EARTH!

VRRT

USING HIS UNCANNY MACHINES, *THOUSANDS OF YEARS MORE ADVANCED* THAN ANYTHING ON EARTH, HE BEGINS TO CONVERT HIS *BRAIN-WAVES*...INTO EARTHLING WRITING!

CHOOOOM

AND SOON HIS WEIRD TASK IS *COMPLETED!*

THERE! IN THIS *NEW* VERSION, JESUS REALLY IS A *NOBODY. NOBODY* LIKES HIM!

HE'S A REAL *PAIN* IN THE NECK TO A LOT OF PEOPLE WITH BETTER *CONNECTIONS* THAN HE HAS!

The BIBLE II

The BIBLE II

BUT HE STILL GETS TO SAY ALL THE LOVELY AND PUZZLING THINGS HE SAID IN ALL THE *OTHER GOSPELS!*

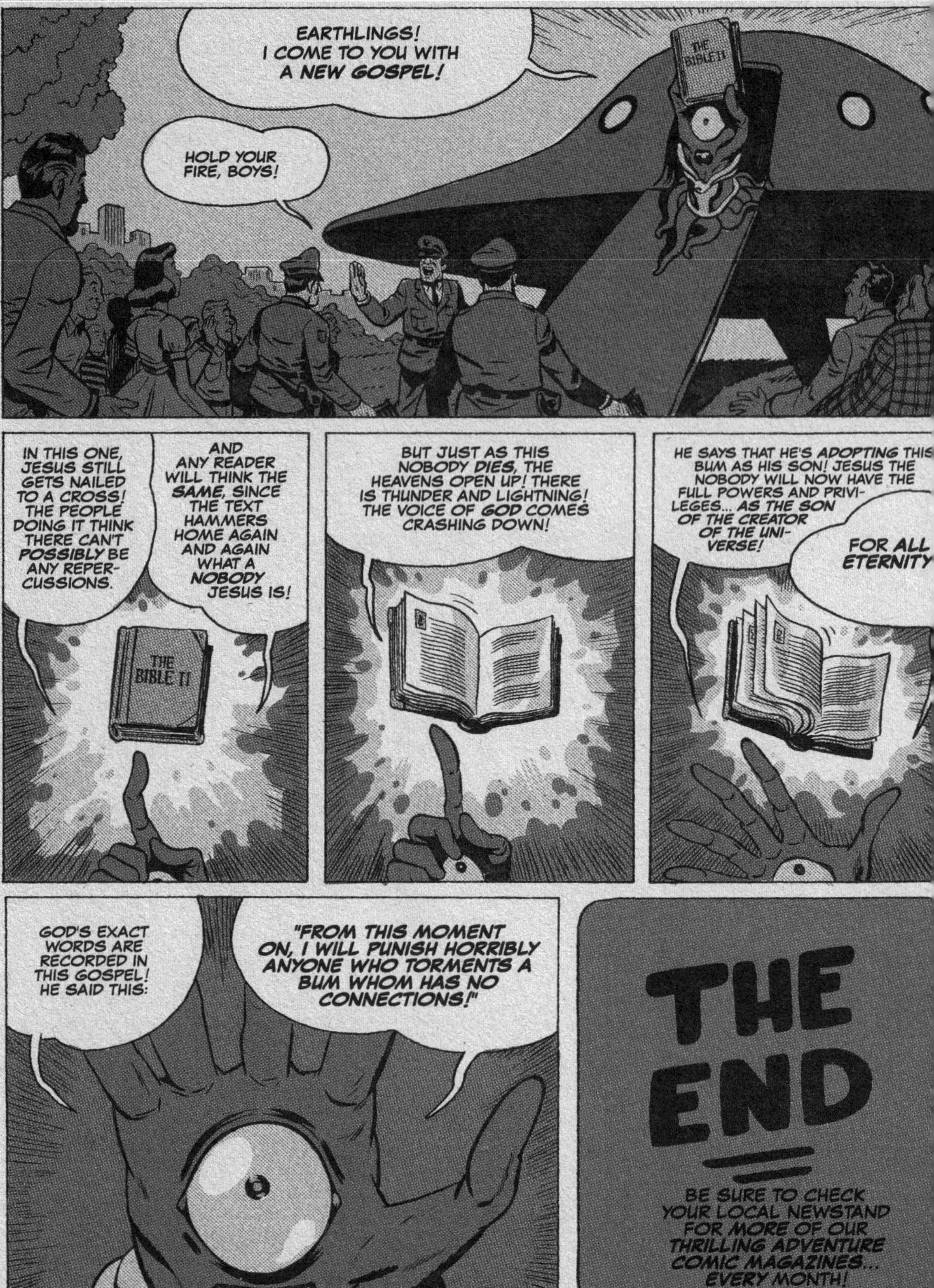
EARTHLINGS! I COME TO YOU WITH A NEW GOSPEL!
THE BIBLE II
HOLD YOUR FIRE, BOYS!
IN THIS ONE, JESUS STILL GETS NAILED TO A CROSS! THE PEOPLE DOING IT THINK THERE CAN'T POSSIBLY BE ANY REPERCUSSIONS.
AND ANY READER WILL THINK THE SAME, SINCE THE TEXT HAMMERS HOME AGAIN AND AGAIN WHAT A NOBODY JESUS IS!
THE BIBLE II
BUT JUST AS THIS NOBODY DIES, THE HEAVENS OPEN UP! THERE IS THUNDER AND LIGHTNING! THE VOICE OF GOD COMES CRASHING DOWN!
HE SAYS THAT HE'S ADOPTING THIS BUM AS HIS SON! JESUS THE NOBODY WILL NOW HAVE THE FULL POWERS AND PRIVILEGES... AS THE SON OF THE CREATOR OF THE UNIVERSE!
FOR ALL ETERNITY
GOD'S EXACT WORDS ARE RECORDED IN THIS GOSPEL! HE SAID THIS:
"FROM THIS MOMENT ON, I WILL PUNISH HORRIBLY ANYONE WHO TORMENTS A BUM WHOM HAS NO CONNECTIONS!"
THE END
BE SURE TO CHECK YOUR LOCAL NEWSTAND FOR MORE OF OUR THRILLING ADVENTURE COMIC MAGAZINES... EVERY MONTH!

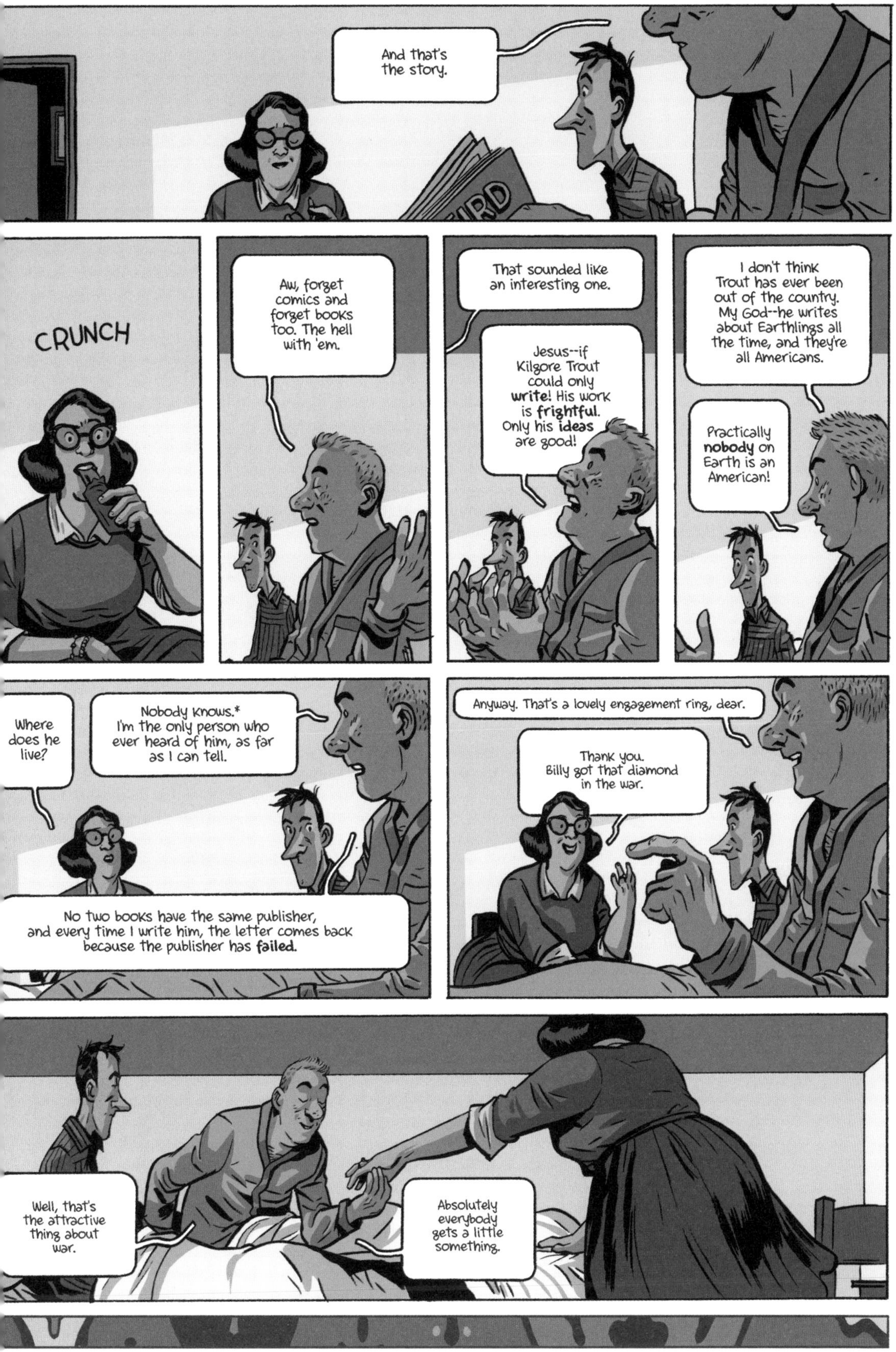
And that's the story.
CRUNCH
Aw, forget comics and forget books too. The hell with 'em.
That sounded like an interesting one.
Jesus--if Kilgore Trout could only **write**! His work is **frightful**. Only his **ideas** are good!
I don't think Trout has ever been out of the country. My God--he writes about Earthlings all the time, and they're all Americans.
Practically **nobody** on Earth is an American!
Where does he live?
Nobody knows.* I'm the only person who ever heard of him, as far as I can tell.
No two books have the same publisher, and every time I write him, the letter comes back because the publisher has **failed**.
Anyway. That's a lovely engagement ring, dear.
Thank you. Billy got that diamond in the war.
Well, that's the attractive thing about war.
Absolutely everybody gets a little something.

*With regard to the whereabouts of Kilgore Trout: he actually lived in Ilium, Billy's hometown, friendless and despised. Billy would meet him by and by.

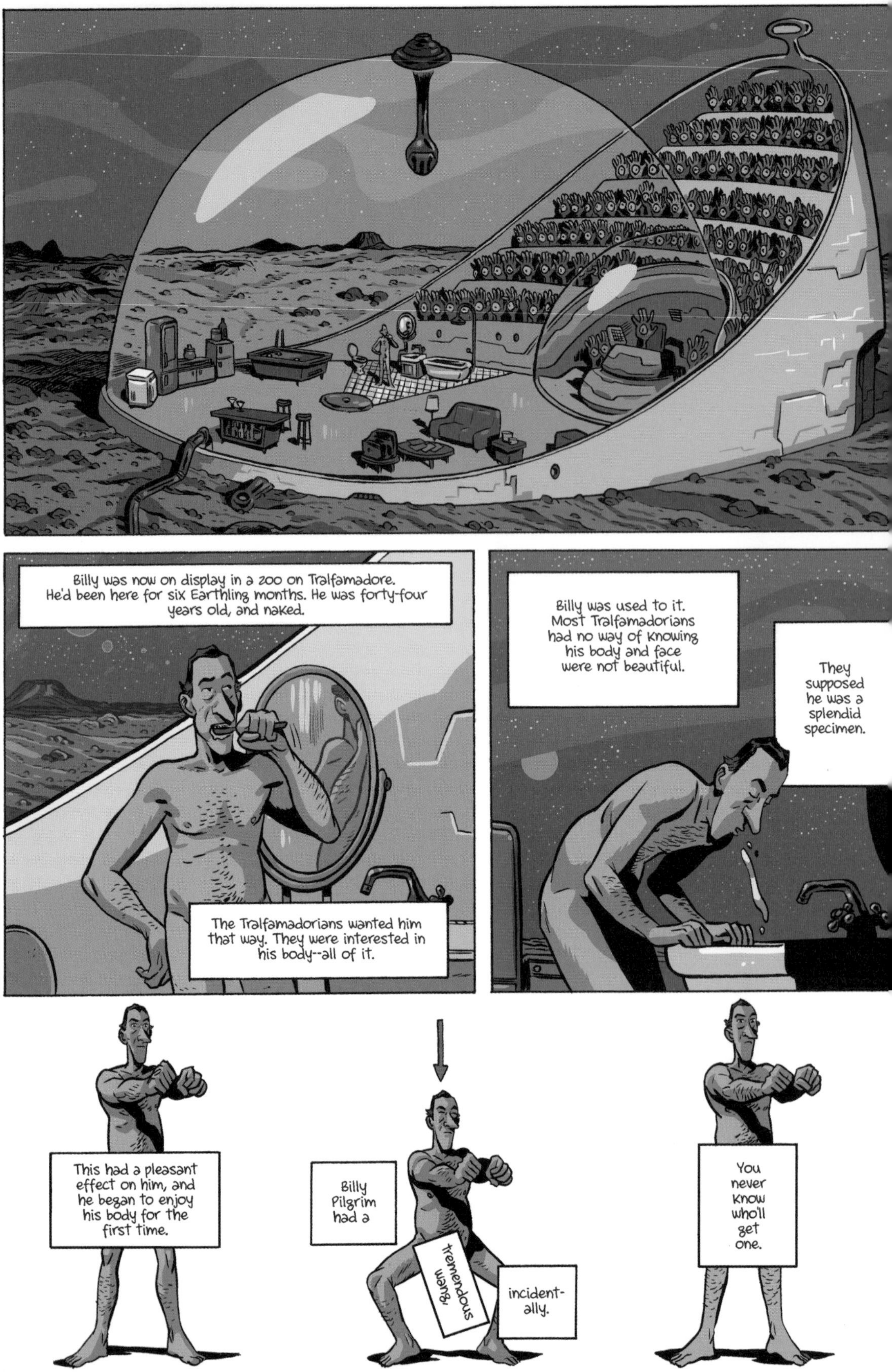

Billy was now on display in a zoo on Tralfamadore. He'd been here for six Earthling months. He was forty-four years old, and naked.
The Tralfamadorians wanted him that way. They were interested in his body--all of it.
Billy was used to it. Most Tralfamadorians had no way of knowing his body and face were not beautiful.
They supposed he was a splendid specimen.
This had a pleasant effect on him, and he began to enjoy his body for the first time.
Billy Pilgrim had a
tremendous wang,
incident-ally.
You never know who'll get one.

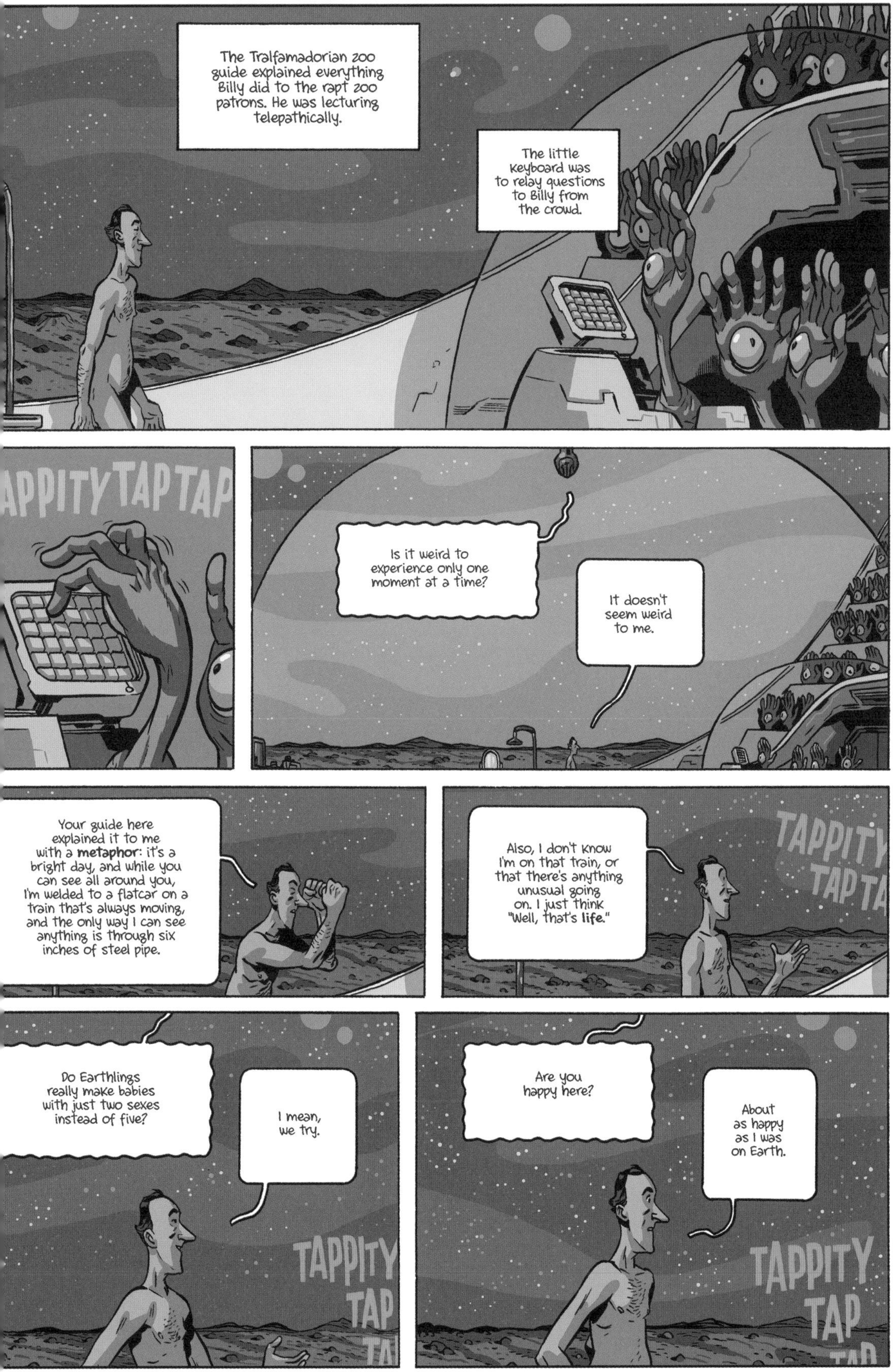
The Tralfamadorian zoo guide explained everything Billy did to the rapt zoo patrons. He was lecturing telepathically.
The little keyboard was to relay questions to Billy from the crowd.
TAPPITY TAP TAP
Is it weird to experience only one moment at a time?
It doesn't seem weird to me.
Your guide here explained it to me with a **metaphor**: it's a bright day, and while you can see all around you, I'm welded to a flatcar on a train that's always moving, and the only way I can see anything is through six inches of steel pipe.
Also, I don't know I'm on that train, or that there's anything unusual going on. I just think "Well, that's **life**."
TAPPITY TAP TA
Do Earthlings really make babies with just two sexes instead of five?
I mean, we try.
TAPPITY TAP
Are you happy here?
About as happy as I was on Earth.
TAPPITY TAP

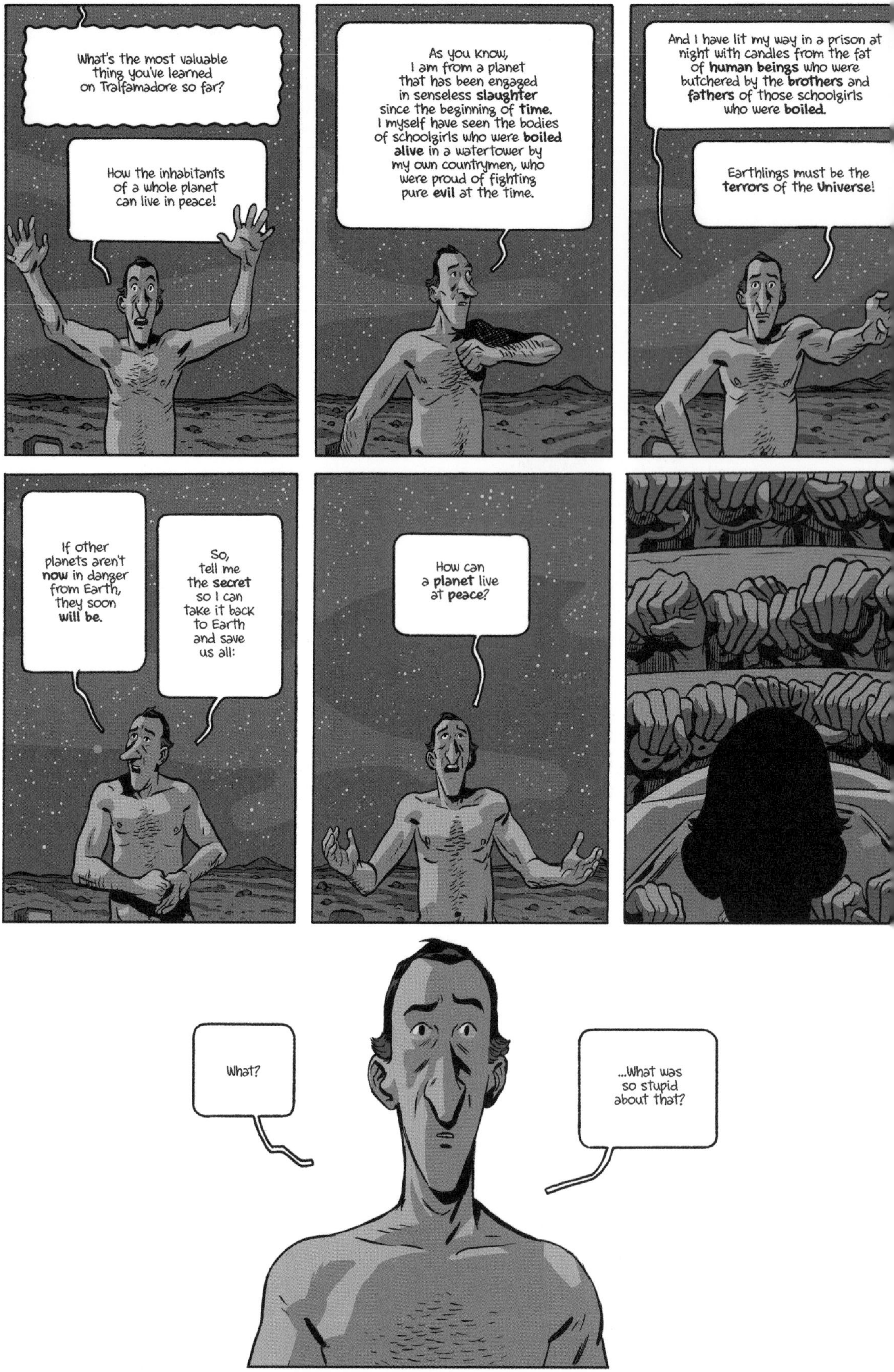
What's the most valuable thing you've learned on Tralfamadore so far?
How the inhabitants of a whole planet can live in peace!
As you know, I am from a planet that has been engaged in senseless **slaughter** since the beginning of **time.** I myself have seen the bodies of schoolgirls who were **boiled alive** in a watertower by my own countrymen, who were proud of fighting pure **evil** at the time.
And I have lit my way in a prison at night with candles from the fat of **human beings** who were butchered by the **brothers** and **fathers** of those schoolgirls who were **boiled.**
Earthlings must be the **terrors** of the **Universe**!
If other planets aren't **now** in danger from Earth, they soon **will be.**
So, tell me the **secret** so I can take it back to Earth and save us all:
How can a **planet** live at **peace**?
What?
...What was so stupid about that?

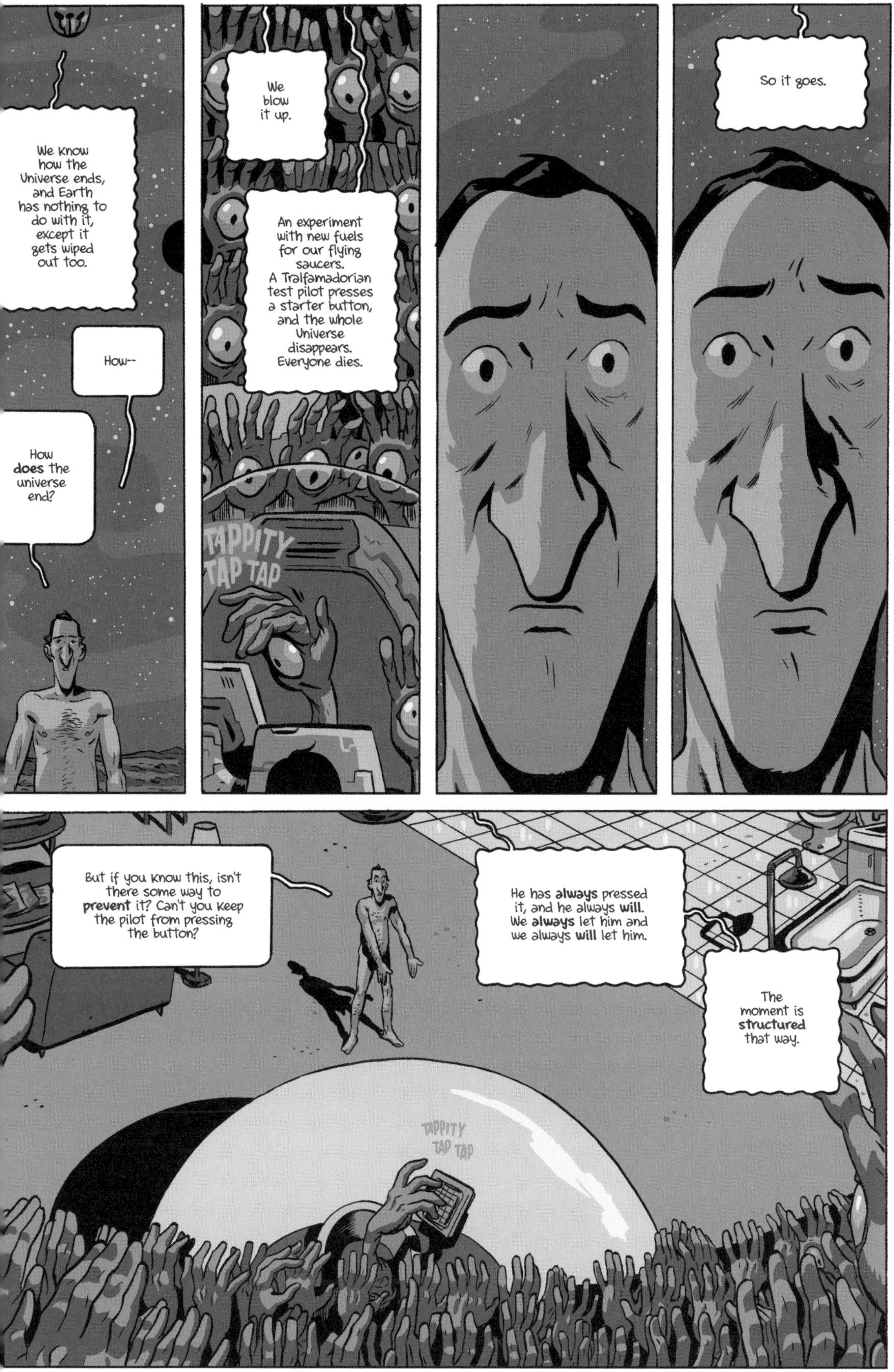
We know how the Universe ends, and Earth has nothing to do with it, except it gets wiped out too.
How--
How **does** the universe end?
We blow it up.
An experiment with new fuels for our flying saucers. A Tralfamadorian test pilot presses a starter button, and the whole Universe disappears. Everyone dies.
TAPPITY TAP TAP
So it goes.
But if you know this, isn't there some way to **prevent** it? Can't you keep the pilot from pressing the button?
He has **always** pressed it, and he always **will**. We **always** let him and we always **will** let him.
The moment is **structured** that way.
TAPPITY TAP TAP

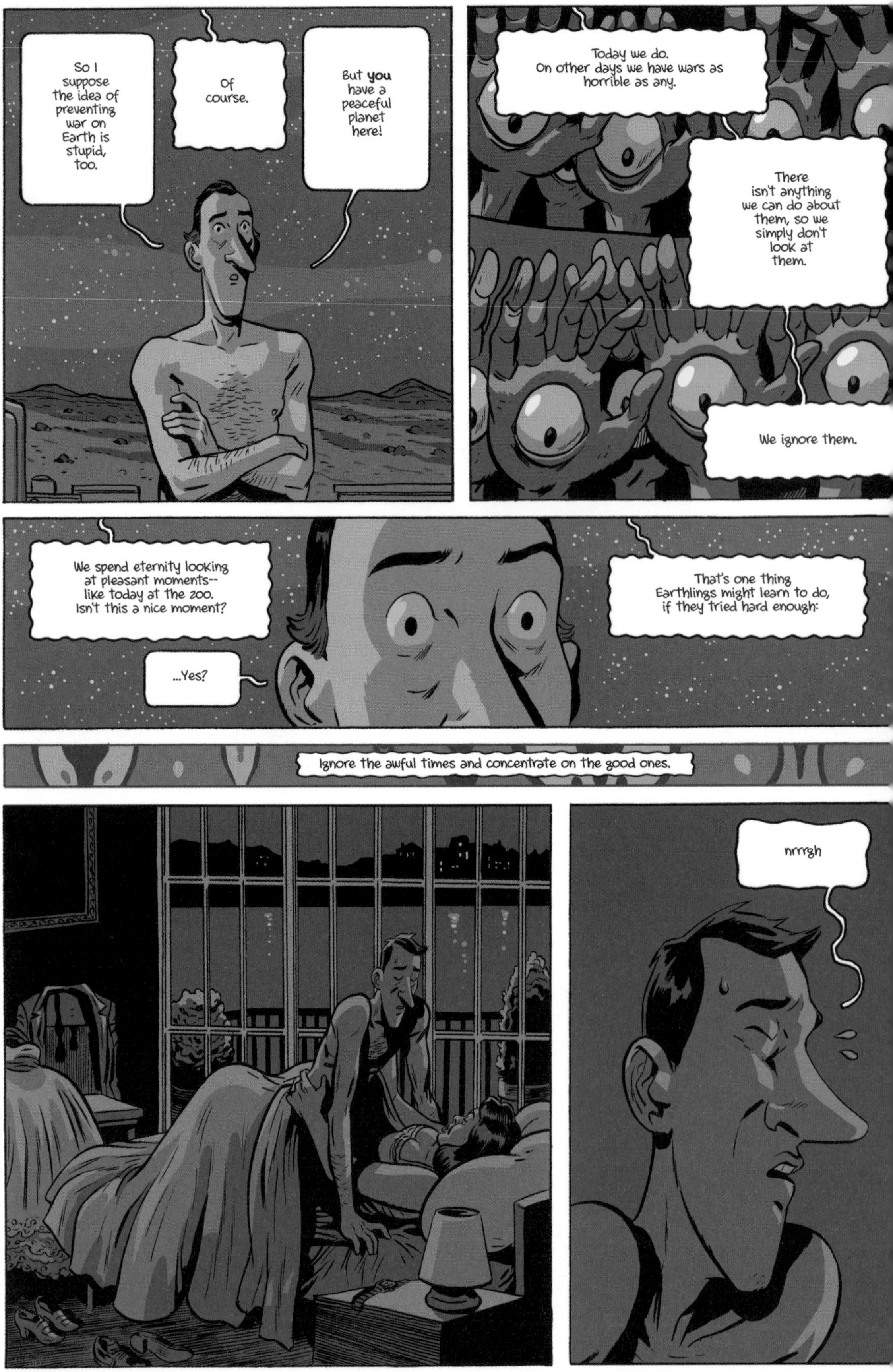
So I suppose the idea of preventing war on Earth is stupid, too.
Of course.
But **you** have a peaceful planet here!
Today we do. On other days we have wars as horrible as any.
There isn't anything we can do about them, so we simply don't look at them.
We ignore them.
We spend eternity looking at pleasant moments-- like today at the zoo. Isn't this a nice moment?
...Yes?
That's one thing Earthlings might learn to do, if they tried hard enough:
Ignore the awful times and concentrate on the good ones.
nrrrgh

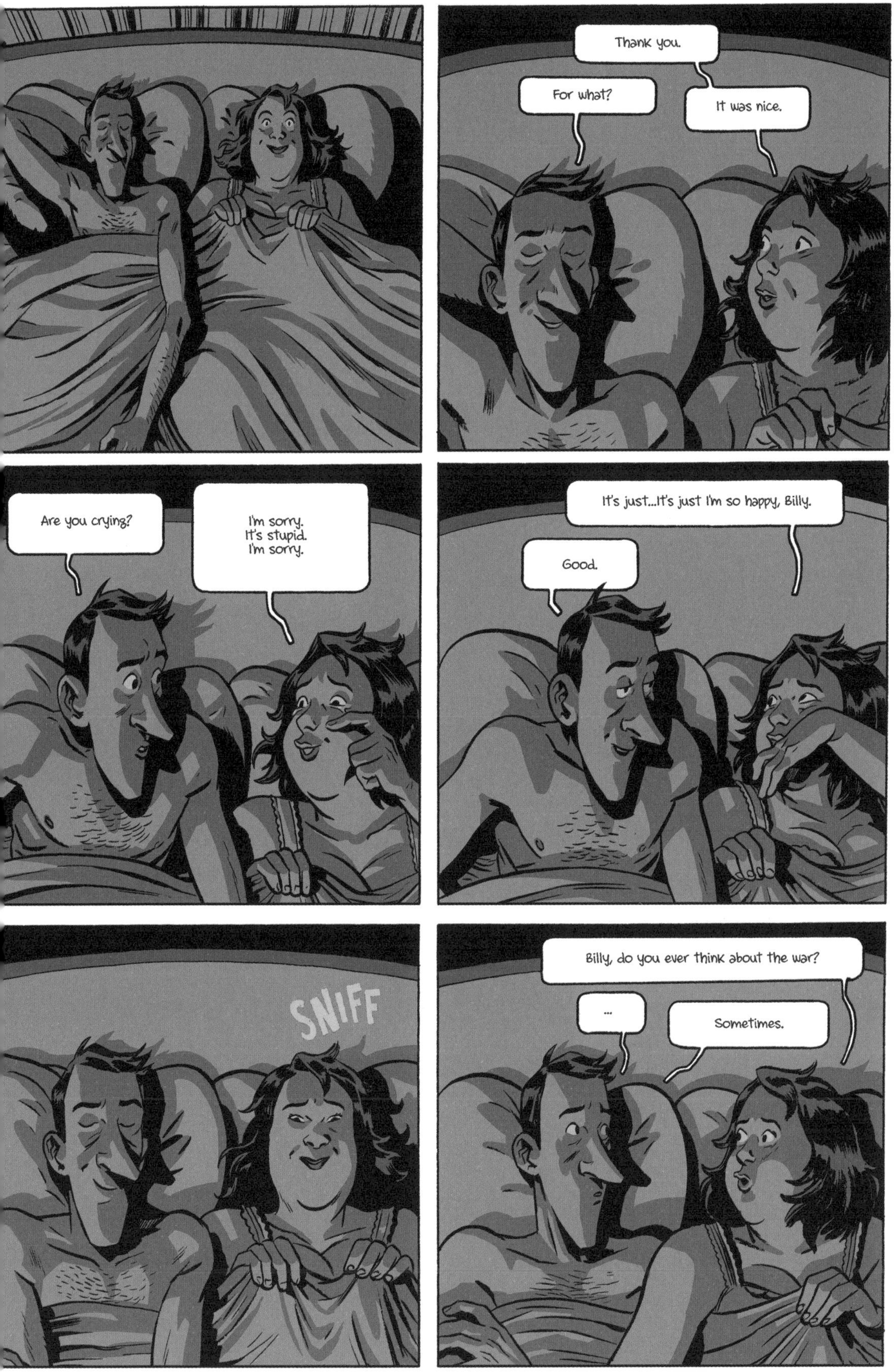
Thank you.
For what?
It was nice.
Are you crying?
I'm sorry.
It's stupid.
I'm sorry.
It's just...It's just I'm so happy, Billy.
Good.
SNIFF
Billy, do you ever think about the war?
...
Sometimes.

You must have secrets. About the war. Or, not secrets, I guess, but things you don't want to talk about.

No.

That was a lie, of course. Billy was full of secrets.

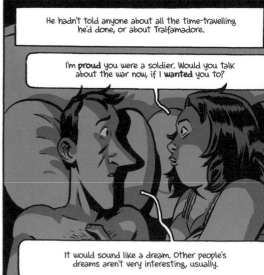

He hadn't told anyone about all the time-travelling he'd done, or about Tralfamadore.

I'm **proud** you were a soldier. Would you talk about the war now, if I **wanted** you to?

It would sound like a dream. Other people's dreams aren't very interesting, usually.

I heard you tell Father one time about a German firing squad.

Um.

You had to bury him? And he saw you with your shovels before he was shot?

Yes.

Did he **say** anything? Was he scared?

No. They had him doped up. He was sort of glassy-eyed.

Excuse me. I need to take a leak.

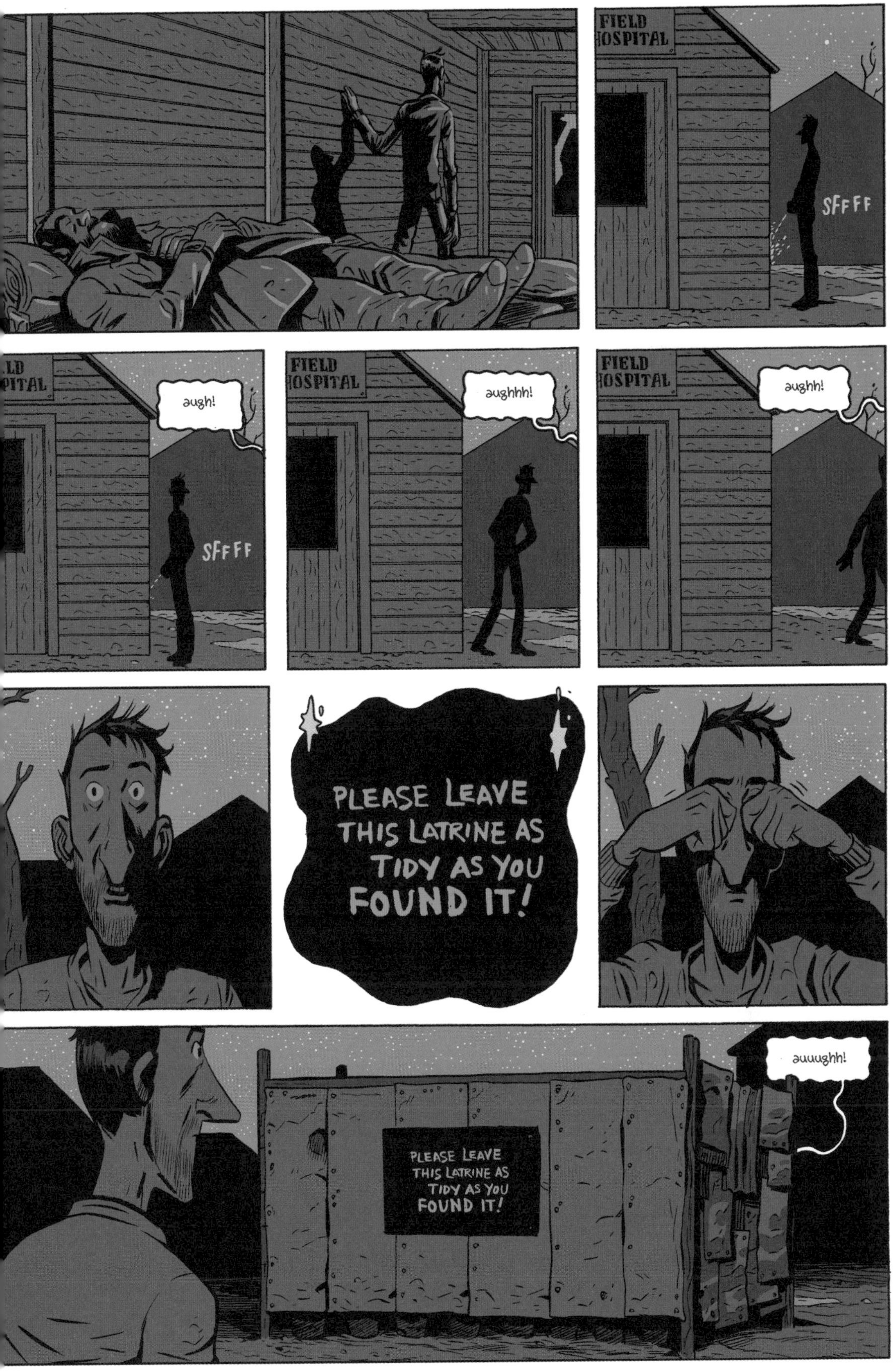
FIELD HOSPITAL
SFFFF
augh!
SFFFF
aughhh!
aughh!
PLEASE LEAVE THIS LATRINE AS TIDY AS YOU FOUND IT!
PLEASE LEAVE THIS LATRINE AS TIDY AS YOU FOUND IT!
auuughh!

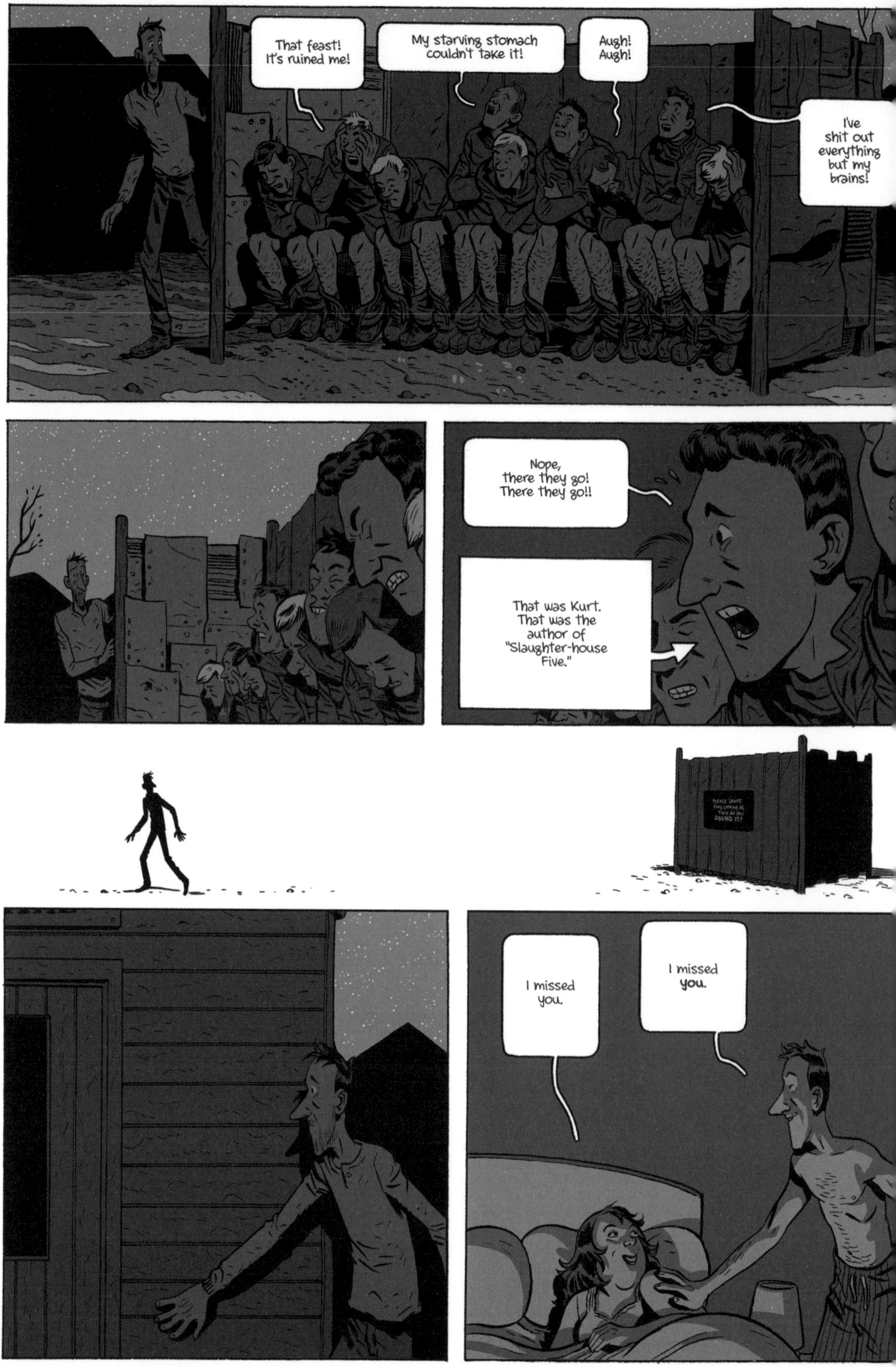
That feast! It's ruined me!
My starving stomach couldn't take it!
Augh! Augh!
I've shit out everything but my brains!
Nope, there they go! There they go!!
That was Kurt. That was the author of "Slaughter-house Five."
I missed you.
I missed **you.**

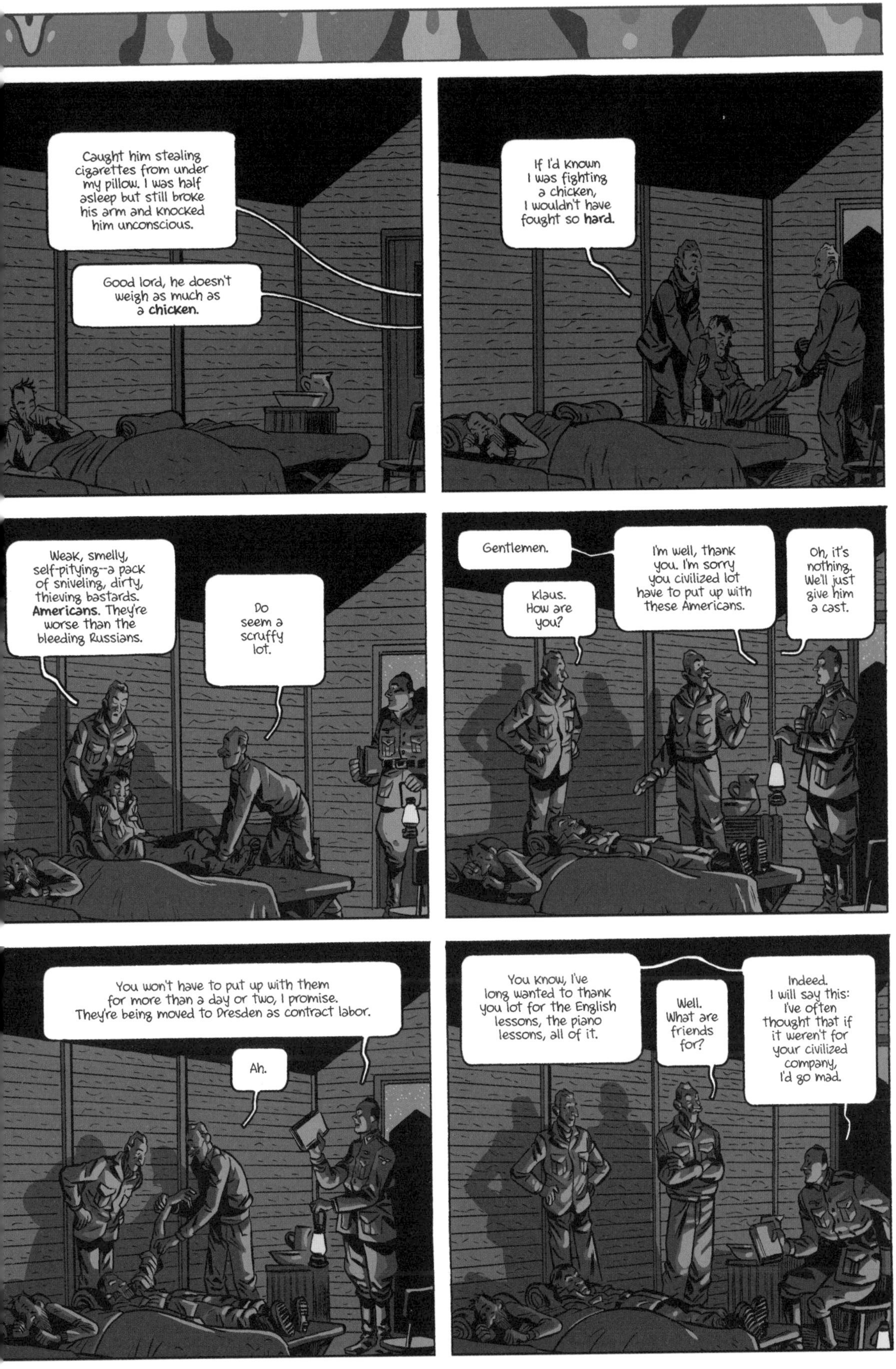
Caught him stealing cigarettes from under my pillow. I was half asleep but still broke his arm and knocked him unconscious.
Good lord, he doesn't weigh as much as a **chicken.**
If I'd known I was fighting a chicken, I wouldn't have fought so **hard.**
Weak, smelly, self-pitying--a pack of sniveling, dirty, thieving bastards. **Americans.** They're worse than the bleeding Russians.
Do seem a scruffy lot.
Gentlemen.
Klaus. How are you?
I'm well, thank you. I'm sorry you civilized lot have to put up with these Americans.
Oh, it's nothing. We'll just give him a cast.
You won't have to put up with them for more than a day or two, I promise. They're being moved to Dresden as contract labor.
Ah.
You know, I've long wanted to thank you lot for the English lessons, the piano lessons, all of it.
Well. What are friends for?
Indeed. I will say this: I've often thought that if it weren't for your civilized company, I'd go mad.

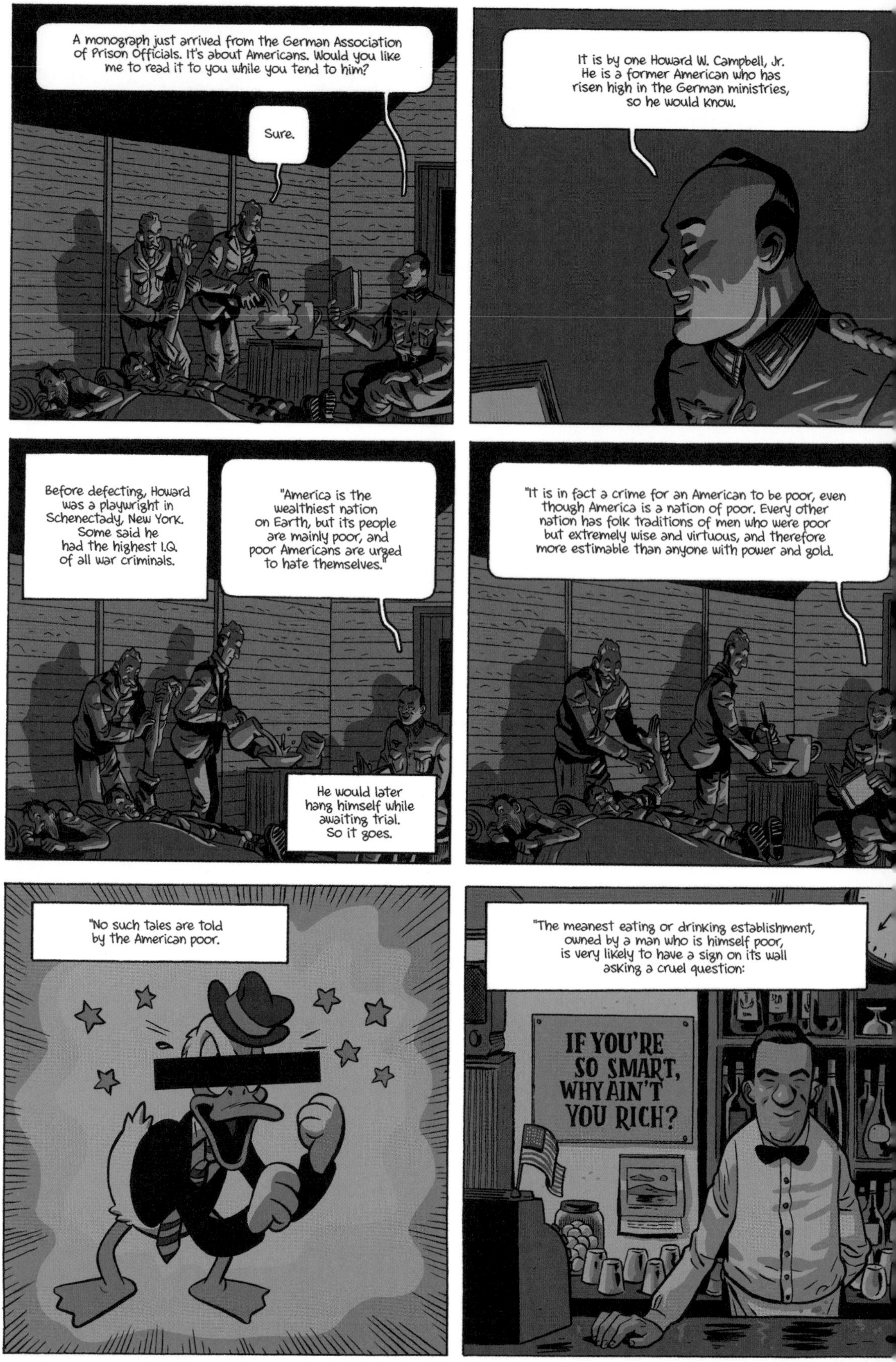
A monograph just arrived from the German Association of Prison Officials. It's about Americans. Would you like me to read it to you while you tend to him?
Sure.
It is by one Howard W. Campbell, Jr. He is a former American who has risen high in the German ministries, so he would know.
Before defecting, Howard was a playwright in Schenectady, New York. Some said he had the highest I.Q. of all war criminals.
"America is the wealthiest nation on Earth, but its people are mainly poor, and poor Americans are urged to hate themselves."
He would later hang himself while awaiting trial. So it goes.
"It is in fact a crime for an American to be poor, even though America is a nation of poor. Every other nation has folk traditions of men who were poor but extremely wise and virtuous, and therefore more estimable than anyone with power and gold.
"No such tales are told by the American poor.
"The meanest eating or drinking establishment, owned by a man who is himself poor, is very likely to have a sign on its wall asking a cruel question:
IF YOU'RE SO SMART, WHY AIN'T YOU RICH?

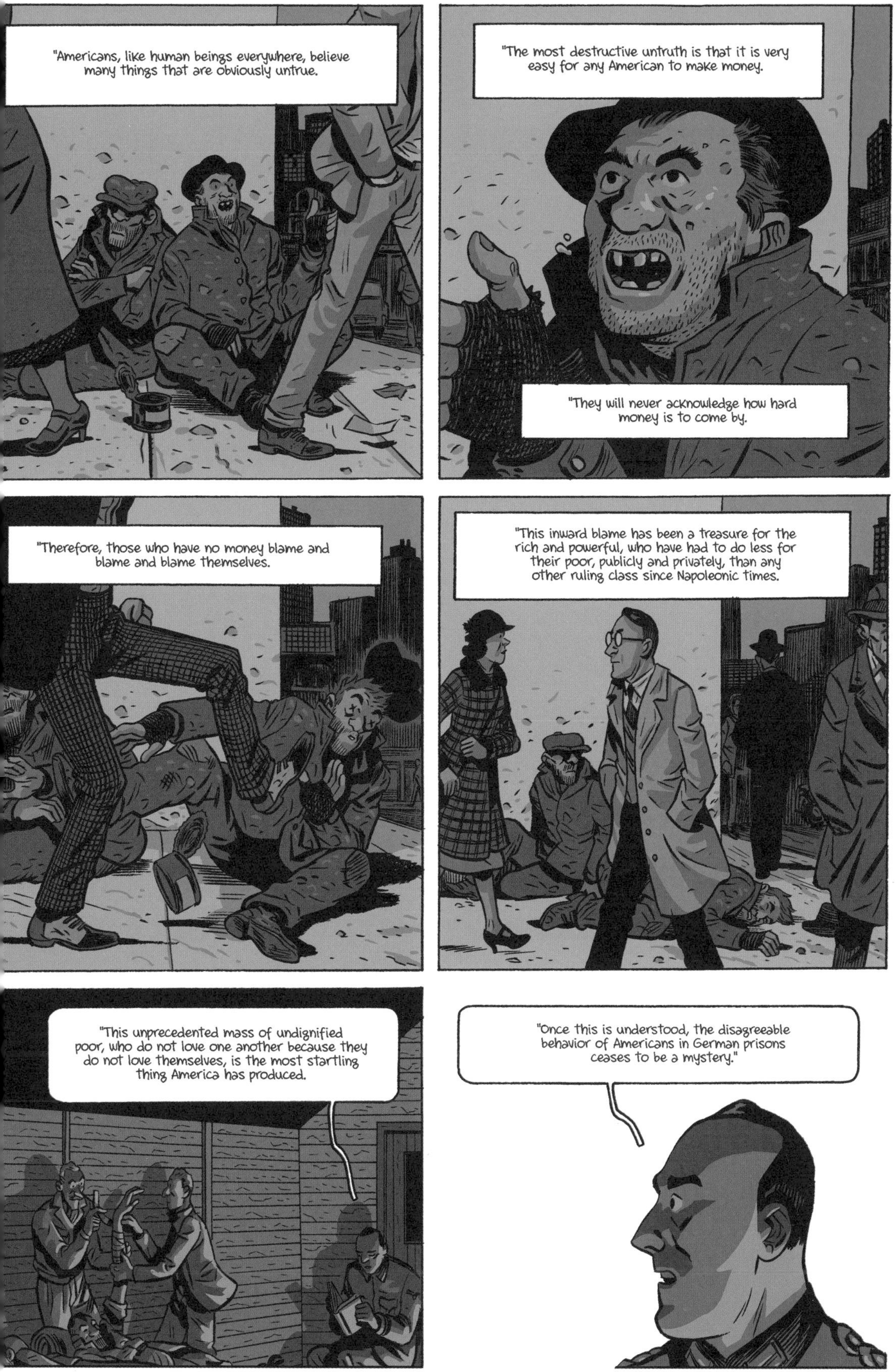
"Americans, like human beings everywhere, believe many things that are obviously untrue.
"The most destructive untruth is that it is very easy for any American to make money.
"They will never acknowledge how hard money is to come by.
"Therefore, those who have no money blame and blame and blame themselves.
"This inward blame has been a treasure for the rich and powerful, who have had to do less for their poor, publicly and privately, than any other ruling class since Napoleonic times.
"This unprecedented mass of undignified poor, who do not love one another because they do not love themselves, is the most startling thing America has produced.
"Once this is understood, the disagreeable behavior of Americans in German prisons ceases to be a mystery."

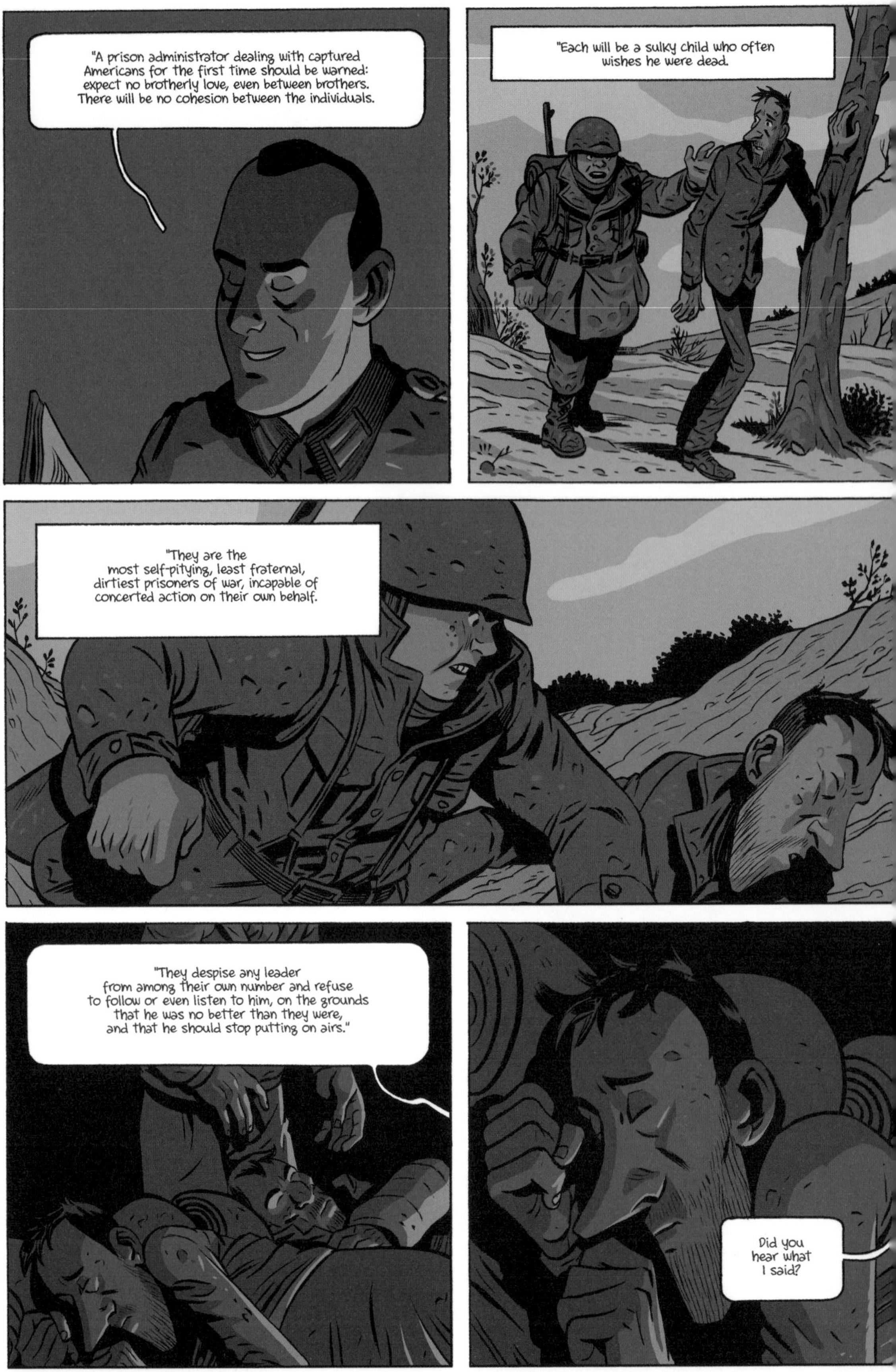
"A prison administrator dealing with captured Americans for the first time should be warned: expect no brotherly love, even between brothers. There will be no cohesion between the individuals.
"Each will be a sulky child who often wishes he were dead.
"They are the most self-pitying, least fraternal, dirtiest prisoners of war, incapable of concerted action on their own behalf.
"They despise any leader from among their own number and refuse to follow or even listen to him, on the grounds that he was no better than they were, and that he should stop putting on airs."
Did you hear what I said?

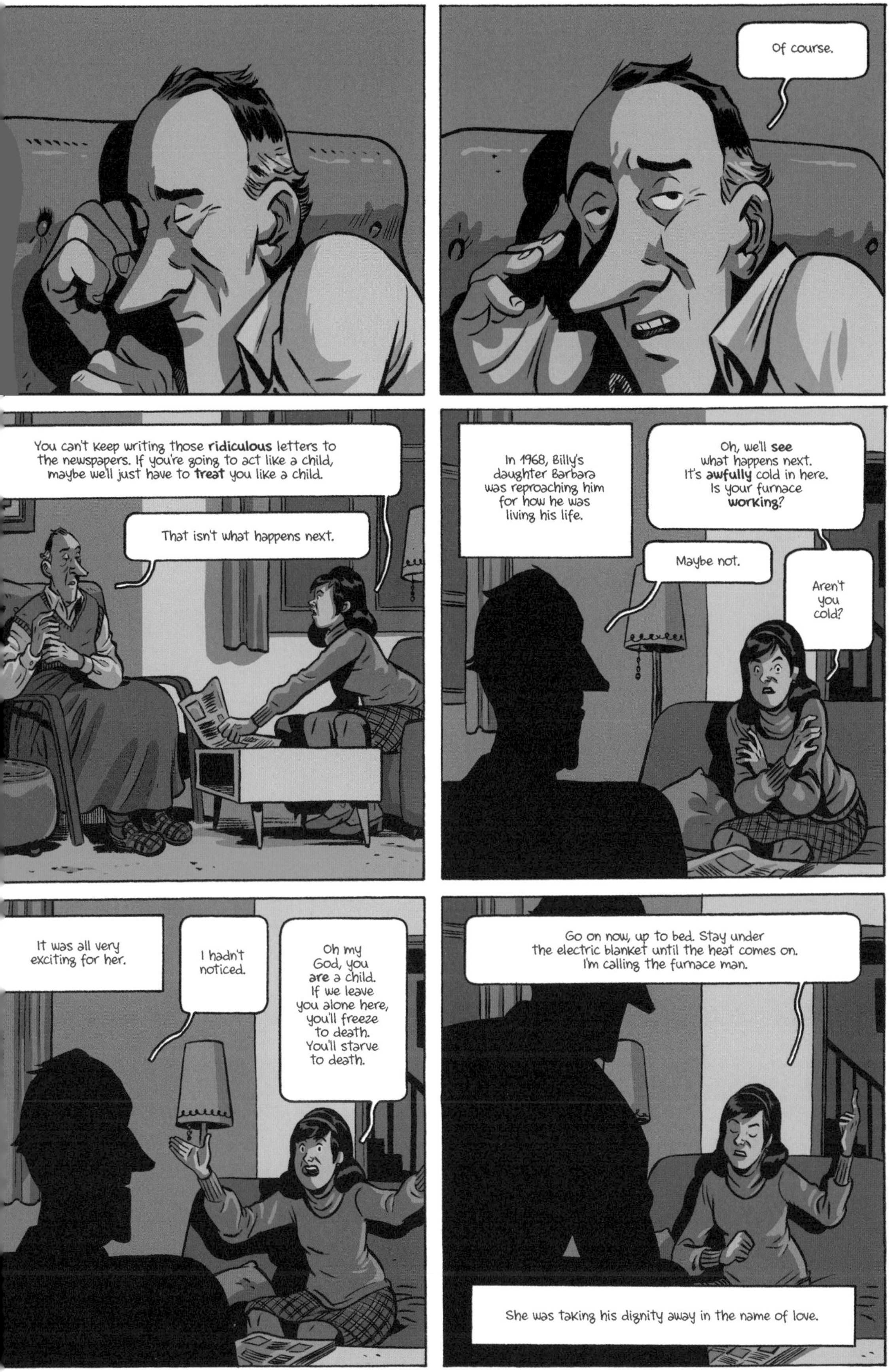
Of course.
You can't keep writing those **ridiculous** letters to the newspapers. If you're going to act like a child, maybe we'll just have to **treat** you like a child.
That isn't what happens next.
In 1968, Billy's daughter Barbara was reproaching him for how he was living his life.
Oh, we'll **see** what happens next. It's **awfully** cold in here. Is your furnace **working**?
Maybe not.
Aren't you cold?
It was all very exciting for her.
I hadn't noticed.
Oh my God, you **are** a child. If we leave you alone here, you'll freeze to death. You'll starve to death.
Go on now, up to bed. Stay under the electric blanket until the heat comes on. I'm calling the furnace man.
She was taking his dignity away in the name of love.

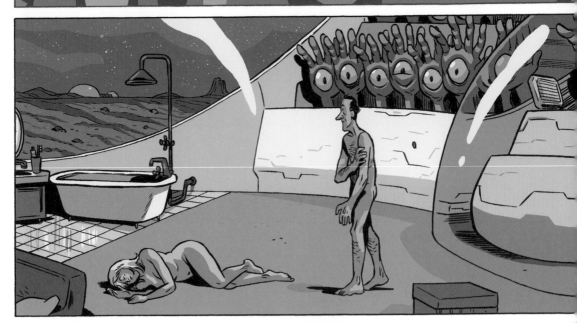

Eugh.

Everything is all right. Please don't be afraid.

W--

Where am I?

You've been kidnapped, like me. You're on the planet Tralfamadore, in their zoo. We're their human exhibit.

If we decide to, the Tralfamadorians are hoping to see us mate.

What are you talking about? You're not making sens--

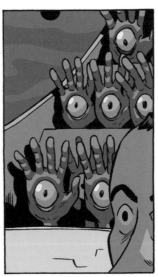

AAAHHHHHH!!

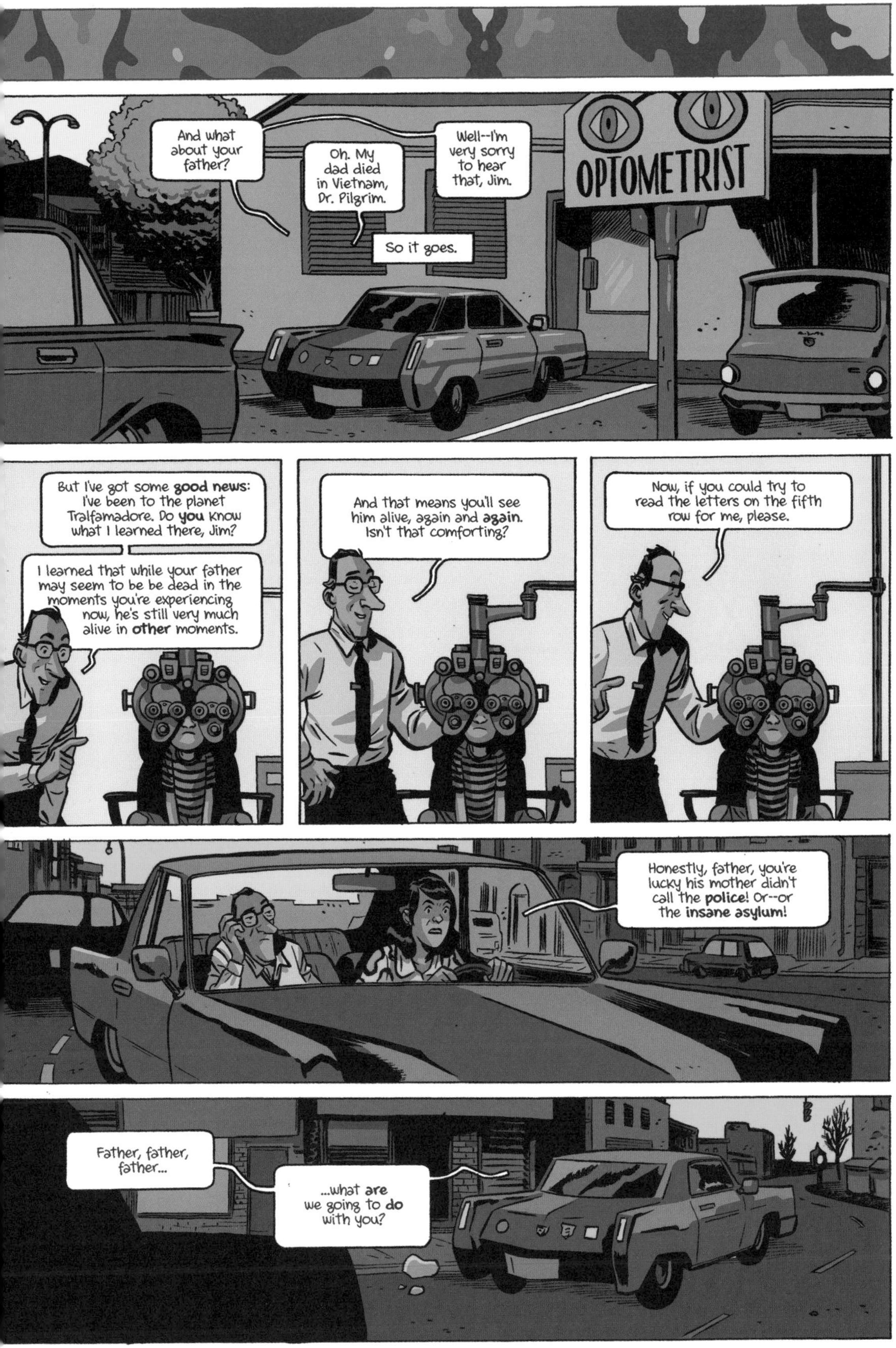
And what about your father?
Oh. My dad died in Vietnam, Dr. Pilgrim.
Well--I'm very sorry to hear that, Jim.
So it goes.
OPTOMETRIST
But I've got some **good news**: I've been to the planet Tralfamadore. Do **you** know what I learned there, Jim?
I learned that while your father may seem to be be dead in the moments you're experiencing now, he's still very much alive in **other** moments.
And that means you'll see him alive, again and **again**. Isn't that comforting?
Now, if you could try to read the letters on the fifth row for me, please.
Honestly, father, you're lucky his mother didn't call the **police**! Or--or the **insane asylum**!
Father, father, father...
...what **are** we going to **do** with you?

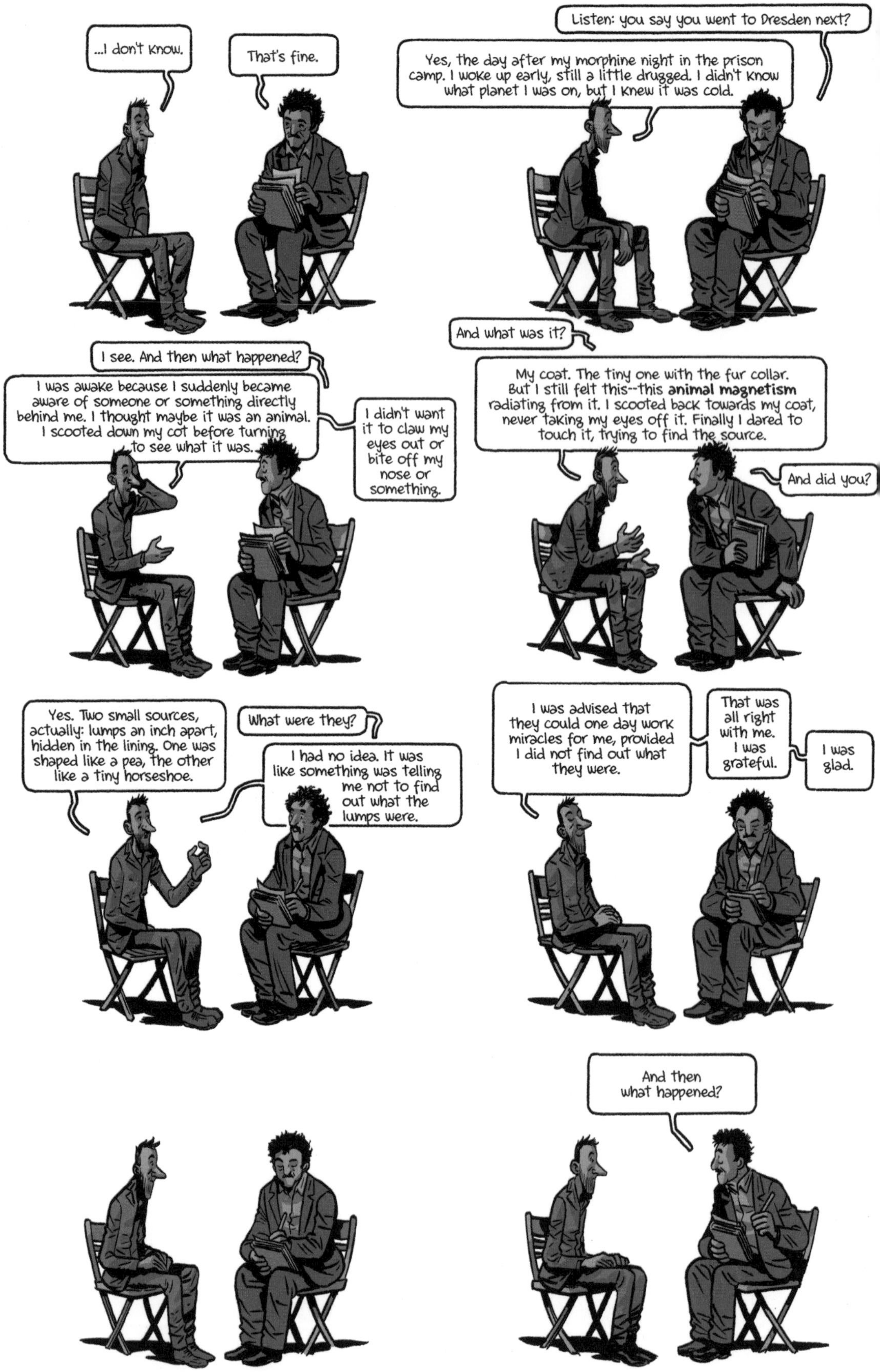
...I don't know.
That's fine.
Listen: you say you went to Dresden next?
Yes, the day after my morphine night in the prison camp. I woke up early, still a little drugged. I didn't know what planet I was on, but I knew it was cold.
I see. And then what happened?
I was awake because I suddenly became aware of someone or something directly behind me. I thought maybe it was an animal. I scooted down my cot before turning to see what it was.
I didn't want it to claw my eyes out or bite off my nose or something.
And what was it?
My coat. The tiny one with the fur collar. But I still felt this--this **animal magnetism** radiating from it. I scooted back towards my coat, never taking my eyes off it. Finally I dared to touch it, trying to find the source.
And did you?
Yes. Two small sources, actually: lumps an inch apart, hidden in the lining. One was shaped like a pea, the other like a tiny horseshoe.
What were they?
I had no idea. It was like something was telling me not to find out what the lumps were.
I was advised that they could one day work miracles for me, provided I did not find out what they were.
That was all right with me. I was grateful.
I was glad.
And then what happened?

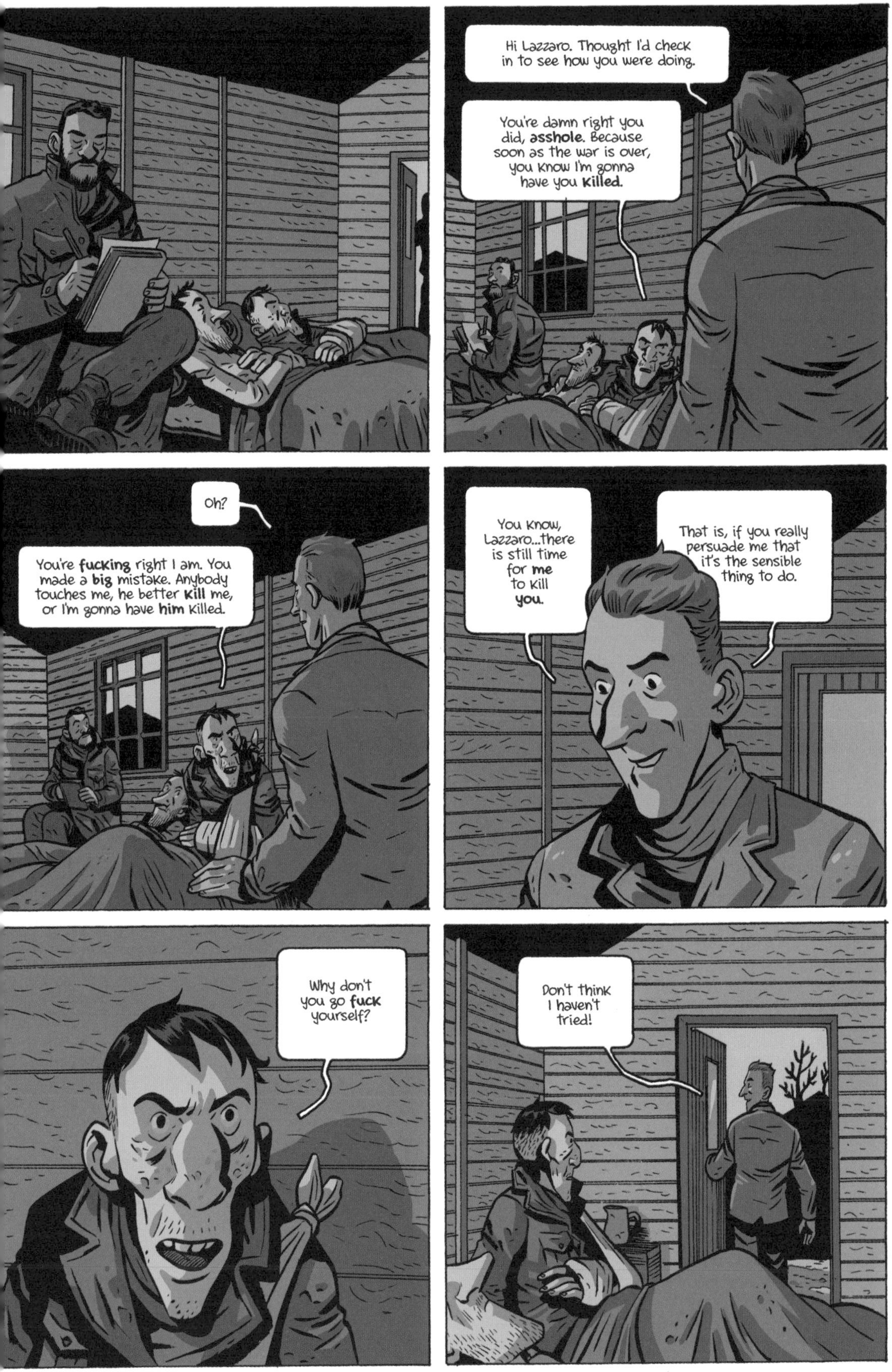
Hi Lazzaro. Thought I'd check in to see how you were doing.
You're damn right you did, **asshole**. Because soon as the war is over, you know I'm gonna have you **killed**.
Oh?
You're **fucking** right I am. You made a **big** mistake. Anybody touches me, he better **kill** me, or I'm gonna have **him** killed.
You know, Lazzaro...there is still time for **me** to kill **you**.
That is, if you really persuade me that it's the sensible thing to do.
Why don't you go **fuck** yourself?
Don't think I haven't tried!

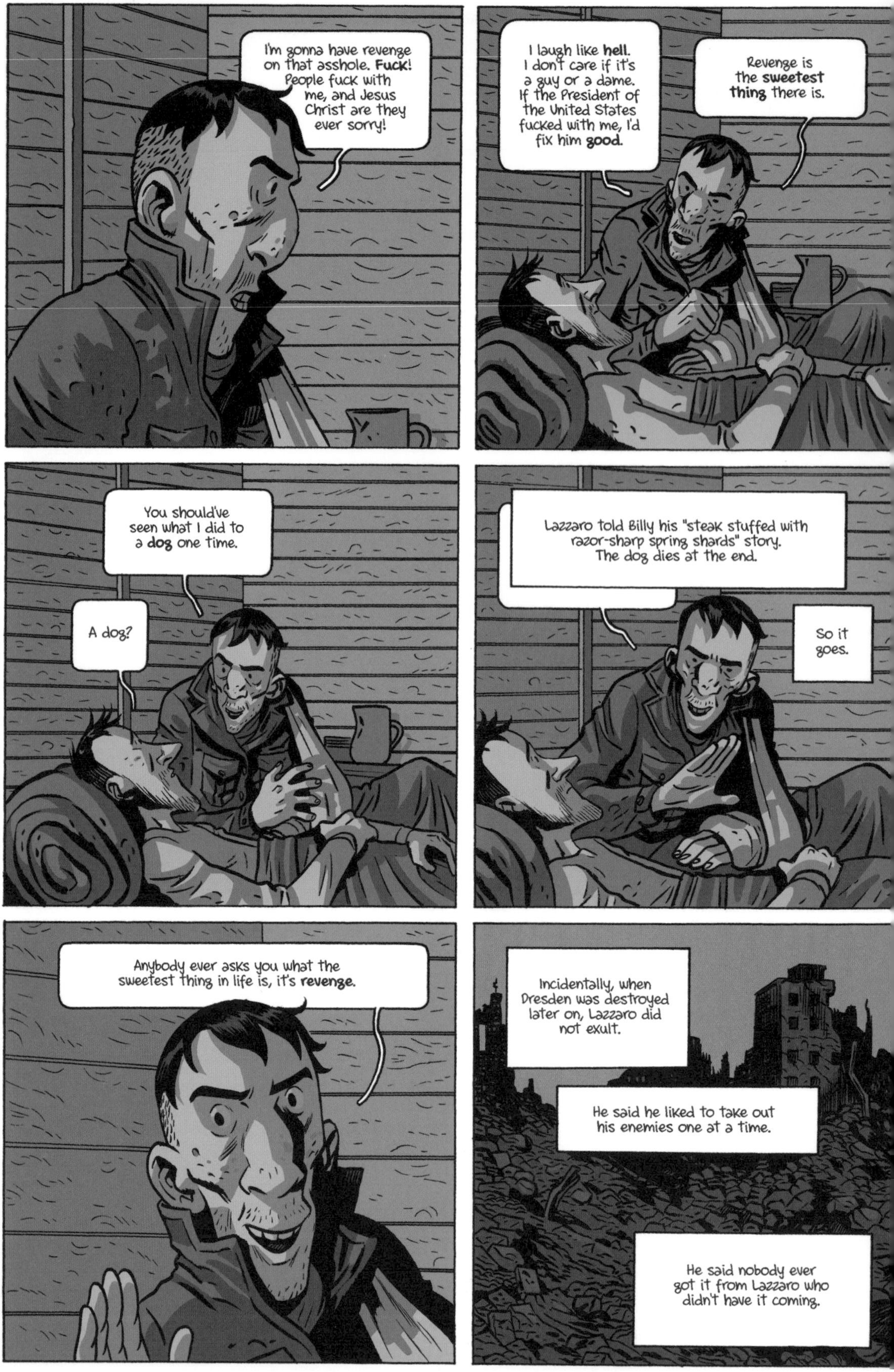
I'm gonna have revenge on that asshole. **Fuck!** People fuck with me, and Jesus Christ are they ever sorry!
I laugh like **hell**. I don't care if it's a guy or a dame. If the President of the United States fucked with me, I'd fix him **good**.
Revenge is the **sweetest thing** there is.
You should've seen what I did to a **dog** one time.
A dog?
Lazzaro told Billy his "steak stuffed with razor-sharp spring shards" story. The dog dies at the end.
So it goes.
Anybody ever asks you what the sweetest thing in life is, it's **revenge**.
Incidentally, when Dresden was destroyed later on, Lazzaro did not exult.
He said he liked to take out his enemies one at a time.
He said nobody ever got it from Lazzaro who didn't have it coming.

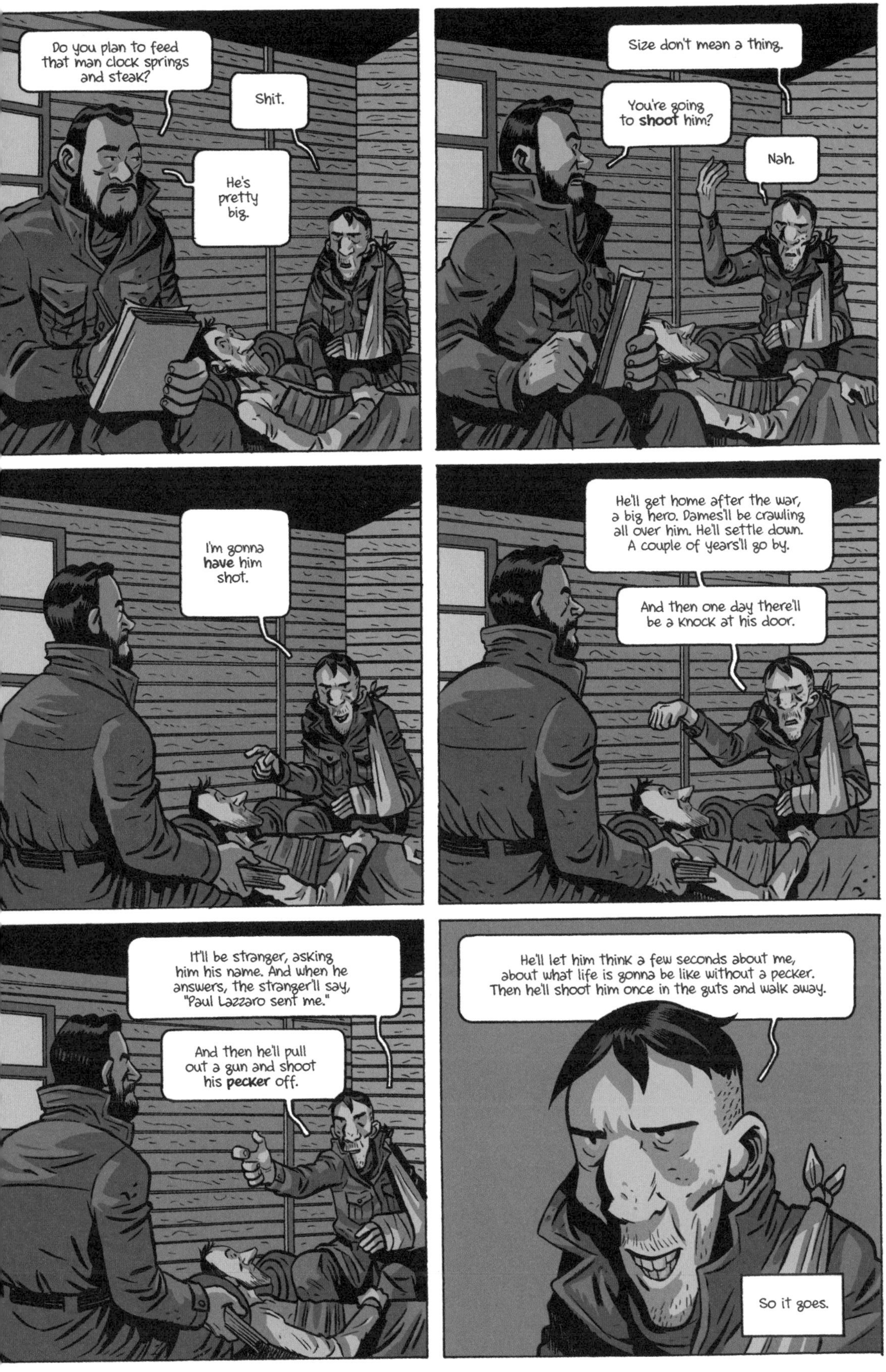
Do you plan to feed that man clock springs and steak?
Shit.
He's pretty big.
Size don't mean a thing.
You're going to **shoot** him?
Nah.
I'm gonna **have** him shot.
He'll get home after the war, a big hero. Dames'll be crawling all over him. He'll settle down. A couple of years'll go by.
And then one day there'll be a knock at his door.
It'll be stranger, asking him his name. And when he answers, the stranger'll say, "Paul Lazzaro sent me."
And then he'll pull out a gun and shoot his **pecker** off.
He'll let him think a few seconds about me, about what life is gonna be like without a pecker. Then he'll shoot him once in the guts and walk away.
So it goes.

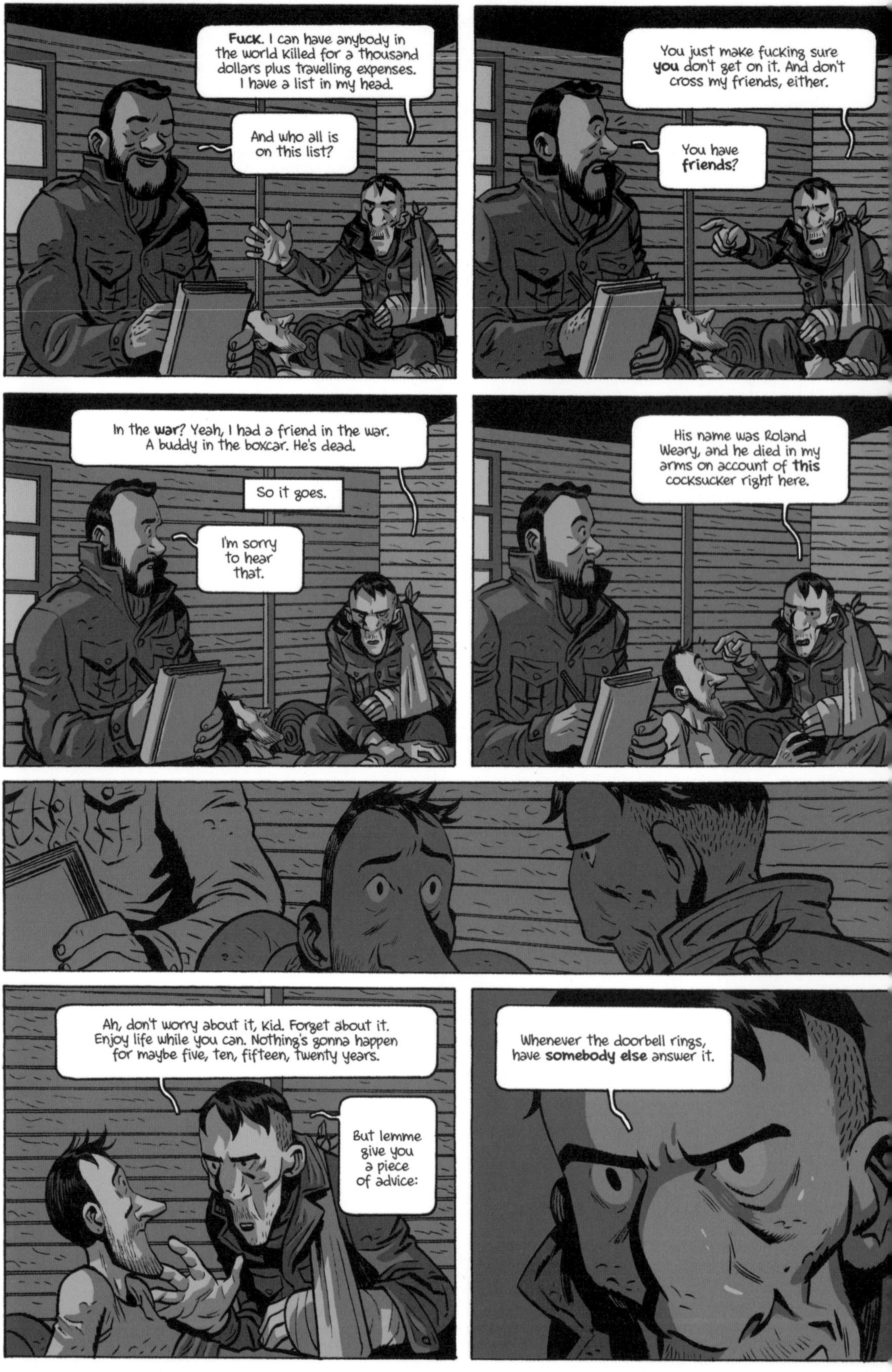
Fuck. I can have anybody in the world killed for a thousand dollars plus travelling expenses. I have a list in my head.
And who all is on this list?
You just make fucking sure **you** don't get on it. And don't cross my friends, either.
You have **friends?**
In the **war?** Yeah, I had a friend in the war. A buddy in the boxcar. He's dead.
So it goes.
I'm sorry to hear that.
His name was Roland Weary, and he died in my arms on account of **this** cocksucker right here.
Ah, don't worry about it, kid. Forget about it. Enjoy life while you can. Nothing's gonna happen for maybe five, ten, fifteen, twenty years.
But lemme give you a piece of advice:
Whenever the doorbell rings, have **somebody else** answer it.

hat really is
the way I'm
going to die,
too. I've seen
my own death
many times.

I even
described
it to a tape
recorder in
my safe
deposit box.

I, Billy Pilgrim, **will** die, have always died, and always **will** die on February 13, 1976. At the time of my death, the United States has been divided into twenty petty nations, so that it will never again be a **threat** to world peace. I am in Chicago, which has been rebuilt after being hydrogen bombed by the Chinese.

So it goes.

The whole city is all brand new then. I'm there in Chicago, under a giant dome, to address a capacity crowd on the subject of flying saucers and the true nature of time.

Many years ago, a certain man promised to have me killed. He is an old man now, living not far from here. He is insane, and tonight he will keep his promise.

I will be dead within the hour.

But it is high time I was dead! And if that makes you sad, if you think death is a terrible thing, then you have not understood a word I said. It has been time for me to be dead for a little while--and then live again!

Farewell, hello, farewell, hello!

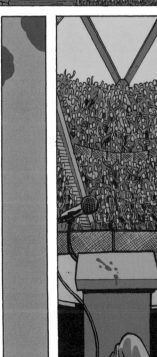

So it goes.

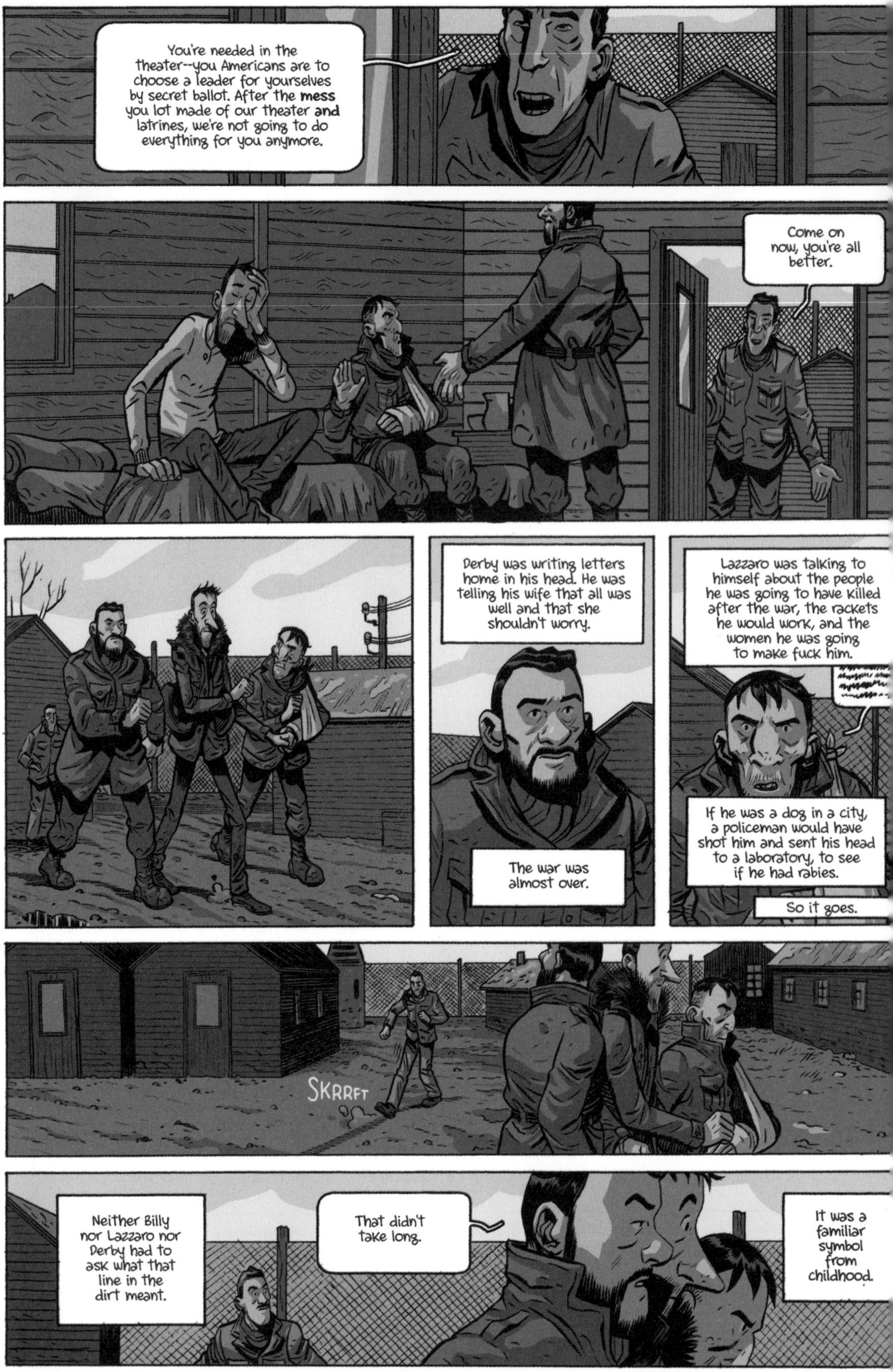
You're needed in the theater--you Americans are to choose a leader for yourselves by secret ballot. After the **mess** you lot made of our theater **and** latrines, we're not going to do everything for you anymore.
Come on now, you're all better.
Derby was writing letters home in his head. He was telling his wife that all was well and that she shouldn't worry.
The war was almost over.
Lazzaro was talking to himself about the people he was going to have killed after the war, the rackets he would work, and the women he was going to make fuck him.
If he was a dog in a city, a policeman would have shot him and sent his head to a laboratory, to see if he had rabies.
So it goes.
SKRRFT
Neither Billy nor Lazzaro nor Derby had to ask what that line in the dirt meant.
That didn't take long.
It was a familiar symbol from childhood.

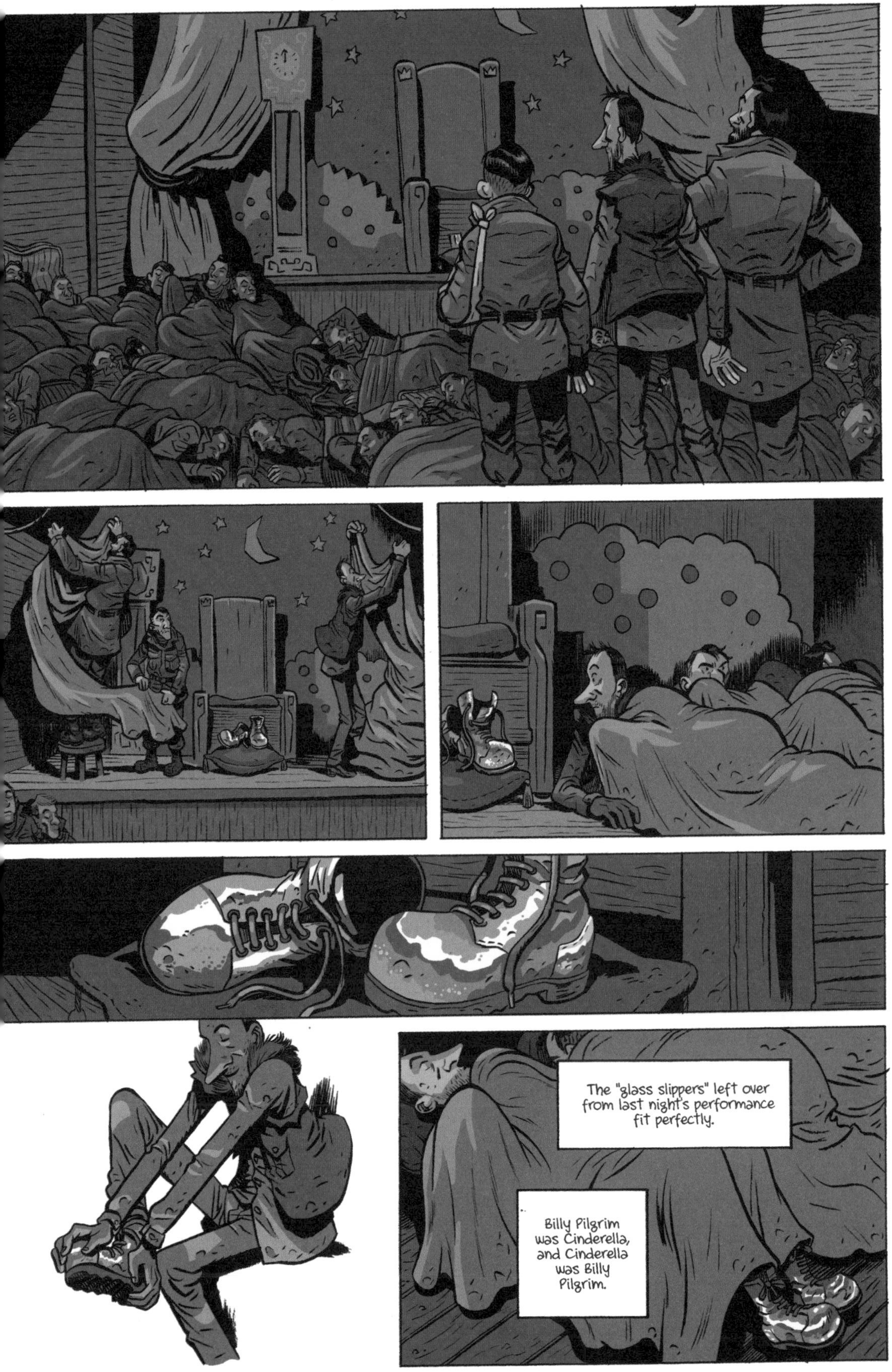

The "glass slippers" left over from last night's performance fit perfectly.
Billy Pilgrim was Cinderella, and Cinderella was Billy Pilgrim.

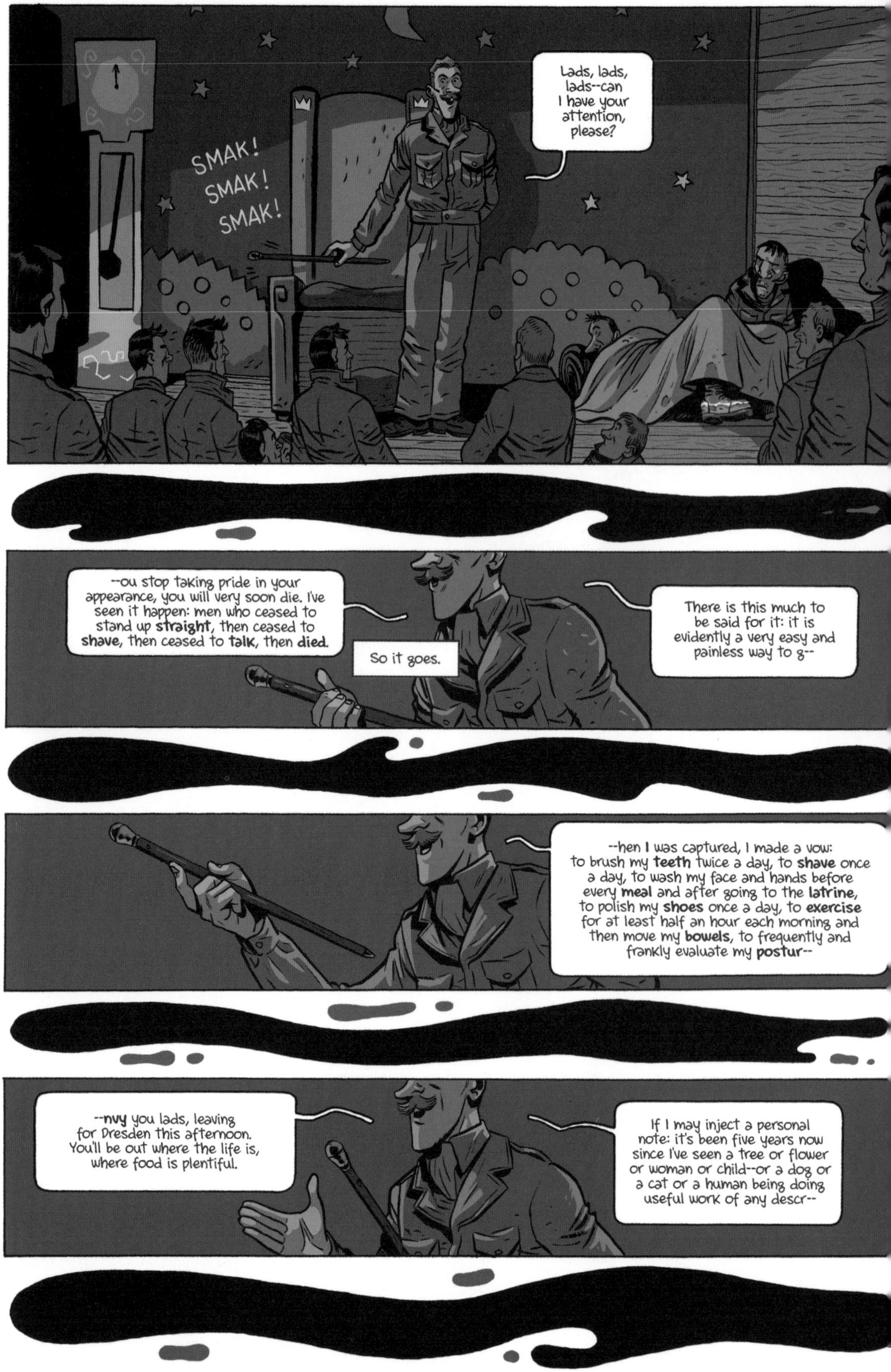
Lads, lads, lads--can I have your attention, please?
SMAK! SMAK! SMAK!
--ou stop taking pride in your appearance, you will very soon die. I've seen it happen: men who ceased to stand up **straight**, then ceased to **shave**, then ceased to **talk**, then **died**.
So it goes.
There is this much to be said for it: it is evidently a very easy and painless way to g--
--hen **I** was captured, I made a vow: to brush my **teeth** twice a day, to **shave** once a day, to wash my face and hands before every **meal** and after going to the **latrine**, to polish my **shoes** once a day, to **exercise** for at least half an hour each morning and then move my **bowels**, to frequently and frankly evaluate my **postur**--
--**nvy** you lads, leaving for Dresden this afternoon. You'll be out where the life is, where food is plentiful.
If I may inject a personal note: it's been five years now since I've seen a tree or flower or woman or child--or a dog or a cat or a human being doing useful work of any descr--

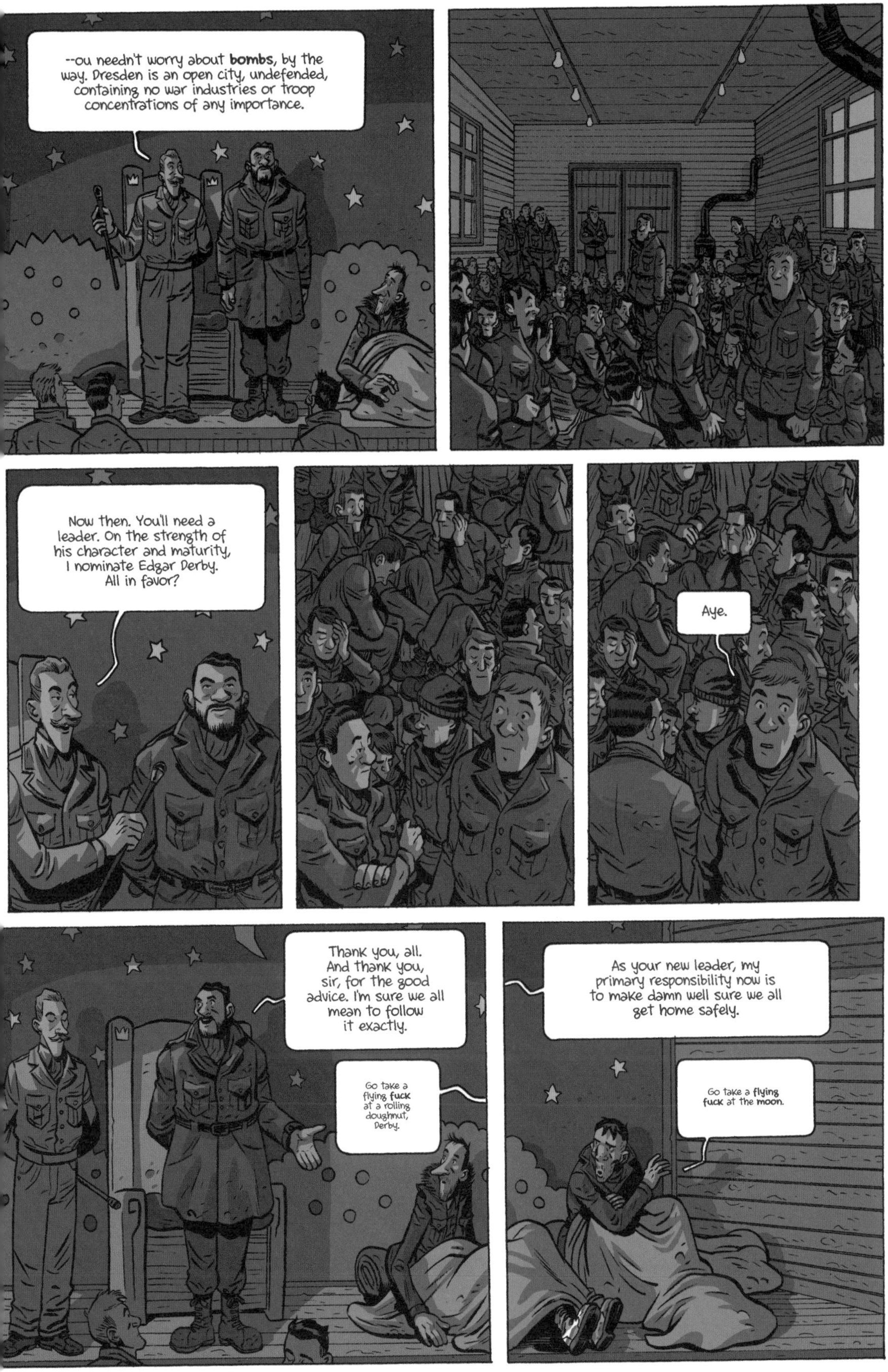
--ou needn't worry about **bombs**, by the way. Dresden is an open city, undefended, containing no war industries or troop concentrations of any importance.
Now then. You'll need a leader. On the strength of his character and maturity, I nominate Edgar Derby. All in favor?
Aye.
Thank you, all. And thank you, sir, for the good advice. I'm sure we all mean to follow it exactly.
Go take a flying **fuck** at a rolling doughnut, Derby.
As your new leader, my primary responsibility now is to make damn well sure we all get home safely.
Go take a **flying fuck** at the **moon**.

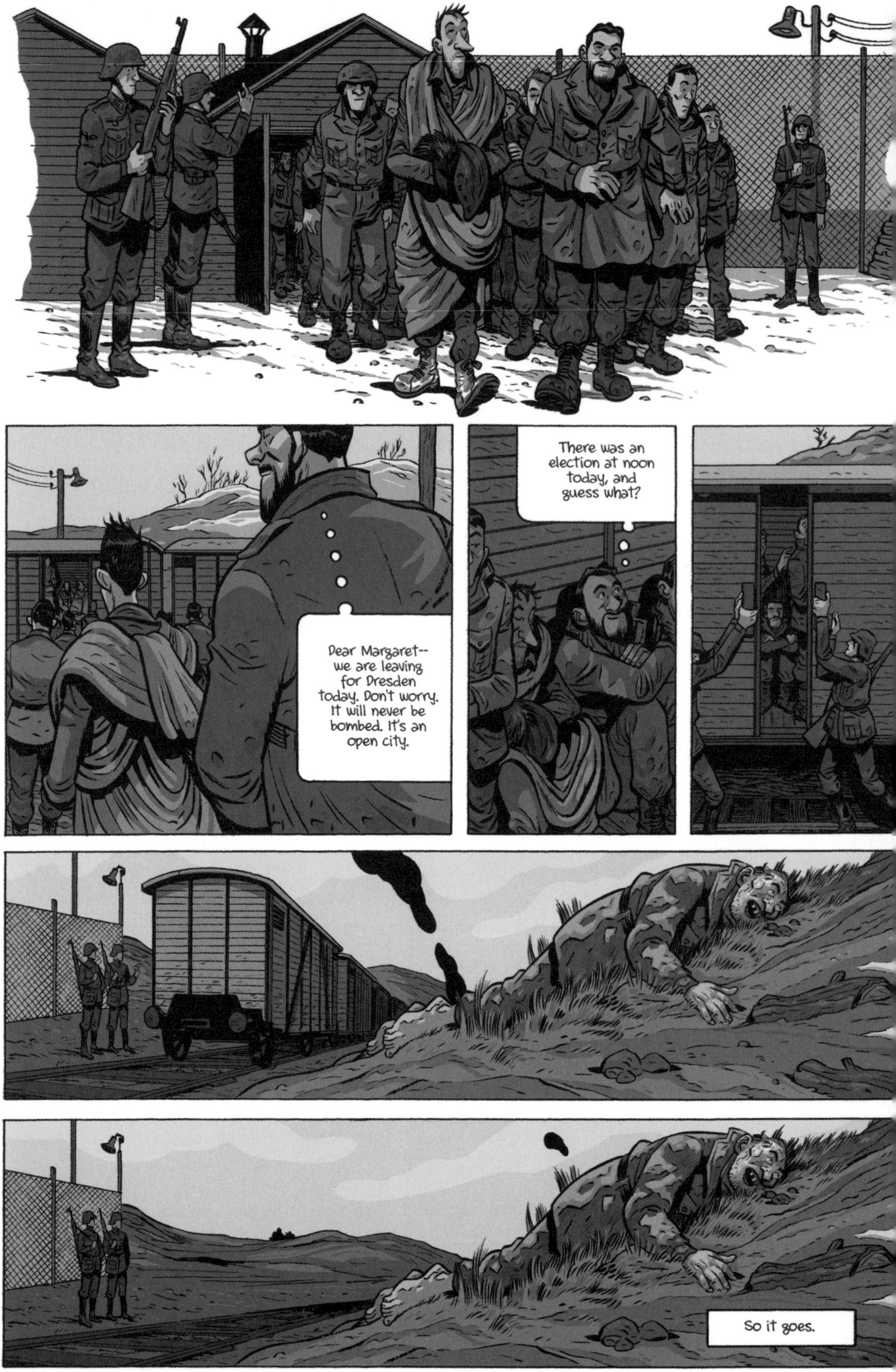
Dear Margaret--
we are leaving
for Dresden
today. Don't worry.
It will never be
bombed. It's an
open city.
There was an
election at noon
today, and
guess what?
So it goes.

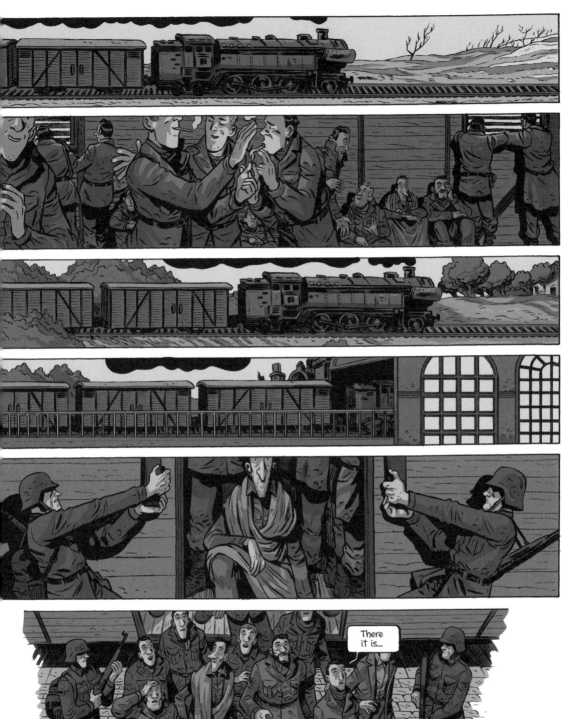

There
it is...

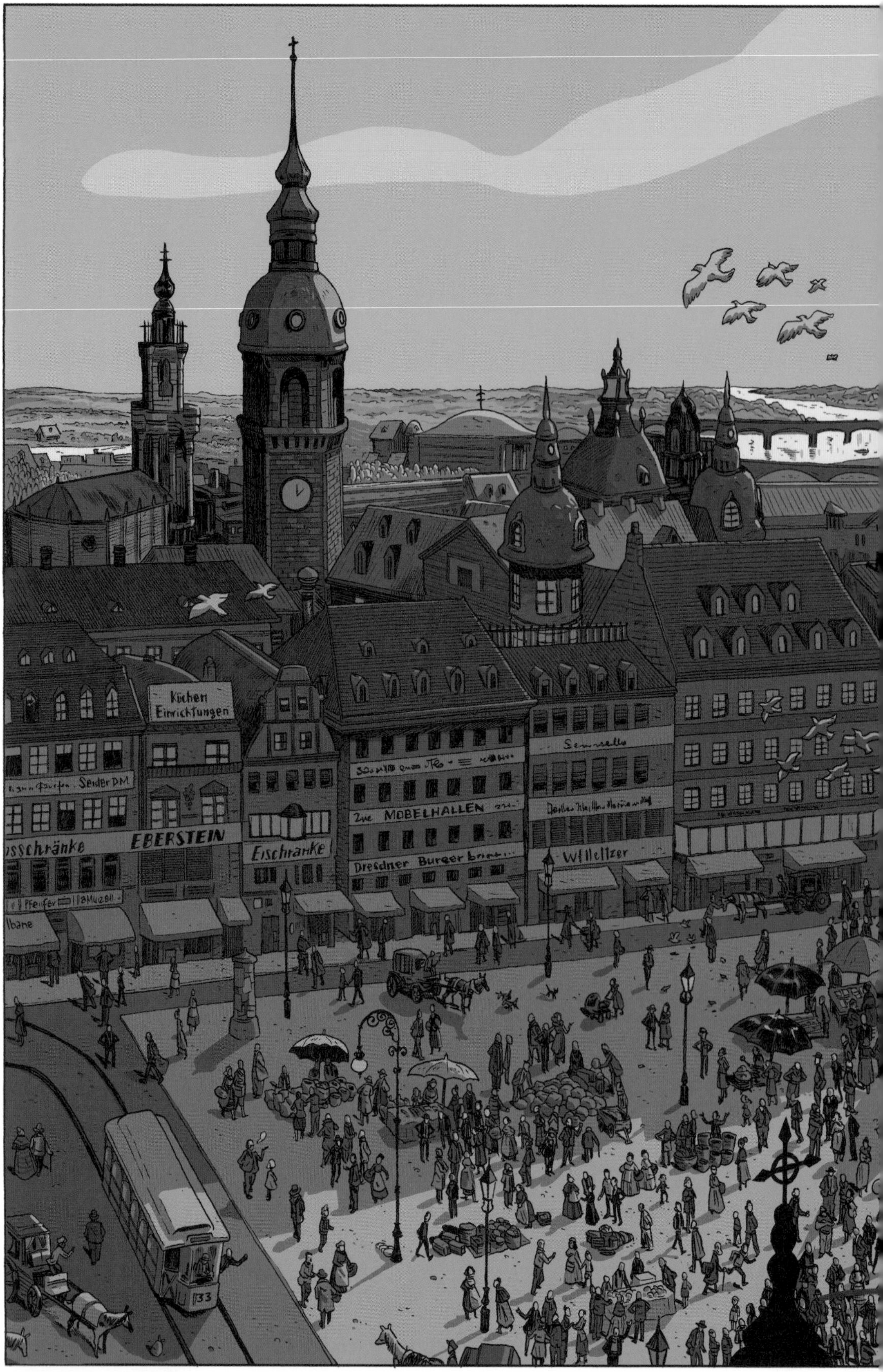
Küchen Einrichtungen
EBERSTEIN
Eischranke
MOBELHALLEN
133

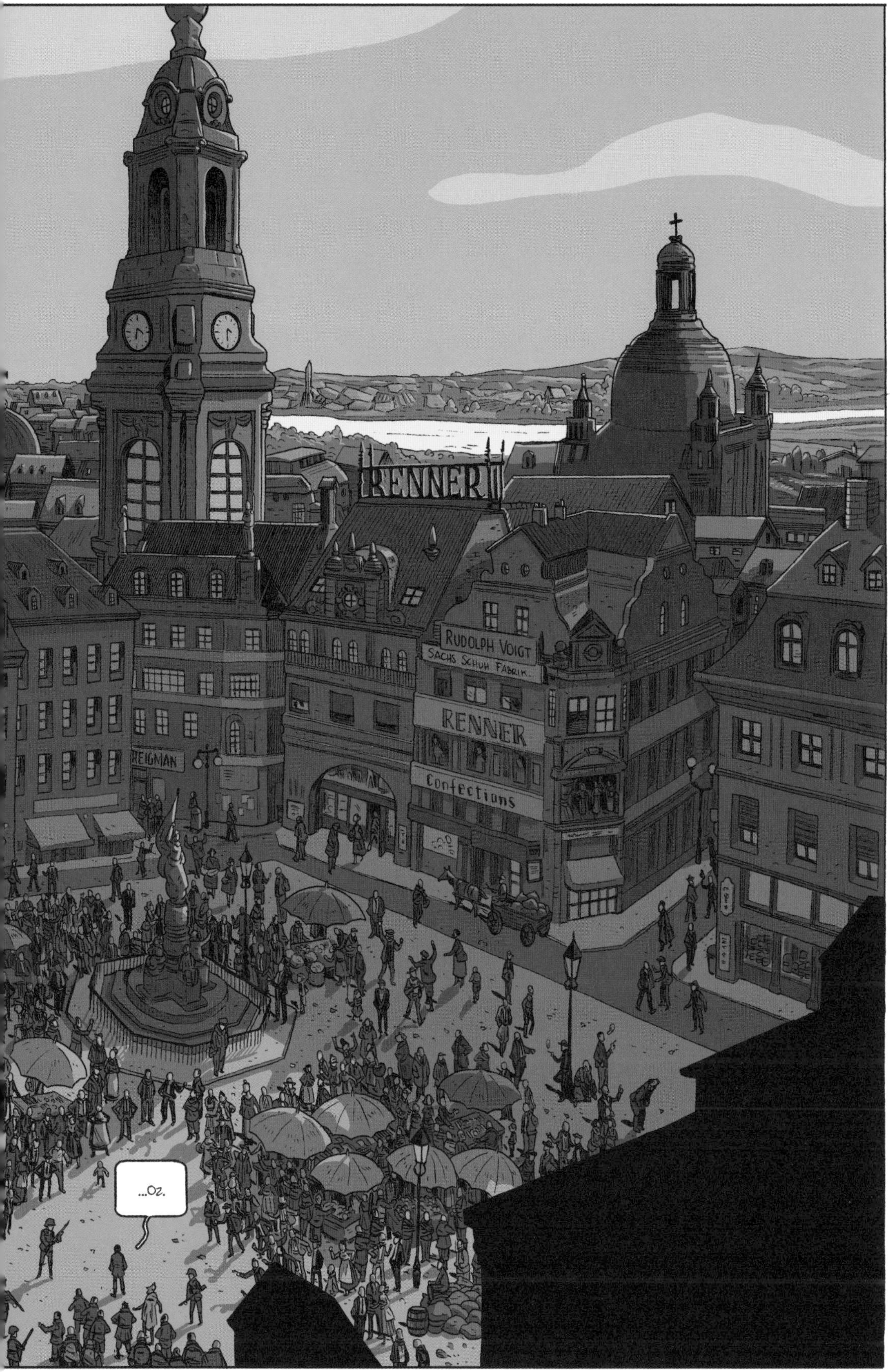
RENNER
RUDOLPH VOIGT
SACHS SCHUH FABRIK
RENNER
Confections
REIGMAN
...Oz.

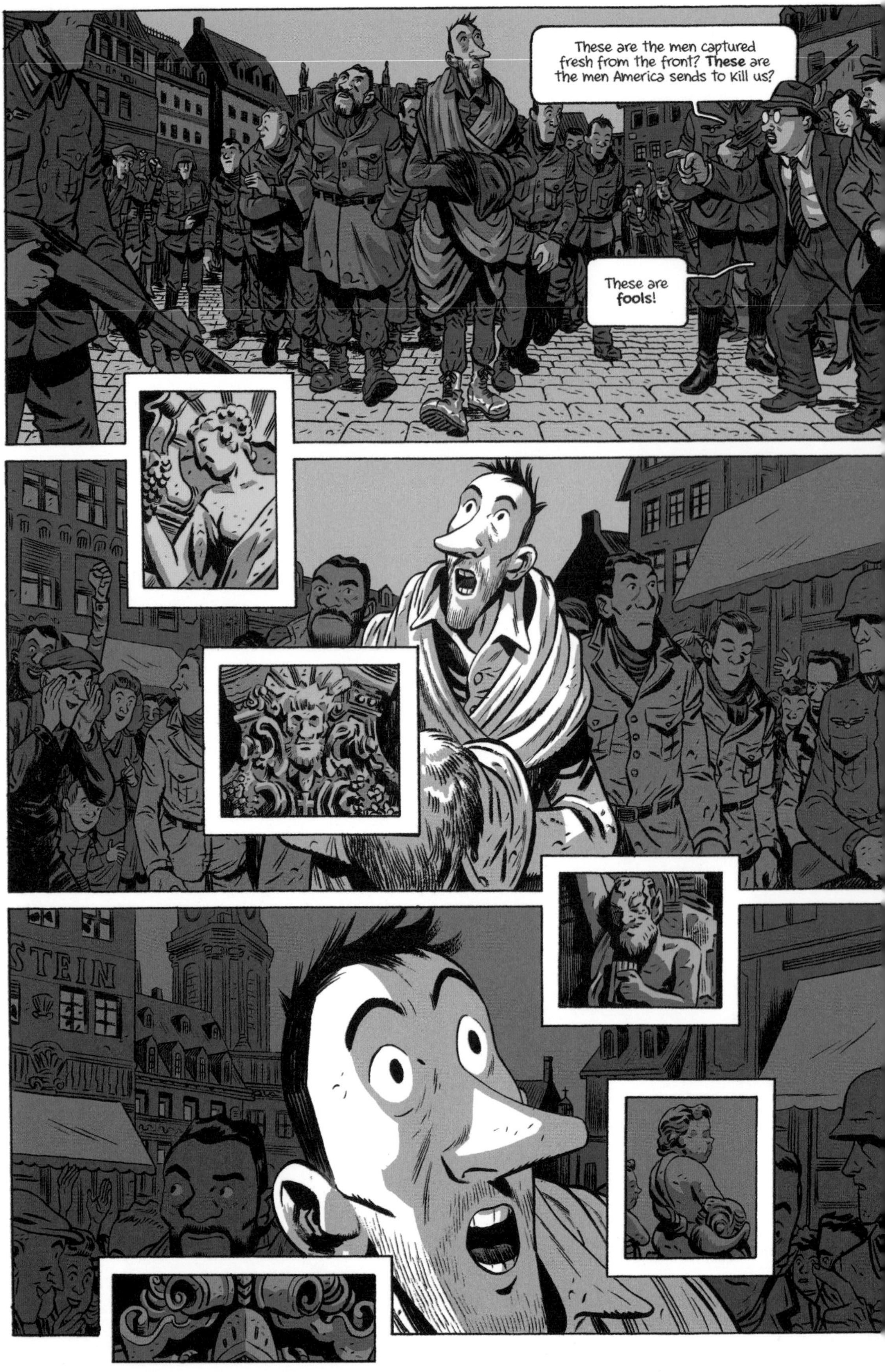
These are the men captured fresh from the front? **These** are the men America sends to kill us?
These are **fools**!
STEIN

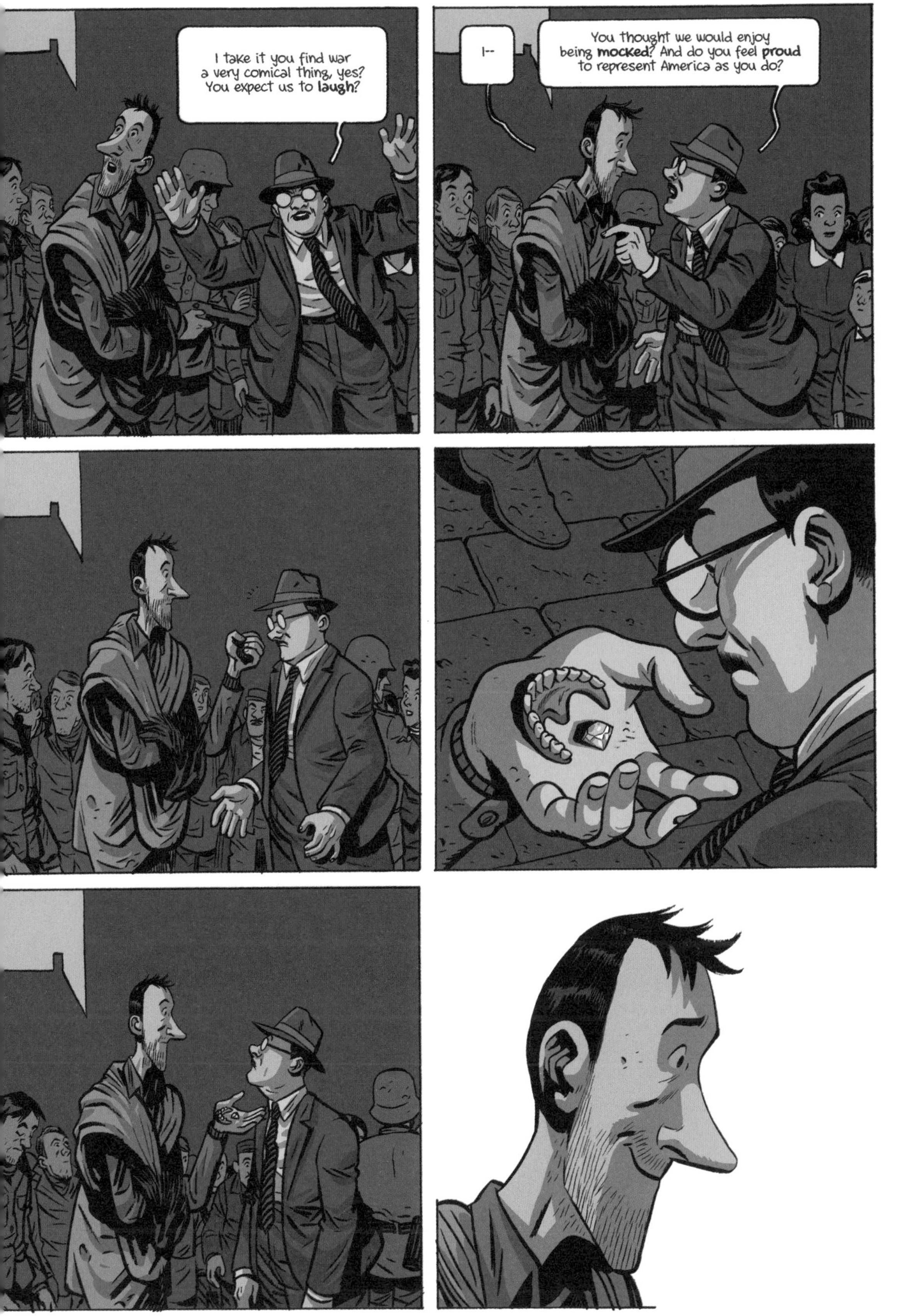
I take it you find war a very comical thing, yes? You expect us to **laugh**?
I--
You thought we would enjoy being **mocked**? And do you feel **proud** to represent America as you do?

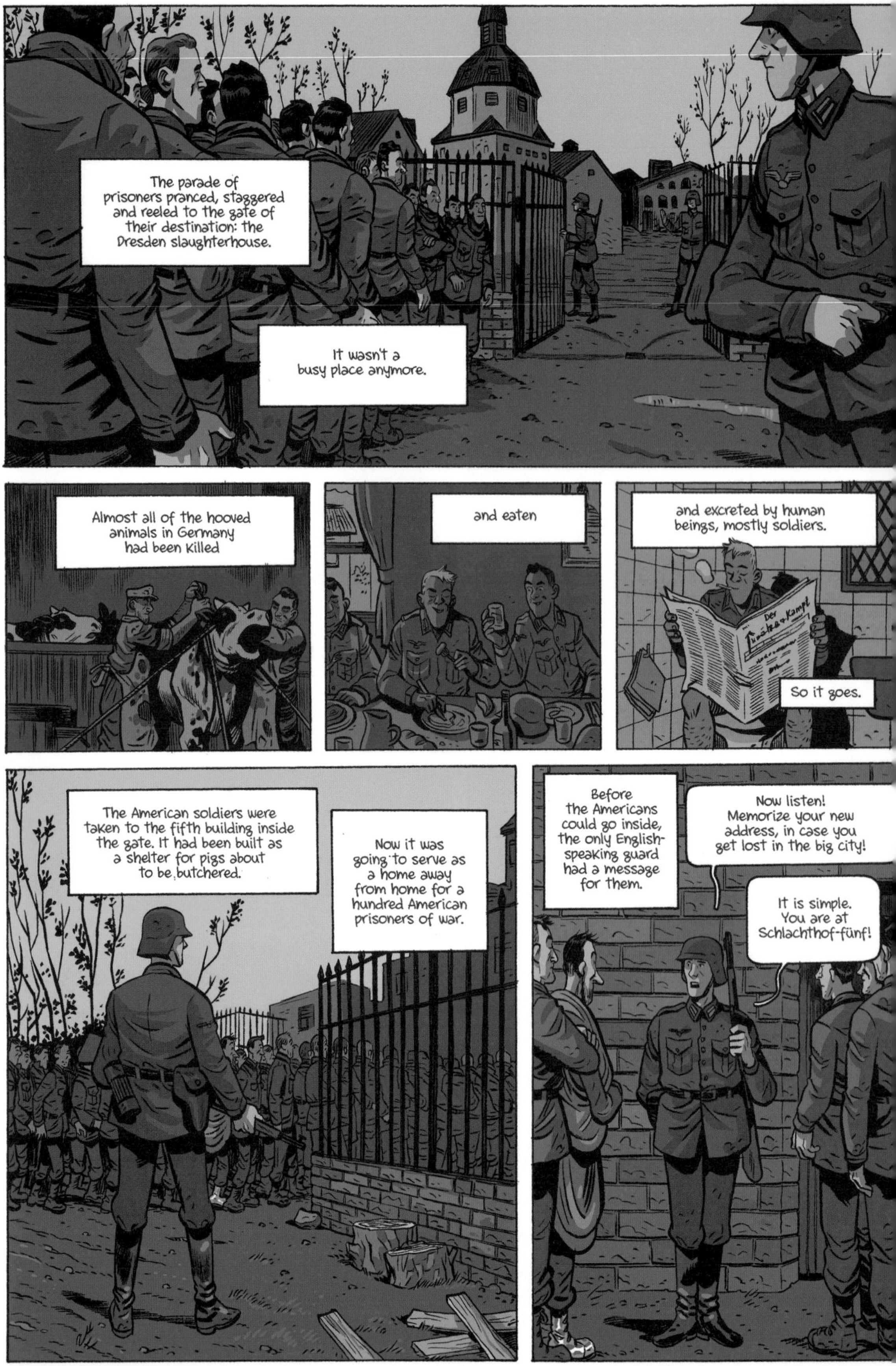
The parade of prisoners pranced, staggered and reeled to the gate of their destination: the Dresden slaughterhouse.
It wasn't a busy place anymore.
Almost all of the hooved animals in Germany had been killed
and eaten
and excreted by human beings, mostly soldiers.
So it goes.
The American soldiers were taken to the fifth building inside the gate. It had been built as a shelter for pigs about to be butchered.
Now it was going to serve as a home away from home for a hundred American prisoners of war.
Before the Americans could go inside, the only English-speaking guard had a message for them.
Now listen! Memorize your new address, in case you get lost in the big city!
It is simple. You are at Schlachthof-fünf!

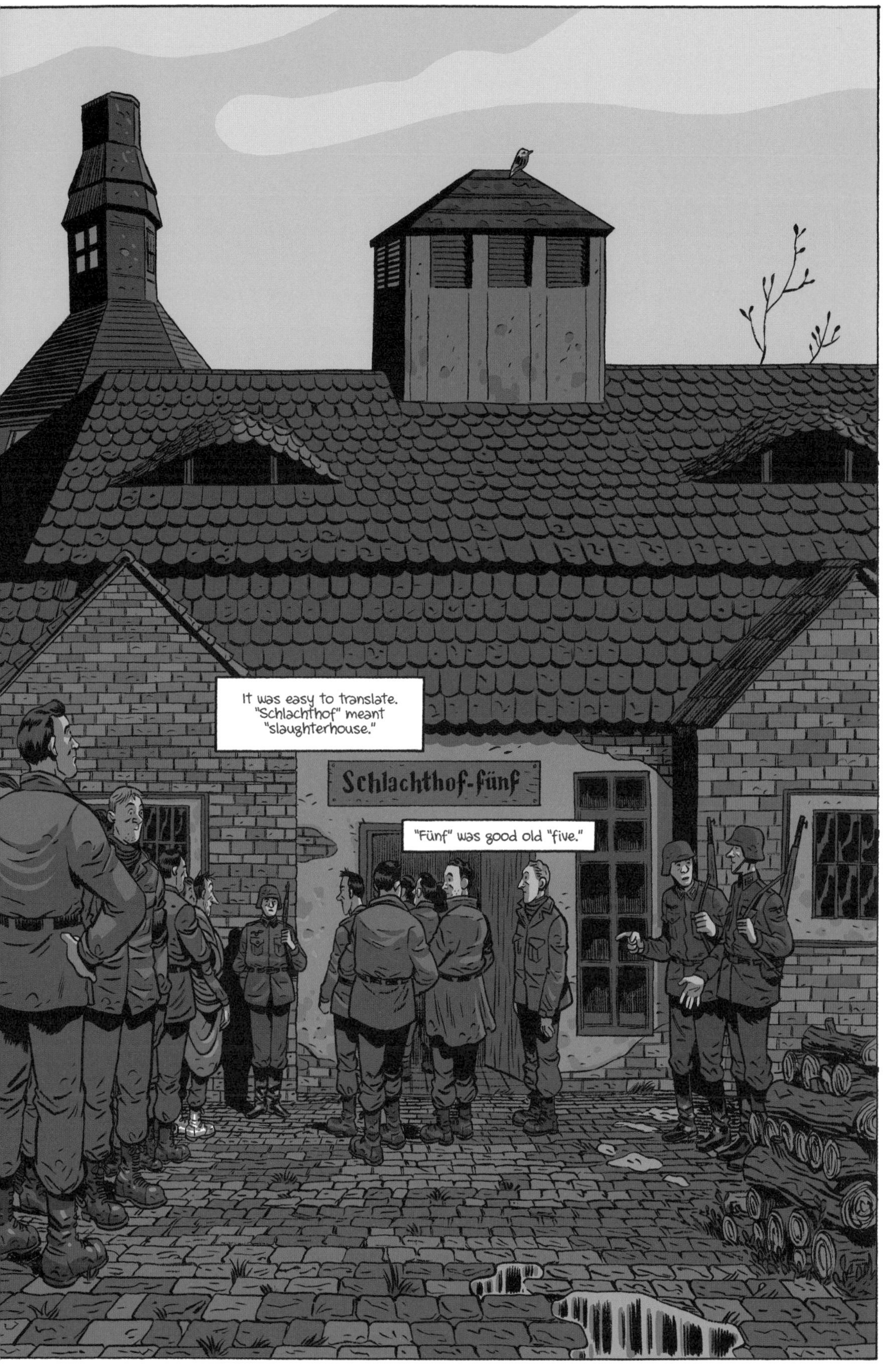
It was easy to translate. "Schlachthof" meant "slaughterhouse."
Schlachthof-fünf
"Fünf" was good old "five."

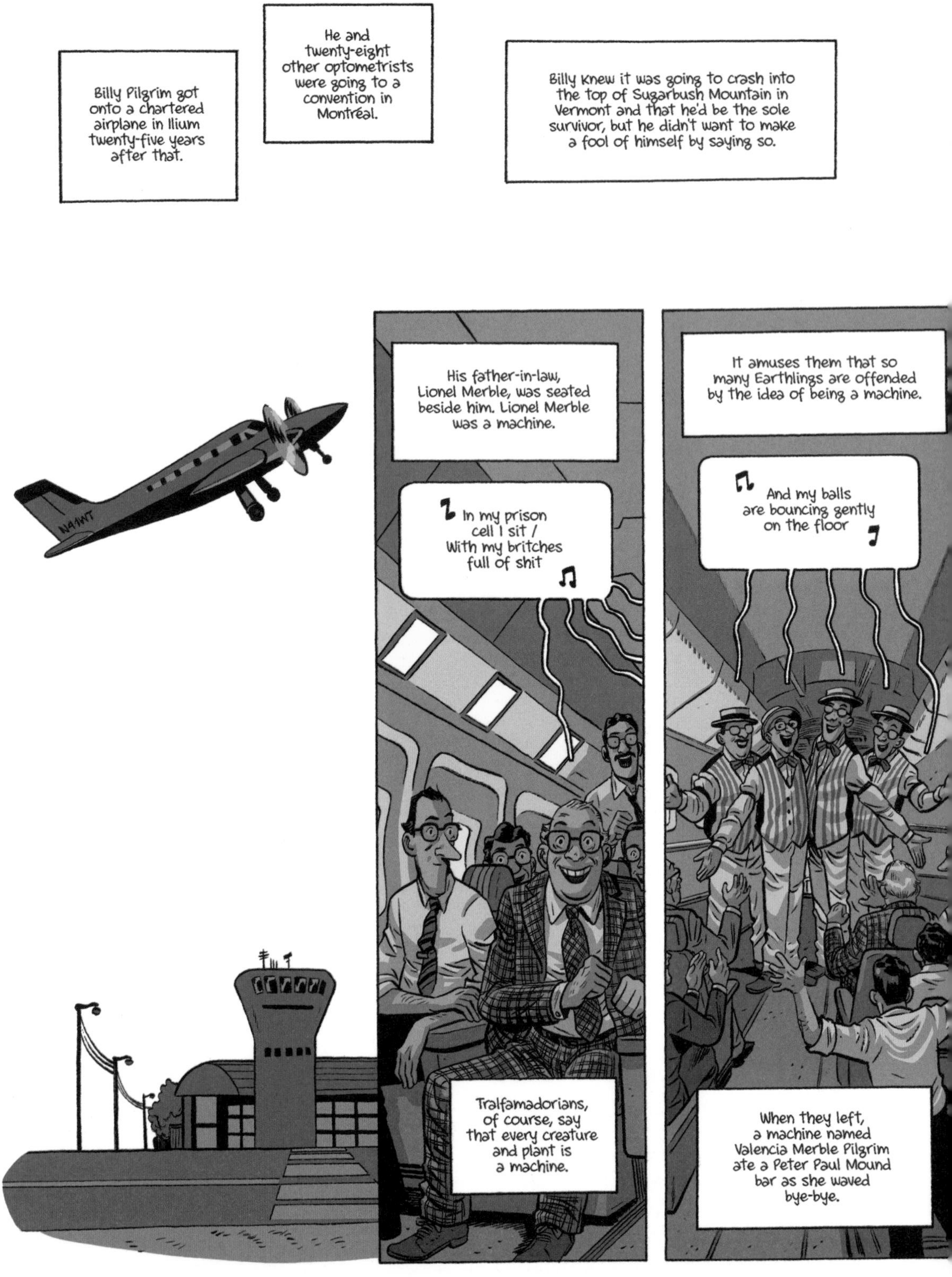
Billy Pilgrim got onto a chartered airplane in Ilium twenty-five years after that.
He and twenty-eight other optometrists were going to a convention in Montréal.
Billy knew it was going to crash into the top of Sugarbush Mountain in Vermont and that he'd be the sole survivor, but he didn't want to make a fool of himself by saying so.
N41WT
His father-in-law, Lionel Merble, was seated beside him. Lionel Merble was a machine.
In my prison cell I sit / With my britches full of shit
Tralfamadorians, of course, say that every creature and plant is a machine.
It amuses them that so many Earthlings are offended by the idea of being a machine.
And my balls are bouncing gently on the floor
When they left, a machine named Valencia Merble Pilgrim ate a Peter Paul Mound bar as she waved bye-bye.

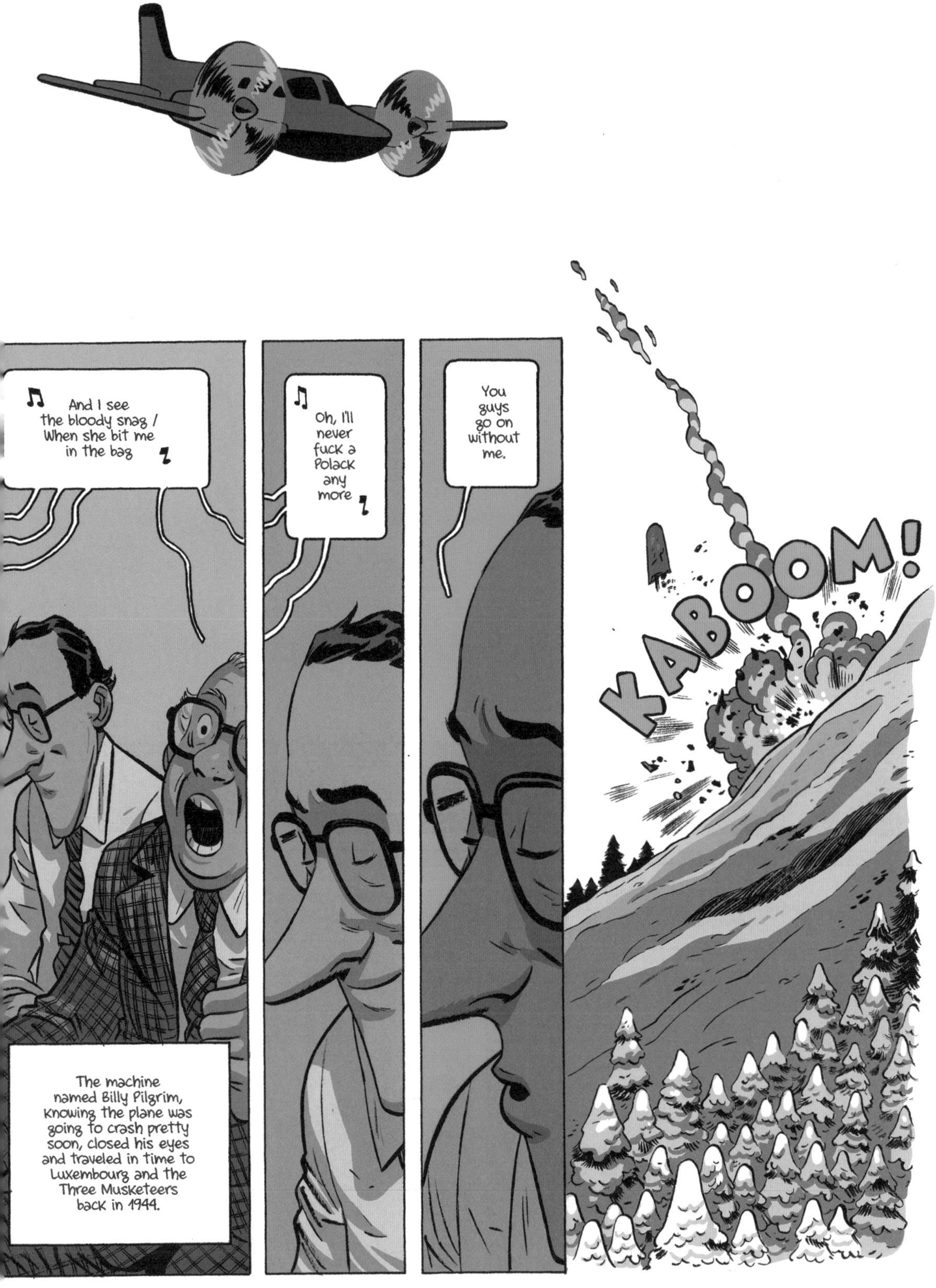

♫ And I see the bloody snag / When she bit me in the bag ♪
♫ Oh, I'll never fuck a Polack any more ♪
You guys go on without me.
The machine named Billy Pilgrim, knowing the plane was going to crash pretty soon, closed his eyes and traveled in time to Luxembourg and the Three Musketeers back in 1944.
KABOOM!

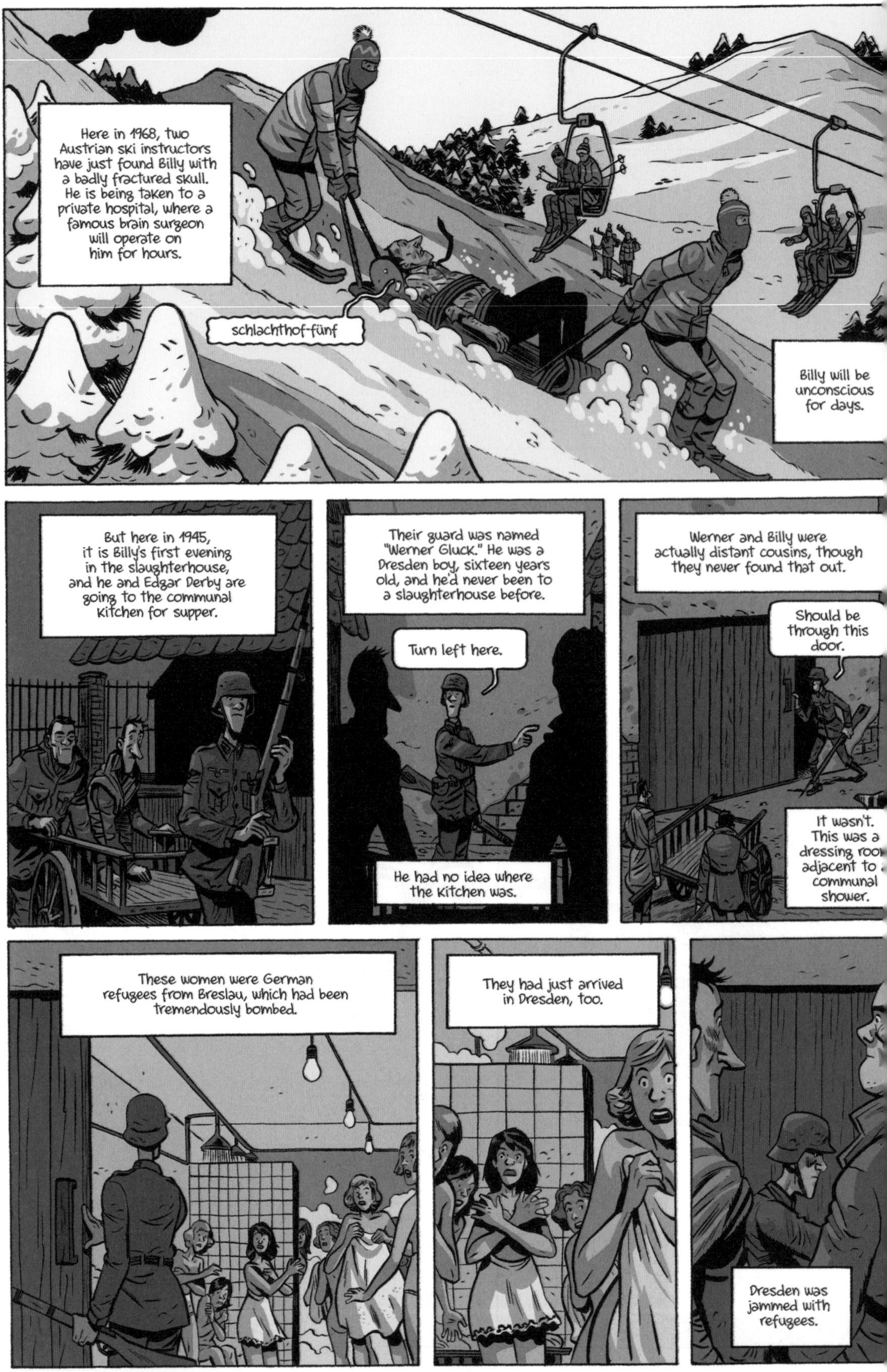
Here in 1968, two Austrian ski instructors have just found Billy with a badly fractured skull. He is being taken to a private hospital, where a famous brain surgeon will operate on him for hours.
schlachthof-fünf
Billy will be unconscious for days.
But here in 1945, it is Billy's first evening in the slaughterhouse, and he and Edgar Derby are going to the communal kitchen for supper.
Their guard was named "Werner Gluck." He was a Dresden boy, sixteen years old, and he'd never been to a slaughterhouse before.
Turn left here.
He had no idea where the kitchen was.
Werner and Billy were actually distant cousins, though they never found that out.
Should be through this door.
It wasn't. This was a dressing roo adjacent to communal shower.
These women were German refugees from Breslau, which had been tremendously bombed.
They had just arrived in Dresden, too.
Dresden was jammed with refugees.

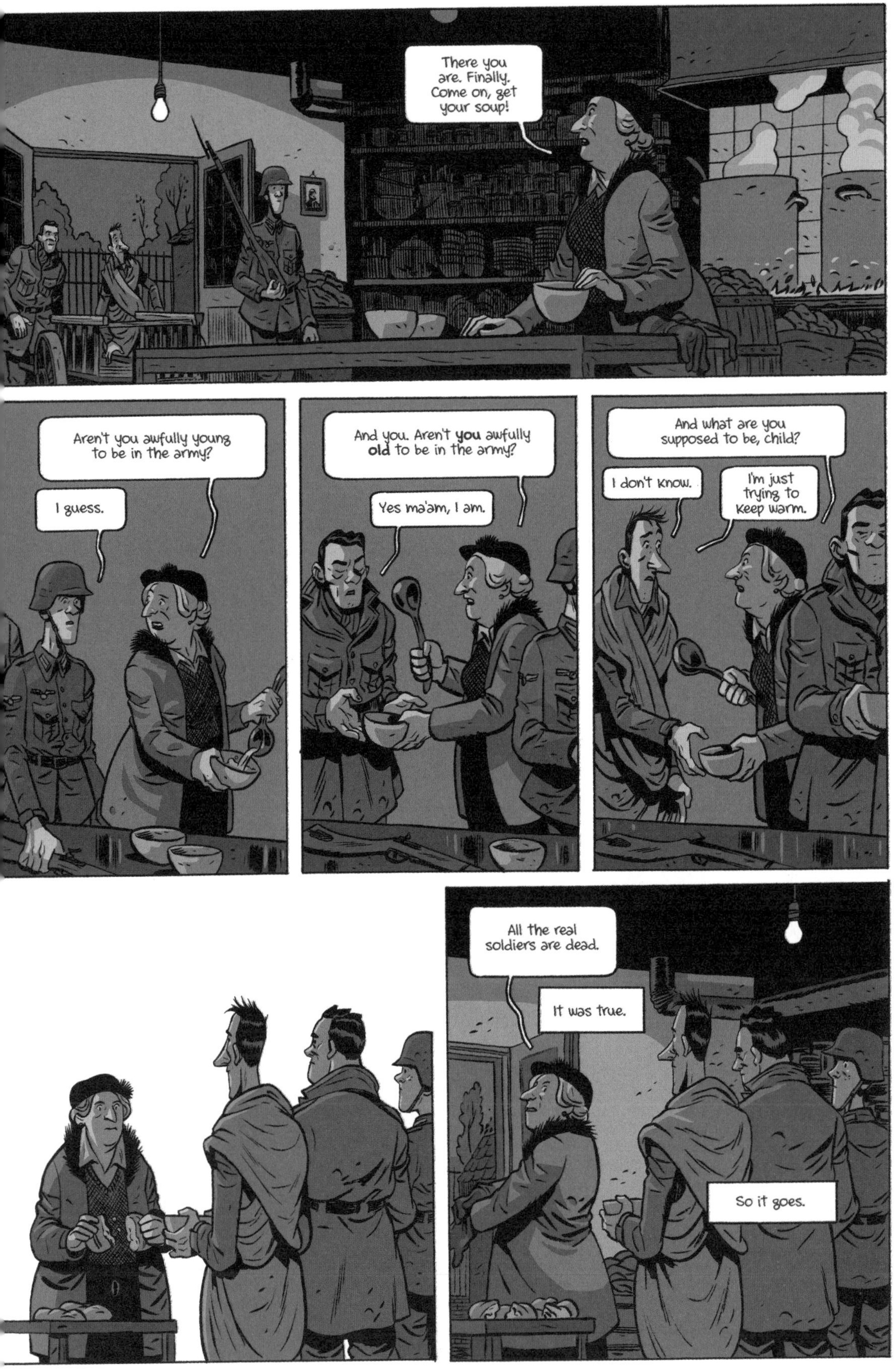

There you are. Finally. Come on, get your soup!
Aren't you awfully young to be in the army?
I guess.
And you. Aren't **you** awfully **old** to be in the army?
Yes ma'am, I am.
And what are you supposed to be, child?
I don't know.
I'm just trying to keep warm.
All the real soldiers are dead.
It was true.
So it goes.

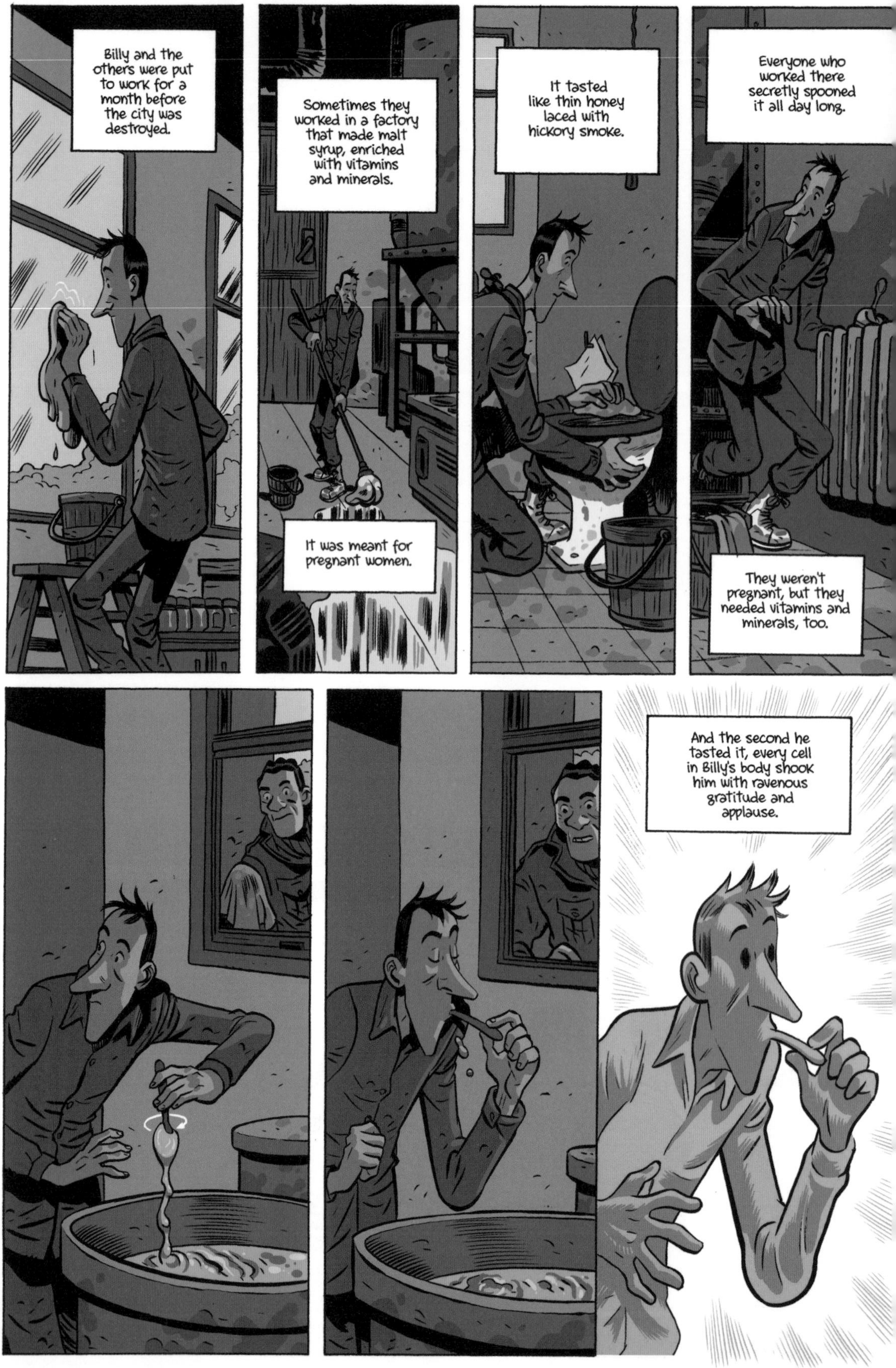
Billy and the others were put to work for a month before the city was destroyed.
Sometimes they worked in a factory that made malt syrup, enriched with vitamins and minerals.
It was meant for pregnant women.
It tasted like thin honey laced with hickory smoke.
Everyone who worked there secretly spooned it all day long.
They weren't pregnant, but they needed vitamins and minerals, too.
And the second he tasted it, every cell in Billy's body shook him with ravenous gratitude and applause.

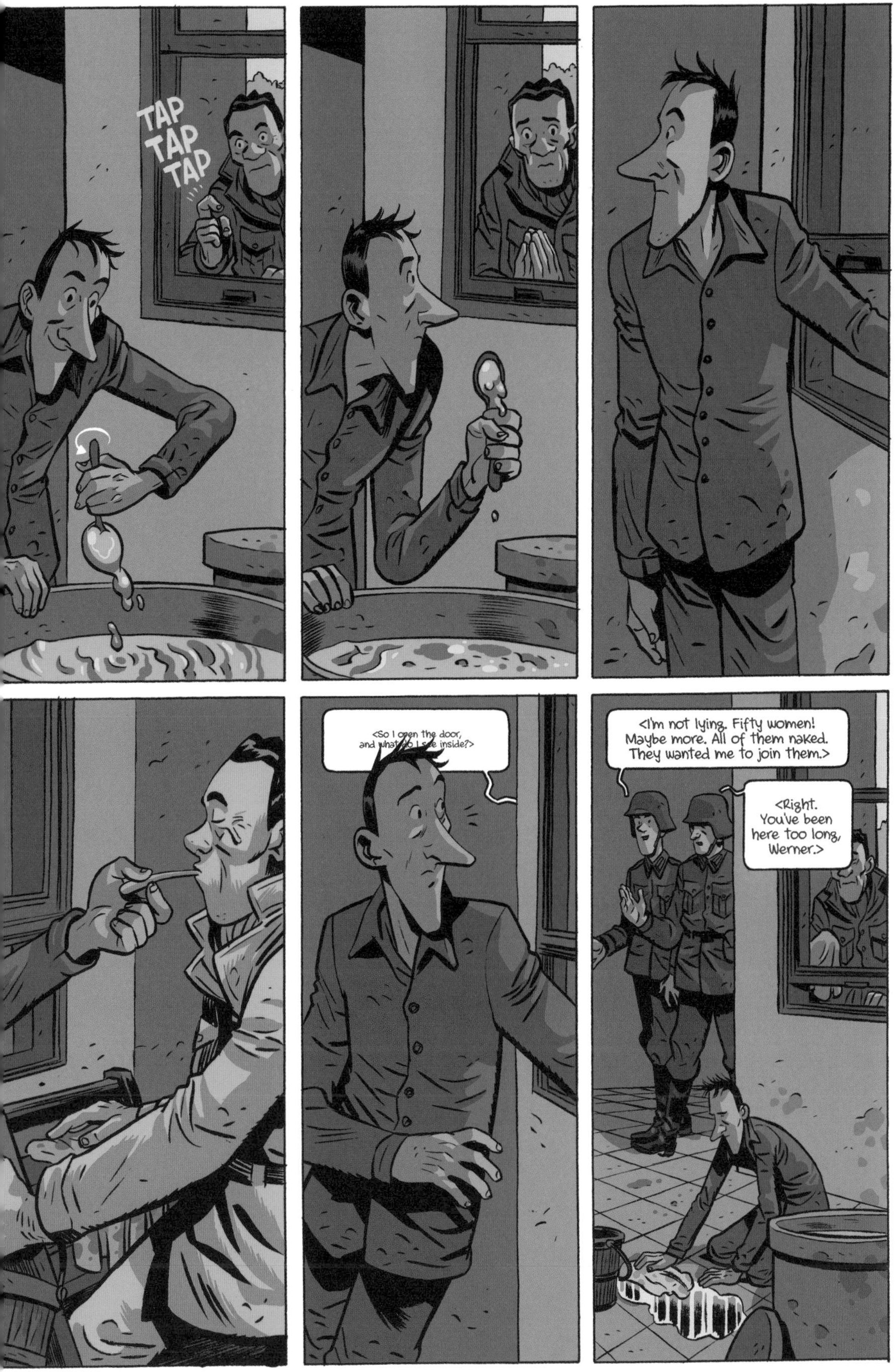
TAP
TAP
TAP
<So I open the door, and what do I see inside?>
<I'm not lying. Fifty women! Maybe more. All of them naked. They wanted me to join them.>
<Right. You've been here too long, Werner.>

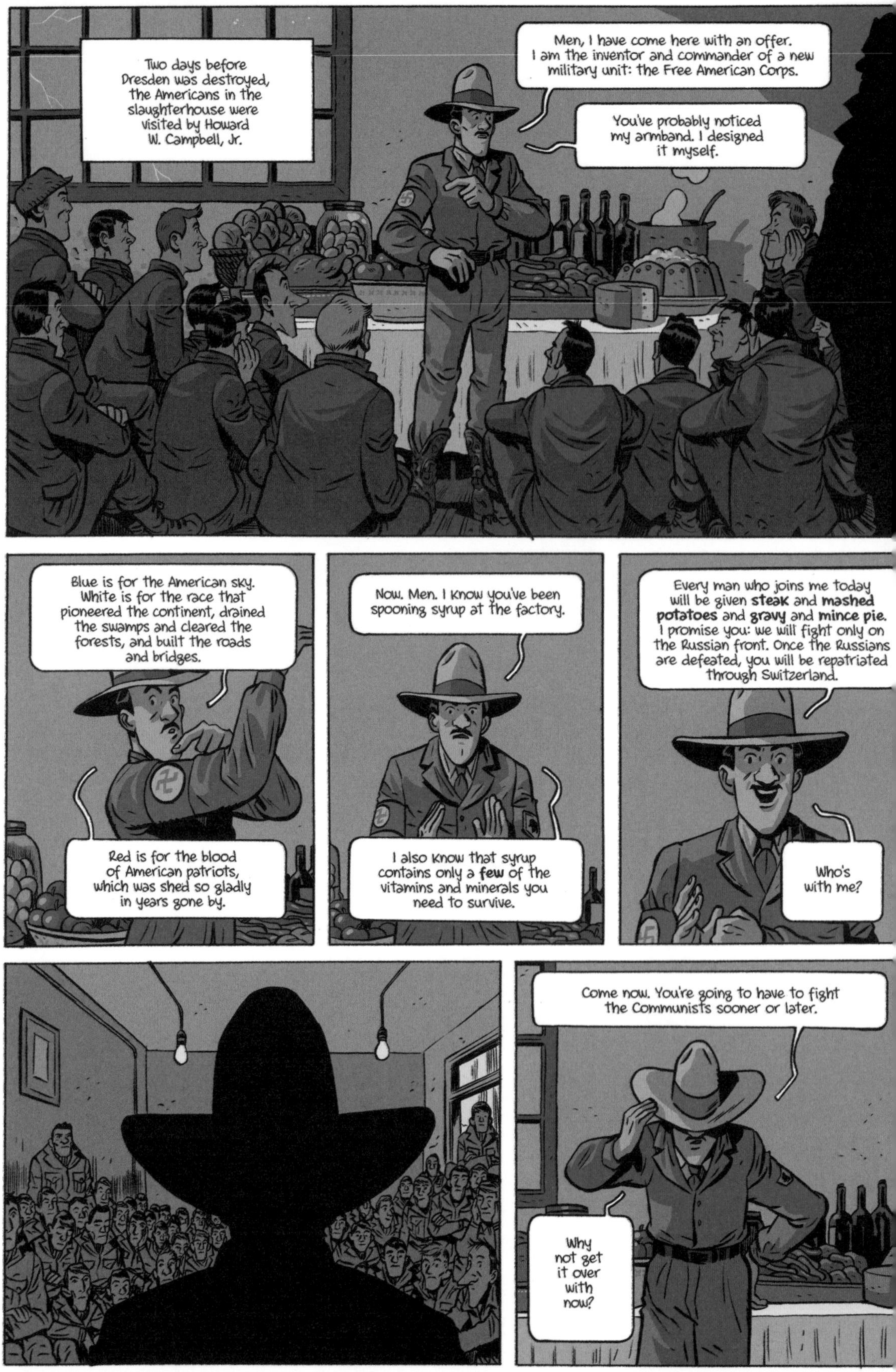
Two days before Dresden was destroyed, the Americans in the slaughterhouse were visited by Howard W. Campbell, Jr.
Men, I have come here with an offer. I am the inventor and commander of a new military unit: the Free American Corps.
You've probably noticed my armband. I designed it myself.
Blue is for the American sky. White is for the race that pioneered the continent, drained the swamps and cleared the forests, and built the roads and bridges.
Red is for the blood of American patriots, which was shed so gladly in years gone by.
Now. Men. I know you've been spooning syrup at the factory.
I also know that syrup contains only a **few** of the vitamins and minerals you need to survive.
Every man who joins me today will be given **steak** and **mashed potatoes** and **gravy** and **mince pie**. I promise you: we will fight only on the Russian front. Once the Russians are defeated, you will be repatriated through Switzerland.
Who's with me?
Come now. You're going to have to fight the Communists sooner or later.
Why not get it over with now?

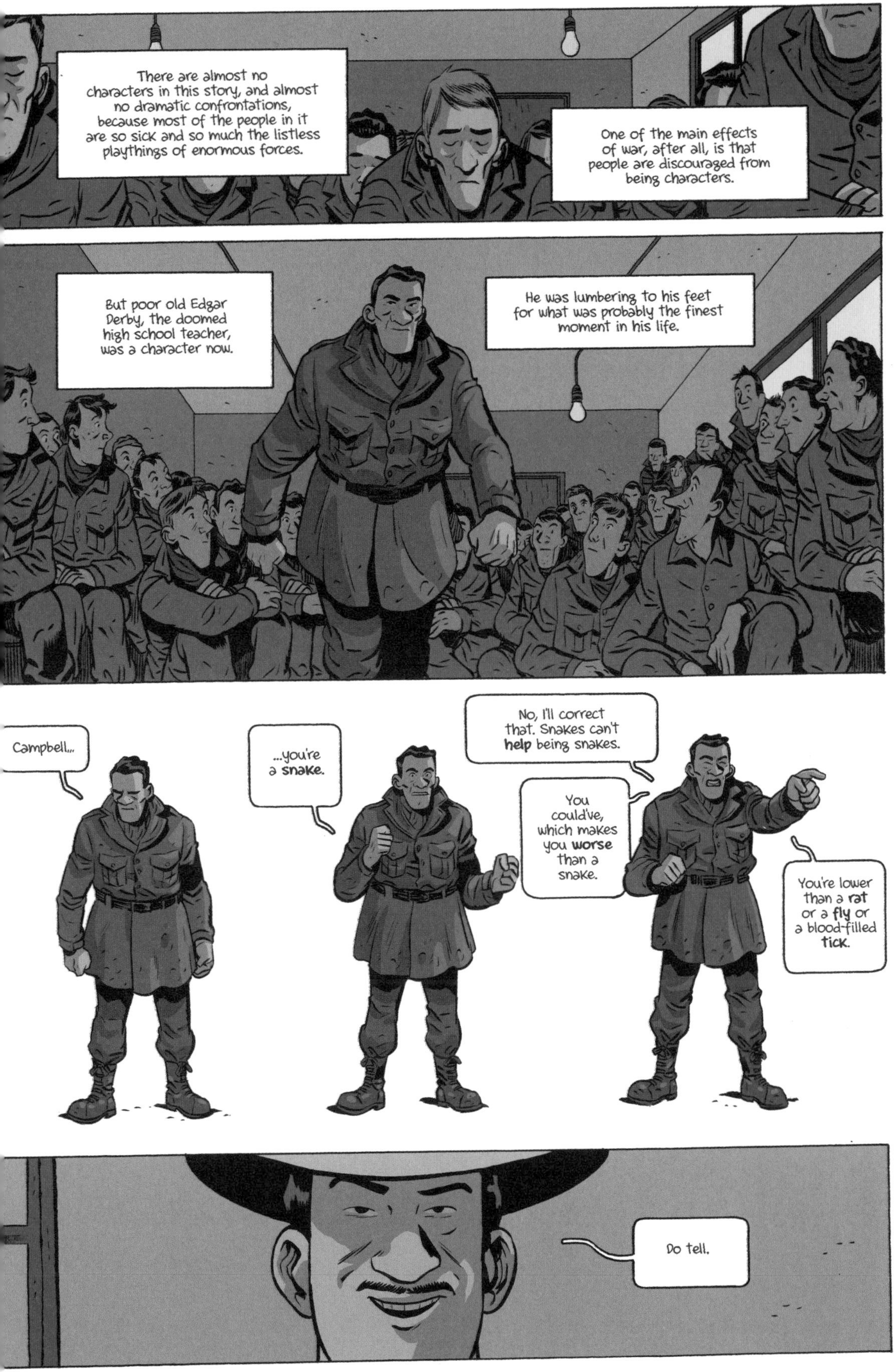
There are almost no characters in this story, and almost no dramatic confrontations, because most of the people in it are so sick and so much the listless playthings of enormous forces.
One of the main effects of war, after all, is that people are discouraged from being characters.
But poor old Edgar Derby, the doomed high school teacher, was a character now.
He was lumbering to his feet for what was probably the finest moment in his life.
Campbell...
...you're a **snake**.
No, I'll correct that. Snakes can't **help** being snakes.
You could've, which makes you **worse** than a snake.
You're lower than a **rat** or a **fly** or a blood-filled **tick**.
Do tell.

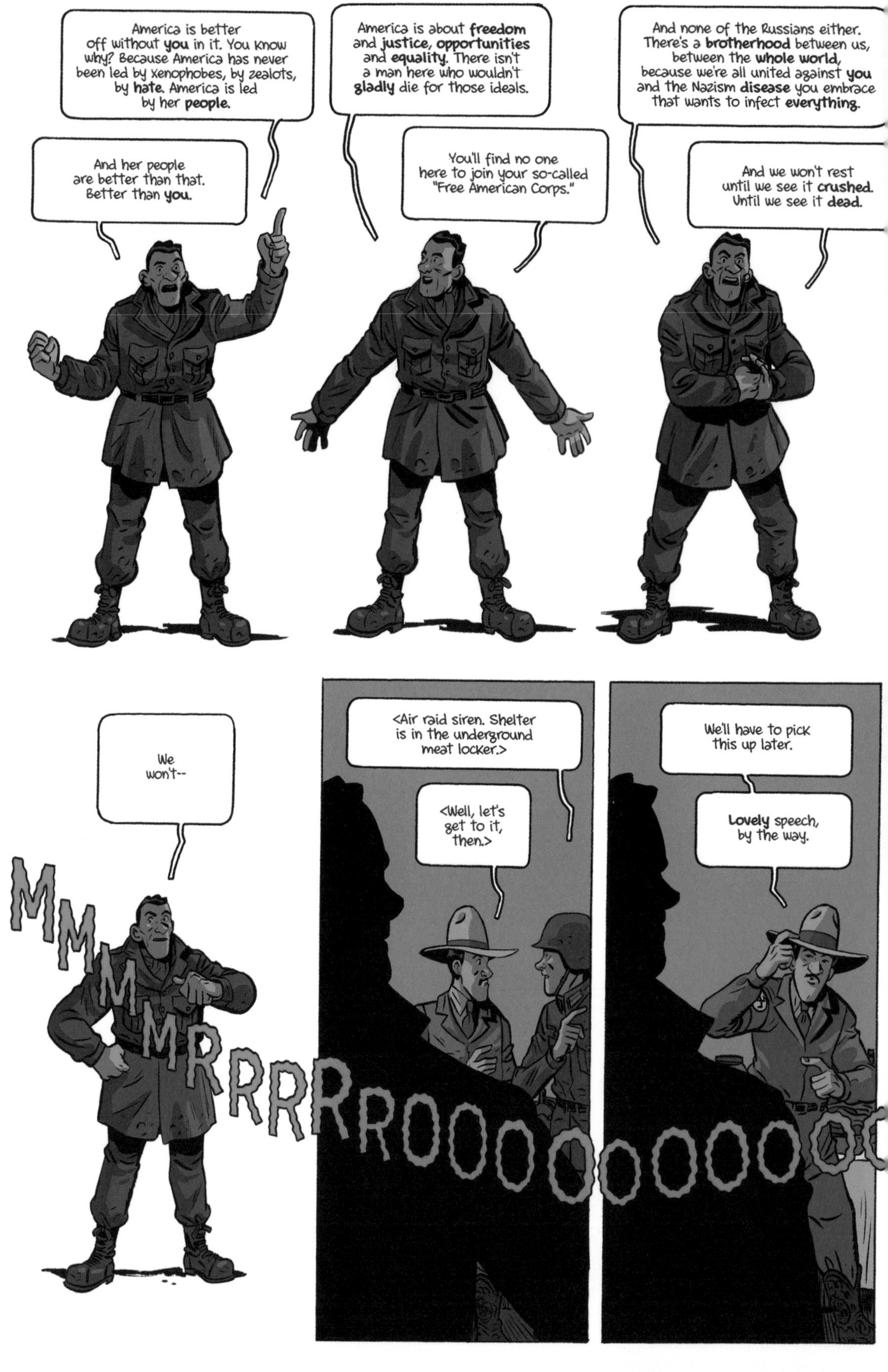
America is better off without you in it. You know why? Because America has never been led by xenophobes, by zealots, by hate. America is led by her people.
And her people are better than that. Better than you.
America is about freedom and justice, opportunities and equality. There isn't a man here who wouldn't gladly die for those ideals.
You'll find no one here to join your so-called "Free American Corps."
And none of the Russians either. There's a brotherhood between us, between the whole world, because we're all united against you and the Nazism disease you embrace that wants to infect everything.
And we won't rest until we see it crushed. Until we see it dead.
We won't--
MMMMMRRRRROOOOOOOOOO
<Air raid siren. Shelter is in the underground meat locker.>
<Well, let's get to it, then.>
We'll have to pick this up later.
Lovely speech, by the way.

Nothing happened that night.

<I assume you've read my books, or at least the poems.>

<Yes sir. I've seen your comedy about America.>

<Ah, yes. "Fortune's Folly." Tell me, how did you like it?>

It was the next night that over twenty-five thousand people in Dresden would die.

So it goes.

What **are** we going to **do** with you?

I don't know.

I **know** you don't know. God! You know who I could just Kill?

Who could you kill?

That--that **writer** friend of yours, putting these ideas in your head. What's his name?

Fish something?

Trout.

Right, **Trout**.

I could just kill **Kilgore Trout**.

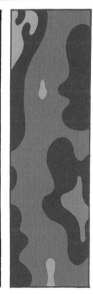

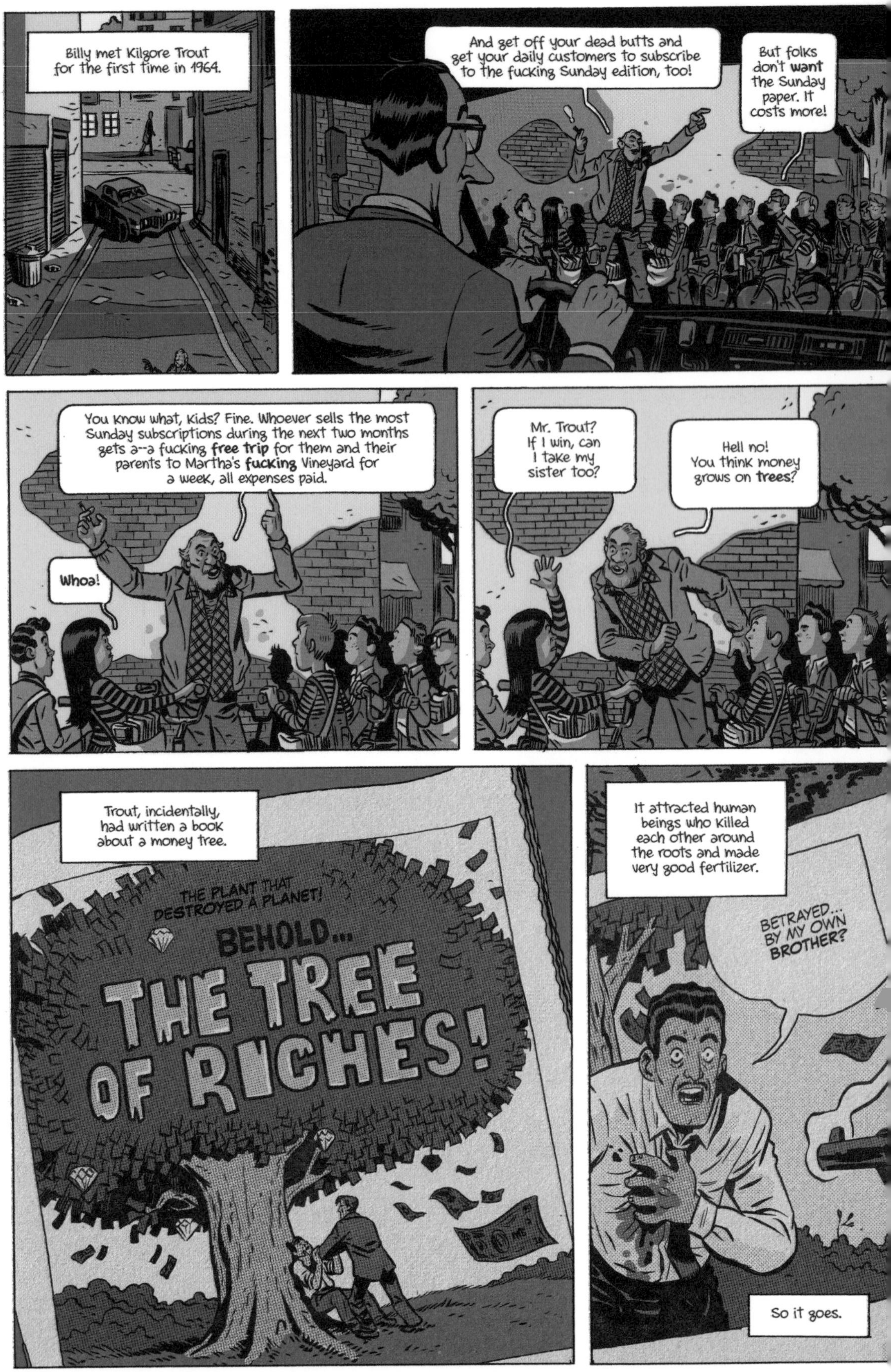

Billy met Kilgore Trout for the first time in 1964.
And get off your dead butts and get your daily customers to subscribe to the fucking Sunday edition, too!
But folks don't **want** the Sunday paper. It costs more!
You know what, kids? Fine. Whoever sells the most Sunday subscriptions during the next two months gets a--a fucking **free trip** for them and their parents to Martha's **fucking** Vineyard for a week, all expenses paid.
Whoa!
Mr. Trout? If I win, can I take my sister too?
Hell no! You think money grows on **trees?**
Trout, incidentally, had written a book about a money tree.
THE PLANT THAT DESTROYED A PLANET!
BEHOLD...
THE TREE OF RICHES!
It attracted human beings who killed each other around the roots and made very good fertilizer.
BETRAYED... BY MY OWN BROTHER?
So it goes.

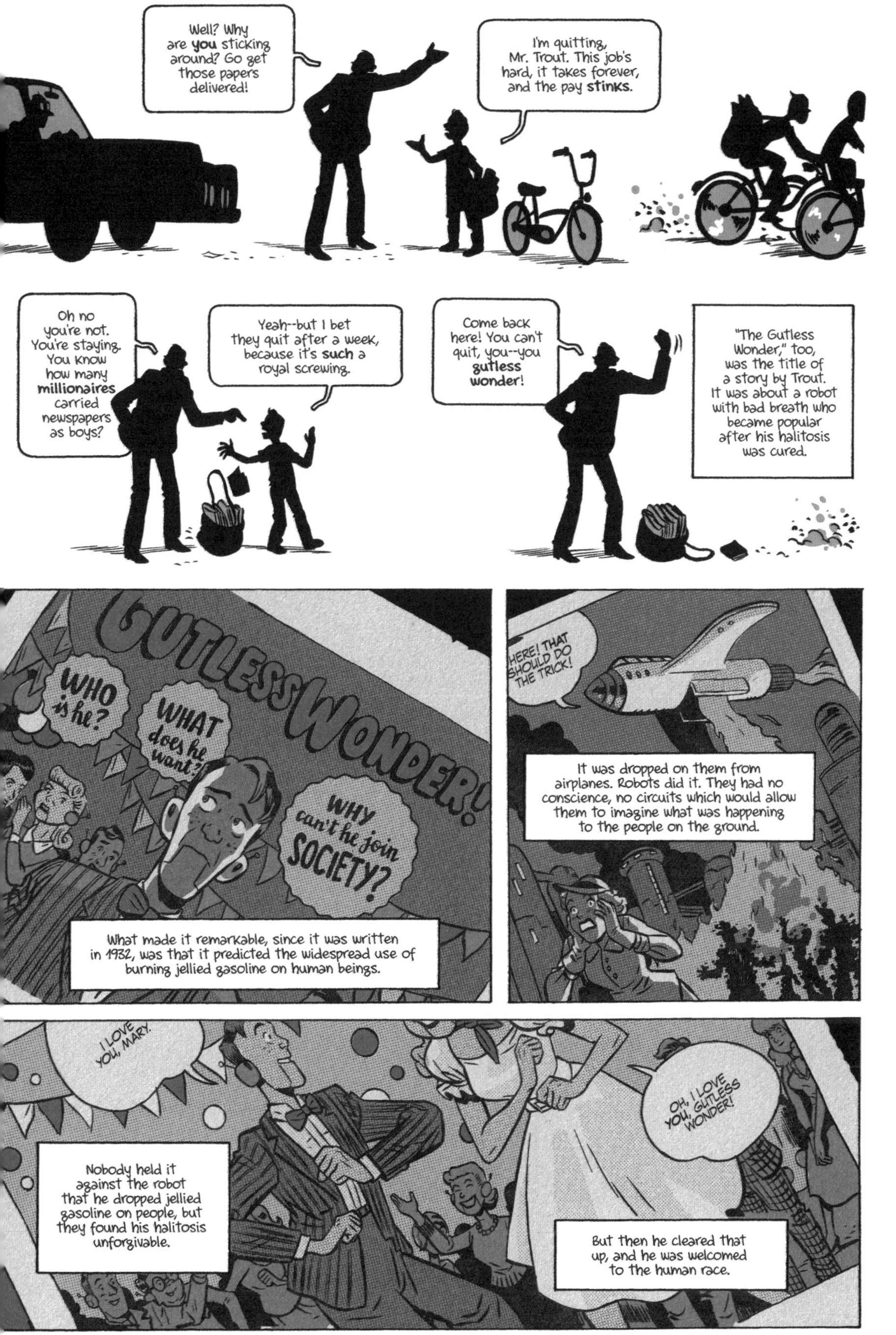
Well? Why are you sticking around? Go get those papers delivered!
I'm quitting, Mr. Trout. This job's hard, it takes forever, and the pay stinks.
Oh no you're not. You're staying. You know how many millionaires carried newspapers as boys?
Yeah--but I bet they quit after a week, because it's such a royal screwing.
Come back here! You can't quit, you--you gutless wonder!
"The Gutless Wonder," too, was the title of a story by Trout. It was about a robot with bad breath who became popular after his halitosis was cured.
GUTLESS WONDER!
WHO is he?
WHAT does he want?
WHY can't he join SOCIETY?
What made it remarkable, since it was written in 1932, was that it predicted the widespread use of burning jellied gasoline on human beings.
HERE! THAT SHOULD DO THE TRICK!
It was dropped on them from airplanes. Robots did it. They had no conscience, no circuits which would allow them to imagine what was happening to the people on the ground.
I LOVE YOU, MARY.
OH, I LOVE YOU, GUTLESS WONDER!
Nobody held it against the robot that he dropped jellied gasoline on people, but they found his halitosis unforgivable.
But then he cleared that up, and he was welcomed to the human race.

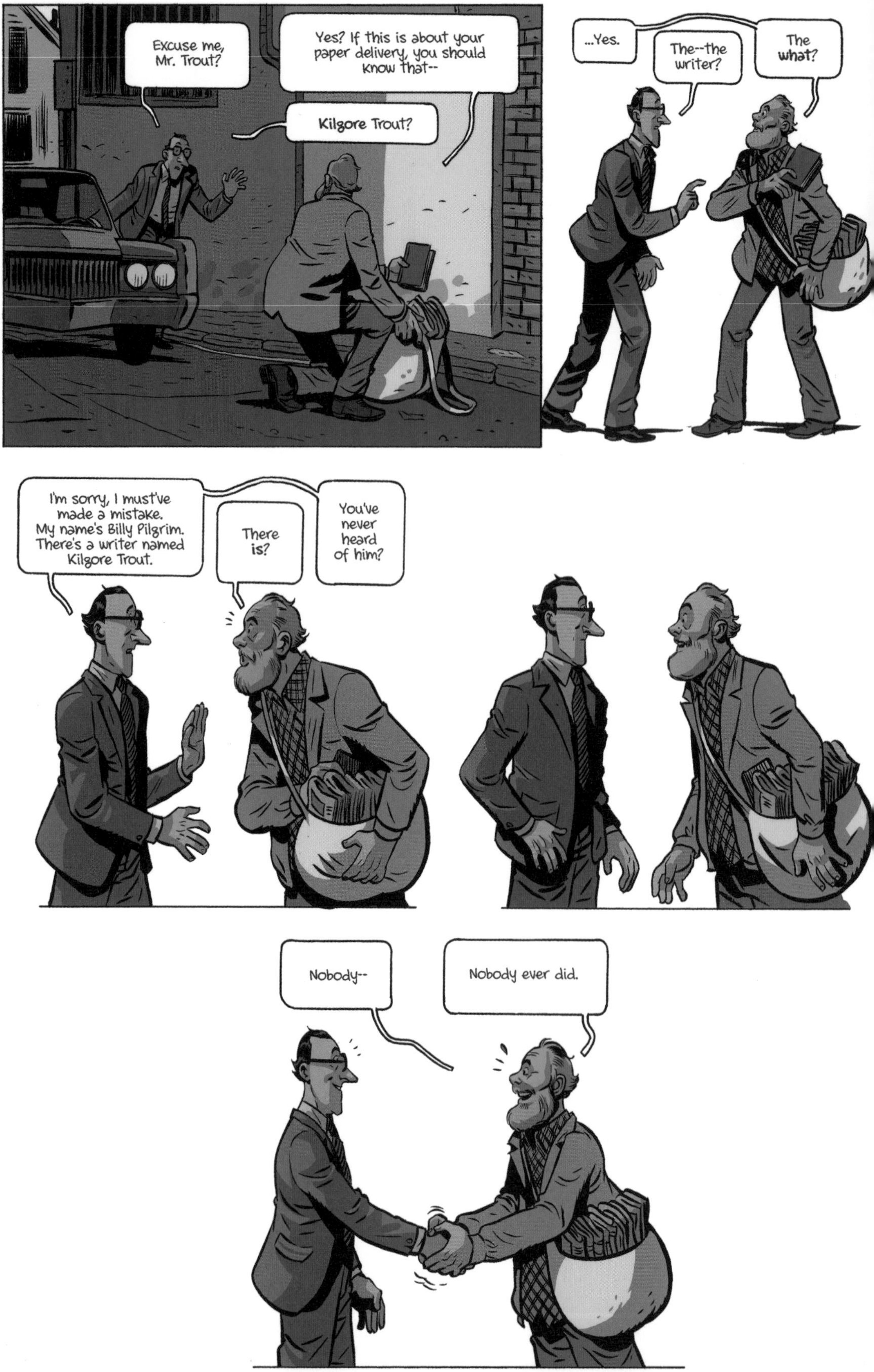
Excuse me, Mr. Trout?
Yes? If this is about your paper delivery, you should know that--
Kilgore Trout?
...Yes.
The--the writer?
The what?
I'm sorry, I must've made a mistake. My name's Billy Pilgrim. There's a writer named Kilgore Trout.
There is?
You've never heard of him?
Nobody--
Nobody ever did.

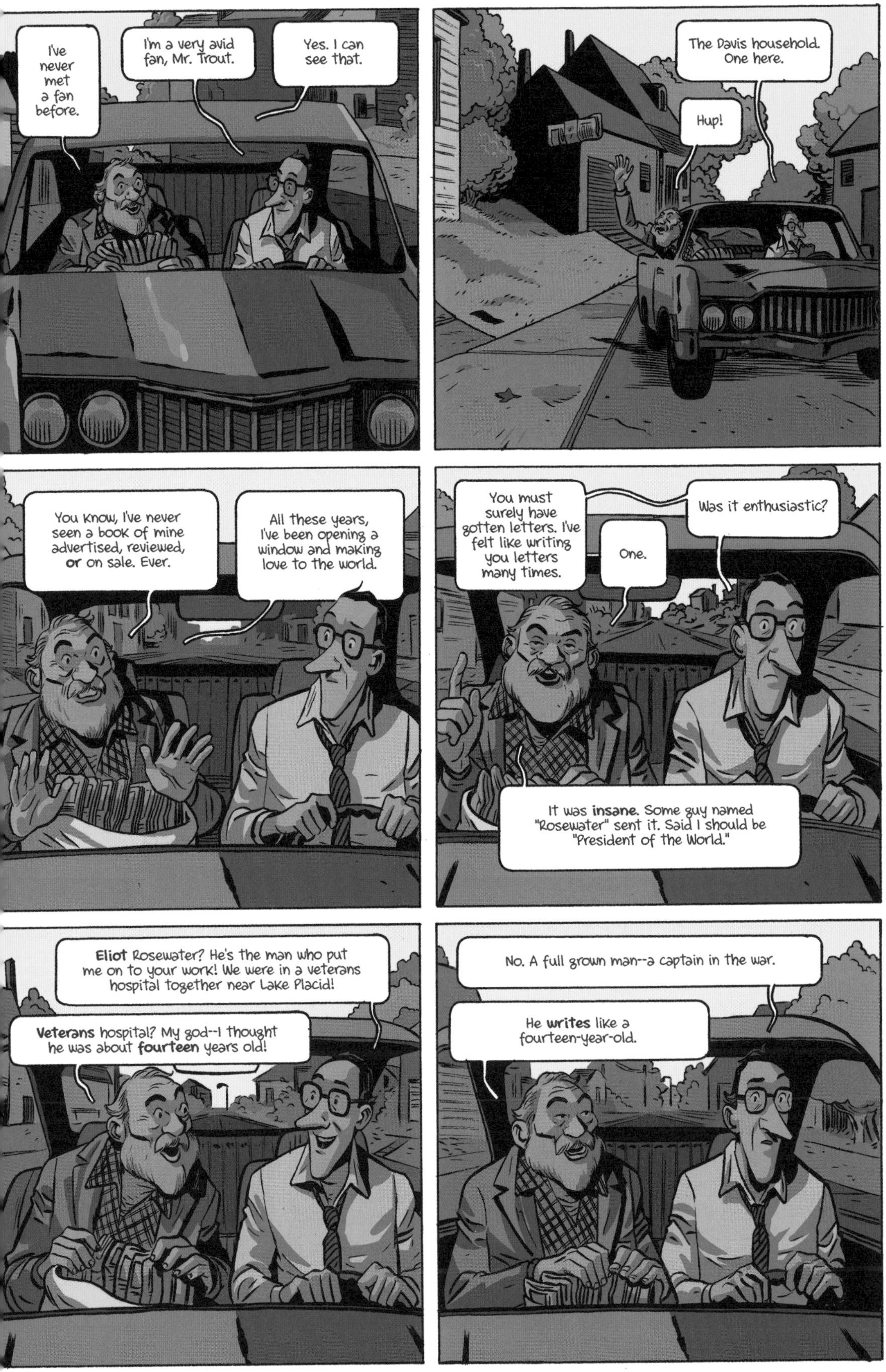
I've never met a fan before.
I'm a very avid fan, Mr. Trout.
Yes. I can see that.
The Davis household. One here.
Hup!
You know, I've never seen a book of mine advertised, reviewed, **or** on sale. Ever.
All these years, I've been opening a window and making love to the world.
You must surely have gotten letters. I've felt like writing you letters many times.
One.
Was it enthusiastic?
It was **insane.** Some guy named "Rosewater" sent it. Said I should be "President of the World."
Eliot Rosewater? He's the man who put me on to your work! We were in a veterans hospital together near Lake Placid!
Veterans hospital? My god--I thought he was about **fourteen** years old!
No. A full grown man--a captain in the war.
He **writes** like a fourteen-year-old.

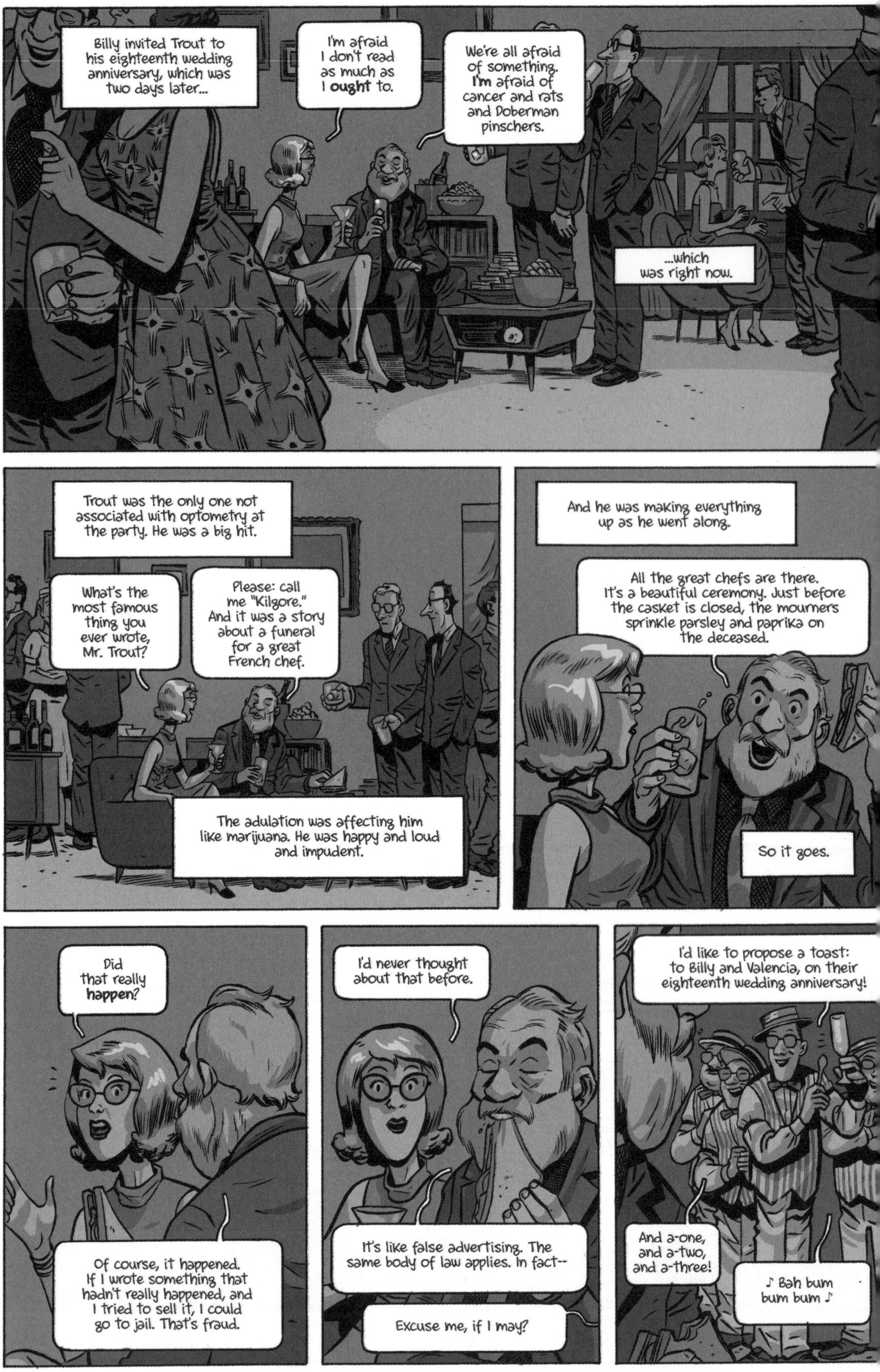

Billy invited Trout to his eighteenth wedding anniversary, which was two days later...
I'm afraid I don't read as much as I **ought** to.
We're all afraid of something. **I'm** afraid of cancer and rats and Doberman pinschers.
...which was right now.
Trout was the only one not associated with optometry at the party. He was a big hit.
What's the most famous thing you ever wrote, Mr. Trout?
Please: call me "Kilgore." And it was a story about a funeral for a great French chef.
The adulation was affecting him like marijuana. He was happy and loud and impudent.
And he was making everything up as he went along.
All the great chefs are there. It's a beautiful ceremony. Just before the casket is closed, the mourners sprinkle parsley and paprika on the deceased.
So it goes.
Did that really **happen**?
Of course, it happened. If I wrote something that hadn't really happened, and I tried to sell it, I could go to jail. That's fraud.
I'd never thought about that before.
It's like false advertising. The same body of law applies. In fact--
Excuse me, if I may?
I'd like to propose a toast: to Billy and Valencia, on their eighteenth wedding anniversary!
And a-one, and a-two, and a-three!
♪ Bah bum bum bum ♪

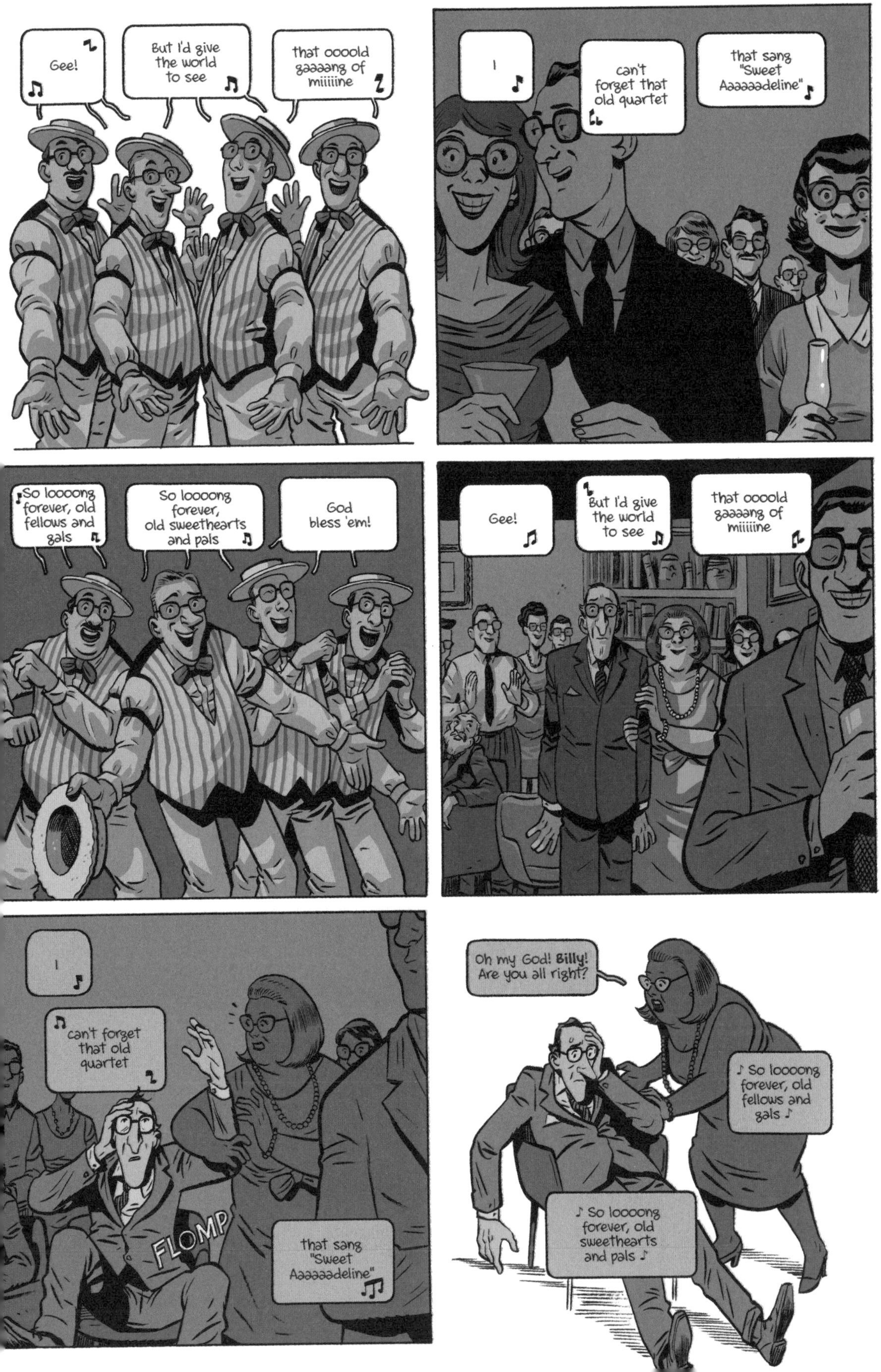
Gee!
But I'd give the world to see
that oooold gaaaang of miiiiine
I
can't forget that old quartet
that sang "Sweet Aaaaaadeline"
So loooong forever, old fellows and gals
So loooong forever, old sweethearts and pals
God bless 'em!
Gee!
But I'd give the world to see
that oooold gaaaang of miiiiine
I
can't forget that old quartet
FLOMP
that sang "Sweet Aaaaaadeline"
Oh my God! **Billy!** Are you all right?
♪ So loooong forever, old fellows and gals ♪
♪ So loooong forever, old sweethearts and pals ♪

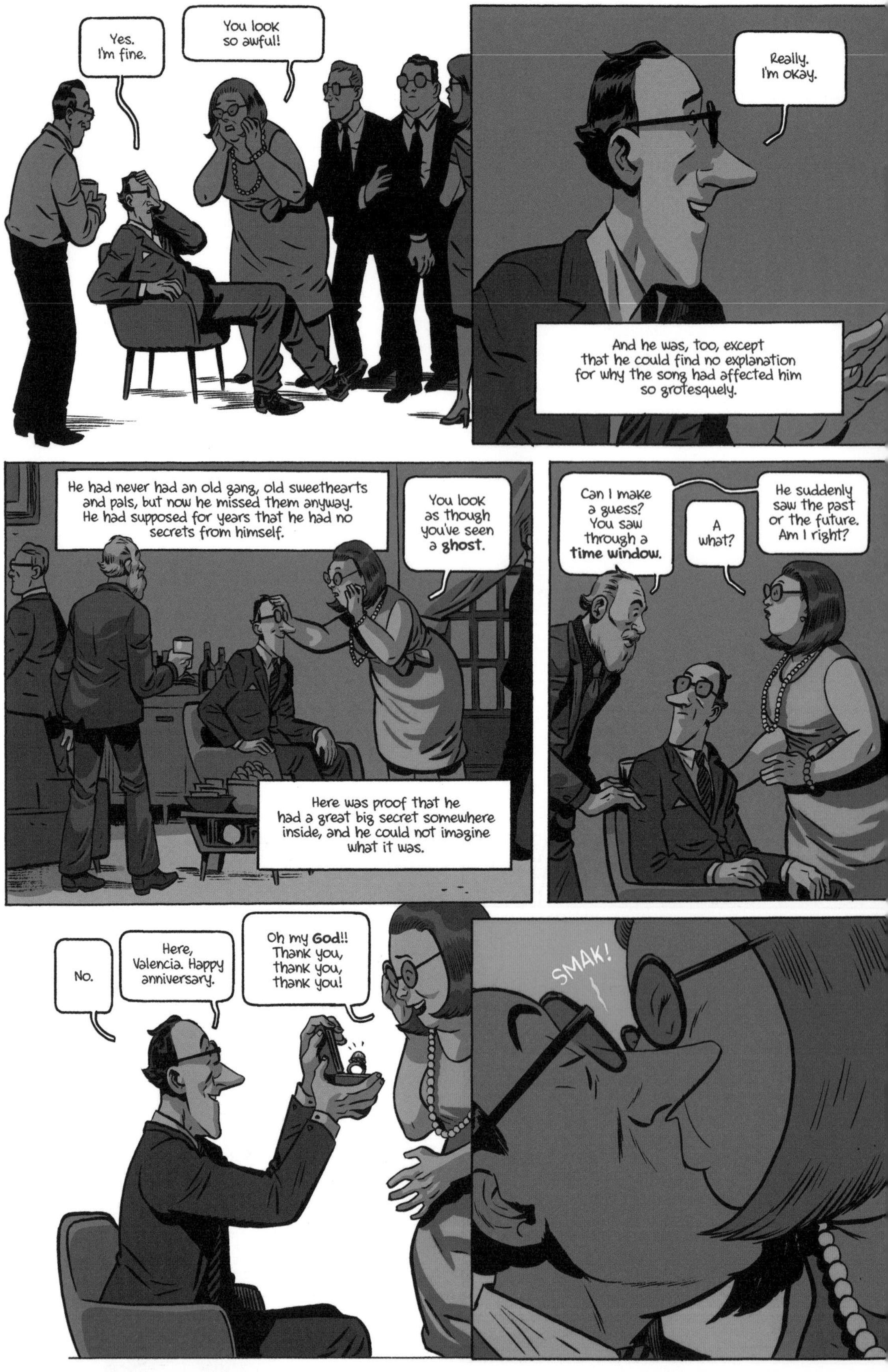
Yes. I'm fine.
You look so awful!
Really. I'm okay.
And he was, too, except that he could find no explanation for why the song had affected him so grotesquely.
He had never had an old gang, old sweethearts and pals, but now he missed them anyway. He had supposed for years that he had no secrets from himself.
You look as though you've seen a **ghost**.
Here was proof that he had a great big secret somewhere inside, and he could not imagine what it was.
Can I make a guess? You saw through a **time window**.
A what?
He suddenly saw the past or the future. Am I right?
No.
Here, Valencia. Happy anniversary.
Oh my **God**!! Thank you, thank you, thank you!
SMAK!

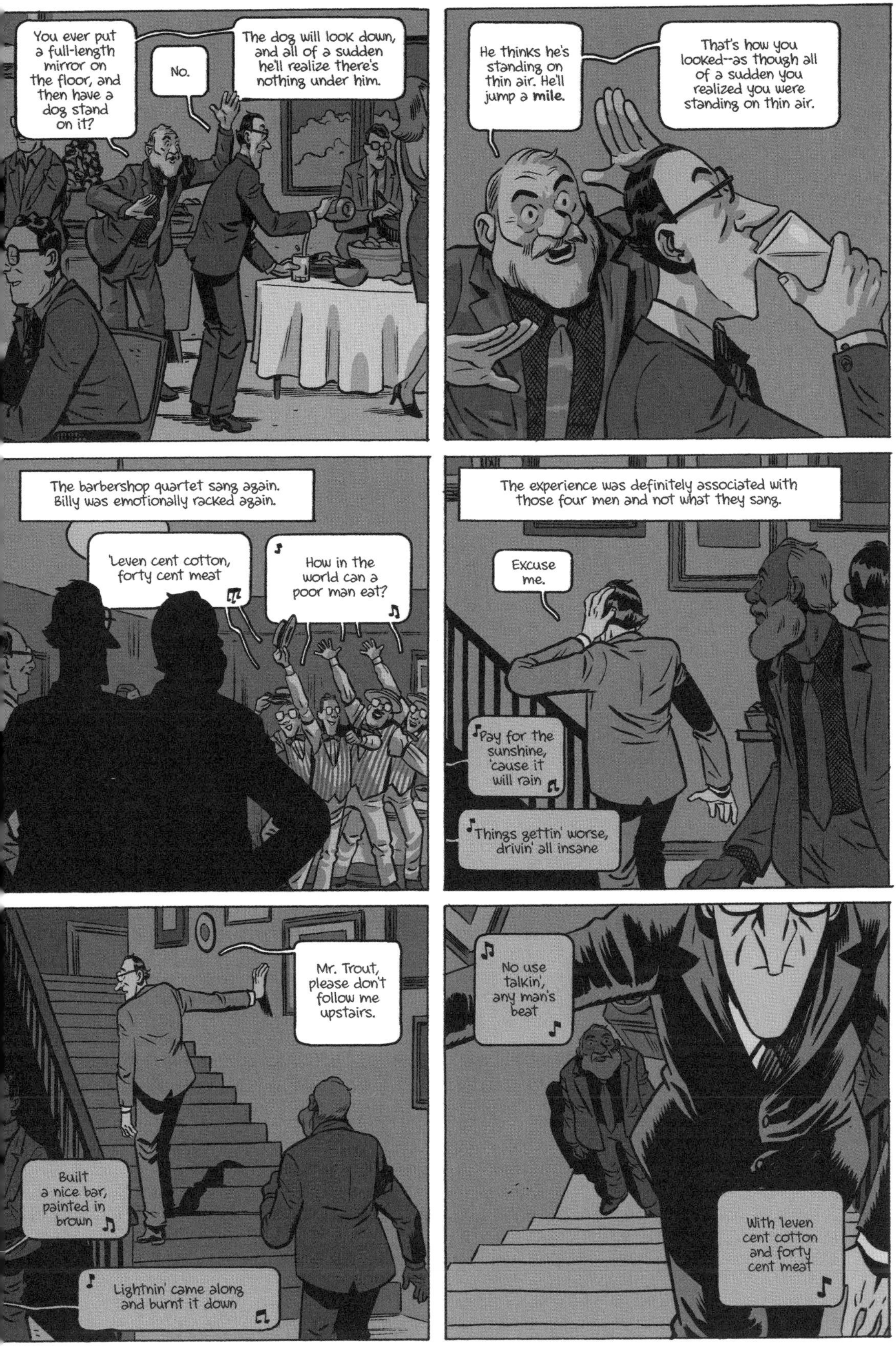
You ever put a full-length mirror on the floor, and then have a dog stand on it?
No.
The dog will look down, and all of a sudden he'll realize there's nothing under him.
He thinks he's standing on thin air. He'll jump a **mile.**
That's how you looked--as though all of a sudden you realized you were standing on thin air.
The barbershop quartet sang again. Billy was emotionally racked again.
'Leven cent cotton, forty cent meat
How in the world can a poor man eat?
The experience was definitely associated with those four men and not what they sang.
Excuse me.
Pay for the sunshine, 'cause it will rain
Things gettin' worse, drivin' all insane
Mr. Trout, please don't follow me upstairs.
Built a nice bar, painted in brown
Lightnin' came along and burnt it down
No use talkin', any man's beat
With 'leven cent cotton and forty cent meat

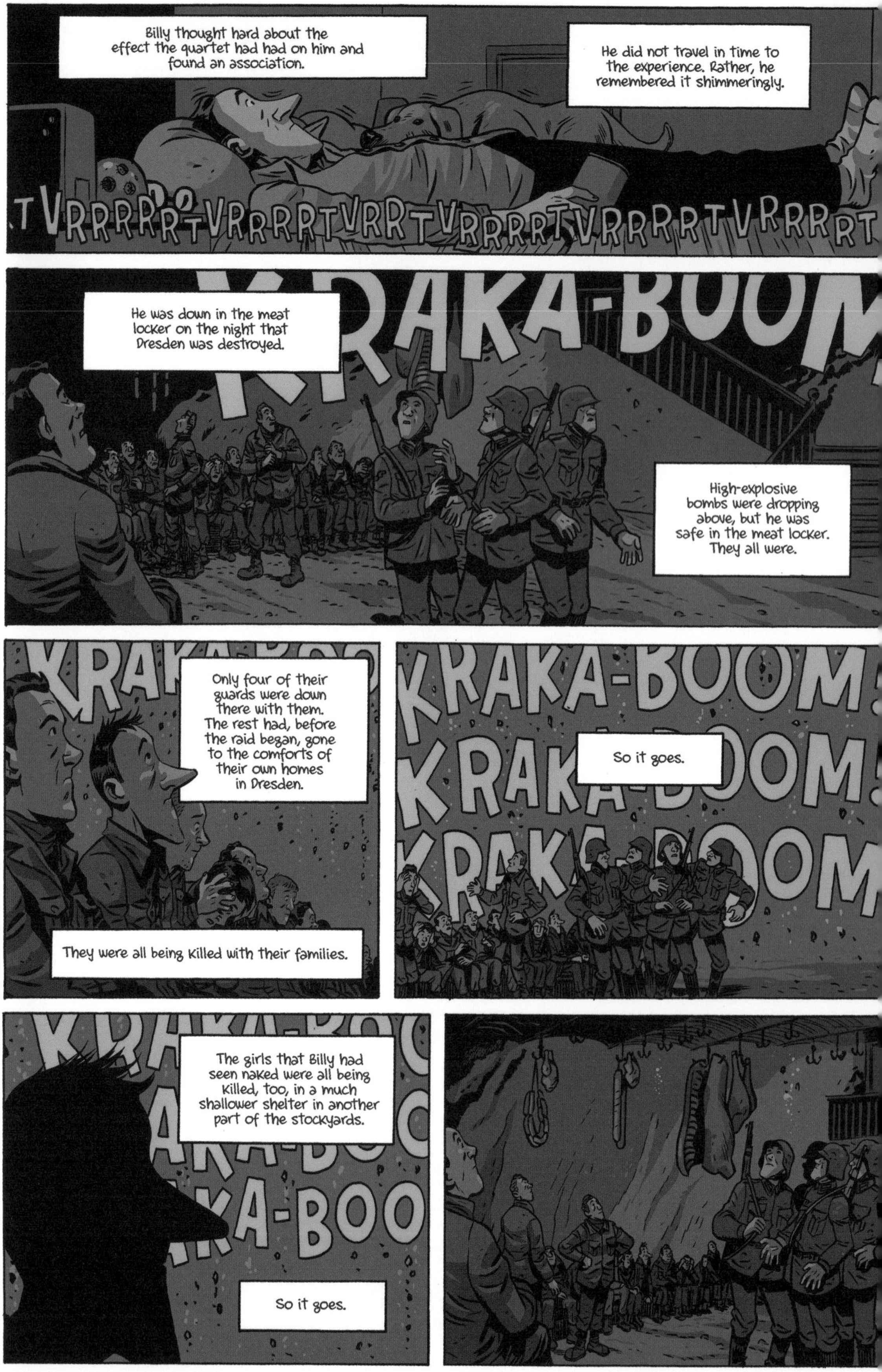
Billy thought hard about the effect the quartet had had on him and found an association.
He did not travel in time to the experience. Rather, he remembered it shimmeringly.
TVRRRRRTVRRRRRTVRRTVRRRRTVRRRRTVRRRRT
KRAKA-BOOM
He was down in the meat locker on the night that Dresden was destroyed.
High-explosive bombs were dropping above, but he was safe in the meat locker. They all were.
Only four of their guards were down there with them. The rest had, before the raid began, gone to the comforts of their own homes in Dresden.
They were all being killed with their families.
KRAKA-BOOM!
So it goes.
The girls that Billy had seen naked were all being killed, too, in a much shallower shelter in another part of the stockyards.
So it goes.

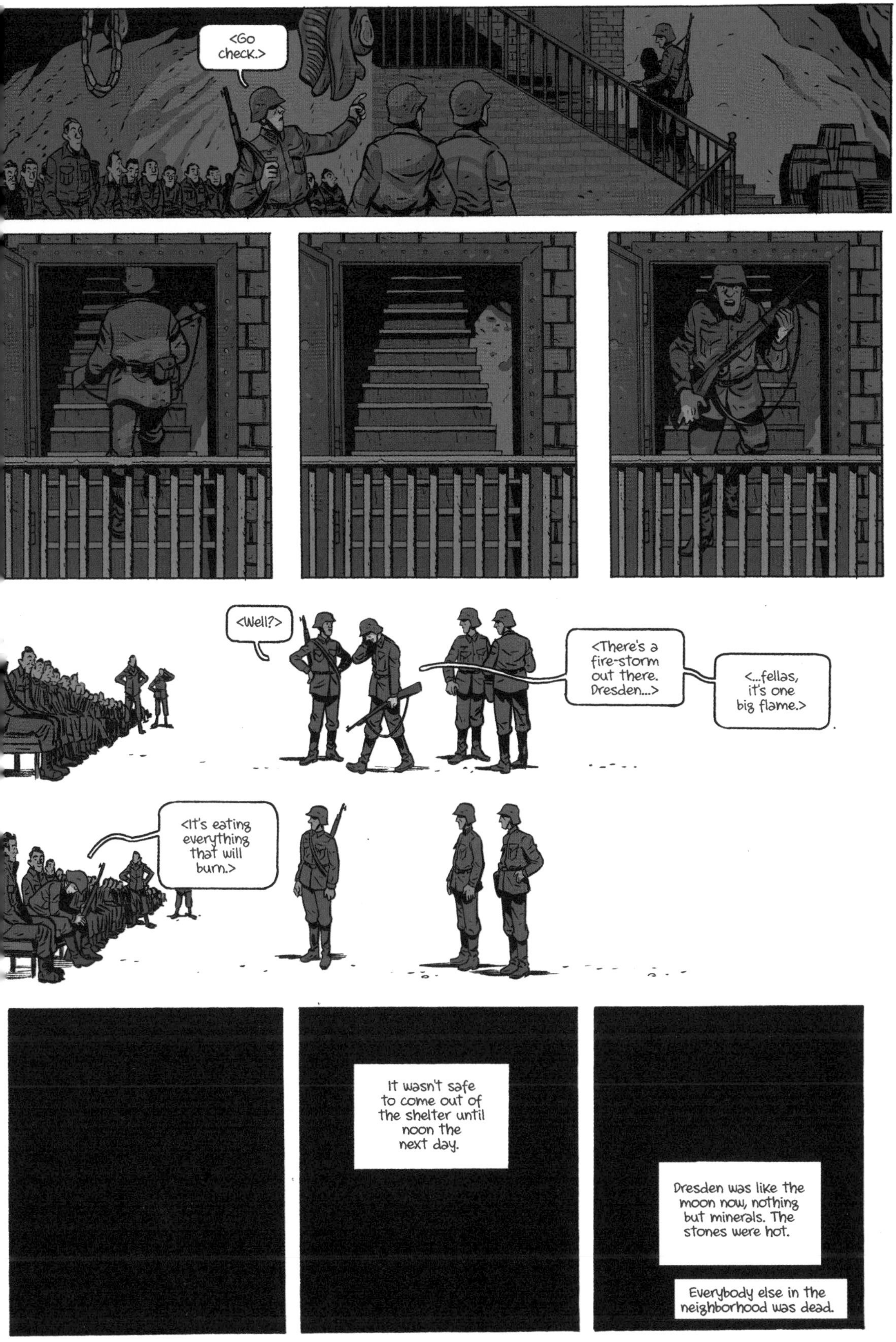

<Go check.>
<Well?>
<There's a fire-storm out there. Dresden...>
<...fellas, it's one big flame.>
<It's eating everything that will burn.>
It wasn't safe to come out of the shelter until noon the next day.
Dresden was like the moon now, nothing but minerals. The stones were hot.
Everybody else in the neighborhood was dead.

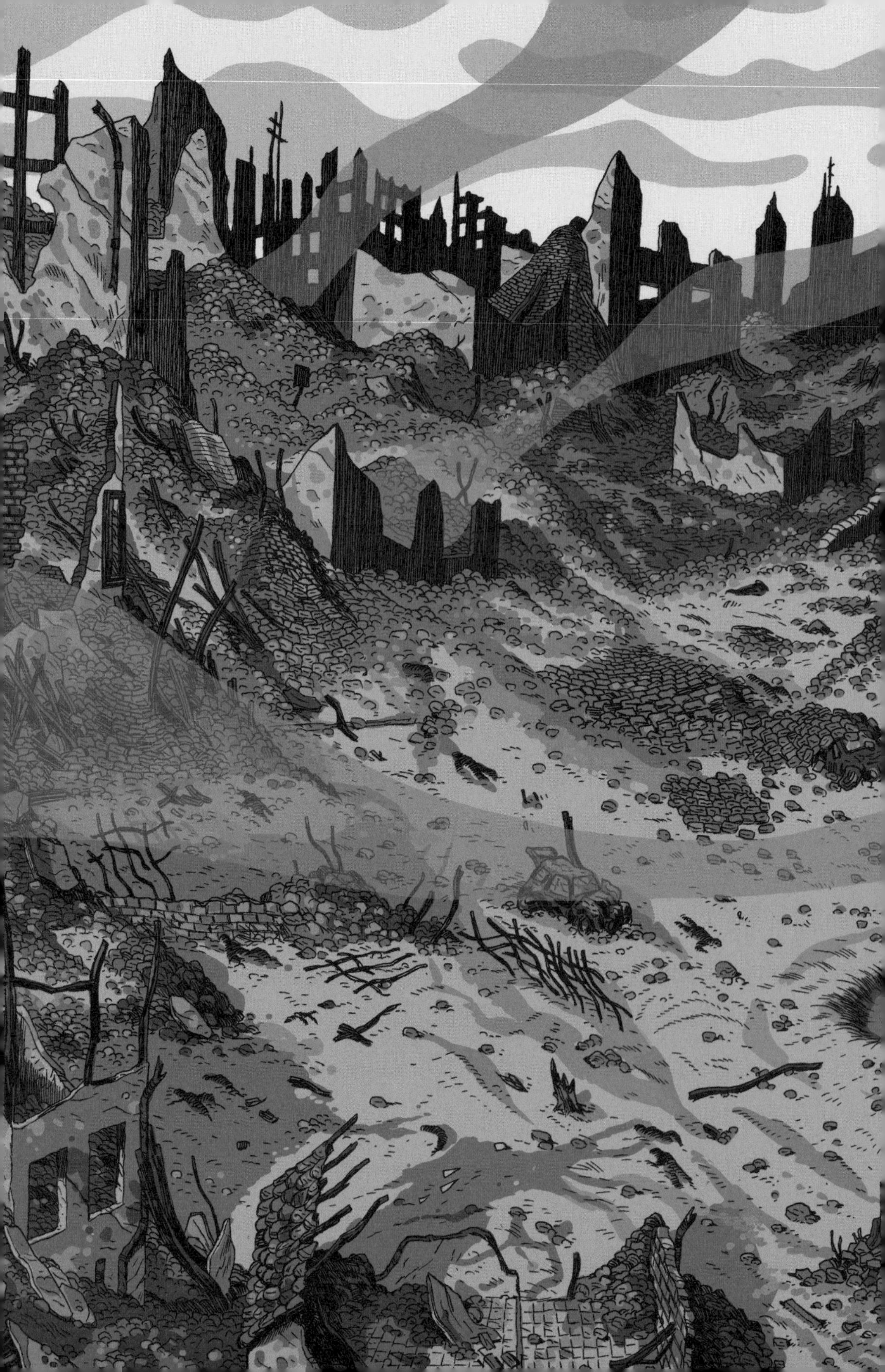

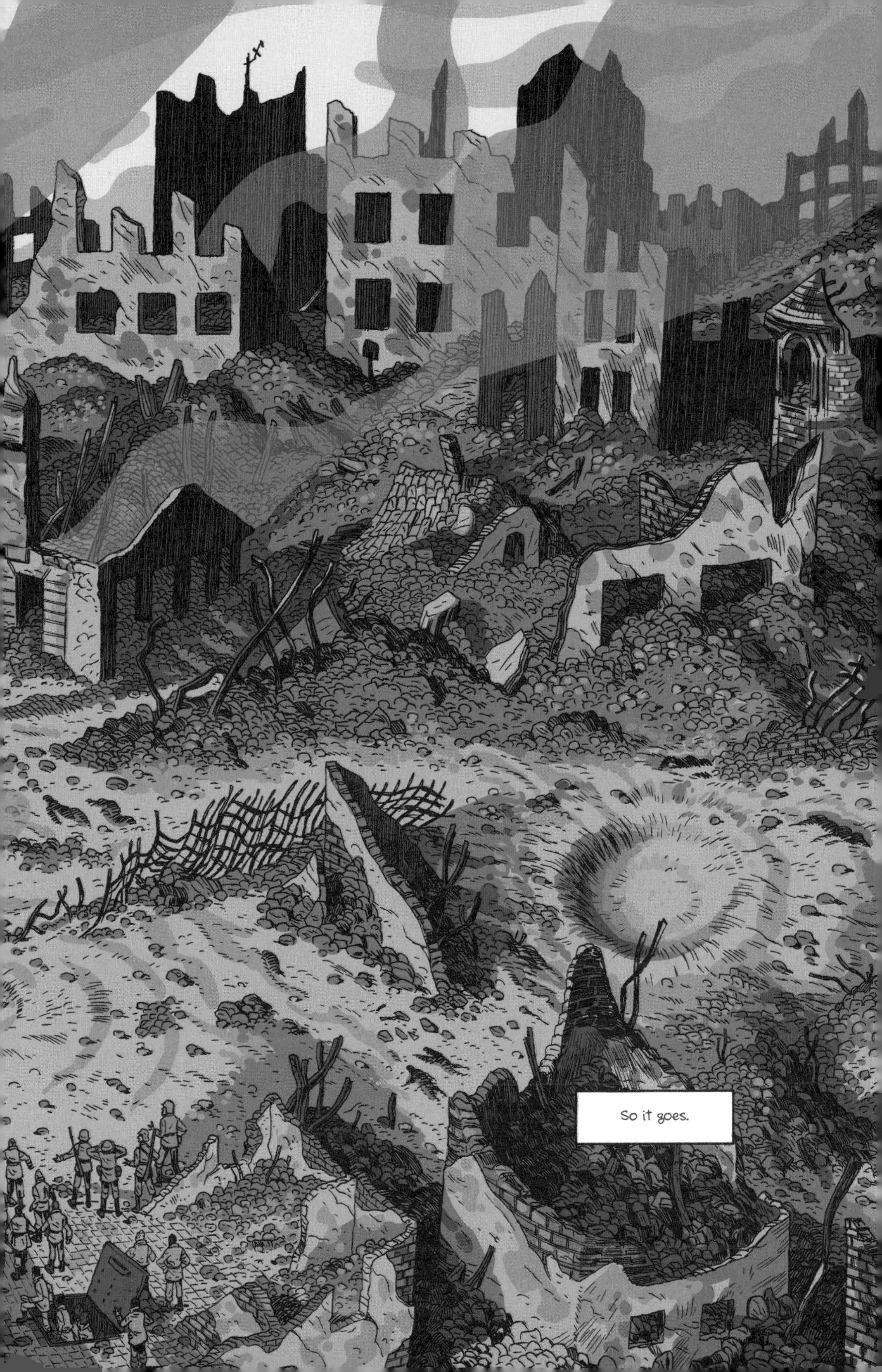
So it goes.

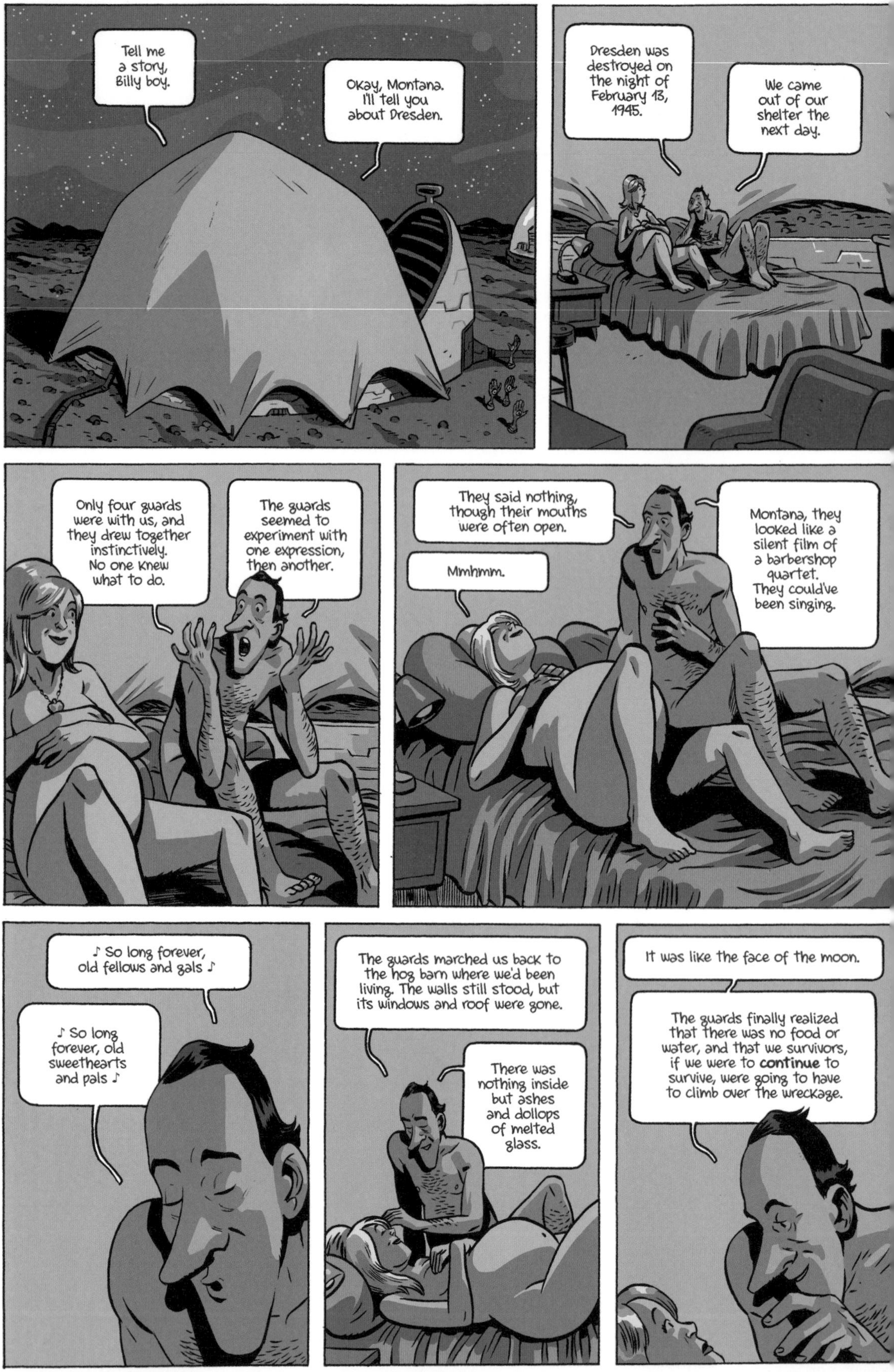

Tell me a story, Billy boy.
Okay, Montana. I'll tell you about Dresden.
Dresden was destroyed on the night of February 13, 1945.
We came out of our shelter the next day.
Only four guards were with us, and they drew together instinctively. No one knew what to do.
The guards seemed to experiment with one expression, then another.
They said nothing, though their mouths were often open.
Mmhmm.
Montana, they looked like a silent film of a barbershop quartet. They could've been singing.
♪ So long forever, old fellows and gals ♪
♪ So long forever, old sweethearts and pals ♪
The guards marched us back to the hog barn where we'd been living. The walls still stood, but its windows and roof were gone.
There was nothing inside but ashes and dollops of melted glass.
It was like the face of the moon.
The guards finally realized that there was no food or water, and that we survivors, if we were to **continue** to survive, were going to have to climb over the wreckage.

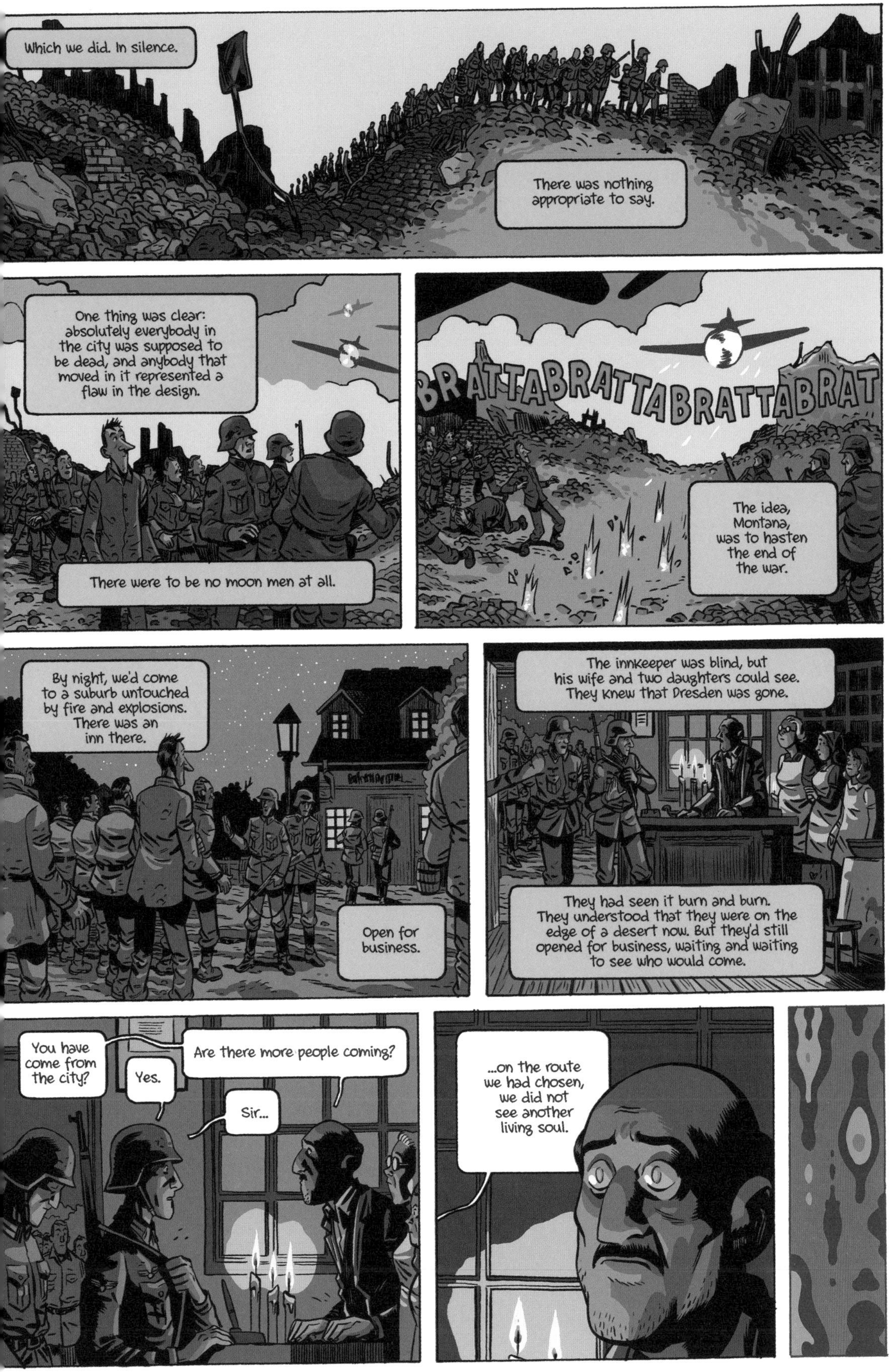
Which we did. In silence.
There was nothing appropriate to say.
One thing was clear: absolutely everybody in the city was supposed to be dead, and anybody that moved in it represented a flaw in the design.
There were to be no moon men at all.
BRATTABRATTABRATTABRAT
The idea, Montana, was to hasten the end of the war.
By night, we'd come to a suburb untouched by fire and explosions. There was an inn there.
Open for business.
The innkeeper was blind, but his wife and two daughters could see. They knew that Dresden was gone.
They had seen it burn and burn. They understood that they were on the edge of a desert now. But they'd still opened for business, waiting and waiting to see who would come.
You have come from the city?
Yes.
Are there more people coming?
Sir...
...on the route we had chosen, we did not see another living soul.

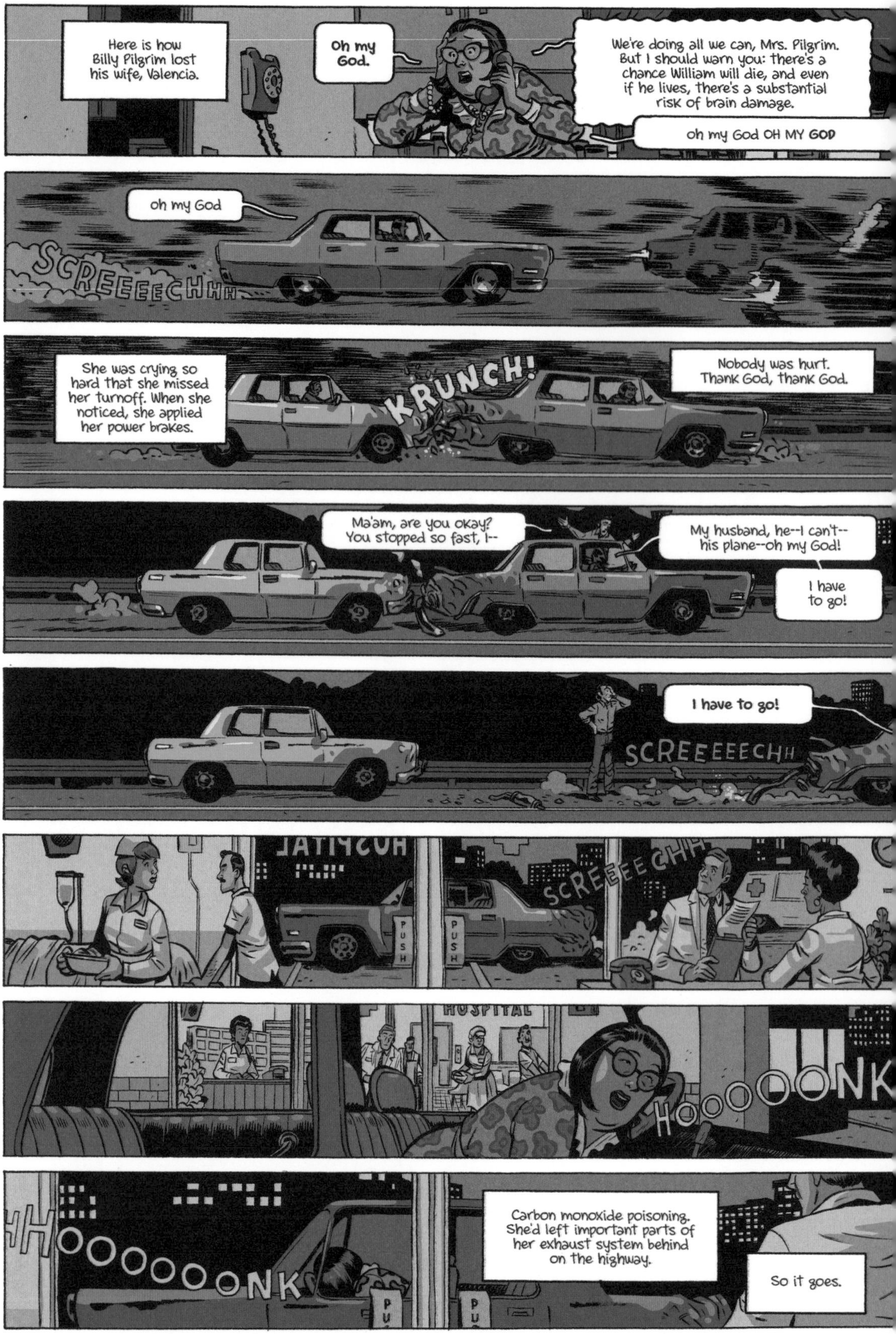
Here is how Billy Pilgrim lost his wife, Valencia.
Oh my God.
We're doing all we can, Mrs. Pilgrim. But I should warn you: there's a chance William will die, and even if he lives, there's a substantial risk of brain damage.
oh my God OH MY GOD
oh my God
SCREEEEECHHH
She was crying so hard that she missed her turnoff. When she noticed, she applied her power brakes.
KRUNCH!
Nobody was hurt. Thank God, thank God.
Ma'am, are you okay? You stopped so fast, I--
My husband, he--I can't-- his plane--oh my God!
I have to go!
I have to go!
SCREEEEECHH
HOSPITAL
SCREEEECHH
PUSH
PUSH
HOSPITAL
HOOOOONK
HHOOOOOOONK
Carbon monoxide poisoning. She'd left important parts of her exhaust system behind on the highway.
So it goes.

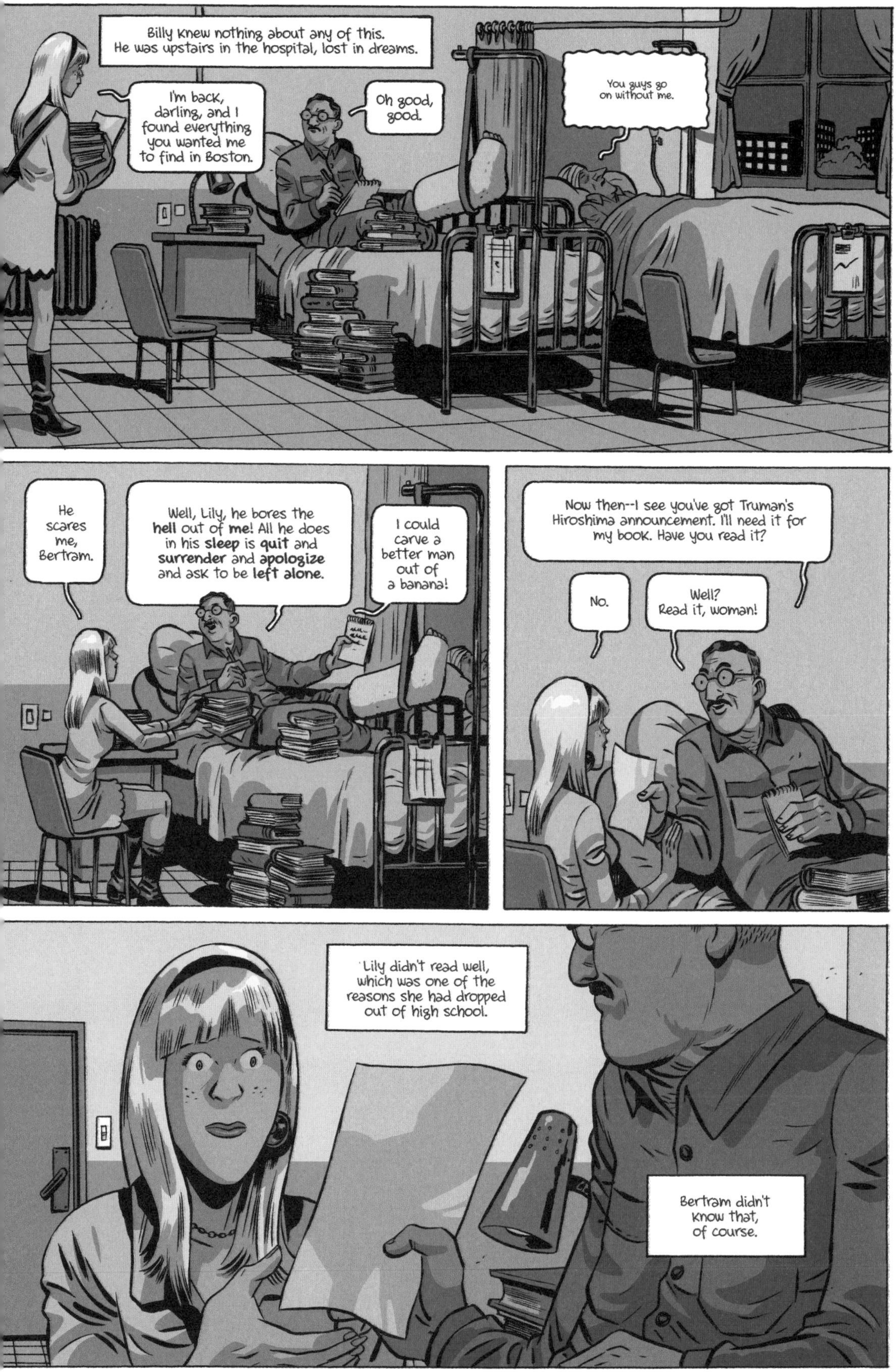
Billy knew nothing about any of this.
He was upstairs in the hospital, lost in dreams.
I'm back, darling, and I found everything you wanted me to find in Boston.
Oh good, good.
You guys go on without me.
He scares me, Bertram.
Well, Lily, he bores the **hell** out of **me**! All he does in his **sleep** is **quit** and **surrender** and **apologize** and ask to be **left alone**.
I could carve a better man out of a banana!
Now then--I see you've got Truman's Hiroshima announcement. I'll need it for my book. Have you read it?
No.
Well? Read it, woman!
Lily didn't read well, which was one of the reasons she had dropped out of high school.
Bertram didn't know that, of course.

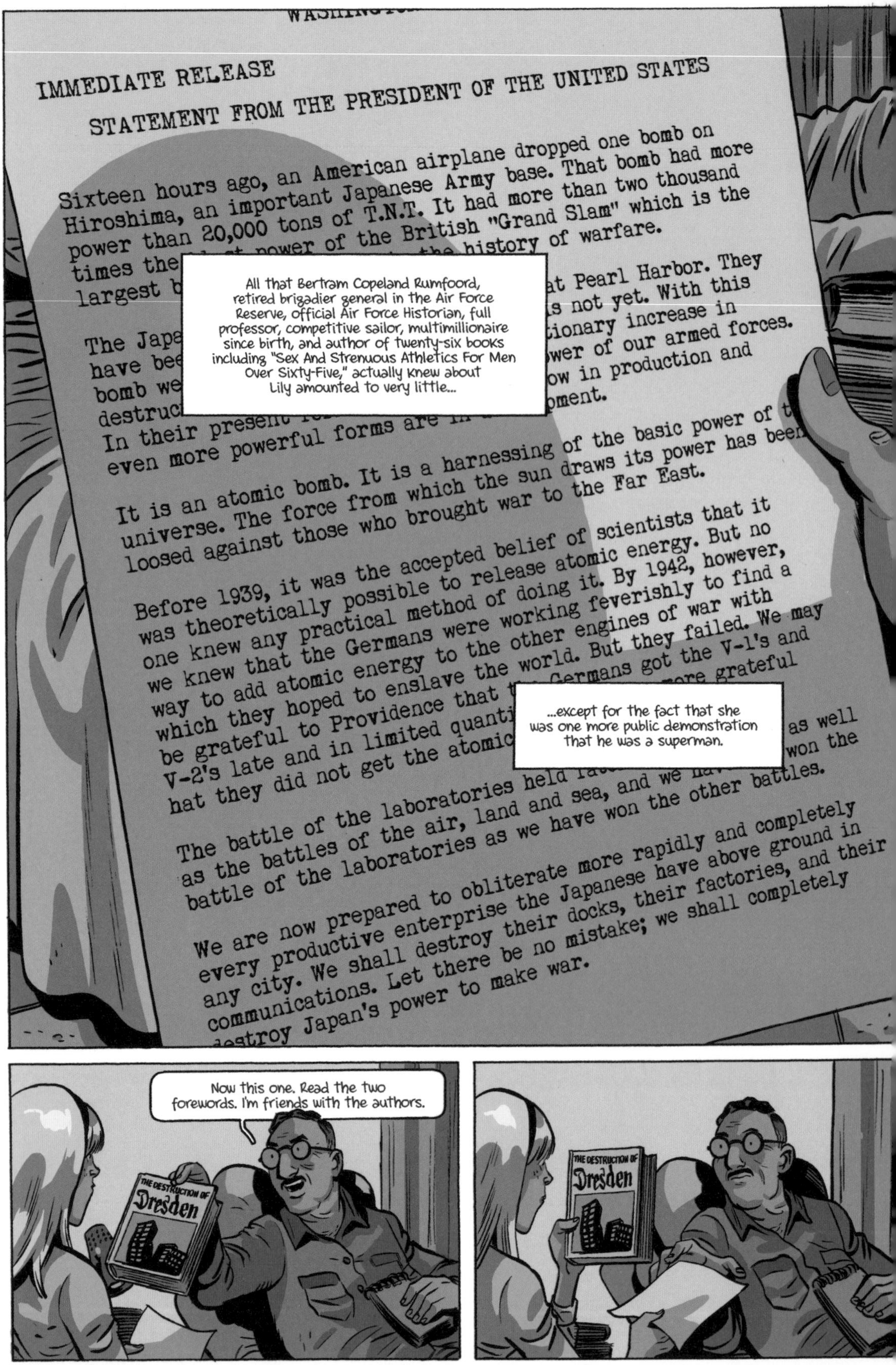
IMMEDIATE RELEASE
STATEMENT FROM THE PRESIDENT OF THE UNITED STATES
Sixteen hours ago, an American airplane dropped one bomb on
Hiroshima, an important Japanese Army base. That bomb had more
power than 20,000 tons of T.N.T. It had more than two thousand
times the
largest b
at Pearl Harbor. They
is not yet. With this
tionary increase in
ower of our armed forces.
ow in production and
pment.
The Japa
have bee
bomb we
destruc
In their present
even more powerful forms are in
All that Bertram Copeland Rumfoord, retired brigadier general in the Air Force Reserve, official Air Force Historian, full professor, competitive sailor, multimillionaire since birth, and author of twenty-six books including "Sex And Strenuous Athletics For Men Over Sixty-Five," actually knew about Lily amounted to very little...
It is an atomic bomb. It is a harnessing of the basic power of t
universe. The force from which the sun draws its power has been
loosed against those who brought war to the Far East.
Before 1939, it was the accepted belief of scientists that it
was theoretically possible to release atomic energy. But no
one knew any practical method of doing it. By 1942, however,
we knew that the Germans were working feverishly to find a
way to add atomic energy to the other engines of war with
which they hoped to enslave the world. But they failed. We may
be grateful to Providence that t
V-2's late and in limited quanti
hat they did not get the atomic
Germans got the V-1's and
more grateful
as well
won the
...except for the fact that she was one more public demonstration that he was a superman.
The battle of the laboratories held
as the battles of the air, land and sea, and we have won the other battles.
battle of the laboratories as we have won the other battles.
We are now prepared to obliterate more rapidly and completely
every productive enterprise the Japanese have above ground in
any city. We shall destroy their docks, their factories, and their
communications. Let there be no mistake; we shall completely
destroy Japan's power to make war.
Now this one. Read the two forewords. I'm friends with the authors.
THE DESTRUCTION OF Dresden
THE DESTRUCTION OF Dresden

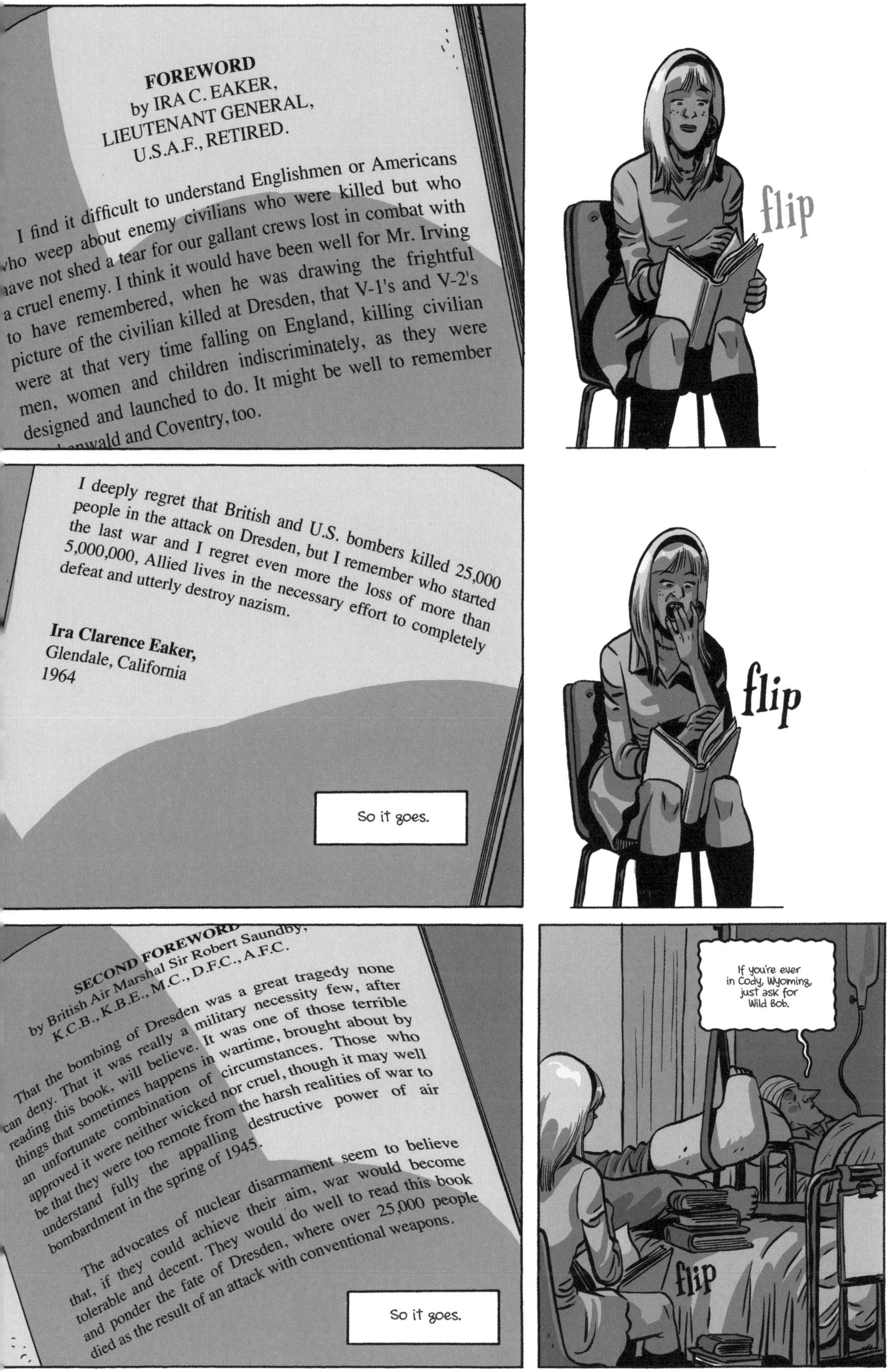
FOREWORD
by IRA C. EAKER,
LIEUTENANT GENERAL,
U.S.A.F., RETIRED.
I find it difficult to understand Englishmen or Americans who weep about enemy civilians who were killed but who have not shed a tear for our gallant crews lost in combat with a cruel enemy. I think it would have been well for Mr. Irving to have remembered, when he was drawing the frightful picture of the civilian killed at Dresden, that V-1's and V-2's were at that very time falling on England, killing civilian men, women and children indiscriminately, as they were designed and launched to do. It might be well to remember
...nwald and Coventry, too.
flip
I deeply regret that British and U.S. bombers killed 25,000 people in the attack on Dresden, but I remember who started the last war and I regret even more the loss of more than 5,000,000, Allied lives in the necessary effort to completely defeat and utterly destroy nazism.
Ira Clarence Eaker,
Glendale, California
1964
So it goes.
flip
SECOND FOREWORD
by British Air Marshal Sir Robert Saundby,
K.C.B., K.B.E., M.C., D.F.C., A.F.C.
That the bombing of Dresden was a great tragedy none can deny. That it was really a military necessity few, after reading this book, will believe. It was one of those terrible things that sometimes happens in wartime, brought about by an unfortunate combination of circumstances. Those who approved it were neither wicked nor cruel, though it may well be that they were too remote from the harsh realities of war to understand fully the appalling destructive power of air bombardment in the spring of 1945.
The advocates of nuclear disarmament seem to believe that, if they could achieve their aim, war would become tolerable and decent. They would do well to read this book and ponder the fate of Dresden, where over 25,000 people died as the result of an attack with conventional weapons.
So it goes.
If you're ever in Cody, Wyoming, just ask for Wild Bob.
flip

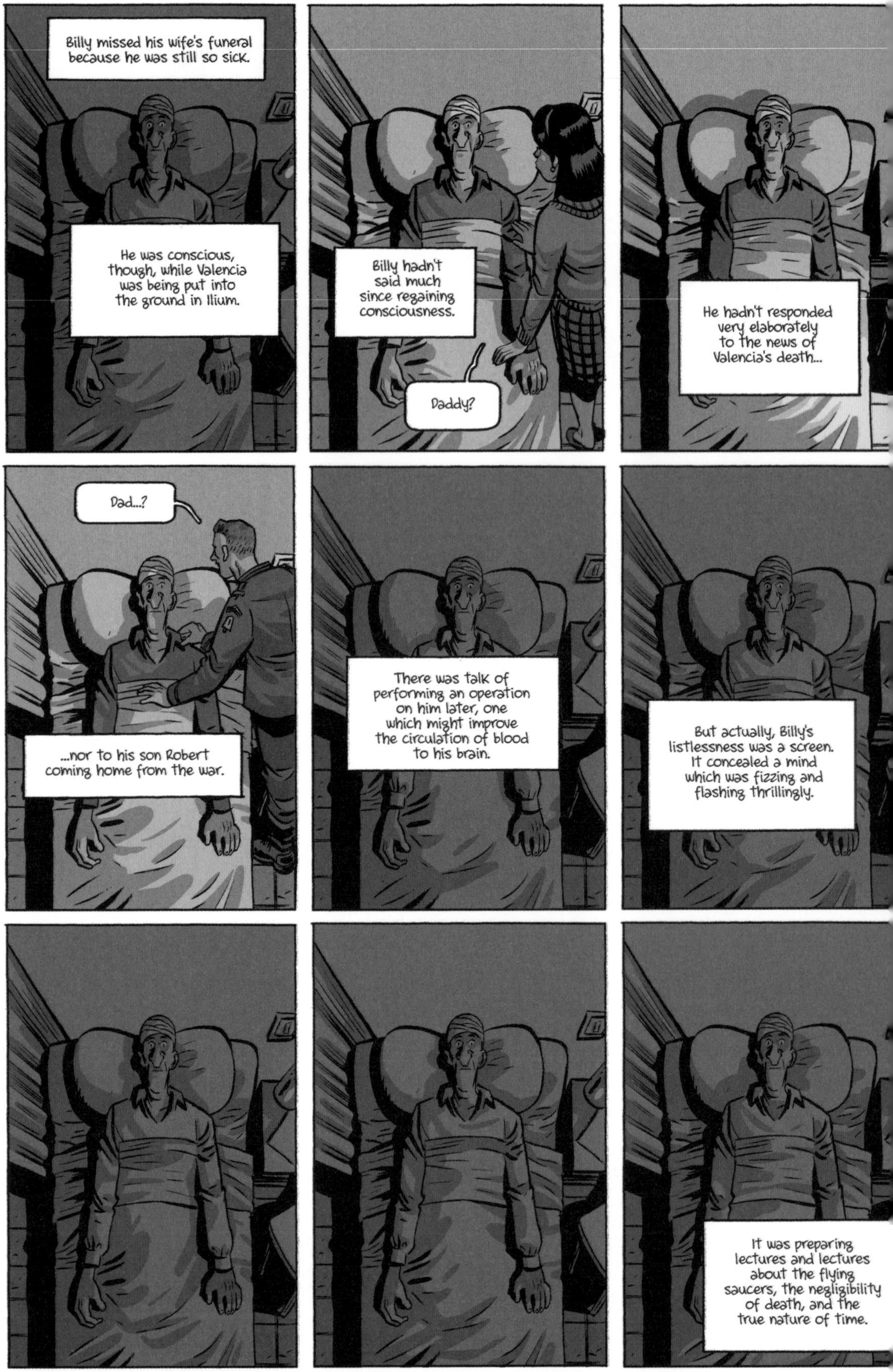
Billy missed his wife's funeral because he was still so sick.
He was conscious, though, while Valencia was being put into the ground in Ilium.
Billy hadn't said much since regaining consciousness.
Daddy?
He hadn't responded very elaborately to the news of Valencia's death...
Dad...?
...nor to his son Robert coming home from the war.
There was talk of performing an operation on him later, one which might improve the circulation of blood to his brain.
But actually, Billy's listlessness was a screen. It concealed a mind which was fizzing and flashing thrillingly.
It was preparing lectures and lectures about the flying saucers, the negligibility of death, and the true nature of time.

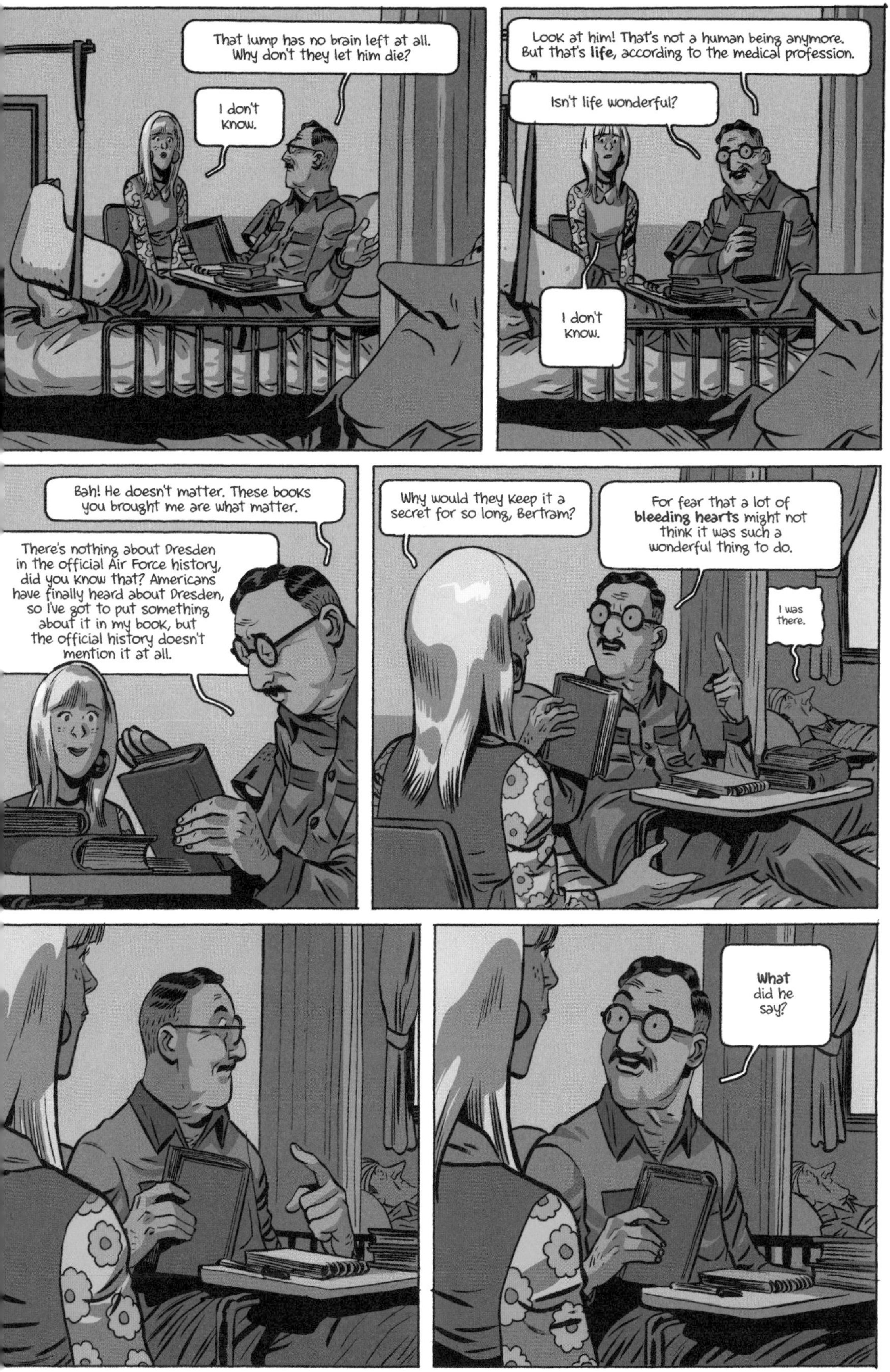

That lump has no brain left at all. Why don't they let him die?
I don't know.
Look at him! That's not a human being anymore. But that's **life**, according to the medical profession.
Isn't life wonderful?
I don't know.
Bah! He doesn't matter. These books you brought me are what matter.
There's nothing about Dresden in the official Air Force history, did you know that? Americans have finally heard about Dresden, so I've got to put something about it in my book, but the official history doesn't mention it at all.
Why would they keep it a secret for so long, Bertram?
For fear that a lot of **bleeding hearts** might not think it was such a wonderful thing to do.
I was there.
What did he say?

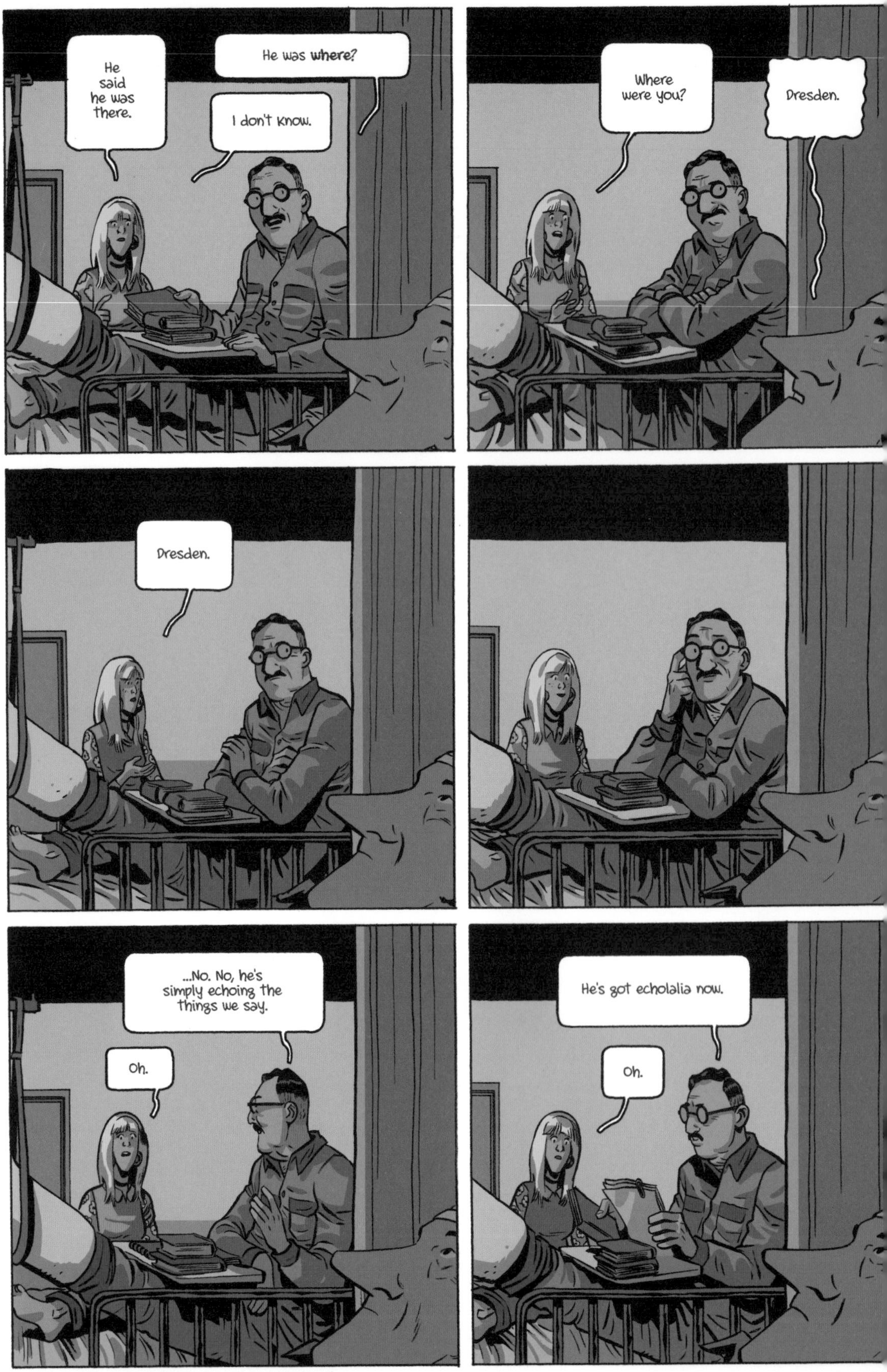
He said he was there.
He was **where**?
I don't know.
Where were you?
Dresden.
Dresden.
...No. No, he's simply echoing the things we say.
Oh.
He's got echolalia now.
Oh.

Rumfoord insisted for several hours that--

Billy has echolalia now.

--and experiments were performed on Billy.

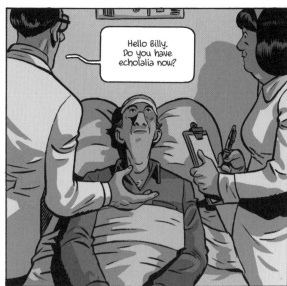

Hello Billy. Do you have echolalia now?

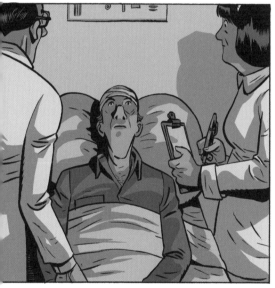

He isn't doing it **now**, obviously. The minute you go away, he'll start doing it again.

Nobody took Rumfoord's diagnosis seriously. The staff thought he was a hateful old man, conceited and cruel.

He often said to them that people who were weak deserved to die.

Whereas the staff, of course, was devoted to the idea that weak people should be helped as much as possible--

--that **nobody** should die.

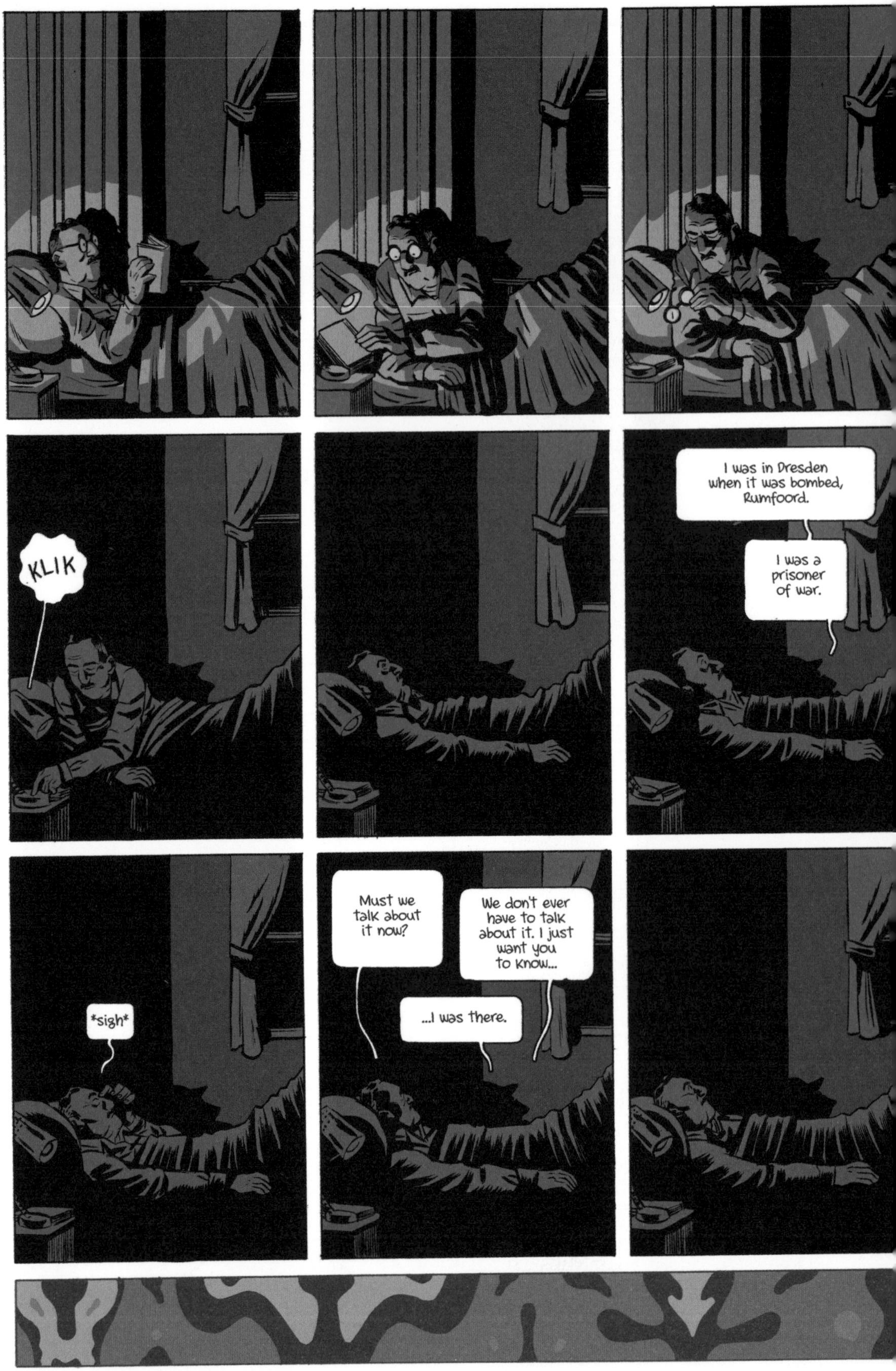
KLIK
I was in Dresden when it was bombed, Rumfoord.
I was a prisoner of war.
sigh
Must we talk about it now?
We don't ever have to talk about it. I just want you to know...
...I was there.

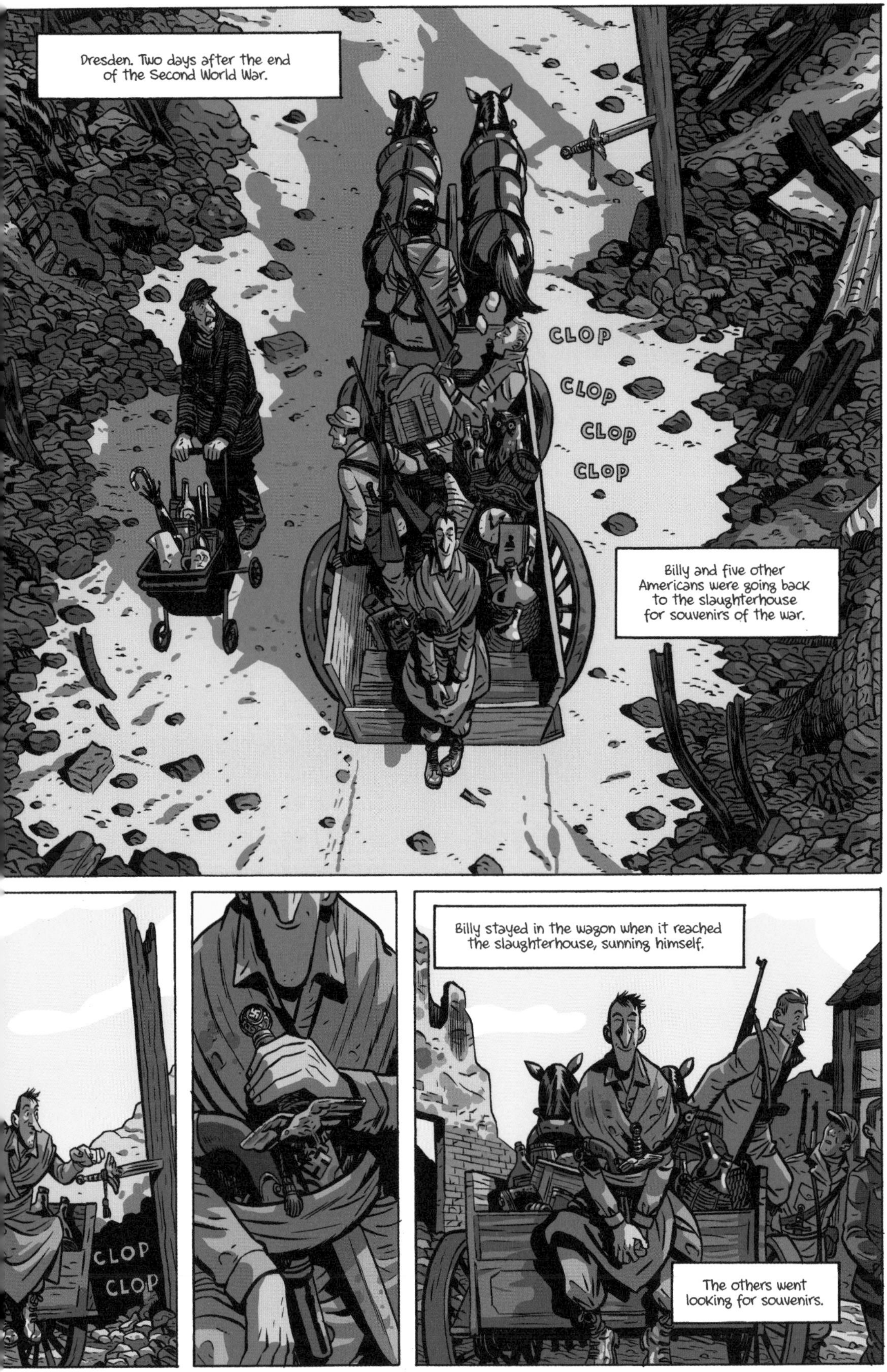
Dresden. Two days after the end of the Second World War.
CLOP
CLOP
CLOP
CLOP
Billy and five other Americans were going back to the slaughterhouse for souvenirs of the war.
CLOP
CLOP
Billy stayed in the wagon when it reached the slaughterhouse, sunning himself.
The others went looking for souvenirs.

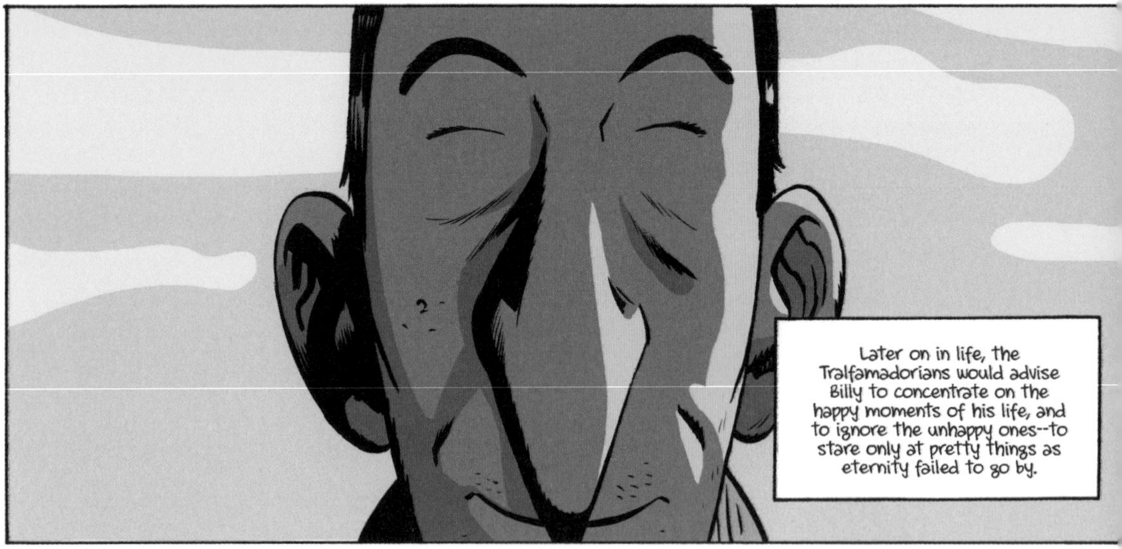
Later on in life, the Tralfamadorians would advise Billy to concentrate on the happy moments of his life, and to ignore the unhappy ones--to stare only at pretty things as eternity failed to go by.

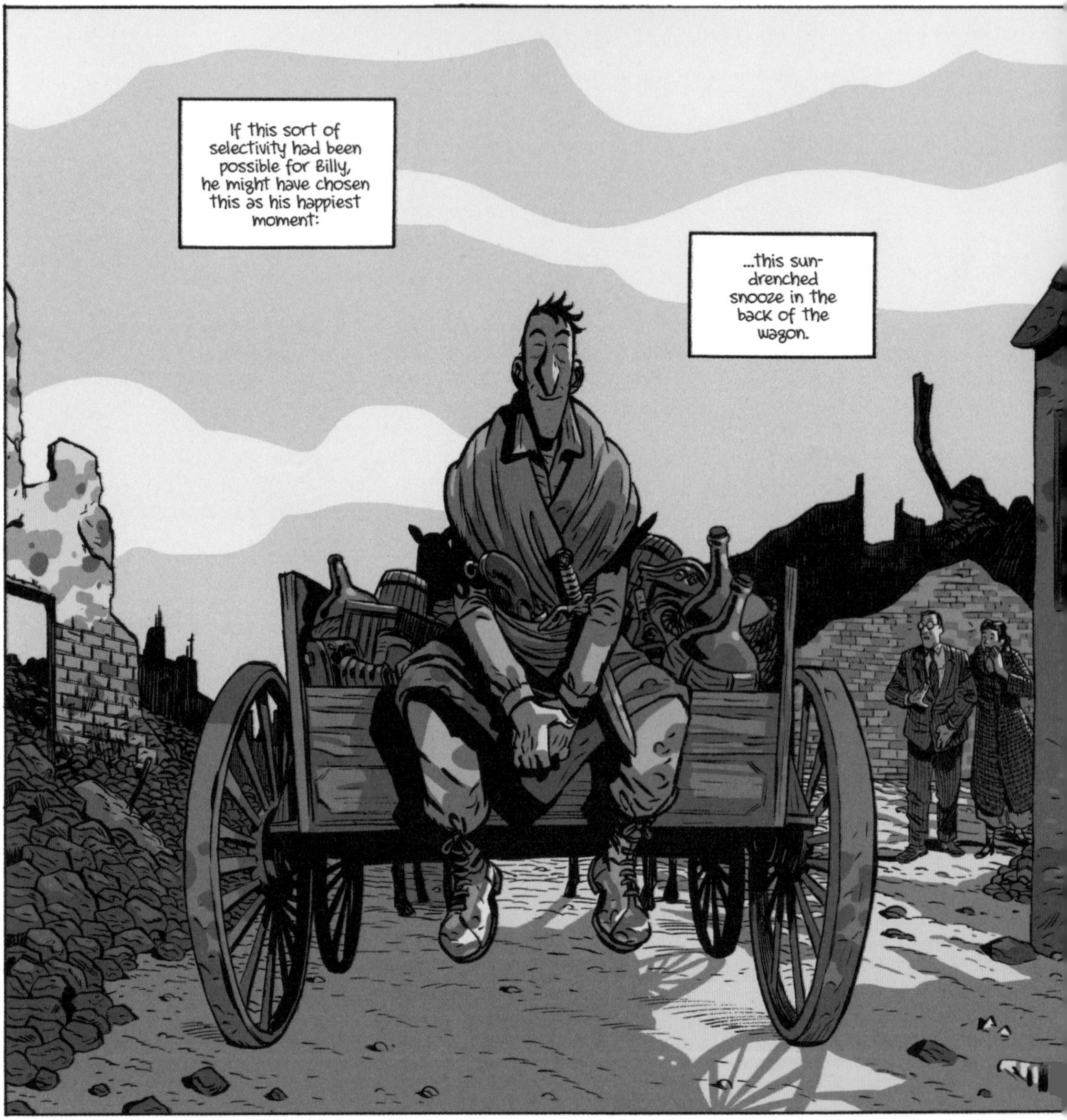
If this sort of selectivity had been possible for Billy, he might have chosen this as his happiest moment:
...this sun-drenched snooze in the back of the wagon.

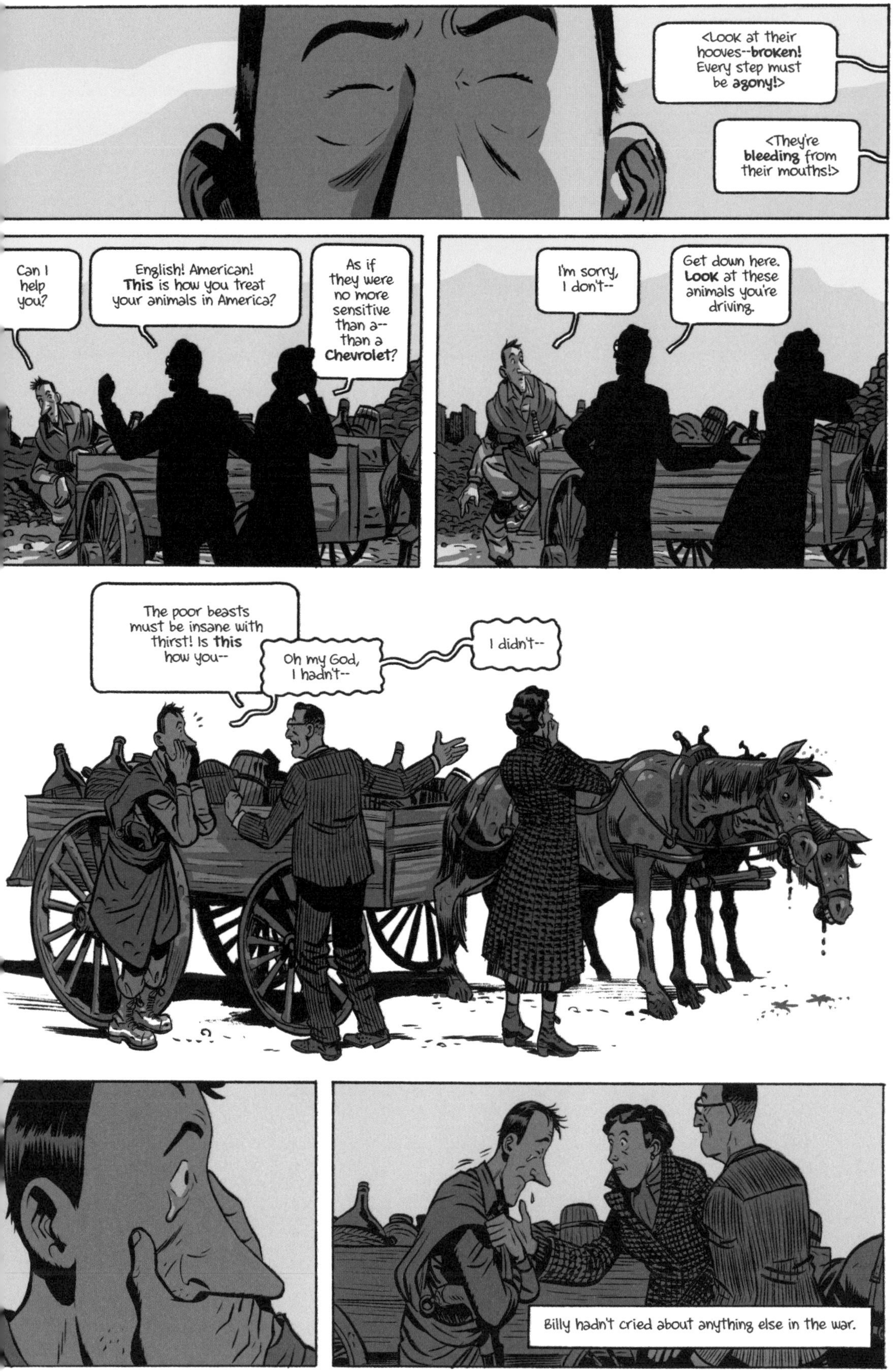
<Look at their hooves--broken! Every step must be agony!>
<They're bleeding from their mouths!>
Can I help you?
English! American! This is how you treat your animals in America?
As if they were no more sensitive than a-- than a Chevrolet?
I'm sorry, I don't--
Get down here. Look at these animals you're driving.
The poor beasts must be insane with thirst! Is this how you--
Oh my God, I hadn't--
I didn't--
Billy hadn't cried about anything else in the war.

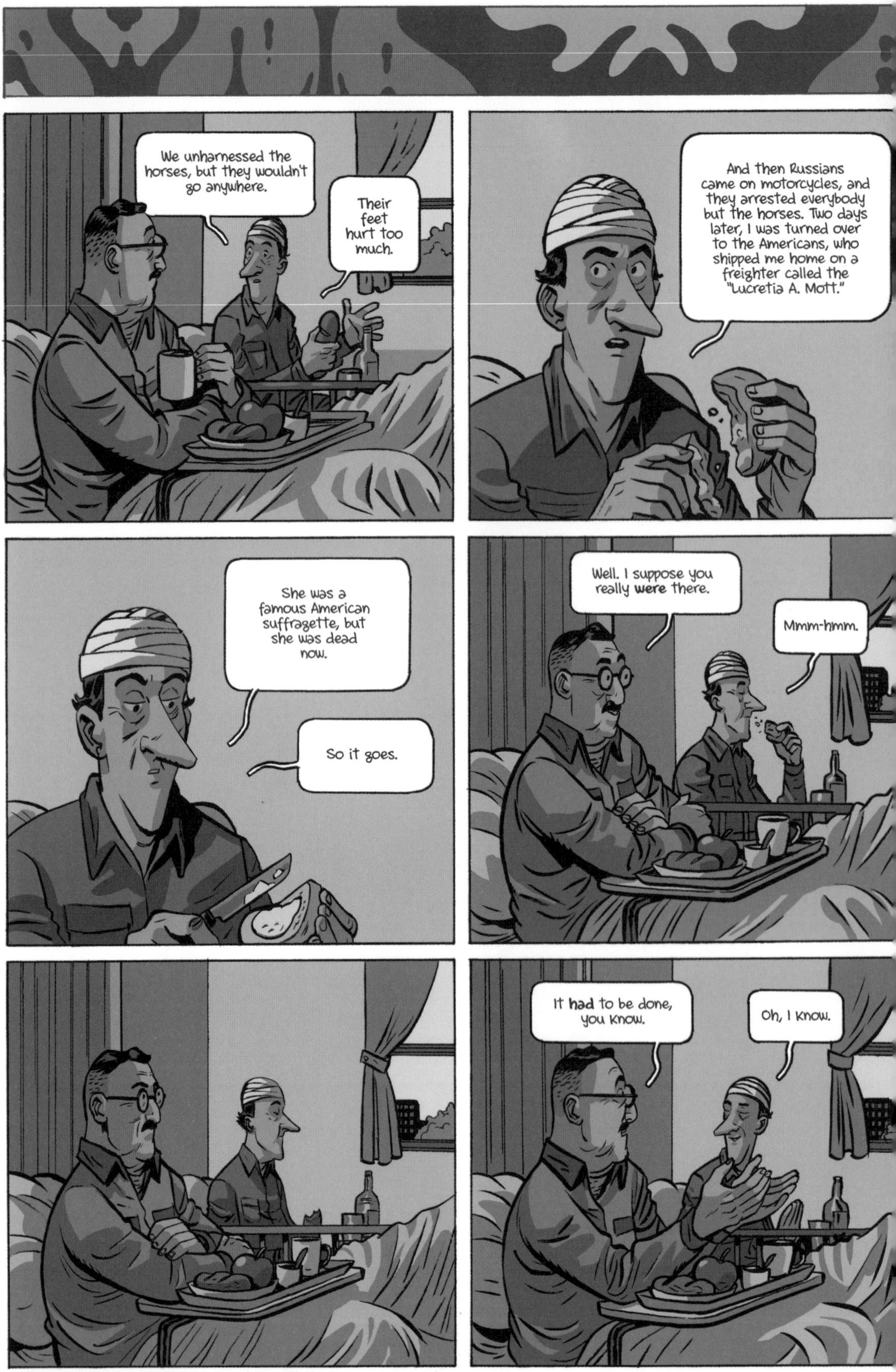
We unharnessed the horses, but they wouldn't go anywhere.
Their feet hurt too much.
And then Russians came on motorcycles, and they arrested everybody but the horses. Two days later, I was turned over to the Americans, who shipped me home on a freighter called the "Lucretia A. Mott."
She was a famous American suffragette, but she was dead now.
So it goes.
Well. I suppose you really **were** there.
Mmm-hmm.
It **had** to be done, you know.
Oh, I know.

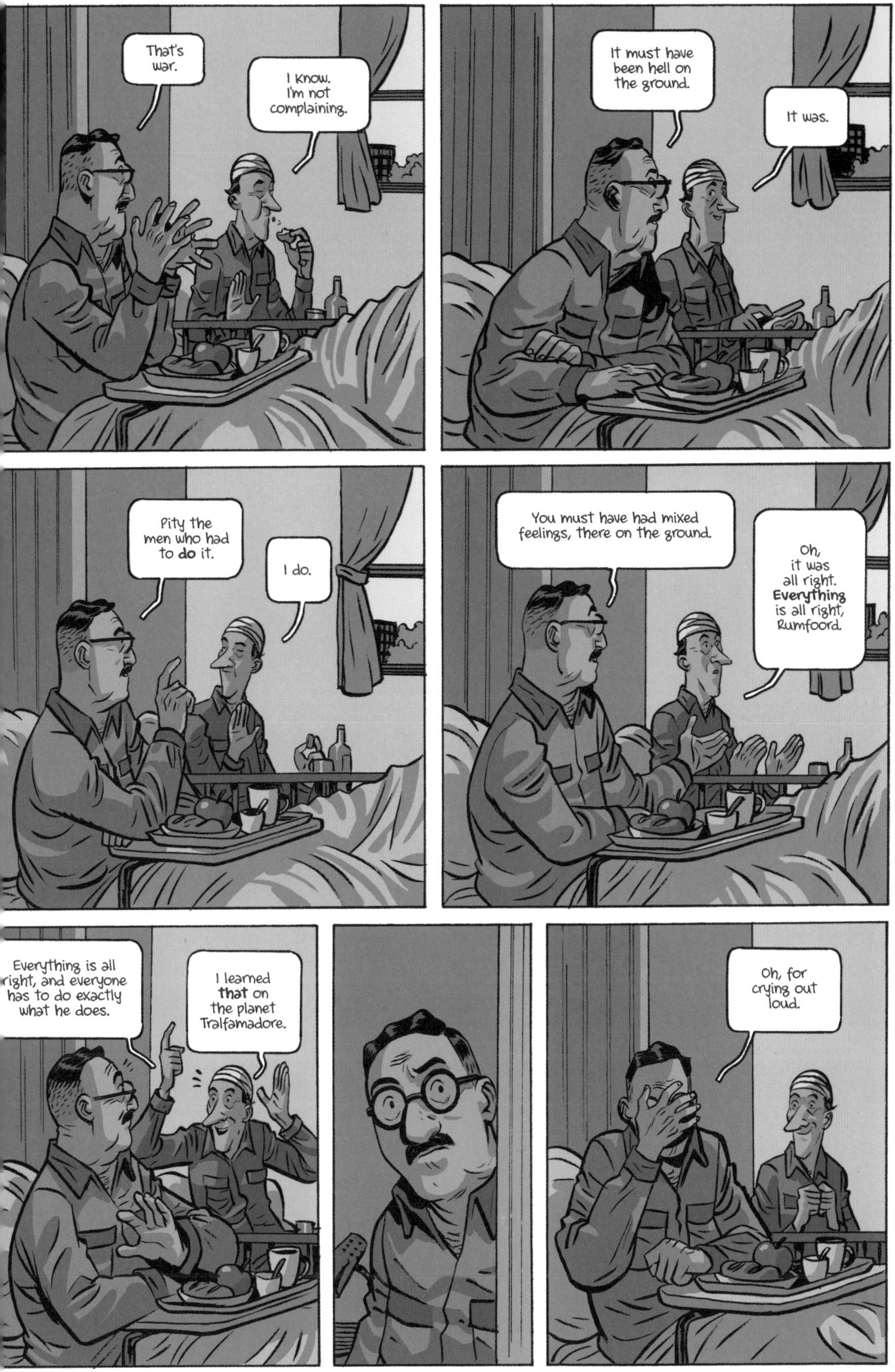
That's war.
I know. I'm not complaining.
It must have been hell on the ground.
It was.
Pity the men who had to **do** it.
I do.
You must have had mixed feelings, there on the ground.
Oh, it was all right. **Everything** is all right, Rumfoord.
Everything is all right, and everyone has to do exactly what he does.
I learned **that** on the planet Tralfamadore.
Oh, for crying out loud.

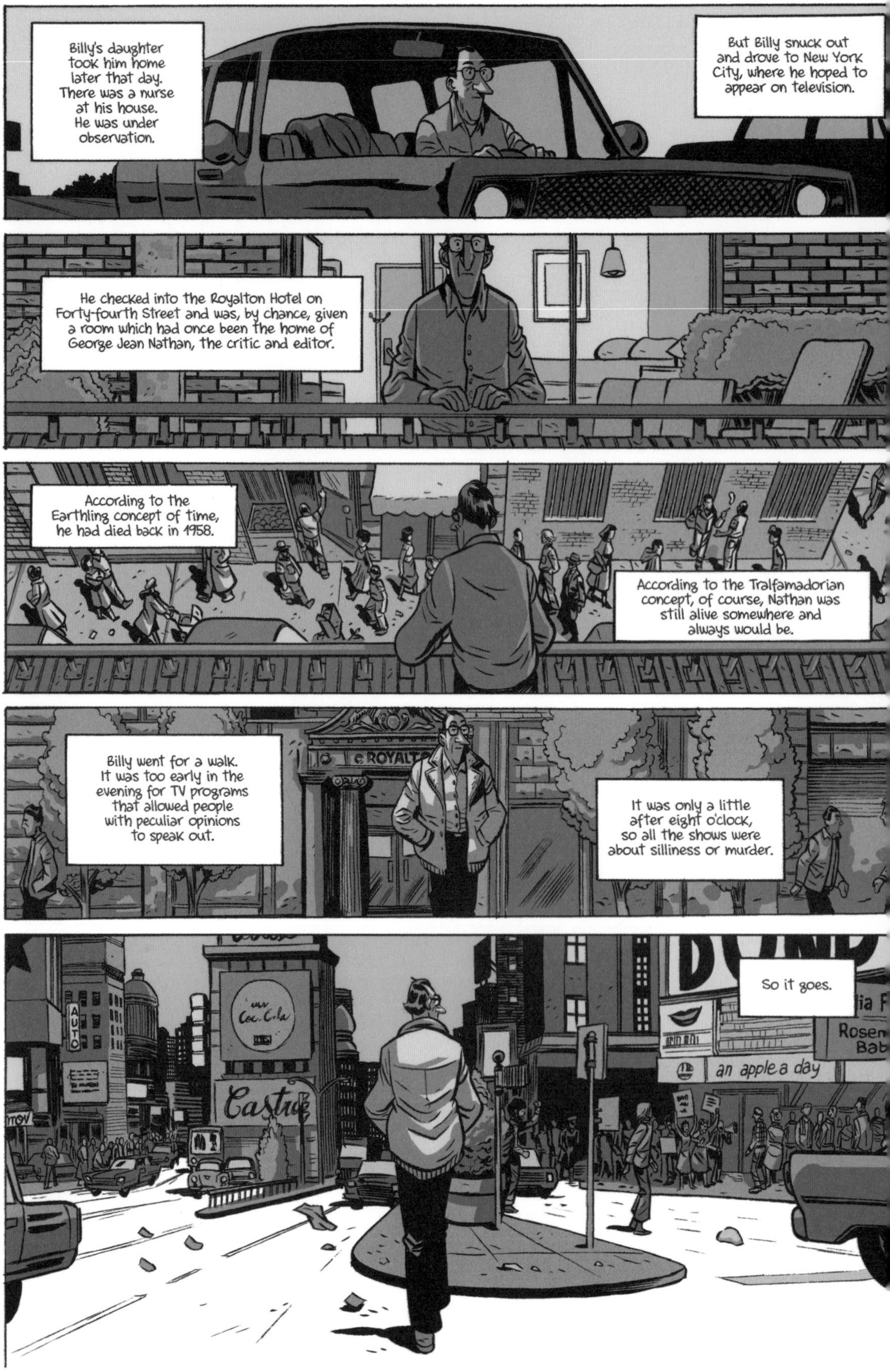
Billy's daughter took him home later that day. There was a nurse at his house. He was under observation.
But Billy snuck out and drove to New York City, where he hoped to appear on television.
He checked into the Royalton Hotel on Forty-fourth Street and was, by chance, given a room which had once been the home of George Jean Nathan, the critic and editor.
According to the Earthling concept of time, he had died back in 1958.
According to the Tralfamadorian concept, of course, Nathan was still alive somewhere and always would be.
Billy went for a walk. It was too early in the evening for TV programs that allowed people with peculiar opinions to speak out.
It was only a little after eight o'clock, so all the shows were about silliness or murder.
So it goes.
an apple a day

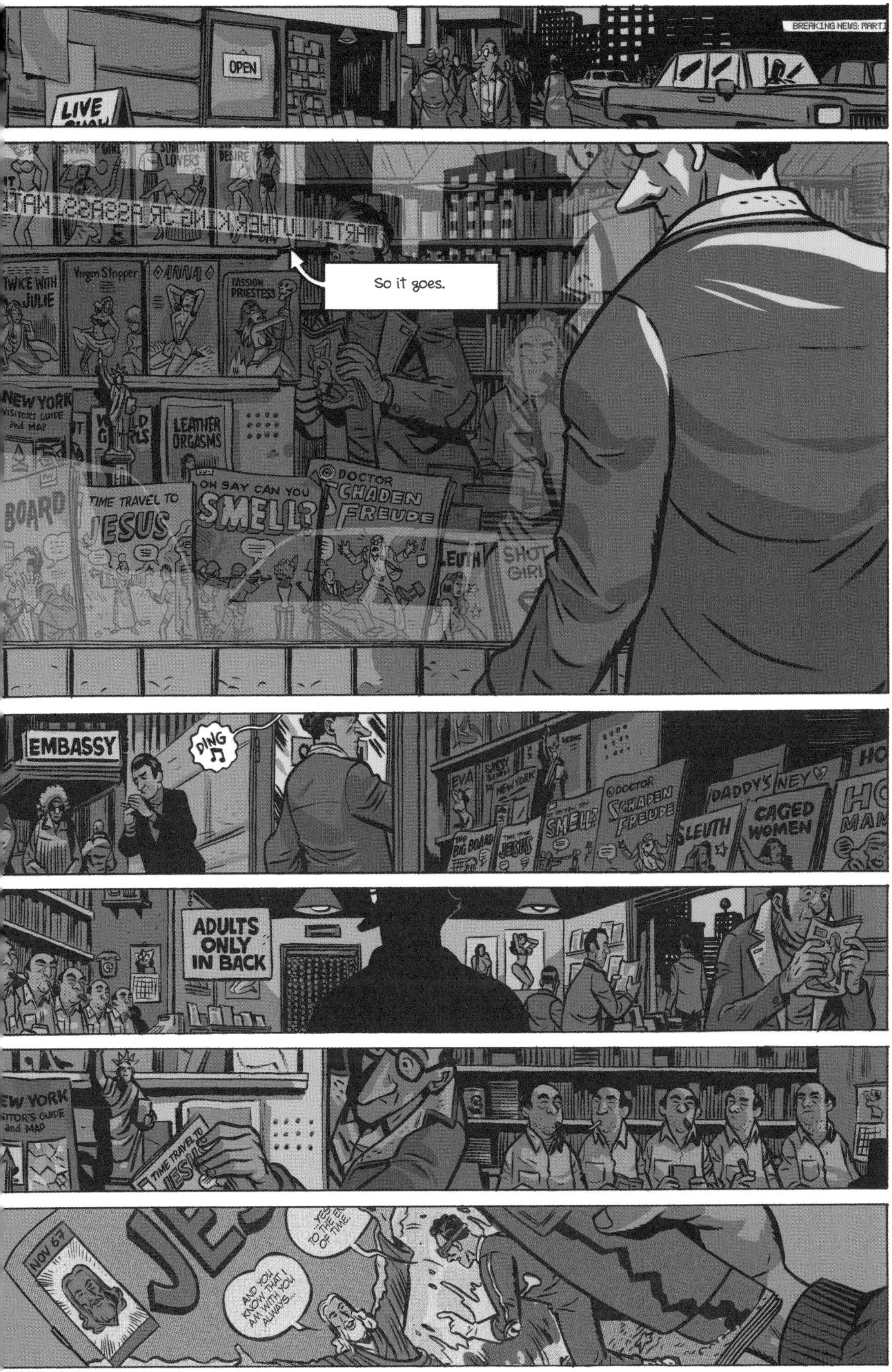

BREAKING NEWS: MARTI
OPEN
LIVE
SWAMP GIRL
SUBURBAN LOVERS
MARTIN LUTHER KING JR. ASSASSINATI
So it goes.
TWICE WITH JULIE
Virgin Stripper
ANNA
PASSION PRIESTESS
NEW YORK VISITOR'S GUIDE and MAP
LEATHER ORGASMS
BOARD
TIME TRAVEL TO JESUS
OH SAY CAN YOU SMELL?
DOCTOR SCHADEN FREUDE
SLEUTH
EMBASSY
DING
DOCTOR SCHADEN FREUDE
DADDY'S
CAGED WOMEN
SLEUTH
ADULTS ONLY IN BACK
NEW YORK VISITOR'S GUIDE and MAP
NOV 67
...YES TO THE END OF TIME.
AND YOU KNOW THAT I AM WITH YOU ALWAYS...

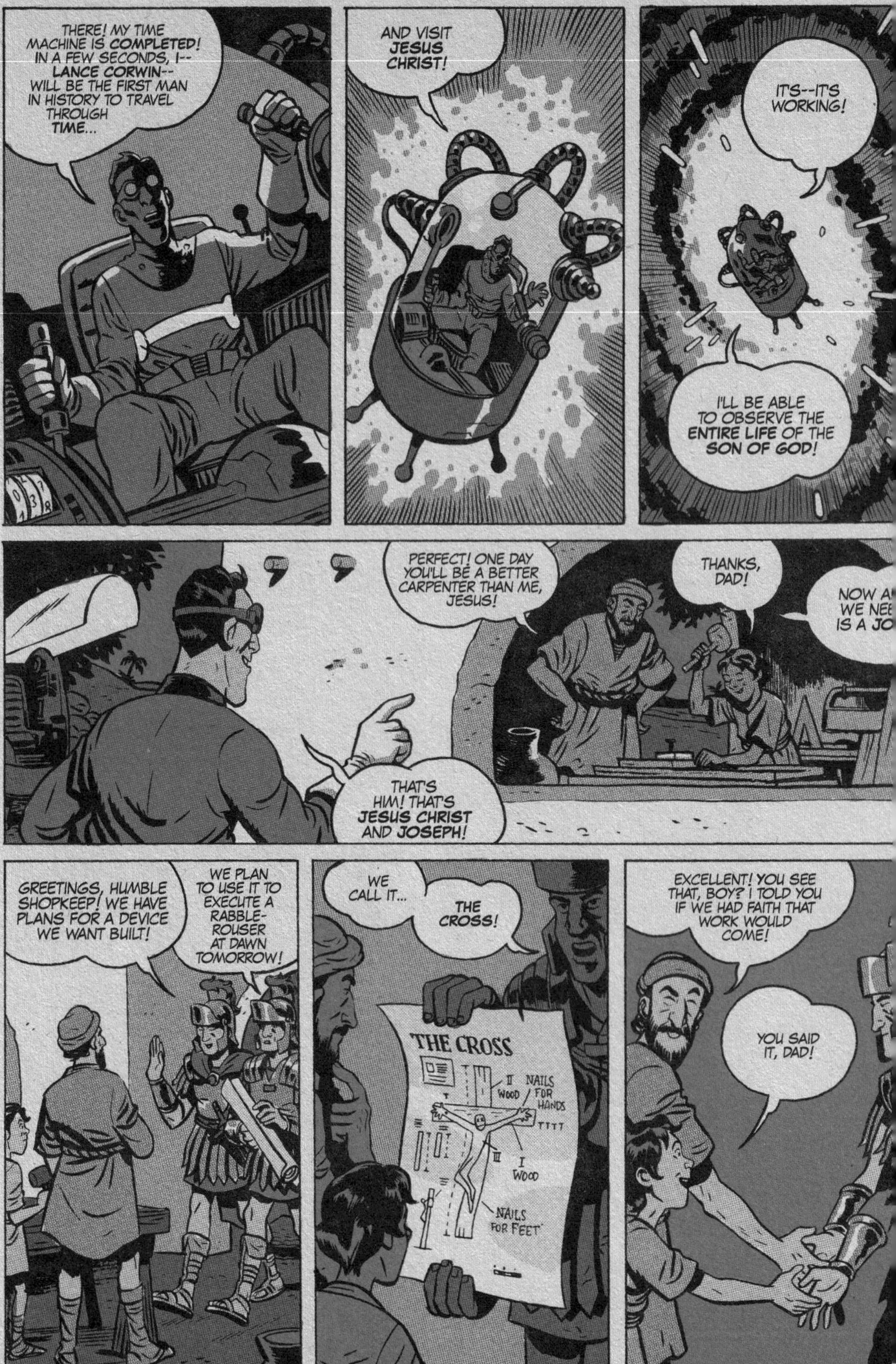

THERE! MY TIME MACHINE IS **COMPLETED!** IN A FEW SECONDS, I-- **LANCE CORWIN**-- WILL BE THE FIRST MAN IN HISTORY TO TRAVEL THROUGH **TIME**...
AND VISIT **JESUS CHRIST!**
IT'S--IT'S WORKING!
I'LL BE ABLE TO OBSERVE THE **ENTIRE LIFE** OF THE **SON OF GOD!**
PERFECT! ONE DAY YOU'LL BE A BETTER CARPENTER THAN ME, JESUS!
THANKS, DAD!
THAT'S HIM! THAT'S **JESUS CHRIST** AND **JOSEPH!**
GREETINGS, HUMBLE SHOPKEEP! WE HAVE PLANS FOR A DEVICE WE WANT BUILT!
WE PLAN TO USE IT TO EXECUTE A RABBLE-ROUSER AT DAWN TOMORROW!
WE CALL IT...
THE CROSS!
THE CROSS
II WOOD
NAILS FOR HANDS
III
I WOOD
NAILS FOR FEET
EXCELLENT! YOU SEE THAT, BOY? I TOLD YOU IF WE HAD FAITH THAT WORK WOULD COME!
YOU SAID IT, DAD!

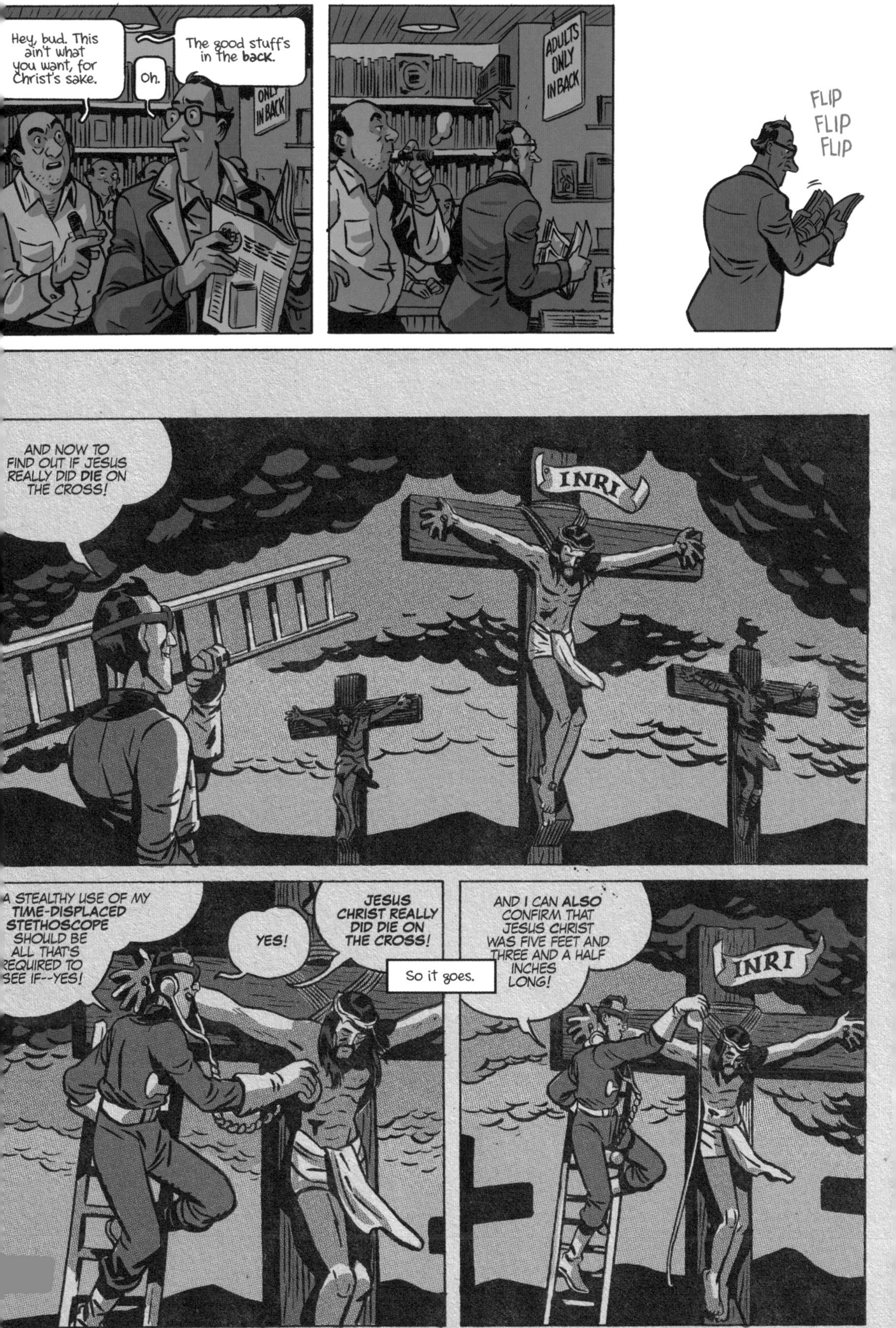
Hey, bud. This ain't what you want, for Christ's sake.
Oh.
The good stuff's in the **back.**
ONLY IN BACK
ADULTS ONLY IN BACK
FLIP FLIP FLIP
AND NOW TO FIND OUT IF JESUS REALLY DID **DIE** ON THE CROSS!
INRI
A STEALTHY USE OF MY **TIME-DISPLACED STETHOSCOPE** SHOULD BE ALL THAT'S REQUIRED TO SEE IF--YES!
YES!
JESUS CHRIST REALLY DID DIE ON THE CROSS!
So it goes.
AND I CAN **ALSO** CONFIRM THAT JESUS CHRIST WAS FIVE FEET AND THREE AND A HALF INCHES LONG!
INRI

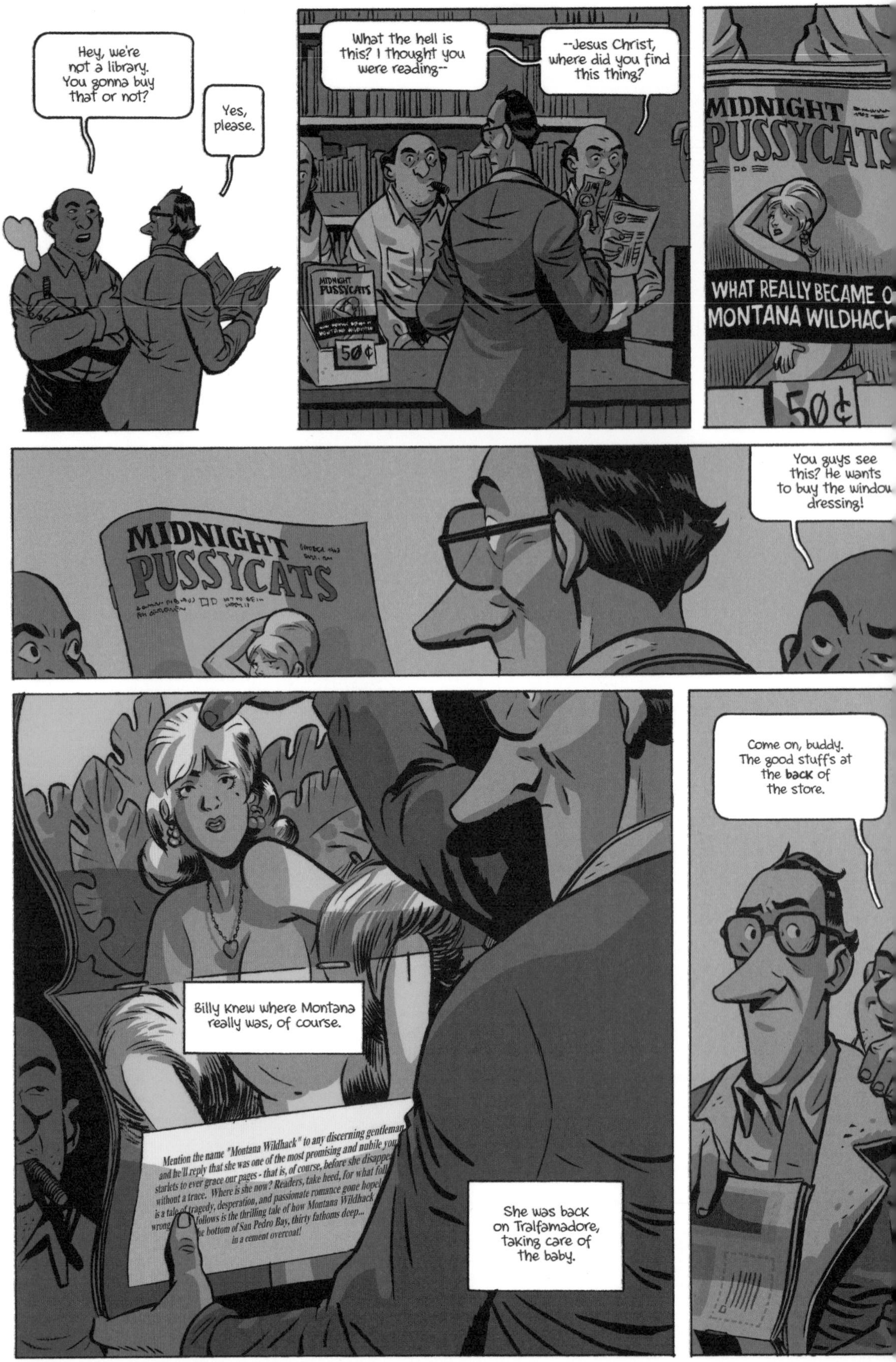
Hey, we're not a library. You gonna buy that or not?
Yes, please.
What the hell is this? I thought you were reading--
--Jesus Christ, where did you find this thing?
MIDNIGHT PUSSYCATS
50¢
MIDNIGHT PUSSYCATS
WHAT REALLY BECAME O
MONTANA WILDHACK
50¢
MIDNIGHT PUSSYCATS
You guys see this? He wants to buy the window dressing!
Billy knew where Montana really was, of course.
Mention the name "Montana Wildhack" to any discerning gentleman
and he'll reply that she was one of the most promising and nubile you
starlets to ever grace our pages - that is, of course, before she disappe
without a trace. Where is she now? Readers, take heed, for what foll
is a tale of tragedy, desperation, and passionate romance gone hopel
wrong follows is the thrilling tale of how Montana Wildhack
he bottom of San Pedro Bay, thirty fathoms deep...
in a cement overcoat!
She was back on Tralfamadore, taking care of the baby.
Come on, buddy. The good stuff's at the back of the store.

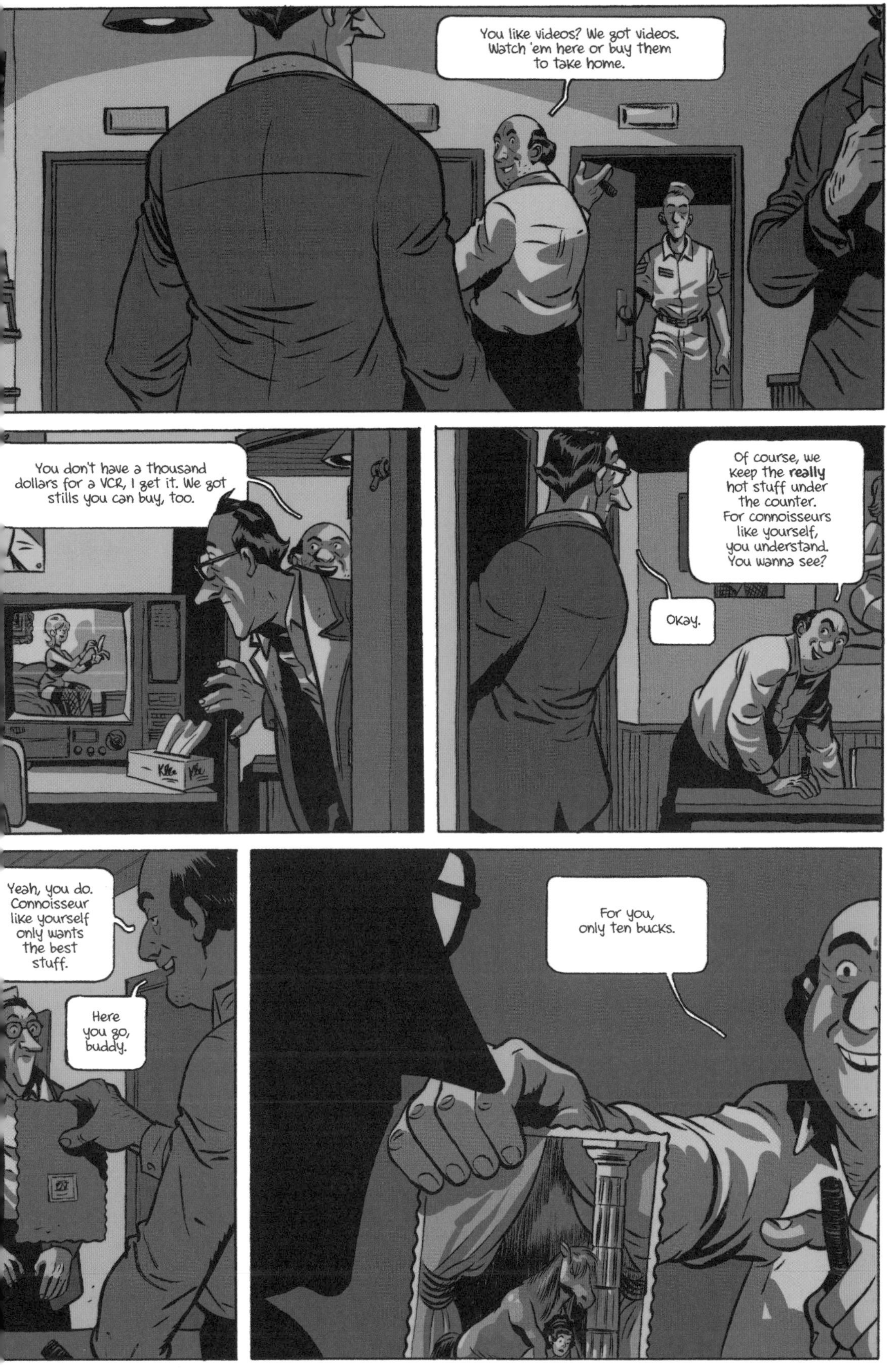
You like videos? We got videos. Watch 'em here or buy them to take home.
You don't have a thousand dollars for a VCR, I get it. We got stills you can buy, too.
Of course, we keep the **really** hot stuff under the counter. For connoisseurs like yourself, you understand. You wanna see?
Okay.
Yeah, you do. Connoisseur like yourself only wants the best stuff.
Here you go, buddy.
For you, only ten bucks.

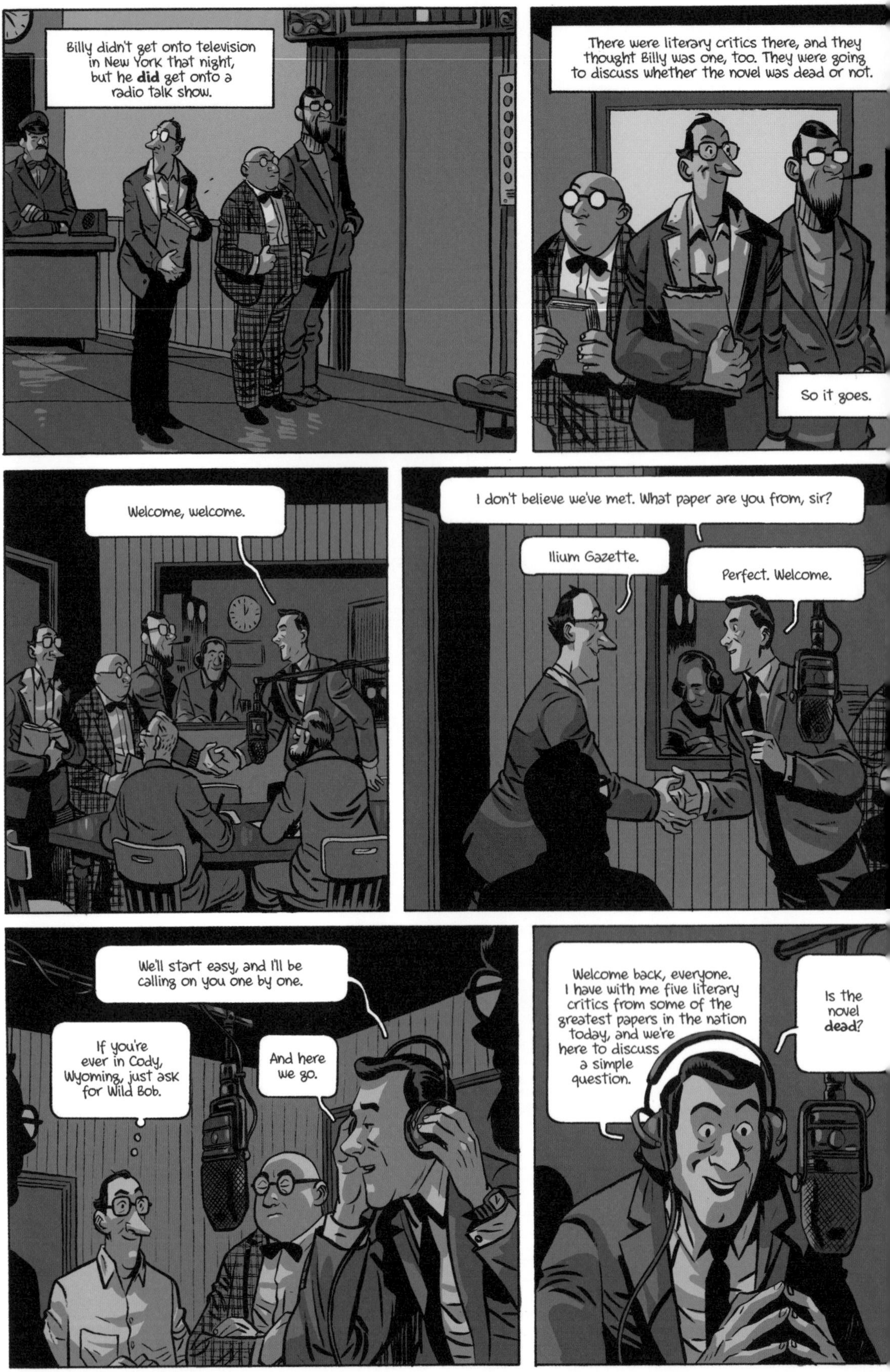
Billy didn't get onto television in New York that night, but he **did** get onto a radio talk show.
There were literary critics there, and they thought Billy was one, too. They were going to discuss whether the novel was dead or not.
So it goes.
Welcome, welcome.
I don't believe we've met. What paper are you from, sir?
Ilium Gazette.
Perfect. Welcome.
We'll start easy, and I'll be calling on you one by one.
If you're ever in Cody, Wyoming, just ask for Wild Bob.
And here we go.
Welcome back, everyone. I have with me five literary critics from some of the greatest papers in the nation today, and we're here to discuss a simple question.
Is the novel **dead**?

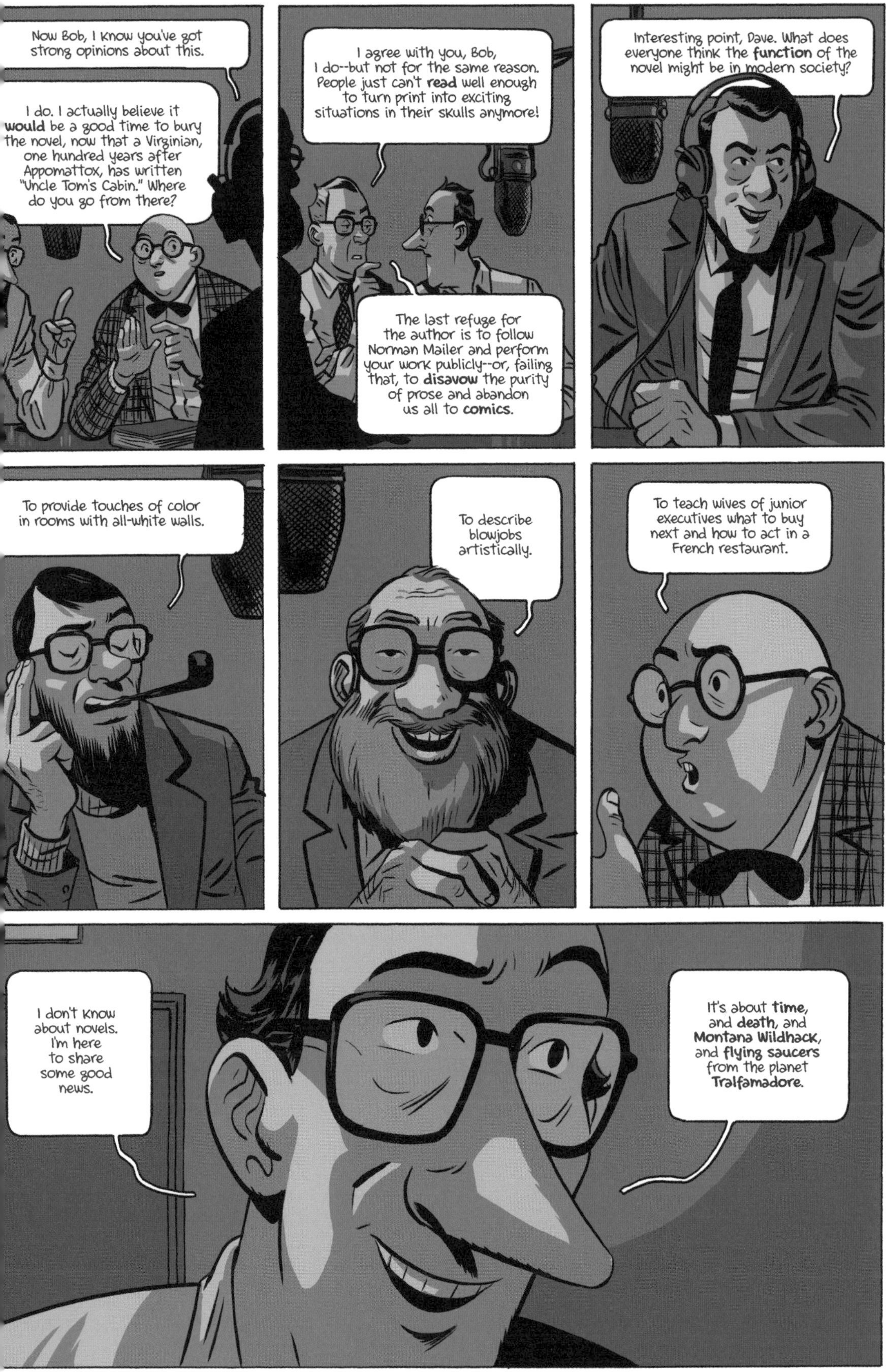
Now Bob, I know you've got strong opinions about this.
I do. I actually believe it **would** be a good time to bury the novel, now that a Virginian, one hundred years after Appomattox, has written "Uncle Tom's Cabin." Where do you go from there?
I agree with you, Bob, I do--but not for the same reason. People just can't **read** well enough to turn print into exciting situations in their skulls anymore!
The last refuge for the author is to follow Norman Mailer and perform your work publicly--or, failing that, to **disavow** the purity of prose and abandon us all to **comics**.
Interesting point, Dave. What does everyone think the **function** of the novel might be in modern society?
To provide touches of color in rooms with all-white walls.
To describe blowjobs artistically.
To teach wives of junior executives what to buy next and how to act in a French restaurant.
I don't know about novels. I'm here to share some good news.
It's about **time**, and **death**, and **Montana Wildhack**, and **flying saucers** from the planet **Tralfamadore**.

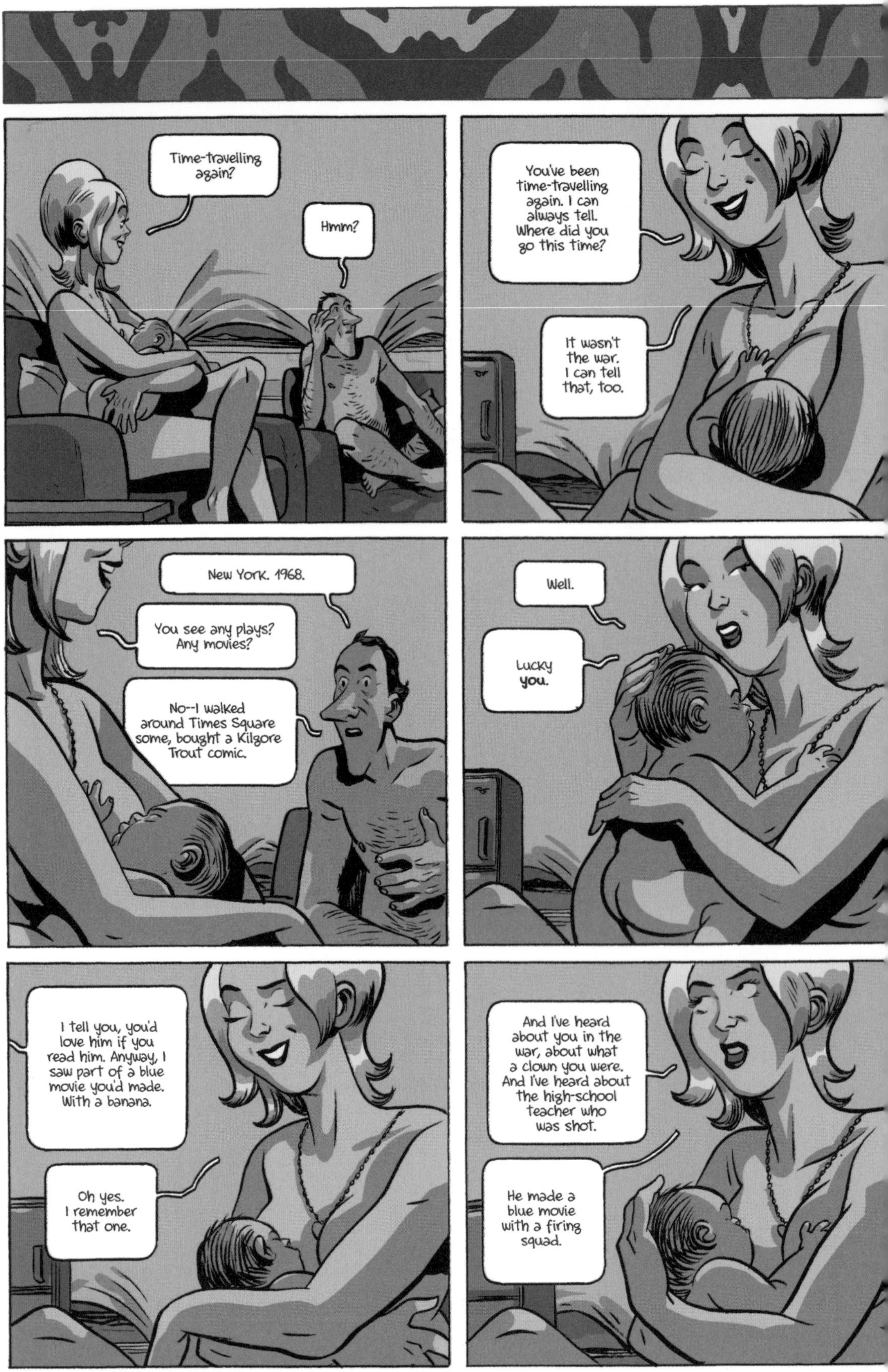
Time-travelling again?
Hmm?
You've been time-travelling again. I can always tell. Where did you go this time?
It wasn't the war. I can tell that, too.
New York. 1968.
You see any plays? Any movies?
No--I walked around Times Square some, bought a Kilgore Trout comic.
Well.
Lucky **you.**
I tell you, you'd love him if you read him. Anyway, I saw part of a blue movie you'd made. With a banana.
Oh yes. I remember that one.
And I've heard about you in the war, about what a clown you were. And I've heard about the high-school teacher who was shot.
He made a blue movie with a firing squad.

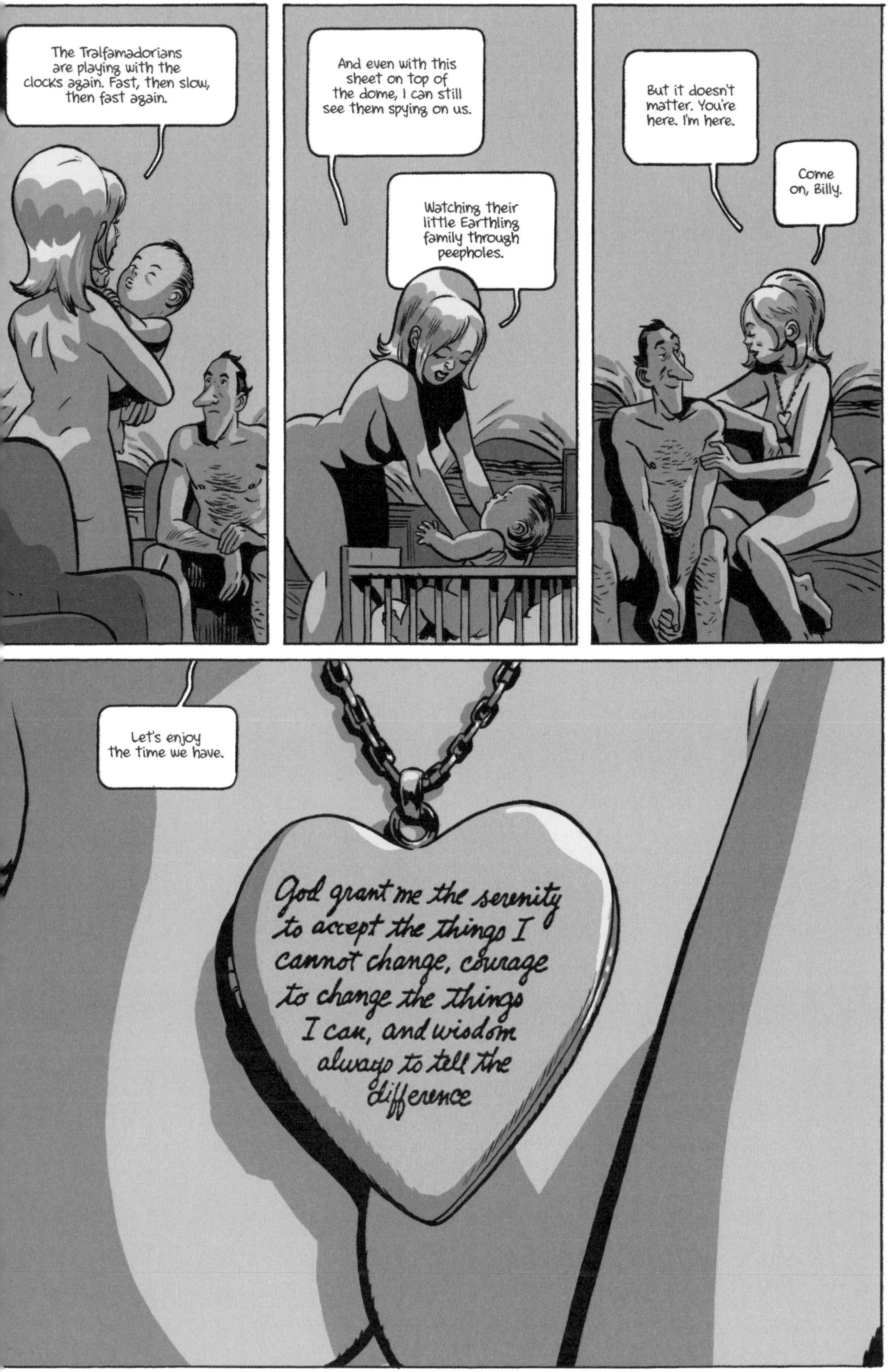
The Tralfamadorians are playing with the clocks again. Fast, then slow, then fast again.
And even with this sheet on top of the dome, I can still see them spying on us.
Watching their little Earthling family through peepholes.
But it doesn't matter. You're here. I'm here.
Come on, Billy.
Let's enjoy the time we have.
God grant me the serenity to accept the things I cannot change, courage to change the things I can, and wisdom always to tell the difference

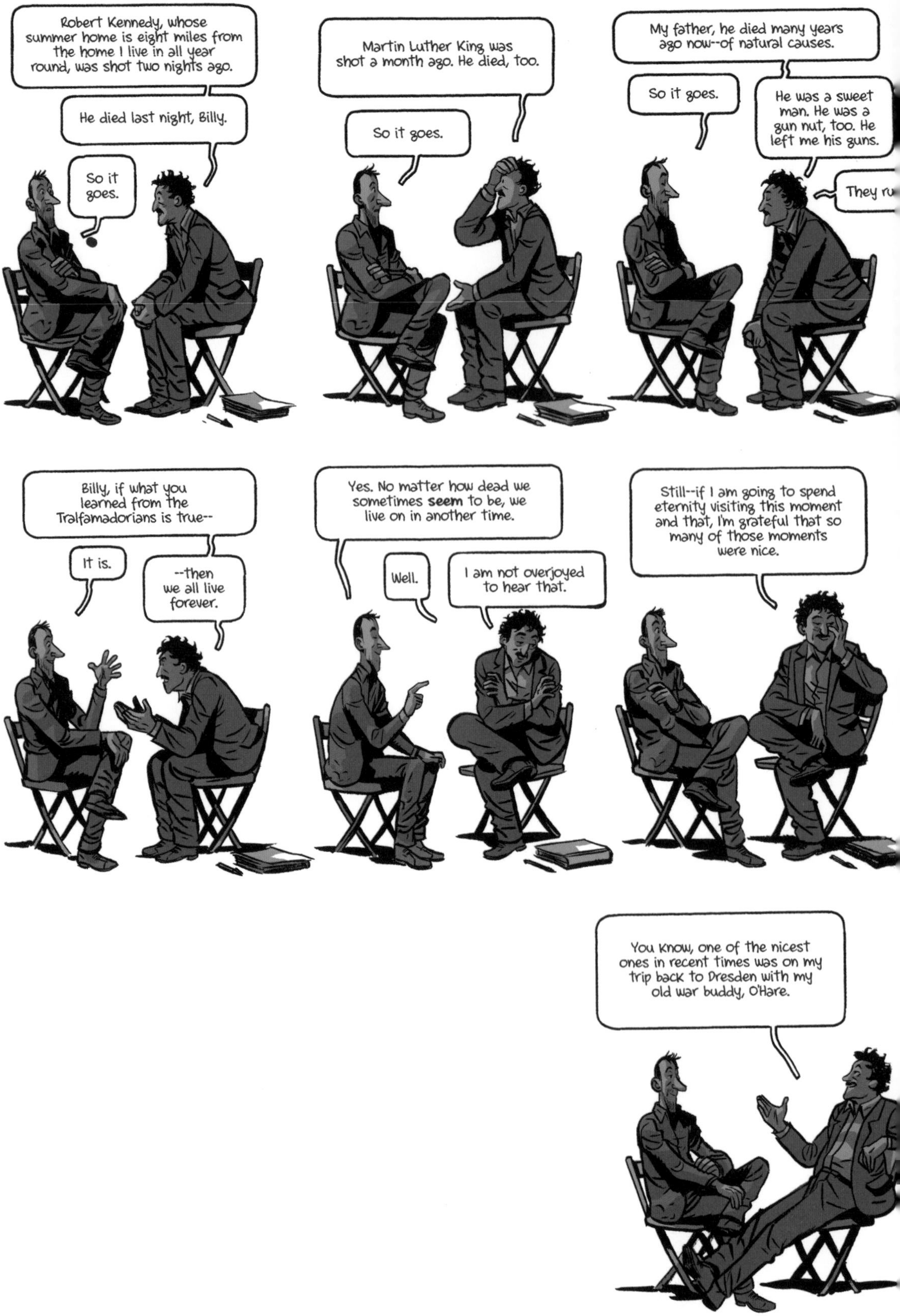
Robert Kennedy, whose summer home is eight miles from the home I live in all year round, was shot two nights ago.
He died last night, Billy.
So it goes.
Martin Luther King was shot a month ago. He died, too.
So it goes.
My father, he died many years ago now--of natural causes.
So it goes.
He was a sweet man. He was a gun nut, too. He left me his guns.
They ru
Billy, if what you learned from the Tralfamadorians is true--
It is.
--then we all live forever.
Yes. No matter how dead we sometimes **seem** to be, we live on in another time.
Well.
I am not overjoyed to hear that.
Still--if I am going to spend eternity visiting this moment and that, I'm grateful that so many of those moments were nice.
You know, one of the nicest ones in recent times was on my trip back to Dresden with my old war buddy, O'Hare.

We took a Hungarian Airlines plane from East Berlin. The pilot smoked a Cuban cigar when the plane was being fueled.

When we took off, there was no talk of fastening seatbelts.

East Germany was down below, and the lights were on.

I imagined dropping bombs on those lights, on those villages and cities and towns.

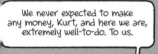

We never expected to make any money, Kurt, and here we are, extremely well-to-do. To us.

To us. And if you're ever in Cody, Wyoming, Bernard, just ask for Wild Bob.

KLINK!

You know, I was trying to look up the population of Dresden, but it's not in this book.

But look at this.

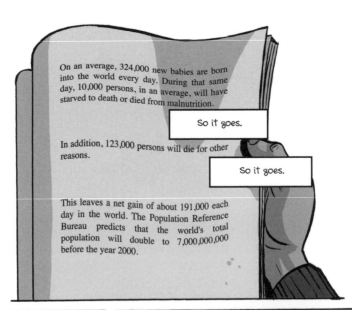

On an average, 324,000 new babies are born into the world every day. During that same day, 10,000 persons, in an average, will have starved to death or died from malnutrition.

So it goes.

In addition, 123,000 persons will die for other reasons.

So it goes.

This leaves a net gain of about 191,000 each day in the world. The Population Reference Bureau predicts that the world's total population will double to 7,000,000,000 before the year 2000.

I suppose they will all want dignity.

Yes.

I suppose they will.

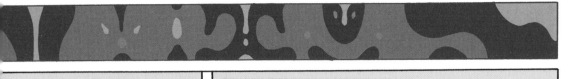

Billy Pilgrim was travelling back to Dresden too, but he was going to 1945.

He and the rest of the Americans were being marched into the ruins by their German guards.

Prisoners of war from many lands came together that morning in Dresden.

It had been decreed that the digging for bodies was to begin.

And so the digging began.

Most of the holes came to nothing-- to pavement, or to boulders so huge they would not move.

But finally, Billy and his partners found something. Their digging had unearthed a hole, an area of darkness and space beneath their feet.

The German soldier would be gone a long time. When he finally came back, he would report dozens of bodies inside, unmarked, sitting on benches.

Thus began the first corpse mine in Dresden.

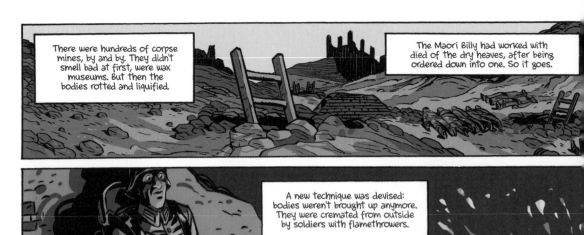

There were hundreds of corpse mines, by and by. They didn't smell bad at first, were wax museums. But then the bodies rotted and liquified.

The Maori Billy had worked with died of the dry heaves, after being ordered down into one. So it goes.

A new technique was devised: bodies weren't brought up anymore. They were cremated from outside by soldiers with flamethrowers.

Somewhere in there, poor old Edgar Derby was caught with a teapot he'd taken. He was arrested for plundering. He was tried and shot.

So it goes.

And somewhere in there it was springtime. The corpse mines were closed down. The soldiers all left to fight the Russians.

Billy and the rest of his group were locked up in the inn's stable.

And then, one morning, they got up to discover that the door was unlocked.

World War Two in Europe was over.

Billy and the rest wandered out onto the shady street. There was nothing going on out there, no traffic of any kind.

Birds were talking.

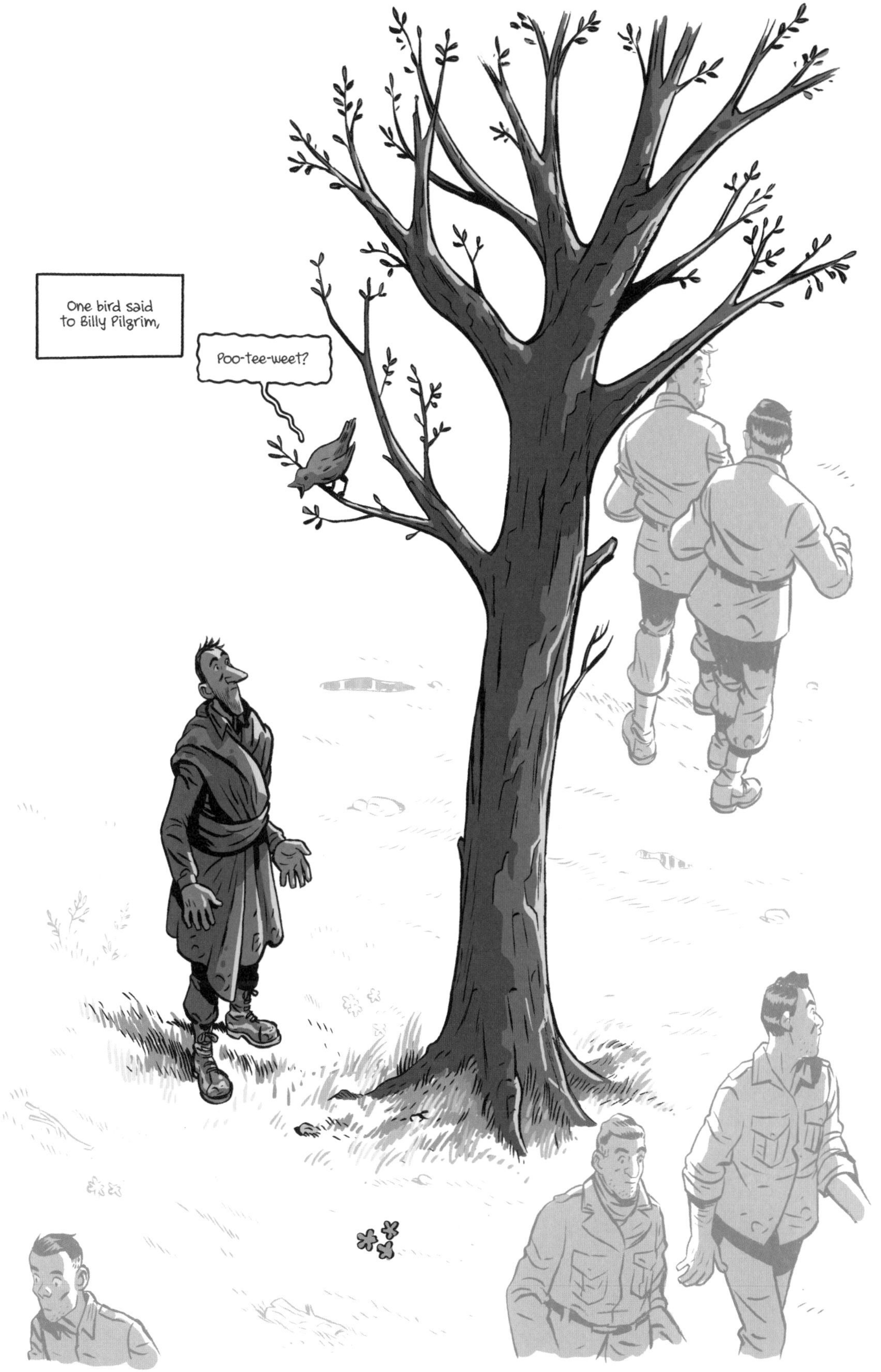
One bird said to Billy Pilgrim,
Poo-tee-weet?

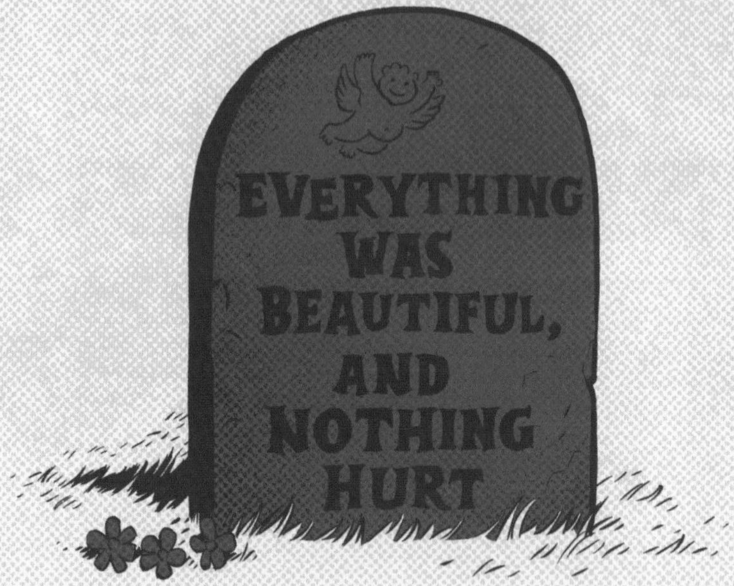
EVERYTHING
WAS
BEAUTIFUL,
AND
NOTHING
HURT

"I think you guys are going to have to come up with a lot of wonderful new lies, or people just aren't going to want to go on living."

—Eliot Rosewater

KURT VONNEGUT

Kurt Vonnegut's black humor, satiric voice, and incomparable imagination first captured America's attention in *The Sirens of Titan* in 1959, and established him as "a true artist" *(The New York Times)* with *Cat's Cradle* in 1963. He was, as Graham Greene declared, "one of the best living American writers." Kurt Vonnegut died in 2007.

RYAN NORTH

Ryan North is the writer responsible for *Dinosaur Comics*, the Eisner and Harvey Award-winning *Adventure Time* comic book series for BOOM! Studios, the bestselling anthology series *Machine of Death*, and the *New York Times* bestselling and Eisner-Award winning *Unbeatable Squirrel Girl* series for Marvel Comics. North has also written a *New York Times* bestselling series of choose-your-own-adventure books based on Shakespeare's classic plays *Romeo and Juliet* and *Hamlet*. His latest book, *How to Invent Everything*, is nothing less than a complete cheat sheet for civilization. North currently resides in Toronto, Canada.

ALBERT MONTEYS

Albert Monteys is a Spanish graphic novelist and illustrator, best known for his work in *El Jueves*, a weekly satirical magazine that he directed from 2006 until 2011. Monteys also created the series *Carlitos Fax* for the children's magazine *Mister K*. In 2014, he founded a satirical monthly publication *Orgullo y Satisfacción (Pride and Satisfaction)* with several other cartoonists, and began to publish a science fiction comic, *¡Universo! (Universe!)* in Panel Syndicate, winning a 2017 Eisner Award nomination for Best Digital Comic.

People aren't supposed to look back.
I'm certainly not going to do it anymore.

DISCOVER
GROUNDBREAKING TITLES

FRANK "BIG BLACK" SMITH
BIG BLACK
STAND AT ATTICA
JARED REINMUTH
AMÉZIANE
Four days in 1971 changed the course of American history.

LEV GROSSMAN
LILAH STURGES PIUS BAK
THE MAGICIANS
NEW CLASS

FROM THE NEW YORK TIMES BESTSELLING AUTHOR OF BAD FEMINIST
ROXANE GAY
TRACY LYNNE OLIVER
THE SACRIFICE OF DARKNESS
REBECCA KIRBY
JAMES FENNER

KURT VONNEGUT
with RYAN NORTH & ALBERT MONTEYS
SLAUGHTER
or the children's crusade
HOUSE-FIVE
a graphic novel adaptation

SABAA TAHIR
WITH NICOLE ANDELFINGER & SONIA LIAO
A THIEF AMONG THE TREES
• AN EMBER IN THE ASHES GRAPHIC NOVEL •

EMEI BURELL
WE SERVED THE PEOPLE
MY MOTHER'S STORIES

ARCHAIA

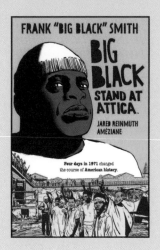

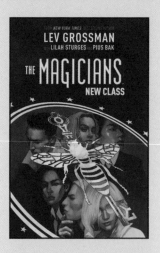

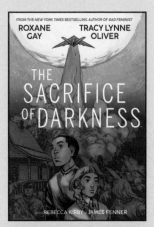

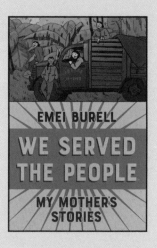

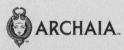

AVAILABLE AT YOUR LOCAL COMICS SHOP AND BOOKSTORE

To find a comics shop in your area, visit www.comicshoplocator.com

WWW.**BOOM-STUDIOS**.COM

Big Black: Stand at Attica
Frank "Big Black" Smith, Jared Reinmuth, Améziane
ISBN: 978-1-68415-479-1 | $19.99 US

The Magicians: New Class
Lev Grossman, Lilah Sturges, Pius Bak
ISBN: 978-1-68415-565-1 | $19.99 US

The Sacrifice of Darkness
Roxane Gay, Tracy Lynne Oliver, Rebecca Kirby
ISBN: 978-1-68415-624-5 | $24.99 US

Slaughterhouse-Five
Kurt Vonnegut, Ryan North, Albert Monteys
ISBN: 978-1-68415-625-2 | $24.99 US

A Thief Among the Trees: An Ember in the Ashes Graphic Novel
Sabaa Tahir, Nicole Andelfinger, Sonia Liao
ISBN: 978-1-68415-524-8 | $19.99 US

We Served the People: My Mother's Stories
Emei Burell
ISBN: 978-1-68415-504-0 | $24.99 US

Bear
Ben Queen, Joe Todd-Stanton
ISBN: 978-1-68415-531-6 | $24.99 US

Girl on Film
Cecil Castellucci, Vicky Leta, Melissa Duffy, V. Gagnon, Jon Berg
ISBN: 978-1-68415-453-1 | $19.99 US

Happiness Will Follow
Mike Hawthorne
ISBN: 978-1-68415-545-3 | $24.99 US

The Man Who Came Down the Attic Stairs
Celine Loup
ISBN: 978-1-68415-352-7 | $14.99 US

Waves
Ingrid Chabbert, Carole Maurel
ISBN: 978-1-68415-346-6 | $14.99 US